Using

Windows® 95

Using

Windows® 95

Ed Bott

Using Windows® 95

Library of Congress Catalog No.: 95-70640

ISBN: 0-7897-0092-1

97   96   95   6   5   4   3   2

Interpretation of the printing code: the rightmost double-digit number is the year of the book's printing; the rightmost single-digit number, the number of the book's printing. For example, a printing code of 95-1 shows that the first printing of the book occurred in 1995.

Screen reproductions in this book were created using Collage Plus from Inner Media, Inc., Hollis, NH.

Credits

President
Roland Elgey

**Vice President
and Publisher**
Marie Butler-Knight

Associate Publisher
Don Roche, Jr.

Editorial Services Director
Elizabeth Keaffaber

Managing Editor
Michael Cunningham

Director of Marketing
Lynn E. Zingraf

Senior Series Editor
Chris Nelson

Publishing Managers
Don Roche, Jr.
Joseph B. Wikert

Acquisitions Editors
Jenny L. Watson
Lori A. Jordan

Product Directors
Lisa D. Wagner
Robin Drake

Production Editor
Nancy E. Sixsmith

Novice Reviewer
Beth Lucas

**Assistant Product
Marketing Manager**
Kim Margolius

Technical Editor
Bruce Wynn

Acquisitions Coordinator
Tracy M. Williams

Operations Coordinator
Patty Brooks

Editorial Assistants
Jill Byus
Carmen Phelps

Book Designer
Ruth Harvey

Cover Designer
Robin Brandenburg

Production Team
Amy Cornwell, Chad Dressler,
Amy Gornik, Karen L. Gregor,
Daryl Kessler, Beth Lewis,
Brenda Sims, Jody York

Indexer
Brad Herriman

Composed in *ITC Century*, *ITC Highlander*, and *MCPdigital* by Que Corporation.

To my mother, of course, who is now working on her third generation of computer experts.

About the Author

Ed Bott, the author of Que's *Using Microsoft Office 4*, is Senior Contributing Editor of *PC/Computing* magazine. With two monthly columns and frequent cover stories on Microsoft Windows and other topics, his is one of the most recognized "voices" in the computing industry.

Acknowledgments

A book like this doesn't just write itself. In this case, it took the coordinated efforts of a tremendously talented group of people to pull all the pieces together in record time, without worrying about silly details like sleep.

Literally dozens of people—editors, artists, graphic designers, proofreaders, and others —worked on this project, and it's impossible to thank them all. So let me single out a few whose efforts were especially meaningful to me.

Product Development Specialists Robin Drake and Lisa Wagner deserve a standing ovation for their tireless efforts in making sure that each chapter was the best it could be.

Production Editor Nancy Sixsmith single-handedly kept several Indianapolis coffee vendors in the black for months as she put in long hours of overtime on this project. Her attention to detail and appreciation of the rhythm of the English language is nothing short of amazing.

A special thank you to Acquisitions Editor Jenny Watson who convinced everyone that this project could be completed in record time—then helped us pull it off.

An extra-special thank you to Associate Publisher Don Roche for his tireless support and infectious enthusiasm.

Que also thanks Michael O'Mara for his important contributions to this book.

We'd Like to Hear from You!

As part of our continuing effort to produce books of the highest possible quality, Que would like to hear your comments. To stay competitive, we *really* want you, as a computer book reader and user, to let us know what you like or dislike most about this book or other Que products.

You can mail comments, ideas, or suggestions for improving future editions to the address below, or send us a fax at (317) 581-4663. For the online inclined, Macmillan Computer Publishing has a forum on CompuServe (type **GO QUEBOOKS** at any prompt) through which our staff and authors are available for questions and comments. The address of our Internet site is **http://www.mcp.com** (World Wide Web).

In addition to exploring our forum, please feel free to contact me personally to discuss your opinions of this book: I'm **74404,3307** on CompuServe, and I'm **lwagner@que.mcp.com** on the Internet.

Thanks in advance—your comments will help us to continue publishing the best books available on computer topics in today's market.

Lisa D. Wagner
Product Development Specialist
Que Corporation
201 W. 103rd Street
Indianapolis, Indiana 46290
USA

Contents at a Glance

Table of Contents

*Getting around in
Windows 95
see page 11*

Windows 3.1 Upgraders' Guide (So You've Used Windows Before?)

*Why is
there an
arrow on
this icon?*

see page 18

2 How Windows Works

What happens when I start up Windows?

see page 48

Pick the right tool for the job...

see page 69

3 Windows and Your PC

4 Help! Fast Answers, Straight from the Source

*What do I
need to run
Windows 95?*

see page 81

Part II: Controlling Windows

5 Basic Mousing Around

6 My Computer and Everything Inside It

I'm left-handed. Am I doomed?

see page 109

Understanding disks
see page 117

7 Organizing Your Files and Keeping Them Neat

Oops! I didn't mean to delete that file!

see page 145

8 Opening and Closing Windows

9 Moving Windows Around (and Moving Around in Windows)

*Windows hot spots
see page 165*

*What do I do
with these
menus?*

see page 178

10 Talking to Windows: Menus and Dialog Boxes

Part III: Working with Applications

11 Setting Up New Programs (DOS and Windows)

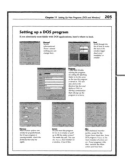

Setting up a DOS
program
see page 205

*What to
do when
the boss is
away...*

see page 224

*Can I cut
and copy
with a DOS
program?*

see page 231

12 What Do All these Free Programs Do?

13 Using Windows to Tie It All Together

Decorate your Desktop

see page 243

Part IV: Making Windows Work the Way You Do

14 Changing the Way Windows Looks

15 Putting Your Favorite Things Where You Want Them

*Make the
Start menu
easier to
work from...*

see page 267

*Taskbar in
your way?
Hide it!*

see page 272

Part V: Out of the PC, Onto the Page: Printing and Fonts

16 Printing Perfect Pages

17 Making Text Stand Out with Fonts

Ready to print?

see page 288

*Understanding fonts
see page 303*

*What is
multimedia?*

see page 320

Part VI: Lights, Camera, Action: Multimedia and More Fun

18 The Amazing, Talking, Singing, Exploding PC

*Using a
laptop?
Look here!*

see page 333

19 Mobile Computing: Taking Your Show On the Road

Part VII: Communicating with the Rest of the World

*What good is
a CD-ROM?*

see page 345

*How does
Windows
know who
I am?*

see page 363

The Inbox
see page 385

How do I join the Internet?

see page 401

Can't get the dang thing to work? Check here!

see page 427

Part VIII: Troubleshooting Windows 95

*Menus
mumbo-jumbo...*

see page 435

*Long file
names
causing you
headaches?*

see page 439

*I think my
mouse is
drunk...*

see page 445

The Case of the Disappearing Data

see page 450

What about viruses?

see page 463

Part IX: Indexes

Action Index

Index   **473**

Need to know fast? Find it here...

see page 467

Introduction

When I first began working with Microsoft Windows, Joe Montana had only two Super Bowl rings, Bill Gates was still working on his first billion, the hottest PC you could buy was a 386, and people just looked at me funny when I told them about this cool new software from Microsoft.

Every year or two since then there's been a new version of Windows, so you'd think that it would have gotten easier to use during that time. Nope. Every single week I get at least one frantic phone call from a friend or a relative—or even a total stranger. What do all these folks have in common? They can't figure out how their computer works. Specifically, they can't figure out why MS-DOS and Windows 3.1 behave in such bizarre ways. And for the past year, I've been promising them that relief is just around the corner.

It's hard to imagine anything more complicated and frustrating than the combination of good ol' DOS and Windows 3.1. Most sensible people would rather set the time on a VCR while blindfolded than struggle with a DOS prompt. And don't even think of upgrading your old Windows PC with a multimedia kit unless you have a rocket scientist and a witch doctor standing by to help you get it all working together.

But that's all history now, because Windows 95 is here. If you've ever used Windows and DOS before, it's time to celebrate. Put this book down for a minute. Call the neighbors, wake the dog, and dance around the room if you feel like it because you don't have to use DOS anymore. If there's anyone watching, I'm sure they'll understand—especially if they've struggled with DOS, too.

When I first saw Windows 95, back when it was code-named "Chicago," I knew it would be special. And it's turned out exactly that way. Windows 95 is much more intelligently designed, much more consistent, and just plain more fun than the versions of Windows that you've probably learned to live with. But that doesn't mean that Windows 95 will turn you into a computer expert in 20 minutes. This is still a computer, after all, and Windows is still an enormous, complicated program. On the ease-of-use scale, your computer and Windows 95 probably fall somewhere between microwave ovens and VCRs.

Most of the ordinary people I know start shaking at the mere thought of programming a VCR. Well, they'll probably have a little better luck with Windows 95, but it's still guaranteed to cause a few moments of complete befuddlement, where the only thing you can think of is one question:

What do I do now?

Windows has that effect on people. It doesn't matter how smart you are, or how many DOS commands you've memorized, or how many hours you've spent tapping on your PC's keyboard and clicking on your mouse. Everyone who uses a computer for business or pleasure asks that same question, over and over again.

Think of Windows 95 as a giant amusement park, like some sort of Digital Disney World. You can probably have a perfectly enjoyable day with Mickey and Goofy and the gang if you go down to Orlando without a map. But you'll also waste a few hours (at least) while you wander around trying to figure out where everything is. And you might never stumble across the Indiana Jones Adventure if you don't wander down the street where it's located.

The same thing is true of Windows 95. It's big and it's complex. It sprawls across 20-something floppy disks and even fills up a whole CD, if you're lucky enough to get that version. And after you've gone through the pointing, clicking, swapping, and upgrading to get Windows 95 on your PC, you'll probably wonder:

What do I do now?

Windows is filled with nooks and crannies you can explore. There's even a Start button you can click before you try anything else. You can learn a lot about Windows 95 by poking through menus and dialog boxes, clicking mouse buttons, and pressing key combinations. (If you have plenty of spare time and lots of patience, that is.)

What if you don't have the time or the patience to explore Windows 95 like a tourist on vacation? You can use this book as a guidebook to Windows 95. No leisurely strolls through the park here—this book was written specifically to answer one question:

What do I do now?

What makes this book different?

You don't need an advanced degree in engineering or computer science to read this book. If you can tell the difference between the left and right mouse buttons, you've got all the technical background you need.

It's written in plain English, too. I promise not to bury you in detailed explanations and three-letter acronyms (TLAs). After all, you're not studying for a degree in computer science—you're trying to get some work done, with the help of some incredibly powerful and occasionally baffling computer programs.

With Windows and Windows programs, there are always *at least* four different ways to do everything. If you were planning to become a computer expert, you'd expect a computer book to give you step-by-step instructions for each of them. Not this book.

In this book, I focus on results. That means I'll tell you the best way to get each job done. There might be three other ways to do the same thing, but for most people, most of the time, the technique I describe is the one that will get results most quickly.

Oh, and there won't be a quiz.

How do I use this book?

This isn't a textbook. You don't have to start at page 1 and read all the way to the end. It's not a mystery novel, either, so if you want to skip to the last chapter first, be my guest.

You'll probably be surprised at some of the things that Windows 95 can do for you. That's why, if you have the time, it's worth flipping through the chapters, looking at the headings, and searching out the references to the things you do at work. The people who published this book went to a lot of trouble to make sure that those interesting ideas would leap off the page and catch your attention as you browse. (It shouldn't take that long—after all, this isn't one of those 1200-page monster books that helps you build up your biceps every time you lift it.)

This book will come in especially handy when you're not sure where to begin. And if you get stuck, you'll probably find the way out in these pages.

How this book is put together

Some people will use every last feature in their computers. Others will spend most of their time doing the same simple tasks over and over again. It doesn't matter which type you are—you'll find exactly what you're looking for. You could look at this book as a tool to help you learn how Windows 95 can help you work (and play) more effectively. The sections are divided into chapters that get into the specifics of each program. And inside each chapter, you'll find tips, hints, and step-by-step instructions for getting your work done faster without having to ask what to do next.

Windows 3.1 Upgraders' Guide (So You've Used Windows Before?)

If you've used Windows before, this short introduction to Windows 95 is designed to show you around the new version and answer some of your inevitable questions: What's different? What's new? Where did the DOS prompt go? What happened to the Program Manager? Lots of illustrations and screen shots in this section will give you a feel for what to expect right up front.

Part I: Getting Started with Windows

What is Windows? And why should you care? (Presumably, because you want to tell your computer what to do instead of letting it try to run the show.) This section includes a quick overview of how Windows works, introduces all the pieces of your PC, and—most importantly—tells you where to go for more help.

Part II: Controlling Windows

Your mouse has two buttons, and Windows uses both of them. Come here for mouse boot camp, then stick around for the explanation of everything inside My Computer. What are you supposed to do with all those windows, icons, menus, and dialog boxes? The answers are all here.

Part III: Working with Applications

What do you do when you get a new program? How do you make sure your old DOS programs work well with Windows 95? And what are you supposed to do with all those free programs that come with Windows 95? You can go your whole life without knowing what Object Linking and Embedding really does. If you want to try it, though, look at Chapter 13. That's the same place you can get the straight skinny on how to tie all your programs together with the Windows Clipboard.

Part IV: Making Windows Work the Way You Do

All this fun stuff is guaranteed to be 100% productivity-free. If you want to add a picture of Bart Simpson to your Windows desktop, this is the place to look. I'll also show you how to change colors and fonts, and install goofy screen savers. If your boss is looking over your shoulder, show him the *next* chapter, which shows you ways to be amazingly more productive by reorganizing your personal space for maximum efficiency. (Don't worry—you can resume that game of Minesweeper as soon as he's gone.)

Part V: Out of the PC, Onto the Page: Printing and Fonts

First, you add a bunch of slick fonts to Windows so you can dazzle your readers with breathtakingly beautiful documents. Then, you follow a few simple instructions for printing perfect pages. If everything works out, you'll be in the corner office by the end of next week.

Part VI: Lights, Camera, Action: Multimedia and More Fun

The folks in the offices and cubicles around yours won't be happy to hear this. Don't you think it's cool if your PC makes jungle sounds every time you move the mouse? This multimedia stuff also covers movies (but your hard disk probably isn't big enough to handle *Terminator 4*—sorry). Check out the next chapter for hands-on advice on how to use your CD-ROM drive. Did you know you can play music CDs through your multimedia speakers? (Maybe this would be a good place to find the built-in Windows 95 volume control, before your coworkers start a petition.)

Part VII: Communicating with the Rest of the World

All about networks and modems, e-mail and faxes, plus The Microsoft Network and the Internet. Looking to get on the World Wide Web? Windows 95 makes it easy. But beware—they don't call it the World Wide Waste of Time for nothing.

Part VIII: Troubleshooting Windows 95

Questions? Problems? Find answers here!

Part IX: Indexes

Everything you need to look up is found here, including tasks and commands.

Special book elements

This book has a number of special elements and conventions to help you find information quickly—or skip stuff you don't want to read right now.

 TIP **Tips either point out information often overlooked in the** documentation, or help you use your software more efficiently, like a shortcut. Some tips help you solve or avoid problems.

Sidebars are interesting nuggets of information

Sidebars provide interesting, nonessential reading; side-alley trips you can take when you're not at the computer, or when you just want some relief from working. Here, you may find more technical details, funny stories, personal anecdotes, or interesting background information.

CAUTION   **Cautions alert you to potentially dangerous consequences of a** procedure or practice, especially if it could cause serious or even disastrous results (such as loss or corruption of data).

Q&A   *What are Q&A notes?*

Cast in the form of questions and answers, these notes provide you with advice on ways to solve common problems.

❝ Plain English, please!

These notes explain the meanings of technical terms or computer jargon. ❞

Throughout this book, we'll use a comma to separate the parts of a pull-down menu command. For example, to start a new document, you'll choose <u>F</u>ile, <u>N</u>ew. That means "Pull down the <u>F</u>ile menu, and choose <u>N</u>ew from the list."

And if you see two keys separated by a plus sign, such as Ctrl+X, that means to press and hold the first key, press the second key, then release both keys.

Windows 3.1 Upgraders' Guide (So You've Used Windows Before?)

● **In this chapter:**

- **What can I do with Windows 95 that I couldn't do before?**

- **Logging in and starting up**

- **New mouse tricks**

- **Where did my applications go?**

- **Connecting with the outside world**

Windows 95 may seem a little unfamiliar at first, but it won't be long before you'll feel right at home . . . . ⊘

Windows 95 is different, inside and out, from the Windows you've gotten used to. If you found it frustrating to work with files and programs in your old version of Windows, you're not alone. When Microsoft set out to design a brand-new Windows, they asked regular people to work with Windows, and they watched as users struggled to do even simple tasks.

Then they took those lessons to heart and designed a computer operating system that should be easier to use than anything you've ever seen before.

What's new in Windows 95?

Well, Windows 95 is bigger—much bigger—than its predecessor. But it's also more consistent.

There are fewer layers of management in Windows 95. All those middle managers—Program Manager, File Manager, and Print Manager—got pink slips the day Microsoft retired Windows 3.1.

It's a better-looking operating system, if that matters. It's faster, too. (That *does* matter.)

You can forget about DOS and most of its confusing old rules. You don't have to worry about keeping track of complex directory paths anymore, for example, because Windows 95 replaces those directories with folders that open into windows with a double-click.

Eventually, you'll have a whole new class of application programs to choose from, as software manufacturers begin to make Windows 95 versions of their programs. For now, though, you'll probably keep using some of your old programs.

A slick technology called Plug and Play will make it easier to upgrade your computer or add new equipment, should you decide that it makes sense.

In short, if you've been using Windows 3.1 for any length of time, you should expect this new Windows to make life easier and make you more productive.

Getting around in Windows 95

Welcome to the Windows 95 desktop. No matter what you're looking for, you'll start the search here.

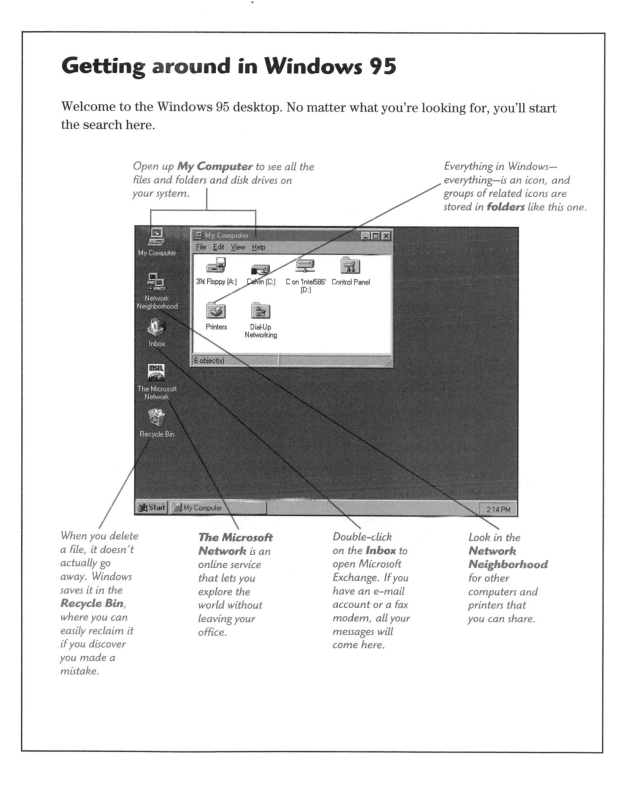

*Open up **My Computer** to see all the files and folders and disk drives on your system.*

*Everything in Windows— everything—is an icon, and groups of related icons are stored in **folders** like this one.*

*When you delete a file, it doesn't actually go away. Windows saves it in the **Recycle Bin**, where you can easily reclaim it if you discover you made a mistake.*

***The Microsoft Network** is an online service that lets you explore the world without leaving your office.*

*Double-click on the **Inbox** to open Microsoft Exchange. If you have an e-mail account or a fax modem, all your messages will come here.*

*Look in the **Network Neighborhood** for other computers and printers that you can share.*

This section isn't intended to be a complete set of instructions for Windows 95. Instead, the idea is to introduce Windows 95 and show you how it's different from the Windows you already know how to use.

If you see something that catches your eye, look in the margin for a pointer to the chapter that covers that feature in more detail. Windows 95 is big and complicated, with a wealth of new features, but it's also extremely consistent.

How does it all work? I'm glad you asked…

Sign in here…

If you're used to staring at a C:\> prompt and typing **WIN** to start Windows, it's time to learn a new daily routine. When you flip the big red switch each morning, Windows 95 bypasses DOS completely. The only thing you'll have to type is your password. Windows expects you to log on each time you start up; if you're hooked up to a local area network, you can connect to everything with a single login (see fig. 1).

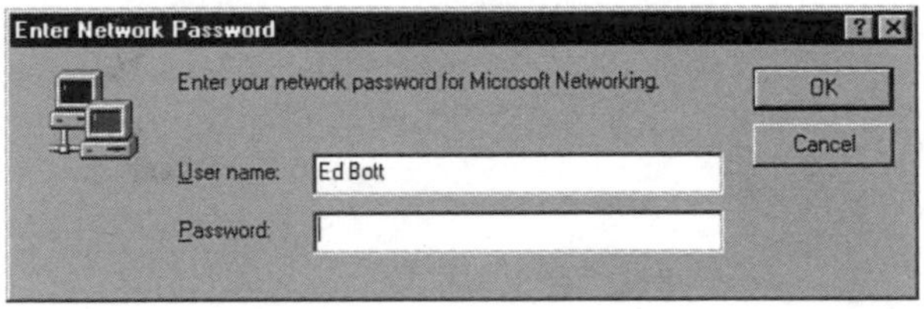

Fig. 1

Every time you start up Windows, you have to log in. The dialog box you see may look a little different, depending on your network configuration.

Enter Network Password	? ☒
Enter your network password for Microsoft Networking.	OK
	Cancel
User name: Ed Bott	
Password:	

If you aren't connected to any network and you want to avoid messing with logging in, the first time you're asked to choose a password, just press Enter. (Don't enter a password at all.) From then on, when you start Windows, it'll just start—it won't ask you for a password. If you've already chosen a password, you can get rid of it using the Passwords icon in the Control Panel. Open the Passwords window and change your password to nothing— no spaces, no letters, nothing.

 TIP **If you're on a Novell NetWare network, you may see a different** login box, including a box where you can enter the name of your login server. If you have no networking installed at all, you can bypass the login screen completely.

What does the Start button do?

Learn about starting up Windows 95, using the Start menu, and getting around in your programs in Chapters 1 and 2.

When you first start up Windows 95, your first question will probably be, "What happened to Program Manager?" (Don't worry—we'll get to that in a second.) Your second question will probably be, "What happens when I click the Start button?"

There are only seven options on the Start menu, but it's hard to think of a thing you *can't* do when you click here (see figs. 2 and 3). Think of the Start menu as Windows 95's central business district. From here, every side road leads to another interesting destination packed with surprises.

Fig. 2
The Start menu. You can get nearly anywhere from here, although it may take a few clicks...

The **Programs** menu replaces the Windows 3.1 Program Manager. Click here, and your program groups cascade off in a series of new menus that open to the right.

Windows remembers the **Documents** you've opened recently. To pick up where you left off yesterday, just look on this menu.

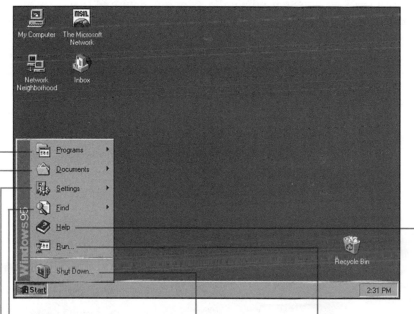

If something in Windows isn't working exactly the way you'd like, click on the **Settings** menu to twiddle knobs and dials until you've got it right. The Control Panel is here, as are any printers you have access to.

Can't track down that file? Even if you don't remember the name, the new **Find** menu can help you narrow down your search. All you have to know is a stray fact or two about the file (if you're positive it contained the word "asparagus," for example, and you know you saved it last April, you'll find it in seconds).

Don't just push that big red switch to turn off your PC! Use the **Shut Down** command to make sure all your data is safe.

The **Run** dialog box lets you type in the name of a program or a folder to open it instantly. Handy for the mouse-phobic.

Need **Help?** The built-in Windows instruction book lets you find step-by-step instructions and explanations for every common task.

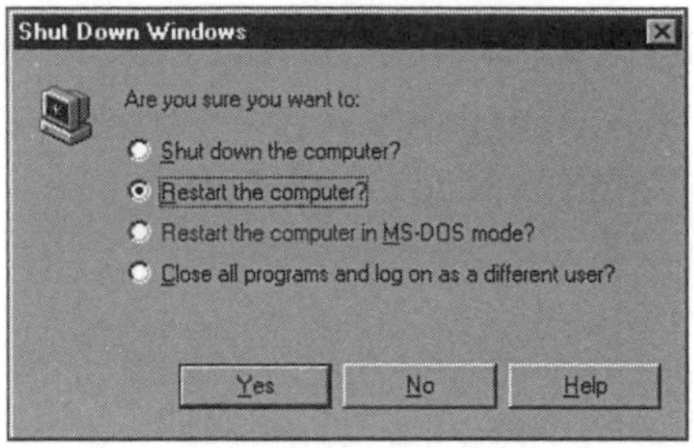

Fig. 3
What's the opposite of "Open Sesame?" The last option on the Start menu lets you shut down Windows quickly and safely.

Teach your old mouse new tricks

See Chapter 5 for the full story on mousing around.

If you've used Windows for any length of time, you already know how to use the mouse. With this version of Windows, you'll find yourself using the mouse even more for quick tasks and shortcuts:

- **Selecting** a group of files is easier. When you need to select a bunch of things, use the mouse to throw an imaginary lasso around everything you need.

- You probably never used the right mouse button in Windows 3.1, but it gets a full aerobic workout in Windows 95. Whenever you're not sure what to do next, point to an unfamiliar object and right-click to pop-up **shortcut menus** like the one in figure 4.

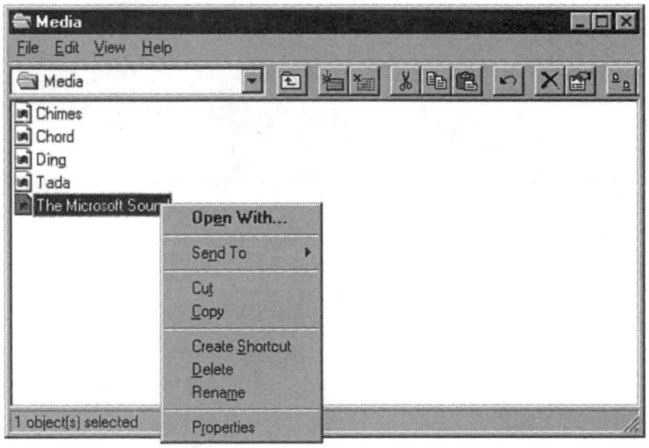

Fig. 4
When in doubt, point and click the *right* mouse button. Practically every object you can think of has one of these useful shortcut menus attached to it.

- **Dragging-and-dropping** is the preferred way to get work done. Drag files from one folder to another to move or copy them, and drop file icons on top of a printer icon to put them on paper with the least amount of fuss. If you use the right mouse button to drag an icon around, you'll get a shortcut menu like the one in figure 5.

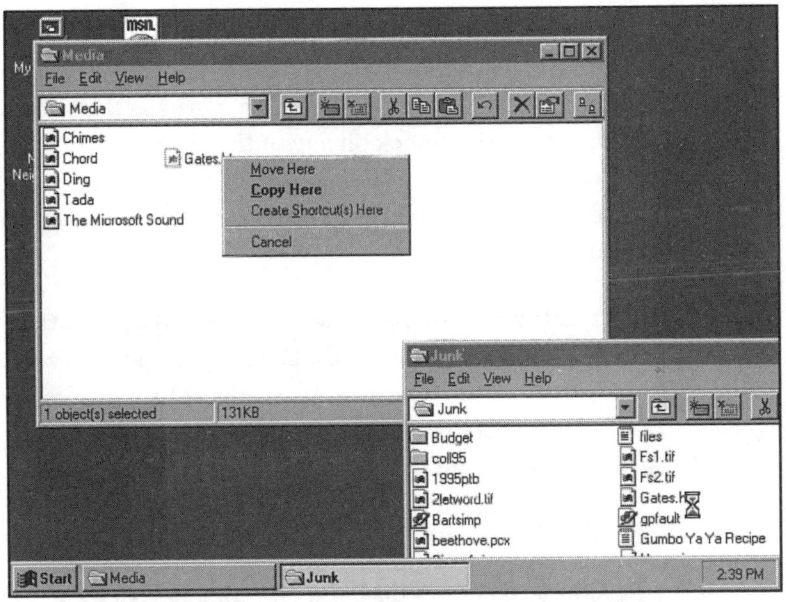

Fig. 5

Drag an icon from here to there, and you can't be sure exactly what's going to happen. Use the right mouse button instead, and this pop-up menu lets you tell Windows exactly what you want it to do.

Switch programs with the taskbar

Attention, couch potatoes! If you can switch channels with your television's remote control, you can switch between all the Windows programs you have running at any given time.

The taskbar stays anchored at the bottom of the desktop, where it's always visible. (You can drag it to any edge of the screen, if you prefer.) Every program that's running right now and every folder that's open gets its own button on the taskbar.

With Windows 3.1, you had to clear windows out of the way before you could find the one you were looking for, and you were never quite sure where all those windows hid when you needed them most. With Windows 95, it doesn't matter how many windows you have open: look for its name on the taskbar, click the button, and watch as the window floats to the top of the stack (see fig. 6).

Fig. 6
Every running program appears on the taskbar, which is always visible on the edge of the desktop. Click on any button to bring that window to the top of the pile.

> Memo to Turner - WordPad

> Start | Printers | Inbox - Micr... | HP LaserJe... | **Memo to...** | 2:49 PM

The more windows you open, the more crowded the taskbar becomes and the less of each name you see there. To overcome this, you can increase the taskbar's height by dragging its top edge upward.

Don't overlook one of the coolest features of the taskbar. At the far right, just to the left of the clock, you'll occasionally see a tiny status icon for part of your system: a printer, a modem, perhaps the volume control on your sound card. Right-click on any of these icons; you'll usually be surprised by the results. Use the volume control to turn off your multimedia speakers instantly, for example, before someone in the next room begins complaining about the racket.

TIP **If you learned to switch between applications using the keyboard** shortcut Alt+Tab, you'll be happy to know it works in Windows 95, too. When you have more than one program running (or several folders open), hold down the Alt key and keep holding it down as you Tab from one program to the next. When you find the one you're looking for, release both keys to switch to that window.

Icons and folders: Windows' building blocks

Learn how to organize your files and icons in Chapter 7.

If you've used Windows 3.1 for any length of time, you've learned that **icons** are small pictures you click to start a program. You've also learned that you can arrange icons into groups within Program Manager. In Windows 3.1, you won't find icons anywhere else, and you can't put one group inside another to keep your desktop neat.

Windows 95 is completely different. For starters, *everything* is an icon:
every file, every program, every printer, and every computer on your
company's local area network. To keep all those files neatly organized,
Windows arranges them into **folders**. You can organize your data files the
same way, even creating new folders inside folders. When you've learned
how to work with one icon and one folder, you've mastered the most
essential Windows skill of all.

What's inside that icon?

In Windows 3.1, you can learn a few basic facts about a file by looking at it:
the name, when it was created, how big it is, that sort of thing. Windows 95
lets you do the same thing (and a whole lot more) with properties sheets.
When you point to most icons and click the right mouse button, a quick
menu appears. Choose the Properties command and a fact-packed box like
the one in figure 7 pops up.

Fig. 7

The Properties menu
always brings up a
sheet of information
like this one. The exact
details you'll see
change from icon to
icon, depending on
the type of object
you're pointing to.

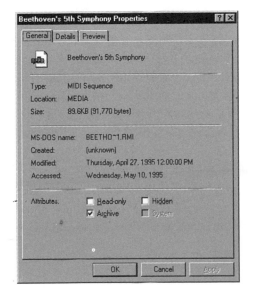

One of the most useful choices on the right-mouse menu is the Quick
Viewer. When you see Quick View on the shortcut menu of a document, you
can ask Windows to show you the document itself, even if you don't have a
copy of the program that created the document. (The Quick View utility is
available only on the CD version of Windows 95.)

Why is there an arrow in the corner of some icons?

Let's say one of your favorite programs is buried in a folder inside a folder inside another folder inside three more folders. Every time you want to start that program, you double-click so many times you're thinking of applying for an index-finger transplant. To make things easier, you could move the program to a more convenient location, but that's not very good file management. It's also not necessary. The better solution is to create a **shortcut** to the program and put it right on your desktop.

Shortcuts are tremendously useful things, and they're everywhere in Windows 95. To get a feeling for the way a shortcut works, think of how you might organize a library for maximum efficiency. Would you shelve the new John Grisham novel in the fiction section? With the law books? Or in the action-adventure aisle? If you were willing to pay for three copies, you could put one in each section, but that would be wasteful. Instead, you could keep one copy in the fiction section, and place a cross-reference in the other two sections telling patrons to ask a clerk to bring them Grisham's latest.

When you put a shortcut on your desktop, it looks just like the original, except for a small arrow in the lower left corner. But it's actually only a pointer to another icon, and no matter how big the original file is, a shortcut occupies only a tiny piece of your hard disk. When you double-click on the shortcut, Windows goes searching for the original (the **target** is the official name) and calls it up, just as if you'd clicked on the original.

Folders

There's nothing complicated about folders. Just as you use manila folders to keep related pieces of paper together, you use Windows folders to keep related icons together. Folders always act the same, although you can take your choice of four different ways to view the icons inside, as you can see in figure 8.

 TIP   If you're used to File Manager, you'll like the Details view best of a all. With this arrangement of icons, you can click on the column headings to sort by the values in that column. Click again to sort in reverse order.

Fig. 8
One folder, four views.
Anytime you see a
window filled with
icons, you can have
your choice of four
icon arrangements. The
toolbar is optional.

Closing and resizing windows with the new buttons

Chapter 9 has all the details about working with windows.

It's OK to keep lots of windows open, especially given how easy it is to switch between windows using the taskbar. But you will occasionally want to clear windows out of the way or close them completely. With Windows 3.1, closing a window is a big hassle. With Windows 95, it's a snap to shrink a window to an icon, expand it to its full size, or shut it down completely. Just look in the top right corner of the window for one of these four buttons:

 The **Close** button is shaped like an X, as in, "Cross this off the list, please."

 To keep the window running, but remove all traces of it from the desktop, use the **Minimize** button. This has the same effect as stuffing the entire contents of the window into its taskbar button. When you need the window again, just click on the taskbar.

 On the other hand, if you want to devote all your attention to a window, click its **Maximize** button. That tells Windows to expand the window to fill every square inch of space on your monitor.

 When you want the maximized application to return to a normal window, click the **Restore** button.

Where did my applications go?
Will they still run?

When you upgrade your old copy of Windows 3.1 to Windows 95, your old Windows programs should keep working just as they always did. (There are a few exceptions, such as utility programs intended to make your hard disk run faster, but most people shouldn't have to worry about them.)

Your older programs will probably work, but that doesn't mean they'll behave exactly the same as new Windows 95 programs. In fact, if you don't recognize the difference between old Windows programs and new ones, you might run into problems. Here's what to watch out for.

What's the difference between new Windows programs and old ones?

If you're paying close attention, you'll notice subtle differences in the way new Windows programs look. Dialog boxes, for example, are likely to have tabbed pages on them, just like the ones in Windows itself.

Not only do they look different, these new Windows programs also act different than their predecessors.

You can use long file names

When you open or save a file using a new Windows program like **WordPad** (the word processor that comes with Windows), you can enter a long file name that helps you (or anyone else) see at a glance exactly what's inside the file. Older Windows programs don't know how to read those long file names; they're still stuck with the old DOS file name rules. With these old programs, your file name has to be eight characters or fewer, not counting an optional three-letter extension tacked onto the end.

So what happens if you've created a file with a long name, and then you open it with an older program that doesn't speak that language? If your long file name was a WordPad document called Letter to my accountant, 8-24-95, the old program will chop off all but the first six characters of the name, and then tack on two extra characters of its own, making the name LETTER~1.DOC. Not very informative, is it?

Why did the old program add the .DOC extension to the end of the file name? Actually, it was there all along, but Windows 95 hides those extensions when it knows what type of file you're working with. Because it knows that files ending in .DOC can be opened with WordPad, it simply shows you the name. If you want to see the extensions, just select View, Options from My Computer or Windows Explorer, click the View tab, and then deselect the checkbox marked Hide MS-DOS file extensions for file types that are registered.

New and improved dialog boxes

For more info on dialog boxes, see Chapter 10.

Every time you open or save a file with a new Windows 95 program, you'll use a slick dialog box like the one shown in figure 9. When one of these dialog boxes is open, you can do all sorts of cool things with the icons inside it.

- To add a new folder, right-click anywhere in the window, and choose New, Folder.

- To delete a file, right-click on its icon, and choose Delete.

- To give a file a different name (perhaps so you can save your new file under that name instead), select the file, and then click on its name and start typing.

In short, anything you can do in a folder window, you can do in one of these dialog boxes.

More dragging-and-dropping

New Windows 95 programs typically let you drag-and-drop icons in much more flexible ways than older programs do. They also take better advantage of shortcuts, which means you can mail a network or Microsoft Network shortcut to someone else who uses the same system, and know that they'll be able to open it.

Extra crash protection

New Windows programs use 32 bits at a time instead of 16 bits. That means that, in theory at least, they're a little more crash-resistant than older programs. With either type of program, though, if a bug causes your computer to lock up, you can recover by pressing Ctrl+Alt+Del, looking in the list for a program that has stopped responding (see fig. 10), then shutting it down without harming the rest of your open programs and data files.

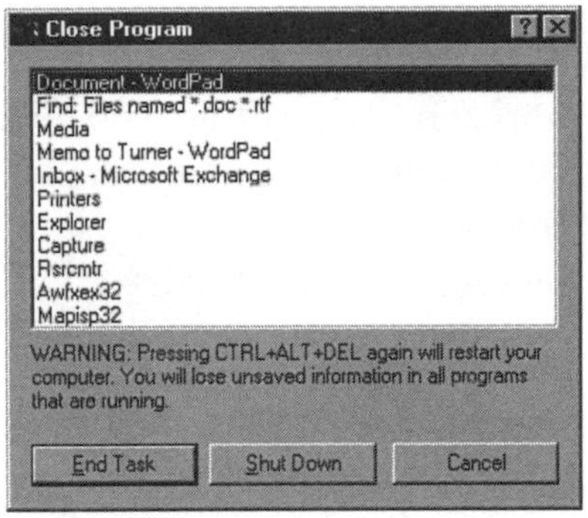

Fig. 10

No kidding—when you press Ctrl+Alt+Del, you can see a list of all the programs you're running right now. If one is misbehaving, you can make it go away with one click.

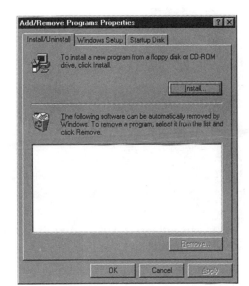

Installing (and uninstalling) new Windows programs

Finally, new Windows programs should be easier to install—and easier to remove later if you decide you don't need them anymore. To take care of either task, open Control Panel and double-click on the Add/Remove Programs icon. The Add/Remove Programs Properties dialog box appears (see fig. 11).

Fig. 11

Use this dialog box to add or remove programs. Newer programs can even include a way for you to uninstall them later.

What about my DOS programs?

*Turn to
Chapter 11
to learn more
about setting up
programs.*

Windows 95 doesn't go through MS-DOS (the old Microsoft operating system) when you start it up, but that doesn't mean it's clueless about DOS programs. On the contrary, some of your old DOS programs that refused to run gracefully under Windows 3.1 may actually perform better under Windows 95.

If you know how to fine-tune the settings of an old DOS program, you can tweak it under Windows 95, too. Just right-click on the program's icon, then choose Properties to see a box like the one in figure 12.

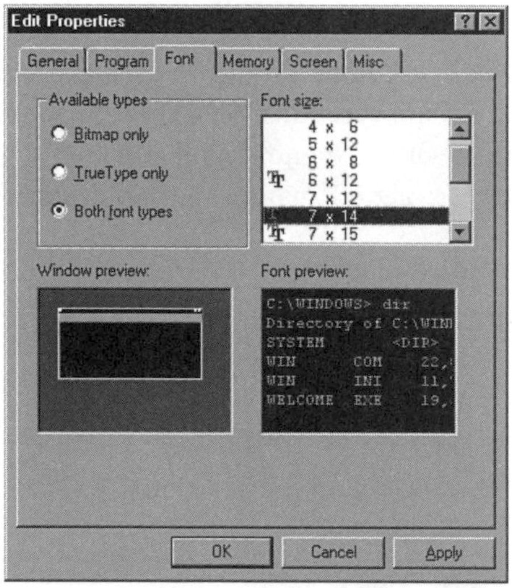

Fig. 12

Most of the stuff in this sheet is strictly for DOS experts. Still, it's nice to know all your old MS-DOS programs will run in a window.

Finally, if your old DOS program keeps giving you fits, try running it in MS-DOS mode. Click on the Start button and choose Shut Down from the Start menu, then check the button next to Restart the computer in MS-DOS mode, and click OK. You won't be able to run any other programs while your DOS program is running, but at least you'll be able to get your work done.

Finding familiar tools

All those middle managers you learned how to deal with in Windows 3.1 are gone in Windows 95. There's no more Program Manager, no File Manager, no Print Manager. The jobs they used to do are now handled by other parts of Windows: the Start button replaced Program Manager, and Explorer replaced File Manager. (There's still a print manager of sorts, though it's not called that anymore—it's just a window with the printer's name.)

What happened to Program Manager?

Click the Start button to pop up the Start menu, and then rest the mouse pointer on the Programs choice. After a second or so, a new menu will cascade off to the right. That's where all your Program Manager groups went.

When you install a new program, instead of creating a Program Manager group, it will create a new folder containing shortcuts for all the new files it wants you to know about, then arrange the new folder on one of the cascading menus.

Unlike Program Manager, you can rearrange these folders so that you have groups inside of groups. That makes it easier to stay organized. (The easy way to do it: right-click on the Start button. Remember, when you're not sure what to do next, point and right-click.)

I used to have 40 program groups fighting for space in my Program Manager window, and too often it was impossible to find anything. With Windows 95, I created a folder called Extras and filled it with all the folders for programs I rarely use. Now, when I call up the Start menu and click on Programs, I see a short, easy-to-follow list of the programs I use all the time (see fig. 13).

Fig. 13
Windows 95 turned the old Program Manager sideways and rear-ranged your groups. Click here to start up any program you've installed.

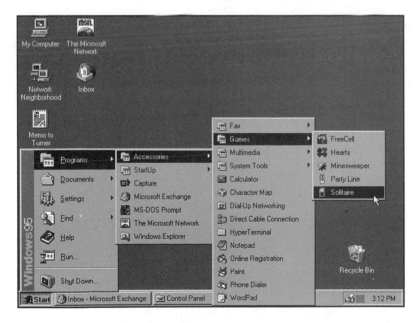

Where's File Manager?

You probably learned how to use the Windows 3.1 File Manager, but I'll bet you never learned to like it. Besides, with those silly eight-character file names, what could you really do with it?

When Microsoft finished Windows 95, File Manager got a gold watch, a hearty handshake, and a one-way ticket to the retirement home. Now, when you want to move, copy, delete, or rename files in Windows 95, you have a lot of choices.

The Windows Explorer: seeing everything at once

There's more about the Windows Explorer in Chapter 7.

The Windows Explorer is about the closest thing Windows 95 offers to the old File Manager. To start it up, click the Start button, choose Programs, and look for Windows Explorer on the first cascading menu. When you first start it up, it will probably look something like the window in figure 14.

Fig. 14

The Windows Explorer replaces File Manager. Click on any drive or folder on the left side, and the right side shows you its contents.

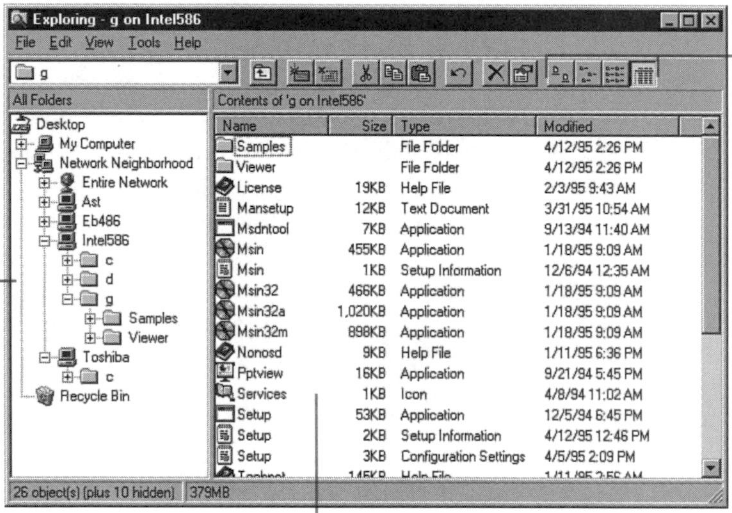

You can scroll up and down through a tree-style listing that includes everything on your computer and on any networks you're attached to. Click on the plus signs to see more detail; click on the minus signs to put all that confusing detail away.

Just as with a folder window, you can change the view of the items in the right pane to Large icons, Small icons, List, or Details.

Windows displays the contents of the folder (or other object) that's currently selected in the tree pane. As you choose new items on the left, the display on the right changes to match.

Folder windows: one at a time

Folder windows work just like the right pane of the Windows Explorer. If you find the Explorer view confusing, this arrangement might be easier to work with. To open a folder window, double-click on My Computer, and then just keep double-clicking. It's shown in figure 15.

Fig. 15

The no-frills version of the Explorer. When you double-click on a drive in the My Computer window, you get one of these windows.

Find, files or folders

Windows 95 includes an amazingly powerful way to track down any object anywhere on your PC, even across a network. All you need to know is a little bit of information about the thing you're looking for.

When you choose Find from the Start menu, you choose to find files and folders, a computer on your network, or a file on the Microsoft Network. Then you'll see a dialog box like the one in figure 16. Enter a part of the name if you know it. If you don't know that much, try clicking on the Advanced tab, and entering a word or phrase that you're certain is in the file you're looking for. You can also tell Windows you want it to restrict its search to files in a certain location (like your Windows folder), or to files created in a certain time period, such as during the month of April, 1995.

After you click the Find Now button, Windows goes to work, poring through files in search of anything that matches what you've described. The search results list at the bottom of the Find window works just like—you guessed it—the Windows Explorer (see fig. 16). You can change the view to large or small icons; sort the files by any column; and even rename, copy, or delete files you see here.

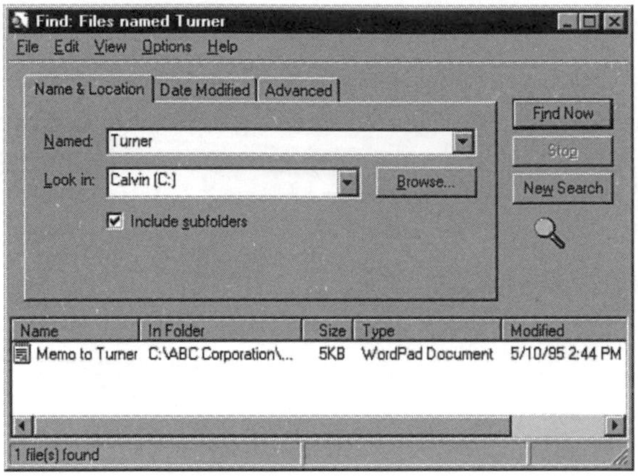

Fig. 16
What happened to that file? Choose Find from the Start menu, and you can find nearly anything, nearly anywhere, even if you can only remember a few sketchy details about it.

Is there still a Control Panel?

Yes, there is still a Control Panel, and it still looks a lot like its Windows 3.1 counterpart. As a cursory glance at the icons in figure 17 shows, you can adjust anything on, in, or around your computer with a few clicks here.

Fig. 17
The new and improved Control Panel lets you pop the hood on Windows and fiddle with your computer's innards.

Figure 18 shows one of the dialog boxes that appears when you click on a Control Panel icon.

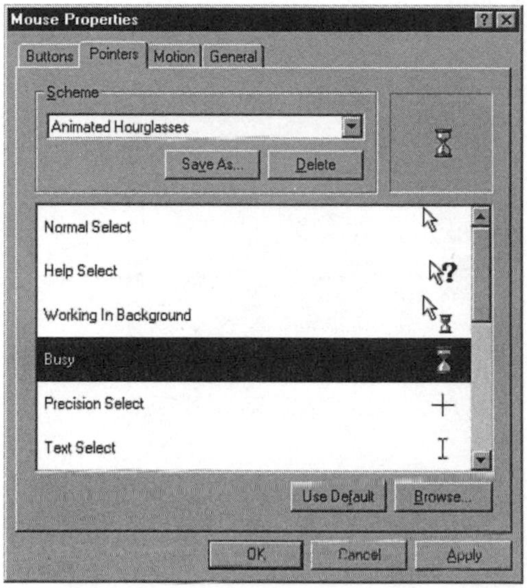

Fig. 18
What can you do with Control Panel? This mini-program lets you replace the boring old hourglass with one that does cartwheels.

How do I add new hardware?

Part VI covers adding multimedia components, and Chapter 22 discusses adding a modem.

Every so often, someone calls me and asks if they should buy a multimedia upgrade kit. If they're using Windows 3.1, I recommend against it in the interest of preserving their sanity. The old Windows forced you to think like a rocket scientist to add even the simplest hardware to a PC. If you're using Windows 95, though, go ahead and tackle that multimedia upgrade. The worst that can happen is you'll be bored, because Windows takes care of most of the work now.

The secret of Windows 95's hardware success is twofold. The first ingredient in the equation is some fancy technology called **Plug and Play**. Basically, every time you turn on your PC, Windows looks at everything inside your PC and compares what it finds against what was there the last time it ran its census. If there's a new device hanging around—like a sound card or CD-ROM drive—it may ask you to insert your original Windows disks, but that's the extent of your involvement.

To make life even easier for Windows, you can use the Add New Hardware Wizard found in the Control Panel (see fig. 19). This mini-program forces Windows to search for new hardware on your PC; it also lets you choose the name of the hardware from a lengthy list of more than 1,000 devices.

Fig. 19

Adding new hardware—like a CD-ROM drive or a sound card—is a lot easier than it used to be, thanks to this wizard.

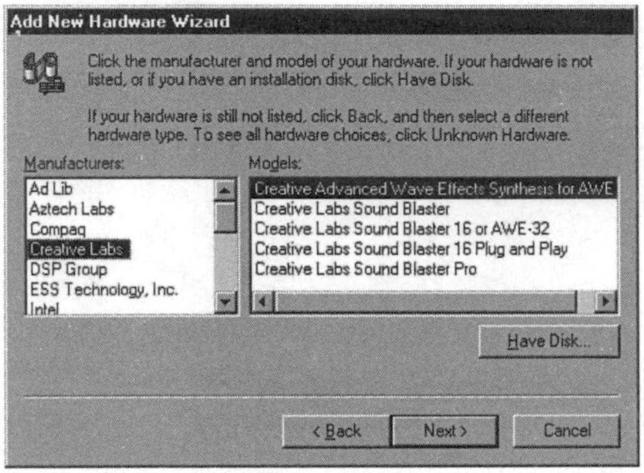

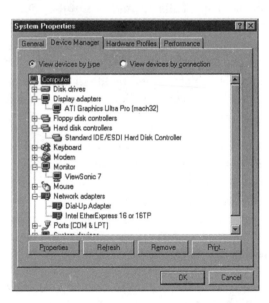

 How do you know what kind of hardware is installed in your PC? If you guessed that it would involve the right mouse button, go to the head of the class. Find the My Computer icon, right-click on it, and choose Properties from the pop-up menu. You'll see a detailed System Properties display like the one in figure 20. Click on the Device Manager tab to see all your hardware up close and personal.

Fig. 20

What kind of hardware is in your PC? Right-click on My Computer, then choose Properties to see this detailed inventory.

How do I set up a printer?

Check out Chapter 16 for more info about printing.

As far as Windows is concerned, a new printer is just another piece of hardware, so it uses its Plug and Play smarts to automatically detect as many printers as it can. If you add a new printer to your work area, click on the Start button, and choose Settings, Printers to open the Printers folder. You can click on the blank printer page to add a new printer from the lengthy list included with Windows 95; after you're done, Windows volunteers to print a test page to make sure that everything's working. Great idea.

Once the printer is installed, it gets its own icon in the Printers folder, and you can check the status of the printer and any jobs by simply double-clicking on it (see fig. 21).

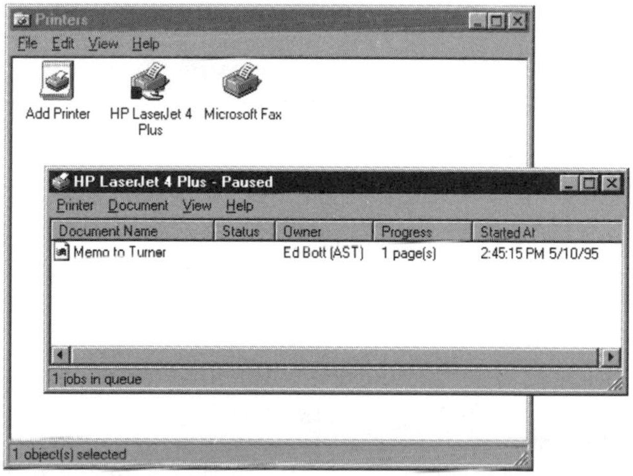

Fig. 21
Click here to set up a new printer, then use this window to check on the status of your print jobs.

How do I add new fonts?

Turn to Chapter 17 for step-by-step instructions for dealing with fonts.

Adding a new font under Windows 3.1 is complicated. Under Windows 95, all you have to do is open the Fonts folder in the Control Panel, then choose File, Install New Font from the pull-down menus. Once the fonts are in place, you can use the same folder to print out font samples or to sort your fonts into groups of typefaces that resemble one another (see fig. 22).

Fig. 22
Look inside the Fonts folder for a detailed look at every font installed on your computer. (So *that's* what Monotype Corsiva looks like!)

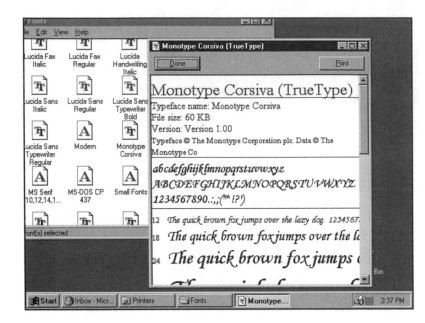

How do I change the look and feel of Windows?

Maybe you changed your Windows 3.1 wallpaper into something flashy or fun. Maybe you even added a screen saver. But there's no comparison with the sheer number of things you can do to make your system look and feel different with the help of Windows 95.

When you right-click on any empty spot on the desktop and choose Properties, Windows pops up the Display properties sheet (see figure 23 for an example of what it might look like).

- **Screen savers** keep snoops from reading whatever you're working on if they walk by when you're not around.

- **Wallpaper** lets you place an image on the desktop.

- You can switch **resolution** —the number of objects you can see on the screen at one time—and **color depth**, which is the number of simultaneous colors you can see. Some of the changes don't require you to even restart Windows, in dramatic contrast to the way these things worked under older versions.

- If you don't like the colors, fonts, and size of everything on the desktop, you can change it here by clicking on the **Appearance** tag.

Fig. 23
Put some personality in
your PC! Right-click
on an empty spot on
the desktop, then
choose Properties to
adjust every detail of
the desktop's look and
feel.

Where do I go for help?

*See Chapter 4 for
Help.*

There's an impressive set of instructions available right on the Start menu.
Stumped? Click Help and then select the Index tab to search for a word (see
fig. 24). You might just find the answer you're looking for.

Fig. 24
Help! There's an
amazing amount of
information in the
Windows 95 Help
system, including
buttons that let you
jump straight to the
dialog box you're
looking for.

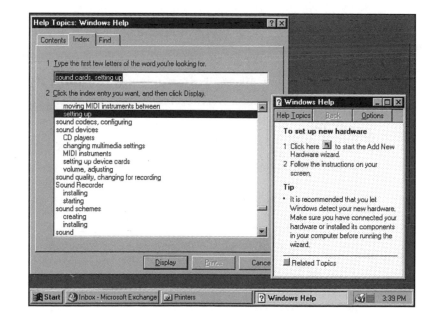

What about those little programs?

Some of the old familiar Windows 3.1 accessories are gone. If you'd like, we can now observe a moment of silence for the Calendar, the Windows Anti-Virus program, and the Cardfile list manager. (If you upgraded over the top of Windows 3.1, those programs may still be hanging around, but there aren't new versions of them.)

But Windows 95 includes enough new and genuinely useful programs and accessories that you'll probably forgive Microsoft for dropping those old programs.

You'll find more details about Windows 95 accessories in Chapter 12

Some accessories that come free with Windows 95 include:

- **WordPad,** a simple word processing program.

- **Paint,** which lets you indulge your artistic tendencies.

- **Phone Dialer**, which dials and tracks phone calls for you.

- **File Transfer** works with certain modems to let you send a file while you are talking to the recipient on the phone.

- **HyperTerminal** is a basic communication package.

- The **CD Player** lets you blast rock and roll (or Bach and Mozart) from your CD-ROM and multimedia speakers.

- The **Volume Control** keeps the neighbors from getting upset at the rock and roll heavy metal part.

- There are a handful of system tools—the **Disk Defragmenter, ScanDisk**, and **DriveSpace**—which help you get the most out of your hard drive.

- And there's a **Backup** program that helps you copy important files to a safe place.

Figure 25 shows the accessories in the Accessories folder.

Fig. 25
Play a CD, write a
memo, dial your
phone. The Windows
95 accessories are
small, free programs
that handle a variety
of odd jobs for you.

Connecting to the outside world

No computer is an island. When you feel like sharing anything from files to ideas, here's where to turn.

Networking

*For more informa-
tion about net-
working with
Windows 95, look
in Chapter 21.*

If you've got a network adapter in your computer, you can easily share files and printers with others. To see what's out there, look in the Network Neighborhood for any other computers or file servers that might be available.

Sharing takes a slight extra step, but it's not difficult. Just right-click on a drive icon in My Computer (if you've installed File Sharing services for your network, the option will be on the pop-up shortcut menu).

The hardest part, although it's a little easier than it used to be, is setting up your network in the first place. Look in Control Panel for the Network icon. Figure 26 shows a network configuration dialog box. If you know a networking expert, offer him or her a case of Jolt cola or a box of chocolate Ho-Hos to come do the work for you.

Fig. 26

There's still way too much techno-babble in these dialog boxes, but if you're willing to slog through the jargon, setting up a network is not that difficult.

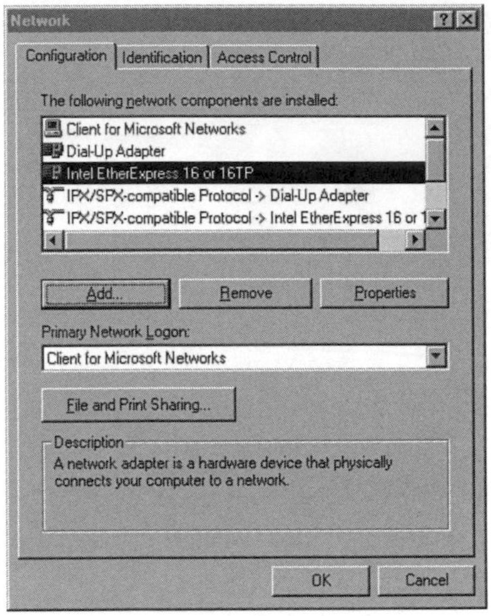

E-mail and faxes

Learn more about communication with e-mail and faxes in Chapter 23.

Once the network is up and running, take advantage of it by using Windows 95's built-in mail program. It's called Microsoft Exchange, and its claim to fame is that all your messages, including faxes people send to your fax modem, arrive in a single place where you should have no trouble managing them (see fig. 27).

Fig. 27

Eventually, all your e-mail and faxes will go here, into the Microsoft Exchange Inbox. With a modem and a Microsoft Network account, you can swap messages with anyone who has an Internet address.

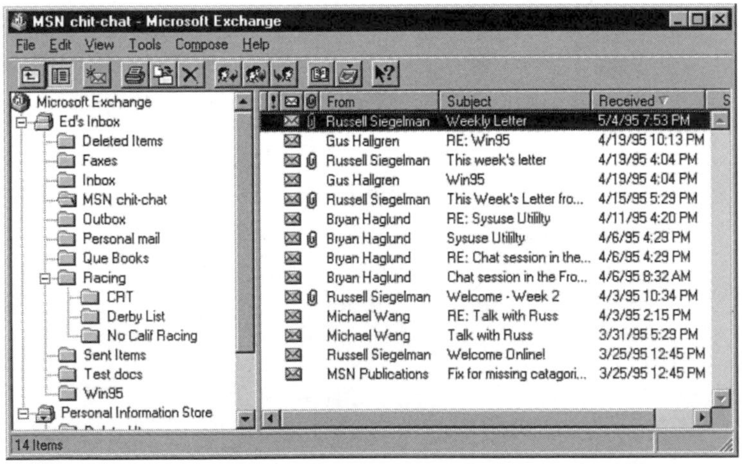

The Microsoft Network

The Microsoft Network is discussed in Chapter 24.

Even if your company doesn't have a network, you can hook up with the outside world by joining The Microsoft Network (see fig. 28). It's not for everyone, and it's not free, but it's one sure way to see how the rest of the world lives.

Fig. 28
Want to go for a spin on the Information Superhighway? Sign up for The Microsoft Network; you can exchange ideas with people all over the world.

I want to take Windows on the road...

Chapter 19 tells you all about mobile computing.

Windows 95 has a lot to offer for notebook users:

- If battery life is an issue, look in the Control Panel (and at the right of the taskbar) for power-management features.

- If your notebook uses a docking station when you're in the office, the Plug and Play support can help you switch effortlessly between docked and undocked modes. You just slip the notebook in and out of its dock as if it were a videotape.

- You can "print" a job even at 35,000 feet—miles away from the nearest printer. Just tell Windows that you want it to store the print job on your hard disk until you get back to the office.

- If you don't have a docking station, the next best thing is a Direct Cable Connection, where you can shuffle files and print jobs back and forth between your desktop and notebook PCs.

- To keep track of those files, use the Briefcase (see fig. 29). When you drag files from your desktop PC into a Briefcase on your notebook, Windows keeps track of both sets of files. The next time you hook th two computers together, it looks on both lists and makes a note of the differences it sees. Then it offers to update the older files with the newer ones. If you've ever struggled to keep two computers in sync, you'll wonder how you ever lived without this feature.

Fig. 29
If you own a notebook PC, check out the Briefcase program, which keeps track of files on two PCs and makes sure you always have the most up-to-date copy.

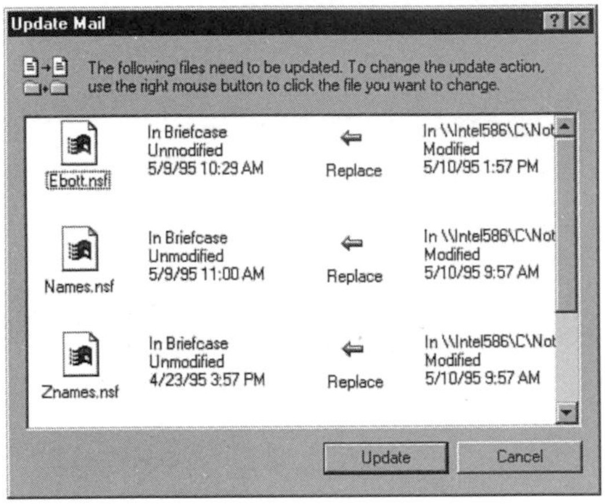

Update Mail

The following files need to be updated. To change the update action, use the right mouse button to click the file you want to change.

[Ebott.nsf]	In Briefcase Unmodified 5/9/95 10:29 AM	⇐ Replace	In \\Intel586\C\Not Modified 5/10/95 1:57 PM
Names.nsf	In Briefcase Unmodified 5/9/95 11:00 AM	⇐ Replace	In \\Intel586\C\Not Modified 5/10/95 9:57 AM
Znames.nsf	In Briefcase Unmodified 4/23/95 3:57 PM	⇐ Replace	In \\Intel586\C\Not Modified 5/10/95 9:57 AM

Update   Cancel

I'm missing one of the pieces of Windows 95!

When you install Windows 95, it asks you to pick from a list of preset installation choices, then makes some intelligent guesses about which programs you might want to use. Most of those guesses will be right, but sooner or later you'll come across a program you want to use that didn't make it onto your PC.

 As long as you have the original disks you used to install Windows 95, it's no problem to update your Windows setup after the fact. Just open Control Panel and choose Add/Remove Programs, then click on the tab headed Windows Setup. You'll work with a screen like the one in figure 30.

- **To add a component,** check the entire box in the scrolling list.

- **To remove a component,** clear the check mark from its box.

- **To choose specific parts of each section,** highlight the entry in the list, and then click the button labeled Details.

Fig. 30

If you can't find a piece of Windows 95, chances are it's not installed on your computer. No problem. Check a few boxes, click a few buttons, swap a disk or two, and you're ready to go.

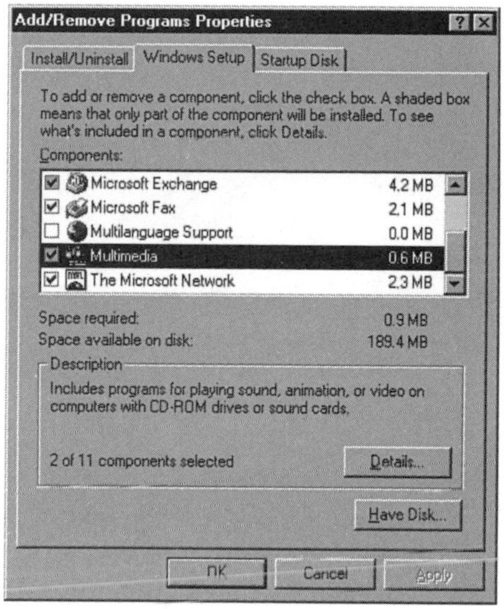

Part I: Getting Started with Windows

1

What Is Windows 95 (and Why Should I Care)?

● **In this chapter:**

- What is Windows, what can it do for me, and why should I care?

- How can Windows help me organize my work?

- How can I make Windows work the way I work?

- Where do I start?

Windows 95 can't solve all your problems, but it CAN make your relationship with your computer friendlier . . . . ⊖

I f you asked a rocket scientist to explain what Windows is, he'd probably tell you that it's a computer operating system with a graphical user interface and a rich set of applications. Whatever *that* means. That definition certainly doesn't give you a clue as to why you'd want to use Windows, does it? So let's try the same question again, this time in plain English.

What is Windows? It's a computer program that helps you organize the work you do with your PC every day. The most obvious part of Windows is the graphical user interface—the colorful screen and the pretty pictures. Once you learn how to move the mouse pointer around the screen, Windows lets you do just about anything by pointing at a picture and clicking a button. That's impressive, but the other half of Windows—the operating system part—is just as amazing.

When you point and click with the mouse, you tell Windows to get to work on your behalf. Behind the scenes, beneath the surface and just out of sight, Windows acts as your personal executive staff, complete with the PC equivalent of file clerks, messengers, switchboard operators, administrative assistants, and a full-time maintenance crew. Best of all, you're the boss: every time you tap a key or click the mouse, this staff swings into action to carry out your requests.

What can Windows do for me?

When you're ready to continue working on that letter you started writing yesterday, just tell Windows the name of the file and it will pop up in a window, ready for you to start typing. Ready to toss out some old files? Just dump them into the Recycle Bin and the housekeeping staff will take care of the rest. When you need to set up a new modem or a laser printer, it's no problem—there's a wizard on the premises to handle most of the hard work. Windows can find a lost file for you, help you keep your company's books, even send a message to a coworker in the next office or a friend halfway around the world, assuming you're connected to some sort of e-mail system.

The Windows 95 desktop

Where do you begin? The most important pieces of Windows are right where you can see them, on the Windows desktop. This desktop works just like the one in your office. You keep the most important work right on top, where you can get to it quickly. Less urgent things get tucked away in folders and file cabinets.

My Computer
Mission Control for your PC and any hardware that's connected to it. Double-click here to see the files, folders, programs, and hardware on your PC.

Network Neighborhood
Every networked PC and printer you're connected to shows up here—whether it's just across the hallway or halfway around the world.

The Microsoft Network
The Microsoft Network offers online bulletin boards, discussion areas, free and cheap software, and many other online features.

The Windows desktop
This is the vacant lot where you build your office. Windows puts a few icons here to get you started; you can keep it uncluttered or drag other icons onto it.

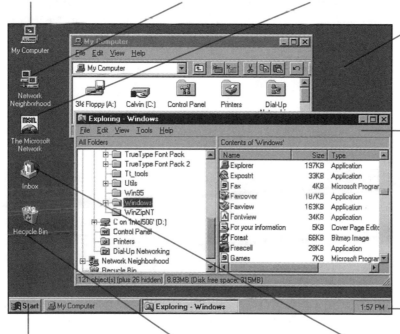

The Windows Explorer
A slightly more complicated view of your files and folders. On one side, there's a list of all the drives and folders on your computer and on the network, arranged like an outline. On the other, there is a list of files in the selected folder.

Start button
Click here to start. When you do, you'll pop up a menu that contains virtually every common task you can perform in Windows 95.

Recycle Bin
When you use Windows 95 to delete a file, it doesn't go away immediately. Instead, your deleted files pile up here until you empty the trash or it gets full.

Inbox (Microsoft Exchange)
Just like the inbox on your real desktop, this is where you can expect to find e-mail messages and faxes from other people (assuming you have a modem, that is).

Taskbar
You'll use the taskbar often: the Start menu to launch programs; buttons to switch quickly between them; and various status icons to tell you what Windows is up to.

Windows makes your life easier—well, at least the part that can be handled by a computer. Inside, it has a collection of specialized programs that work together to keep you as organized as you want to be:

- It's an **operating system**. That means it tells your computer what to do and when to do it.

- It includes a **file system** so you can organize your work.

- It can handle **printing and faxing**, and it even has built-in **electronic-mail** capabilities. You can share your work with other people through hard copy, fax, or a variety of e-mail systems.

- There's a **consistent look and feel** to everything, thanks to a work-shop full of boxes, buttons, toolbars, gizmos, and widgets that other programs can use. The net result? Most programs look a lot alike and work in a similar fashion, so when you learn how to use one program, you can use that knowledge to use other programs, too. That lets you get a lot more work done.

- It lets you do **several things at once**. (If you're easily distracted, this may not be good news!)

- There's some **productivity software**, including a simple word processor, communications programs, and a program you can use to draw or paint pictures.

- There's even some **anti-productivity software**, in the form of games like Solitaire and Freecell.

Why do I need an operating system?

Imagine how chaotic your office would be if your office manager quit tomorrow. The FedEx driver would be wandering the halls looking for someone to sign for all those packages. Telephones would be ringing off the hook. You'd be out of coffee by 9:30.

Without an operating system, things inside your PC would get just as discombobulated, just as fast. Fortunately, the Windows operating system is there to act as a ruthlessly efficient office manager. Windows knows every part of your PC, inside and out, so it can send your work to the right place. (When you ask your PC to print a file, you want it to go to the printer and not the trash can, right? That's the operating system's job.) It also knows all the rules for storing and retrieving files, so you can find your work without a lot of hassle.

The icons and menus in Windows make it easy for you to ask your PC to do some work. The operating system is the part that actually does the work. One without the other would be nearly useless, but together they're an unbeatable combination.

How do I use the Windows desktop?

If you could sweep all the clutter off your desk and spread the computer screen out in front of you, it would be easy to see why the Windows user interface is called the **desktop**. It's a smooth, flat surface that works a lot like your real desktop. It's where you'll keep the tools you need to work with your computer—not a stapler and scissors, but your word processor and spreadsheet, plus the folders full of files they create. Any projects you're working on right now—letters, proposals, budgets, and so on—can sit right here on the desktop if you'd like, or you can tuck them back into their folders and put them neatly away when you're done.

Thanks to the graphical user interface, you don't have to memorize complicated commands (and you don't have to deal with surly error messages when you accidentally mistype a command). Instead, you point to a picture, or an entry on a plain-English list; click the mouse once, and let Windows handle the details.

Things you need to know about Windows

Where do I start? Well, assuming Windows 95 is already installed on your PC, you just turn on your computer. When you press that power switch, a complicated sequence of events starts up.

Depending on the kind of hardware you have, it might take a minute or two for Windows to start up. You'll hear some noises from your hard drive, and if all goes well, you'll see the Windows 95 logo flash on the screen soon enough. Eventually, you'll see the Windows desktop, but there are many processes that go on under the hood first.

What happens when I start up Windows?

Starting up Windows is like opening your office in the morning. You have to go in and turn on the lights, make a fresh pot of coffee, and get the Xerox machine warmed up before you can do any real work. Windows has a lot of the same sort of housekeeping to do. There's a long, long checklist that Windows goes through before it lets you get to work, so it's normal for startup to take a little while. Here's what's going on:

1 The BIOS check. It's your PC's version of opening its eyes, stretching, and yawning. The computer checks to make sure that all its senses are intact. Is my memory all here? Is there a hard disk in the house? Any CD-ROMs? OK, next?

> ### 66 *Plain English, please!*
>
> **BIOS** stands for **Basic Input/Output System**. There are a few essential chores that your computer has learned how to do, like add two numbers together or store a bit of information in a place where it can find it again. The BIOS holds the instructions that tell the PC how to perform these basic, crucial tasks. 99

2 Once your PC finds the hard disk, it searches for the simplest Windows startup files. This is the place where Windows keeps track of everything you've asked it to do, including what color you want the background to be and where you want all your icons to sit.

3 The Plug and Play scan. Your computer sends a quick message to other pieces of hardware, like printers and modems and CD-ROM drives. What are we plugged into here?

4 Assuming everything's OK (and it usually is), your PC loads the rest of Windows at this point. If you're on a network, this is the point where you'll have to type in your password.

5 Now that Windows is running, it loads any programs in your **StartUp group**. When you put a program here, you're telling Windows you want it to automatically start up whenever Windows starts up.

6 That wasn't so hard, and it probably didn't take that long, either. At this point, Windows hands the whole thing over to you.

Q&A *My computer won't start up properly. What's wrong?*

It *is* plugged in, isn't it? The monitor's turned on, too, and the brightness and contrast controls are set properly? If you pass those checkpoints, try to restart your computer by pressing the on-off switch. When you see the words `Starting Windows 95`, press the F8 key and choose Safe Mode from the menu. This starts up a special simplified version of Windows. Once you start in Safe Mode, you can try to figure out where the problem is.

Why does Windows use pictures instead of words?

These days, we're surrounded by pictures and graphic images. Everywhere you look—on road signs, on bottles and cans, even in newspapers and magazines—we're replacing words with pictures. Because Windows is **graphical**—that is, it relies on pictures rather than words—it's chock full of tiny images, called **icons**, which are intended to make it easier to use.

Icons are used absolutely *everywhere* in Windows 95, too, so it pays to learn what the different types of icons mean. The contents might be just about anything—a letter to the IRS, a digitized picture of the Mona Lisa, even a recording of Bart Simpson saying "Cool!" Once you learn what an icon means, it really can act as a quick and easy way to start a program or perform a task. Some icons are instantly recognizable; others take a little getting used to:

The icon	What it means in plain English
☠	Poison! Don't even think about eating or drinking this!
👍 👎	Siskel liked it; Ebert hated it. You'll have to decide for yourself.
⌛	Please wait; your computer is busy at the moment.
🖩	Click here to start the Windows Calculator.

Different icons mean different things

If you compare your Windows desktop to the real one in your office, it's easy to find things that work the same way.

Officially, the small pictures you see are called **icons**. We'll discuss each one in more detail in the next section.

Anything that could go on paper—letters, budgets, presentations, and so on—can be stored as a **file** on your PC.

Windows lets you organize your files—everything from quick notes to formal reports—inside the PC equivalent of manila **folders**.

Folders and files are stored on **disks**, which act just like file cabinets (and seem to fill up just as quickly).

What's a GUI?

It's pronounced "gooey," and the acronym stands for the most obvious part of Windows—its graphical user interface.

A **user interface** is simply the way you communicate with a machine. Your microwave oven has a very simple user interface. The 12 buttons on your telephone are the interface between you and your voice-mail system. And *nobody* can figure out the interface of the average VCR.

Some computers use a **command-line interface**, where you type commands at the computer's keyboard (and it beeps back at you when you type a command wrong). Windows is much easier to use because it lets you tell the computer what to do by pointing at pictures on the screen. You don't have to memorize a whole manual full of commands—you just point at what you want and push a button.

When you put it all together, you get a **graphical user interface**. The pictures on the screen are the *graphics*, you're the *user*, and Windows provides the *interface* between you and the computer.

Why do we need a user interface, graphical or otherwise? Because something has to control the computer's operating system, which actually runs the commands and does the work. You don't really need to know much about your computer's operating system—just what kind you have. (It's like knowing whether your car has a stick shift or is an automatic.)

GUIs are powerful, but they demand equally powerful computers, and lots of memory and disk space.

Command-line interfaces are powerful, too, but they're almost impossible for average people to use. That's why GUIs are rapidly showing up everywhere—on cable TV boxes, in cars, even on refrigerators and washing machines!

What's going on inside My Computer?

I don't know about you, but I'd rather give my PC a friendly name, like Calvin, Hobbes, or Elvis. Unfortunately, someone at Microsoft decided that my computer (and your computer and, in fact, everyone's computer) would get the same dull, generic name: My Computer. Sigh.

We'll figure out how to change the computer's name later. For now, let's look at the useful tasks you can accomplish when you look underneath. The My Computer icon is your window on the most important pieces of your system—the disk drives, the printers, and all the knobs and levers that make it run smoothly (see fig. 1.1). What can you do here? Plenty.

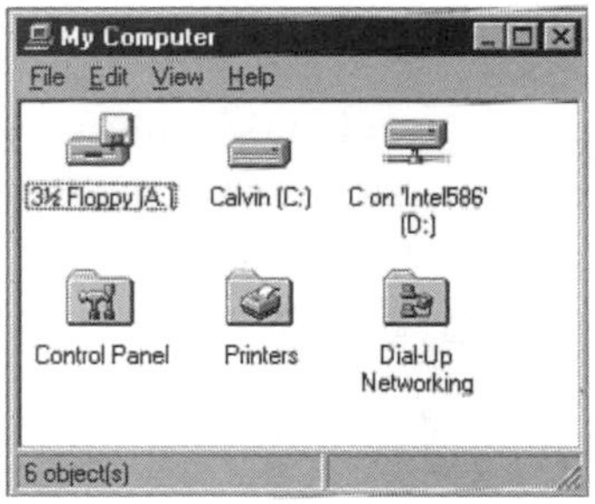

Fig. 1.1

This is My Computer, the place to turn when you want to find a file, set up a printer, or change your PC's settings.

Get the inside story on disks of every kind

How much free space is left on your hard disk? Find out here. This is the place where you can ask Windows to attach an electronic "label" to your disks, as well. From here, you can also turn on file sharing, so that someone else on a network can use the files on your hard disk (if you're on a network). It's also where you turn *off* sharing, or add a secret password so that Bob in Accounting cannot poke around in your hard disk. ("No way, pal. Uh-uh. You're not sharing *this* hard disk.") You can fiddle with a CD-ROM disk from remote control here—pop it out or lock it up, your choice. And it's one of many places in Windows where you can find a file, copy a file, or delete a file.

Ask the wizard to set up a printer!

Imagine how awkward life would be if you had to schlep your monitor down the hall every time you wanted to show someone this quarter's budget spreadsheet. That's why printers are the most important pieces of computer hardware, next to your PC, and that's why they get their own folder in the My Computer window. There's a built-in wizard that walks you, step-by-step, through the process of setting up a new printer. After it's been set up, this is the place you'll change the settings (maybe you added a new paper tray or moved it down the hall). With a few clicks here, you can share a printer with other people on a network; if they're not suitably grateful, you can stop sharing, too. Windows lines up all your print jobs in a list; from here, you can zap backed-up jobs before they ever make it to the printer.

What's under my PC's hood?

The icon called Control Panel may look like a folder, but it's really more like the hood of your car. Pop open the Control Panel, and you can fine-tune just about anything in your PC (see fig. 1.2). Some of the options are incredibly useful. For example, this is where you set the clock your computer uses to keep track of when you saved a file or sent a message.

You might never look at all the Control Panel options, but it's nice to know that Windows has a round-the-clock maintenance crew.

Fig. 1.2

This is where you'll turn for the simplest of tasks, like resetting your computer's clock, and tougher jobs, like installing a new piece of hardware.

Here are just a few of the simple, useful tasks you can perform from here: change the date and time, and tell Windows whether you prefer to see dates displayed in the American or European style. Slow down your mouse pointer and keyboard (or zoom them to Warp Factor 9). Configure a modem or a network.

If you want your sound card to bark every time you get an error message, you've come to the right place. (You'll find the step-by-step procedures in Chapter 18.) And if you want your desktop to look like a hot-dog stand, with a bright yellow and orange background that's so bright you have to pass out Ray-Bans to anyone who passes within five feet, step right this way.

Network Neighborhood? What's that all about?

If you're connected to a local area network, all the computers you're allowed to use get their own icons in your Network Neighborhood. Dig a little deeper and you can see whether the owner of that PC has put a "Share Me" sign on any of his folders or printers. For example, if Bob in Accounting wants you to look over this month's payroll report, he could put the report in a folder, call it "Payroll Reports," and tell Windows that it's OK if you look at it. Now, when you explore the icon for Bob's PC in the Network Neighborhood, you'll see that shared folder.

You can share things, too. If you have a laser printer hooked to your PC and you want your assistant to use it, you tell Windows that it's OK for other people to use it, and your PC and printer will show up in *their* Network Neighborhoods.

You really want a command line?

If you learned to use a PC with MS-DOS on it, you might feel temporarily disoriented when you first dive into Windows. That's normal—the feeling will pass. You'll learn the Windows equivalent of those old DOS commands in nothing flat.

But if you really want to return to the familiar DOS environment, Windows gives you a couple of choices of command lines. Both are accessible directly from the Start menu.

The first is a genuine DOS prompt. Click the Start button, then click on Programs to see its entry in the menu. The DOS Prompt window does everything a DOS user would expect, and then some. Unlike old-fashioned DOS, which insists on filling up your entire screen, this DOS shows up in a window that you can resize and move to fit

your screen. You can type the name of any program—DOS or Windows—and it will start right up. You can also run some of your older DOS programs, although some of them won't work properly with Windows 95.

The other option for anyone who wants to just type a DOS command is the Run command, also found on the Start menu. The Run command gives you a tiny box, big enough to hold a single command, plus a Browse button that lets you search for a specific file to run.

For some tasks, a command prompt is genuinely the fastest way to get the job done. But if you're like most people, the longer you use Windows, the less you'll find yourself craving the comfort of a C:\ prompt.

There's even more at the bottom of the screen

You'd have to be in a coma to miss the Start button. You turn on your PC, and there's the word Start, as big as life. When you first turn on your PC, the Start button's all alone on the bottom of the screen. We'll get to the Start button later, in Chapter 8. For now, though, let's move over a few inches.

Off to the right of the Start button is the **taskbar**, which works a lot like a handyman's tool belt. When you're working around the house, that belt saves you a lot of steps. After you've finished using a hammer or screwdriver, you don't put it back in the toolbox—you hang it on the belt so you can get to it quickly the next time you need it.

The Windows taskbar works the same way: as you begin opening files and setting them aside to work with new ones, the taskbar will fill up with all the programs you're running. When you need to reuse a folder or a program, just check the taskbar to find it fast. We'll look at the taskbar in more detail in Chapter 8.

 TIP   **Because it's possible to move or hide the taskbar, yours may** appear somewhere other than the bottom of the screen; it may even seem to be missing. Don't worry about it. If you want to move it or make it visible again, see Chapter 9.

Windows helps you organize your work

When you're trying to keep track of a complicated project, you use every organizational trick in the book. All your loose papers go into manila folders. You rubber-band thick reports together so they won't be accidentally separated. If the paperwork gets thick enough, you stuff the whole mess into a file-cabinet drawer.

Windows lets you do the exact same thing—only in a much neater and much faster way.

With Windows, it's easy to stay organized. When you write a new letter, for example, you give it a plain-English name, like **Thank-you letter to Bill Jones, April 15**. Each letter goes in the appropriate folder, which also has a plain-English name like April Letters.

And like a great executive assistant, Windows is smart enough to be able to find items that *you* lost. As long as you know some detail, no matter how small, about the file or folder you've lost, Windows can help you find it. Even if you accidentally threw the file into the Recycle Bin (no trash cans here!), there's a fighting chance you can get it back.

CAUTION **If you've thrown away a file by mistake and you want it back,** stop! Before you do anything else, double-click on the Recycle Bin. See Chapter 7 for step-by-step instructions on what to do next.

Shutting down your computer

To turn off your computer, first click on the Start button, then choose Shut Down from the menu. If you have any files you've been working on that haven't been saved yet, Windows will ask you if you want to save them. Just like the startup process, shutting down takes some time, but eventually you'll reach a screen that says it's OK to turn your PC off and quit for the day.

 Q&A *I usually shut down my computer by just pressing the power switch. Is that OK?*

No, it's never OK to press the big red switch unless you've first used the Windows Shut Down command (found on the Start menu). Windows keeps track of all sorts of important information in the background while you work. When you use the Shut Down command, Windows makes sure that that information is saved properly. If you turn off the power before shutting down, you risk losing data.

How can I make Windows work the way I work?

Everybody has a unique way of organizing offices and desktops. Some people like to be surrounded by four-foot stacks of paper; others can't get a thing done unless their desktops are clean enough to eat off of. Well, you can set up your Windows desktop to look and feel just like the one in your real office.

You're used to moving things around on your real desktop, right? If you want the phone on the right, you move it there. You throw all your important papers into a stack on the left? Hey, if it works for you, be my guest.

On the Windows desktop, you can rearrange objects to your heart's content. As long as there's free space, you can set a new object down on the desktop (or even on top of another object). Unlike your real desktop, you can even change the colors and put different labels on most of the objects on this desktop. You can throw away almost anything, too, if you don't need it and don't want it cluttering up your desktop.

66 *Plain English, please!*

Computer gurus (and guru-wannabes) like to talk about objects, because that word sounds so much better than things. It doesn't matter what you call them, though; if you can see something on the screen, it's an object. The most important fact is that objects that look similar usually act alike, too. So, once you learn how one part of Windows works, you can apply that same knowledge later to another, similar object. 99

If you just started Windows for the first time, your Windows desktop is sparkling clean right now. Whether it stays that way is up to you. If you thrive on a little chaos in your working life, go ahead and make this desktop as cluttered as your real one.

2

How Windows Works

● In this chapter:

- In Windows, everything is an icon

- Icons have plain-English names, not cryptic codes

- You store icons in folders

- What happened to DOS? (It's still there...)

Good-bye DOS! Windows 95 uses folders and icons and plain-English names. You don't even have to think about files! . . . . ⊳

I f ou've never used a computer before, you'll need to learn a few
things before Windows 95 makes sense. If you have used a
computer before, you'll need to *unlearn* a few things before Windows 95
makes sense.

Your old computer probably used Microsoft DOS and Windows 3.1 (or
maybe 3.11), which means you had to learn how to think like a computer to
get even the simplest jobs done. It's hard to imagine anything more complicated and frustrating than good ol' DOS. Most sensible people would rather
program a VCR while blindfolded than struggle with a DOS prompt.

With Windows 95, you don't have to look at that ugly old C:\ prompt anymore (as in fig. 2.1—try not to shudder as you view it). You don't have to
type complicated commands to get even the simplest job done. And you
don't have to wrack your brain coming up with eight-character names for
your files. In fact, you don't even have to think about files anymore.

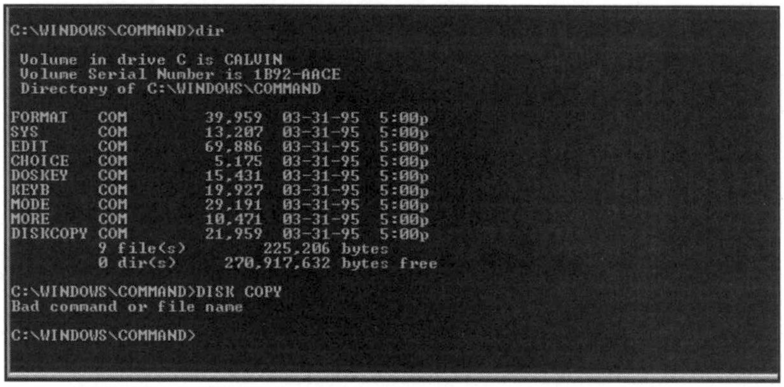

Fig. 2.1

Goodbye, DOS!
Windows uses icons
and folders and plain-
English names instead
of this unfriendly DOS
prompt.

```
C:\WINDOWS\COMMAND>dir
    Volume in drive C is CALVIN
    Volume Serial Number is 1B92-AACE
    Directory of C:\WINDOWS\COMMAND

FORMAT    COM      39,959  03-31-95  5:00p
SYS       COM      13,287  03-31-95  5:00p
EDIT      COM      69,886  03-31-95  5:00p
CHOICE    COM       5,175  03-31-95  5:00p
DOSKEY    COM      15,431  03-31-95  5:00p
KEYB      COM      19,927  03-31-95  5:00p
MODE      COM      29,191  03-31-95  5:00p
MORE      COM      10,471  03-31-95  5:00p
DISKCOPY  COM      21,959  03-31-95  5:00p
         9 file(s)       225,206 bytes
         0 dir(s)    270,917,632 bytes free

C:\WINDOWS\COMMAND>DISK COPY
Bad command or file name

C:\WINDOWS\COMMAND>
```

What happened to my files?

All your files are still there—don't worry about them. The biggest difference
between Windows 95 and DOS is that you get to stop worrying about files.
Instead, start learning how to work with icons because in Windows 95,
everything is an icon.

So, what exactly *is* an icon?

Those small pictures scattered all over your Windows desktop are called
icons. (There's one in fig. 2.2, for instance.) Every icon consists of a picture
and (usually) a text description, like "My Computer" or "Program Files."

Fig. 2.2

Look closely at an icon (like this one for a CD-ROM drive). You'll see that it's made out of dots—32 of them on each side.

Think of each icon as the label on a box that holds something inside your computer. You may have the world's messiest office, but Windows is fussier than Felix Unger. Windows makes sure that everything inside your computer is contained inside one of these icons/boxes. And not just any icon/box, either. There are five distinct types of icons, and each one is reserved for a special kind of data. (After all, it wouldn't do to have your dress shirts and muddy old workboots just shoved into the same drawer, would it?)

Don't let the tiny size fool you, either; Windows can pack an amazing amount of data inside each one of these boxes.

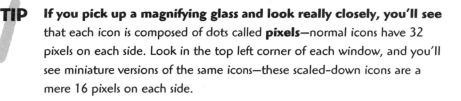

TIP **If you pick up a magnifying glass and look really closely, you'll see** that each icon is composed of dots called **pixels**—normal icons have 32 pixels on each side. Look in the top left corner of each window, and you'll see miniature versions of the same icons—these scaled-down icons are a mere 16 pixels on each side.

How do I make an icon do something?

There's one surefire way to open an icon, and that's to double-click it. (If you're not sure how double-clicking works, skip ahead to Chapter 5.) When you do, the icon opens into a **window**, which is simply another view of what's inside that icon. Depending on the type of icon you double-clicked, you might see a *folder* full of documents, a *program* like Word for Windows, a *document* like an Excel spreadsheet, or a collection of *controls* for all the hardware in and around your PC.

I wonder what this icon does

It's easy to find out: click the right mouse button and choose Properties from the pull-down menu. This lets you look at the icon's Properties sheet (see fig. 2.3). No, it has nothing to do with Donald Trump, and you won't have to pay any taxes on these Properties. Instead, it's Windows' way of providing you with detailed information about the contents of each icon.

Windows makes sure that everything inside your computer is contained inside one of these icon/boxes. And not just any icon/box, either. There are five distinct types of icons, and each one is reserved for a special kind of data:

What It's Called	What It Really Means
Document	A document is the equivalent of one or more pieces of paper, and it is the basic unit of Windows. A document might consist of words or numbers or pictures, or all of them combined.
Program	Programs are the parts of Windows that actually do the work of putting words, numbers, and pictures into documents. They get the coolest icons, too.
Folder	Folders are special places where you can organize a bunch of icons of any kind. If you're the fussy sort, you can even put folders inside of folders inside of folders.
Device	Each piece of your PC—hard drive, printer, mouse, and the like—gets its own icon. Inside, there are knobs and levers to help you fiddle with the device.
Shortcut	A shortcut icon helps you find another icon. The icon you're looking for isn't here, but hang on tight and the shortcut will take you there in a jiffy.

The label underneath is useful, but a bit limited—especially because you fill it out yourself. You've probably had the same experience in your own garage or attic. You wrote "Christmas Ornaments" on the outside of five different boxes. Next December, when you're trying to find the one with the angel for the top of the tree, you'll have to pry each one open and look inside. Unless, of course, you were fussy enough to make a list of each box's contents and tape it to the outside.

Well, Windows *is* that fussy. You can scribble whatever you want underneath the icon, but Windows assigns an inventory clerk to follow along behind you, so that later, when you click the right mouse button, it can hand over a detailed report summarizing the contents of the icon you just clicked.

Tabs along the top let you choose different "pages"
containing different types of information.

Fig. 2.3

What's underneath
that icon? Click the
right mouse button,
and look at the
Properties sheet to
see for yourself.

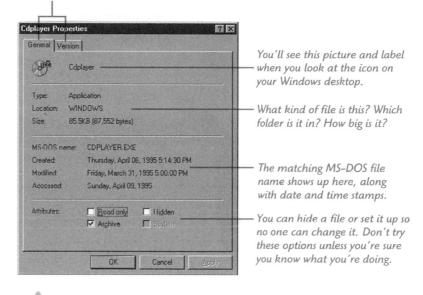

You'll see this picture and label
when you look at the icon on
your Windows desktop.

What kind of file is this? Which
folder is it in? How big is it?

The matching MS-DOS file
name shows up here, along
with date and time stamps.

You can hide a file or set it up so
no one can change it. Don't try
these options unless you're sure
you know what you're doing.

TIP **You can quickly change an icon's label by pressing F2 and then**
typing a new name.

What's on each property sheet? That depends:

- For a **document**, the Properties sheet gives you all the details you'd
  expect from the DOS directory command: name, size, date created, and
  so on. (See the example in fig. 2.3.)

- For a **folder**, you can see at a glance how many items are inside; you
  can also use the Properties sheet to share a folder with someone else on
  your network.

- For a **Windows program**, the label looks nearly the same as a
  document.

- For a **DOS program**, the Properties sheet lets you do all sorts of weird
  and technical things. Don't even think of looking here unless you're
  really a DOS expert!

- For a **device**, the pop-up Properties menu lets you adjust the way Windows works with your hardware. For example, you can kill a print job by double-clicking a printer icon and choosing from a menu.

- For a **shortcut**, the right mouse button displays details about the shortcut and about the original file that it refers to.

CAUTION   **Windows hides things from you, including a lot of the files it** needs to run. With the help of a few DOS tricks, you can easily find these hidden files. But you're better off just leaving them alone. They're hidden for a good reason, and if you accidentally mess with them, you could get your PC so thoroughly confused that it won't run.

What's that arrow in the corner of this icon mean?

The little arrow in the lower left corner of an icon means it's a **shortcut** to an original file. If you've gotten used to DOS and Windows 3.1, you've never seen anything like shortcuts before. But once you learn what they do, you'll find yourself using them everywhere.

Shortcuts work like small push buttons that let you jump straight to a file stored somewhere else. When you double-click a shortcut, you tell Windows to find the **target file** and open it.

Why are shortcuts useful? Well, let's say you crunch numbers for a living. Mind-bogglingly big numbers. Gazillions of numbers. The fastest, easiest way to crunch all those numbers is with the help of the Windows Calculator, but you don't like poking and clicking through all those folders looking for it. No problem—just create a shortcut on your Windows desktop. When you double-click the shortcut, Windows looks inside the shortcut for instructions on where to go next. (They'll probably look a lot like fig. 2.4.) Assuming you've filled in the blanks properly, Windows scurries off in search of the Calculator and opens it up. Easy as 1-2-3.

Fig. 2.4

Fill in the blanks on a shortcut's Properties sheet. Later, when you double-click the shortcut, Windows finds the target file and opens it up instead.

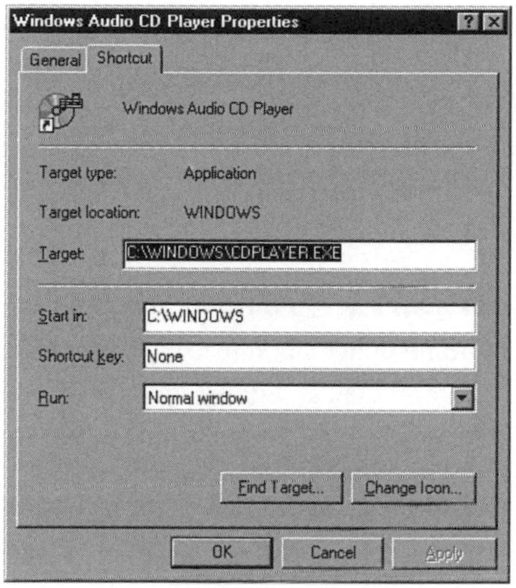

Q&A *Hey! That target file looks a lot like a DOS command! Didn't you say I wouldn't have to type in DOS commands anymore?*

Yes, I did. And no, you don't. You can create a shortcut by simply dragging a file or folder from the Windows Explorer to the desktop, or you can have Windows automatically fill in the blanks for you with the Shortcut Wizard. You can type in commands if you want, but you never have to.

Every icon has a plain-English name

Let's say you're moving across the country, and all of your worldly goods are packed in cardboard boxes. You've got a Magic Marker, but someone just told you that you can only use eight letters (although you can have an extra three letters if you separate it from the eight letters with a dot). "That's ridiculous!" you'd complain. And you'd be right. But that's exactly how DOS has worked for more than a decade.

If you've used DOS, you've learned to compress complex thoughts into ridiculously compact spaces. All the letters you wrote last June, for example, went into a directory called LETTER06, with names like JOHNTHX1.DOC and WLDPRC11.DOC. Who knows what those names meant?

Well, with Windows 95, you don't need to create cryptic eight-letter file names anymore because Windows lets you label your folders and documents with plain-English names of up to 255 characters. (You'll run out of room on the screen before you'll use that many characters.) And won't it be easy to find documents when they have names like Thank-you letter to John Martin, 6-30?

✓ **TIP** **You can make an icon's name up to 255 characters long, and you** can even use some punctuation marks: periods, commas, semicolons, ampersands, parentheses, and dollar signs. There are a handful of characters you can't use to name a file or folder, though. Here are the keys that you're not allowed to use in an icon's name:

: ' " \ / * ? |

What happened to the three-letter file extensions, like .TXT, that you used to tack onto the end of files? They're still there. Whenever possible, though, Windows hides the extensions and gives you a more meaningful explanation. Instead of .TXT, Windows labels those files as Text Documents. Your eight-and-three file and extension names are still there, though, for compatibility with older programs.

You store information in folders

One of the most confusing parts of the good ol' DOS file system is the way it forces you to use complicated directory names. If you wanted to stay organized, the only way to store your data (and then find it again) was to type a mind-boggling path name like C:\WALDO\DATA\LETTERS\JAN95\AARRGGH!

With Windows, you don't need to type in complicated path names because all your files are icons, remember? And they're arranged neatly inside folder icons. Even the desktop, the place where you see My Computer and the Network Neighborhood, is really just a folder that's always open.

Deep down inside, there's not much difference between a folder and a DOS directory, except for the fact that one is easy to use and the other is impossible.

The long and the short of Windows file names

Windows lets you use up to 255 characters to name each icon; that's more room than you get on the average postcard. But when it comes to storing data on your hard disk, Windows still uses the old-fashioned DOS filing system, which is limited to an eight-character name, plus a period and three more letters. You rarely have to worry about the short names, though, because Windows handles the confusing details behind the scenes.

As far as you're concerned, that WordPad file you just finished is called "Letter to the IRS, begging for a four-month extension." As soon as you saved it, Windows converted the long icon names into short file names that follow the DOS rules. First, it trimmed away all the spaces inside (spaces are a no-no for DOS files, but they're A-OK for you to use in Windows 95). It also whacked away everything after the first six characters, and then added a tilde (a squiggly character you'll recognize from high-school Spanish classes), the number 1, a period, and the letters DOC at the end. So your letter's real name, known only to Windows, is LETTER~1.DOC.

Whenever you ask for the file, you double-click an icon labeled with an easy-to-understand name. When Windows gets your message, it looks through its list of short file names to find the one that matches the icon you asked for.

Now, let's say you used WordPad to create another letter in the same folder. This one's called "Letter to our accountant demanding a pretty good explanation!" Windows might try to save this file under the name LETTER~1.DOC, but it won't work—there's already a file by that name, and duplicates aren't allowed. So Windows reaches into its bag of file-naming tricks to come up with a unique name. Add a character here and chop one off there, and you wind up with the next name in the series, LETTER~2.DOC. That name may be meaningless to you and me, but we don't care, because we use the icon's long name.

So far, so good. But what happens when you try to copy a file with a long name to a floppy disk, so you can stick it in a FedEx envelope and send it off to someone else? Well, if you're both using Windows 95, then there's no problem: The long file name is written right on the disk. But if the person at the other end is using DOS or Windows 3.1, then all that information is lost. As far as they're concerned, that file is just called LETTER~1.DOC.

What can I put inside a folder?

Folders hold icons. Most of the folders you'll work with every day will hold icons representing your program files and documents. But folders can also hold other folders. If you want all your work filed in one place, for example, you might create a folder called Projects and fill it with other folders, one for each iron you and your fellow workers have in the fire right now.

This folder-in-a-folder idea isn't difficult to understand. Just think of a typical dresser. Let's say our imaginary dresser has four drawers, and in the top drawer there's a box where we keep socks. When you need a fresh pair of socks, you open the dresser, then open the top drawer, and finally look in the box. Folders work the same way.

If you're the sort who puts different-colored socks in separate drawers, you can put folders inside of folders inside of still other folders, until they're buried so deeply you'll need a backhoe to dig them out. Fortunately, Windows makes it easy to find folders within folders by arranging folders at the top, ahead of any other icons it finds, whenever you open a window.

How do I look inside a folder?

To open up a folder, just double-click it. By default, you'll see the contents of the folder displayed as large icons, like the ones in figure 2.5. You can change to a different view by selecting one from the <u>V</u>iew menu.

Fig. 2.5
Four ways to look at your work: Large icons or Small, List or Details view (more information at your fingertips).

*To see this **Large Icons** view, click here.*

*To see more icons in the same space, click on **Small Icons**. The icons in the folder will still be arranged from left to right.*

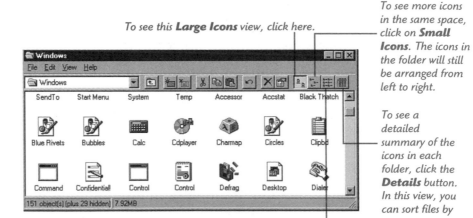

*To see a detailed summary of the icons in each folder, click the **Details** button. In this view, you can sort files by name, type, date and time, or size.*

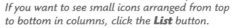

*If you want to see small icons arranged from top to bottom in columns, click the **List** button.*

DOS runs in a box

If you insist, you can still use DOS. (Why would anyone want to? Maybe you have a favorite program and you can't find a Windows version.) From the DOS prompt, you can start DOS and Windows programs, find files, even copy and rename and delete files. You probably won't want to, though, especially if you've used long names for a lot of files and directories. To see those long names from a DOS window, you'll have to remember to enclose the whole path name in quotation marks. Yikes!

Still, if you must, the easy way to get to a DOS prompt is to click the Start button, choose Programs, and then click the entry labeled MS-DOS Prompt.

 TIP **The *MS* in MS-DOS stands for Microsoft, which makes more than** nine out of ten copies of DOS. Other varieties come from IBM, Novell, and Digital Research (DR-DOS). Because Windows 95 is made by Microsoft, it contains a copy of MS-DOS.

 Q&A ***I started a DOS program, and now I can't get back to Windows. What do I do?***

DOS runs in a window most of the time, but you can also start up a full-screen DOS prompt that looks just like you've quit Windows. If you're absent-minded, you might even forget you're still in Windows. Appearances to the contrary, you haven't left Windows. To make the DOS program shrink down into an icon on the taskbar, just press Alt+Tab. To make it go away, get to a DOS prompt, and type **Exit**.

One nice thing about the version of DOS that comes with Windows 95 is that you can make it bigger or smaller, to match your monitor's size and your eyesight. Aim the mouse pointer at the title bar for a DOS window and right-click. From the pop-up menu, choose the word <u>T</u>oolbar. Now you have access to a handy collection of buttons, as well as to a list of different fonts you can use to enlarge or shrink the type inside the DOS window (see fig. 2.6).

 **CAUTION** **If you have an old DOS utilities program like PC Tools or the** Norton Utilities, *don't use it*. You can wind up making a horrible mess of everything on your computer if you try. Get an upgrade designed specifically for Windows 95—most software makers have them.

Fig 2.6
Want to make your
DOS window easier to
read? Right-click the
title bar and click on
the word <u>T</u>oolbar to
produce this collection
of useful buttons and a
drop-down font list.

Your applications all work about the same

Of course, you didn't get a computer so you could simply move files from
folder to folder. Your computer is a tool that lets you get work done. That
means you need **application software** to get that work done. After work
(or whenever the boss is away), you can also use it to relax with a game of
Solitaire or Minesweeper.

Where did CONFIG.SYS and AUTOEXEC.BAT go?

If you've ever struggled with DOS, you've met its
two startup files, CONFIG.SYS and
AUTOEXEC.BAT. They're still here in Windows 95,
but you won't see them nearly as often. Windows
uses them if it must, but it prefers not to.

A lot of the programs that used to clutter up
these files are unnecessary in Windows 95. You
probably had a memory-management program in
your old DOS system, for example. It's not
needed here. Neither is a separate program for
talking with your mouse or hooking you up to a
Novell network.

So why are these two files still around? Because
some kinds of hardware absolutely, positively
have to have their own translation programs,
called **drivers**. If you take their drivers away,
they throw a tantrum and refuse to talk with
Windows until the drivers come back.

Windows does a thorough job of stripping away
unnecessary programs when you first install it, so
you shouldn't need to worry about
AUTOEXEC.BAT or CONFIG.SYS ever again.

66 *Plain English, please!*

> An **application** is a piece of software that helps you do a wide range of business tasks. Your word processor is an application; so is your spreadsheet and your e-mail access software. Tiny application programs that do simple jobs are sometimes called **applets.** 99

The advantage of Windows software is that when you learn how to use one program, you've learned the basics of every Windows program. They all use windows and icons and menus and mouse pointers. Windows also gives you a special tool called the **Clipboard**—with its help, you can copy information (a list of names, perhaps, or a column of numbers) from one place and paste it into another, even if the two applications are completely different.

Finally, Windows lets you work with different applications at the same time. And inside each application you can handle many different data files, also at the same time. As long as you're not overwhelmed by all those windows, it's a great way to get a lot of work done.

Which applications should I use?

That depends on what you want to do. These days, when you buy a new computer you almost always get a suitcase full of software thrown in as part of the deal. You can also buy software just about anywhere. To decide which software is right for you, first ask what kind of work you need to do.

I write letters, reports, and memos

OK, you'll need a **word processor**. The three most popular are Microsoft Word for Windows, Novell's WordPerfect for Windows, and WordPro (formerly called Ami Pro) from Lotus Development.

I crunch numbers and create graphs

Ah, then you'll want a **spreadsheet**. Microsoft Excel, Lotus 1-2-3, and Novell Quattro Pro are the most popular choices. Today's spreadsheets can figure everything from simple addition to the flight plan for the Space Shuttle.

I do a lot of slide presentations

Well, you're in luck, because there's a whole category of software, called **presentation graphics programs**, made just for you. Microsoft PowerPoint and Lotus Freelance Graphics are first-rate programs that let you turn bullet lists into colorful slides.

I manage a mailing list

You can use a spreadsheet for simple lists, but there's a much more powerful tool: a **database manager**. Most database programs are fiendishly hard to use, though, so be careful. Microsoft Access, Lotus Approach, and Borland's Paradox and dBase are the best-known choices.

I just want to track my finances

Then you need Quicken for Windows or Managing Your Money. And at tax time, you'll want their companion programs, TurboTax and TaxCut.

I want to do it all!

If you know that you're going to need several major programs, like a word processor, spreadsheet, and database, consider a **suite**—a bundled package of applications, all by the same manufacturer, which are sold at a big discount. Microsoft Office, Novell Perfect Office, and Lotus SmartSuite are all examples of the latest trend in application software. In each case, you get several big programs, including a word processor, spreadsheet, database manager, and presentation graphics program. Just make sure you have lots of room on your hard disk, because these all-in-one packages typically chew up more than 50 *megabytes* of hard disk space!

66 *Plain English, please!*

A **megabyte** is a unit of measure for computer memory and disk space. Most hard disks sold today are between 100 megabytes and 1 **gigabyte** (1000 megabytes). What's a megabyte? It's a million bytes. What's a **byte**? It's the amount of space taken up by a single character (such as the letter A or the number 2). 99

3

Windows and Your PC

● In this chapter:

- A few words about hardware

- How does Windows know what's inside my PC?

- This PC is so *slow!*

- Do I need a multimedia PC? What is multimedia anyway?

Why do you need to know about hardware? You don't, usually—you just turn on your computer and it works. But sometimes . . . . ▶

You don't need to know what's under your car's hood, at least most of the time. But when it's 12-below-zero and the old clunker won't start, you could be on the road a lot faster if you have a basic understanding of what a spark plug does. It's the same with your computer: if it stops working suddenly, it helps to know which piece you need to bring in for repairs.

And if your PC just seems too slow, it might be because one of the pieces of the hardware team isn't pulling its weight. The PC on your desktop is probably good enough to do everyday work with Windows. But that doesn't mean you're stuck with it. You can make it faster, add extra storage space, or plug in a bigger monitor so you can see more. Thanks to a Windows 95 feature called Plug and Play, it's easier than ever to add new hardware to your system.

What's inside your PC?

You don't need to know every little detail about your PC, like who made the floppy disk drive. You don't need to know who made your car's spark plugs, either, as long as it has a full set. But you should know whether your car has an automatic or manual transmission. And if you know some basic facts about your PC, you'll have a lot easier time when you need to talk with other people about your hardware. Here are some fast facts about common types of hardware:

When They Say...	They Really Mean...	What Windows Uses It for...
CPU	The **central processing unit**, found on a teensy silicon chip inside your computer. Today's most popular chips are the **Pentium** and the **486**; you can run Windows on an old **386**, too, but not on a **286** or **8088**.	This is your PC's brain—the boss that tells all the other pieces what to do every time you press a key or move a mouse. If your CPU is too slow, you get to see the Windows hourglass all the time.
RAM (pronounce it like the sheep)	**Random-access memory**, a short-term storage area for data. Anything that's stored here will vanish—poof!—as soon as you turn the power off, unless you save it on a hard or floppy disk.	Windows carves out a chunk of RAM for everything you do—no matter how big or small. Try to do too much at once, and Windows will tell you it's time to add more RAM or close some windows.

When They Say...	They Really Mean...	What Windows Uses It for...
Hard disk	Long-term storage, where your computer can remember things, even after you turn the power off. All your files, folders, and programs are stored here, the same way TV programs are stored on videotape.	When you double-click on an icon, Windows has to find the icon's data on your hard drive, then copy it into RAM so you can work with it. Even the fastest hard disk is slow compared to the rest of your PC.
Monitor (also called **display,** or **screen,** or sometimes **CRT**)	The part of your PC that looks like a TV screen. Under a powerful magnifying class, you can see that the picture is actually made up of thousands of tiny red, green, and blue dots, called **pixels**.	This is the place where you see your work. Without a monitor, Windows would be useless. A bigger monitor lets you see more at once; a sharper monitor is easier on your eyes.
Video adapter	The hardware that actually puts the things you see on-screen. If you have 20/20 vision and the right monitor, you can use some video cards to shrink windows and icons, so you see even more things at once.	Hey, drawing all those boxes and buttons is hard work. Plain old **video cards** are called **VGA**; fancy video cards are called **Super VGA**. Really expensive video cards get slick brand names.

Windows knows what kind of hardware you have—well, usually

When you start up your PC, the first thing Windows 95 does is look at all the hardware in your system. If there's any housekeeping that needs to be done, this is when it happens. Windows is responsible for making sure that all the parts of your PC get along peacefully (you don't want the phone to start dialing when you click on the Print icon).

What happens when you add a new piece of hardware—like a CD-ROM player, a sound card, a new printer, or a modem? The first time you start Windows after plugging in the new hardware, it should notice that there's a new device, and automatically set it up so it works with all the software and hardware you already have.

Plain English, please!

Why do they call it **Plug and Play**? You plug in the hardware, and
Windows makes sure it plays properly. It may sound like no big deal, but it
is—trust me. If you ever tried to get a multimedia upgrade kit to work with
a PC running Windows 3.1, you'll want to send flowers and candy to the
folks who invented Plug and Play.

Most of the time, Plug and Play makes sure your PC works. But there are
two situations in which you'll need to deal with hardware settings.

Something isn't working!

It might be your CD-ROM, your sound card, or some other device—it doesn't
matter. Before you take your PC in to the repair shop, see if Windows can
help you fix it. Your secret weapon is the **Windows Device Manager**,
which contains a detailed list of every piece of hardware in your PC. If
you're lucky, the problem will show up here first.

To start the Device Manager, follow these steps:

1 Point to the My Computer icon, click the right mouse button, and
      choose Properties from the pop-up menu.

2 Click on the Device Manager tab at the top of the dialog box. You'll see
      a display like the one in figure 3.1. (Yours won't look exactly like mine,
      of course.)

Fig. 3.1
The Windows 95
Device Manager
contains a list of all
the hardware in your
system.

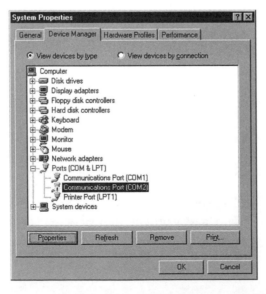

3 Is there a yellow exclamation point over the Device Manager listing for the item you're having trouble with? If so, select that item and click on the button labeled Properties. A new dialog box appears, like the one in figure 3.2.

Fig. 3.2

Whenever you have a problem with hardware, Windows will use its Plug and Play features to try to help you track it down and fix it.

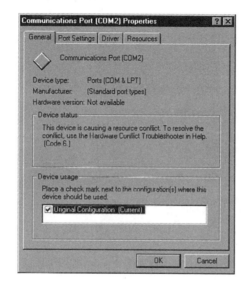

If the dialog box says there's a problem with the hardware, it's time to call for help!

Q&A ***Windows says the device has a resource conflict. What's that mean?***

Basically, a **resource conflict** happens when more than one piece of equipment is trying to use a port or another piece of hardware. Windows 95 has help built in for this problem, in the form of the **Hardware Conflict Troubleshooter**. To start up this wizard, click on the Start button, and choose Help from the menu. On the Contents tab, double-click on Troubleshooting, then click on the entry labeled If you have a hardware conflict. Click on the appropriate button to get the process started, then follow the detailed instructions. (They're written in plain English.)

I have a new device I want to install...

You'll have to plug in the device, but Windows can handle the technical part of it. Double-click on My Computer, then double-click on the Control Panel icon. Finally, double-click on the icon labeled Add New Hardware. You'll see an opening screen for the wizard that handles all the hardware. To begin installing the hardware choose the Next button. The second Wizard box appears (see fig. 3.3).

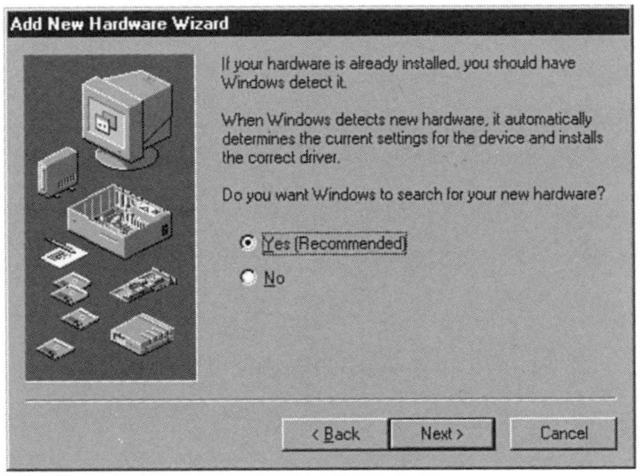

Fig. 3.3

The Add New Hardware Wizard should be your first stop if you plan to install a new device— like a CD-ROM drive, a sound card, or a printer—in your PC.

The whole process is about as simple as PCs get. Be sure to tell Windows you want it to try to detect the new device, and be sure to read the instructions carefully.

TIP **If you're thinking of buying a new hardware feature like a sound** card, look for a Windows 95 logo on the package; if you see one, you can be assured that it will work with your PC. If you don't see the logo, open My Computer and then open the Control Panel window. Double-click on the Add New Hardware icon; and tell Windows you don't want it to search for your new hardware. Click the Next button until you get to the section that lists all the devices. If the sound card you're thinking of buying is listed there, it will probably work just fine with your PC. If it's not there, think twice before buying. And always insist on a money-back guarantee from whoever's selling you the new gadget.

What does all this hardware *do*?

Look carefully at the box Windows 95 comes in, and you'll see a few paragraphs detailing the **minimum hardware configuration** and the **recom-**

mended hardware configuration. If your PC doesn't measure up to the minimum standards, you can't run Windows at all. If it falls short of the recommended level, it will run, but it might be painfully slow. Does Windows work OK for you? Then you shouldn't need to worry about it!

> ## 66 *Plain English, please!*
>
> Because there are so many choices between different components, PCs are almost like snowflakes—no two are exactly alike. Configuration is the catch-all word that refers to the unique combination of parts in your PC. 99

Does my PC have enough horsepower?

If your PC had an engine, the CPU chip and memory would be it. To run Windows, you'll need at least a 386 chip and at least 4M of RAM. But most people will want a little more computer than that.

How do you know how much CPU and memory you have? Watch your PC's screen when you first turn it on; most computers introduce the CPU and inventory memory here. The only trick is converting kilobytes (K) into megabytes (M), and vice versa. There are roughly a thousand kilobytes in one megabyte, so if your PC counts to 4096K when you start it up, you really have 4M. That's the bare minimum you need for Windows—8M is better.

My PC is getting really slow. What could be wrong?

You might be running low on memory. When Windows runs out of RAM, it first tries to use the hard disk to simulate extra memory. Windows takes the chunk of RAM your first program is using and **swaps** it from memory onto the hard disk (which is about a thousand times slower than RAM). That frees up a chunk of RAM for your second program to use, but when you switch back to the first program, Windows has to swap both chunks of data. Add another program, and pretty soon Windows is spending all its time swapping data onto your hard drive and back again instead of running programs. The result is a lot of noise from your hard disk, and a PC that's running in super-slo-mo.

It's a clever fake, but anyone who's ever seen an Elvis impersonator knows there's nothing like the real thing. If your system slows to a crawl too often, you need more memory.

TIP **CPU speed is measured in megahertz, which stands for one million** cycles-per-second. (Each cycle is one little two-step for your CPU; it's not a very complicated move, but since some CPUs can do 100 million of these hokey-pokeys every second, it looks like it's dancing up a storm.) The more megahertz you have, the more muscles your PC can flex: in Windows terms, 20 is slower than a bottle of Heinz ketchup, 100 is faster than a Roger Clemens fastball. If your CPU clocks in at 33MHz or more, you can run Windows just fine.

Sometimes the image seems blurry

To run Windows, you need a color monitor and a VGA card. Windows knows how to identify your video card and set things up so it works properly. Like TVs, monitor screens are measured diagonally. And they're never, ever as big as they claim to be.

CAUTION **There's one place where I draw the line when it comes to saving** money on hardware. I won't settle for a crummy monitor, and you shouldn't, either. We're talking about your *eyes*, for heaven's sake. You're not likely to go blind from using an undersized monitor with a blurry image, but you'll probably go home with a headache every day. If you have to cut corners with a slower PC, that's one thing. But make sure your monitor isn't going to hurt your eyes.

Is my hard disk big enough?

Hard drives are measured in **megabytes,** unless you have a Schwarzenegger-strength system, in which case you might have more than 1000 megabytes, or a **gigabyte** (pronounce it GIG-uh-bite). To run Windows and one additional program, you'll need *at least* an 80M hard drive. And that won't leave a lot of room for your work. Depending on the kind of software you use and the type of data files you create, you may need 200M or more to hold it all.

How much room is left on your hard disk? Look in Chapter 6 for step-by-step instructions on how to find out.

TIP **If you've run out of disk space, you have another option: You can** use Windows' built-in disk-compression program, DriveSpace, to pack nearly twice as much data into the same space. For more details, see Chapter 6.

Don't forget about the floppy disk!

Some older PCs only have one drive, designed to use 5.25-inch disks (you can spot these kind because they're big and soft—you can literally bend them in half). These days, most computers use the smaller 3.5-inch disks. If you don't have one of these floppy drives, get one. It's almost impossible to find new software on the larger disks, and the smaller ones are more reliable and durable anyway.

And, of course, the mouse and keyboard

It may seem obvious, but to run Windows you have to have a mouse and a keyboard.

Unless you spill a Diet Coke on your keyboard there's no real reason to replace it, although these days there are all sorts of wacky keyboard designs to choose from. Most of them look like they survived a 7.1 earthquake, with the keyboard split into two pieces. The theory is that you'll be less likely to get carpal tunnel syndrome if you hold your hands sideways while you type. I have a hard enough time making my two fingers hit the keys when I can see them, so I'll stick with the traditional design, thank you very much.

❝❝ *Plain English, please!*

And, now that I've made my opinion clear, let me add a brief note about the **Microsoft Natural Keyboard**. My Product Director insists that switching to this keyboard helped her get off of the therapist's schedule and back to work, with a tremendous decrease in pain in her wrists from tendonitis. **❞❞**

As for **mice** (which is the plural of mouse, although some people say **mouses** and a few wackos say **meeses,** as in "I hate those meeses to pieces"), you have two basic choices. The dull, conventional mouse that comes with most PCs looks like a bar of soap with a long wire dangling out the back. If you don't like sliding the mouse around on your desktop, with or without a mouse pad, try a **trackball**. Unlike the bar-of-soap mouse, which has a roller on the bottom, the trackball has a roller in the top; the whole thing stays in one place while you twiddle the roller with your thumb.

Trackballs are most popular on notebook PCs, where a long dangling cord is likely to get under the wheels of the drink cart as the flight attendant rolls by. Some notebooks have bizarre mouse substitutes that look like pencil erasers or little pads. Not to worry—the point is still to move the pointer on the screen. As long as there's a left and right button, you're in business.

Q&A   *My mouse is acting funny—it hops and skips across the screen, or leaves little "mouse droppings."*

You probably have a non-Microsoft mouse, and Windows is having trouble communicating with it. Call the store that sold you the mouse (it probably came with your PC) and ask if there's a new driver for Windows 95. (A **driver** is a small software program that tells Windows how to talk to a piece of hardware.) If they say no, demand to exchange it for a new mouse that's compatible with Windows 95.

How to put your work on paper

Printers help you dazzle other people with your brilliant ideas, even if you can't convince them to come around and look over your shoulder at whatever's on your screen. We'll cover printers and how to use 'em with Windows in Chapter 16. Plenty of info there.

Connecting with other computers

Modems let you hook your PC to a telephone line and do all sorts of cool things—send e-mail, find files on your PC at the office without leaving your living room, and cruise up and down the Information Superhighway. We'll talk about modems in Chapter 22.

Network adapters let you hook your PC to another PC so that both computers can share files, folders, printers, and fax modems. Setting up a network is best left to experts, but using them with Windows is really pretty easy. For the gory details, see Chapter 21.

Do you need a multimedia PC?

If you're the one using it, a **multimedia PC** is a powerful tool for adding lifelike sound and video clips to presentations and important documents. If the guy in the next cubicle is using it, though, multimedia is a big waste of money, and if I hear that stupid Homer Simpson sound clip one more time, I'll rip those speakers out of the back of his PC.

Ahem. Multimedia *is* controversial. For most people, it's unnecessary but fun. Typical multimedia PCs include a CD-ROM player, a sound card, and a pair of speakers. We'll cover multimedia in more detail in Chapters 18, 19, and 20.

How much hardware do I need to run Windows?

I was afraid you were going to ask that. You see, the answer is... Well, that depends.

Let's talk for a second about ergonomics

Maybe the most important parts of your PC aren't parts of your PC at all. If you use a computer regularly, you owe it to yourself (and your body) to pay attention to the way you sit in front of your computer.

The human body wasn't designed to handle the stress of nonstop typing. When you twist your body up like a pretzel and pound on a keyboard for hours at a time, the results can be painful, and you can even permanently damage your back, neck, or wrists if you don't use your PC properly.

The most infamous disorder attributed to the stress of computing is called **carpal tunnel syndrome,** which is a specific kind of repetitive stress injury—the symptoms include debilitating pain in the wrists and, in severe cases, permanent nerve damage. How do you avoid this and other unpleasant PC problems? Ask an expert in **ergonomics**—the science of designing human-friendly working environments.

Among other things, an ergonomic expert will tell you the following:

- Use a chair that gives you good back support, and make sure it's the right height.

- Give your wrists a rest, literally, with a padded cushion that sits in front of your keyboard. That way, your wrist muscles won't stretch into unnatural, potentially damaging positions.

- Make sure your monitor is at least two feet away from your face, and that you don't have to stretch your neck to view it properly.

- And take a break at least every half hour. There are even computer programs that will pop up a message every so often to remind you that you've been typing too long.

What do you do with your computer? What kind of data files do you create? How fast is fast enough? How slow is too slow? Do you want instant acceleration, or are you content to mosey along in the slow lane?

See how complicated it gets? Fortunately, there are some pretty easy guidelines to follow, depending on how you plan to use your PC.

The bare minimum

The official Microsoft-approved minimum setup for a Windows PC includes the following pieces:

- At least a 386 CPU (its full name is the **Intel 80386**, but if you actually own one, feel free to use the nickname instead). You can even have a 386SX, which is the Yugo of CPUs, and still run Windows. If your PC has an old 8088 or 286 processor, forget it. By the way, you pronounce these things *eigh-oh-three eight-six* (80386), *three eighty-six ess-ex* (386SX), *two eighty-six* (286), and—most fun of all!—*eighty-eighty-eight* (8088).

- At least 4M of RAM.

- A VGA video card and 14-inch monitor.

- At least 40M of free space on your hard disk.

Now, that's a minimum configuration. If you don't use your PC very often, and if you don't mind waiting, it'll work. But if you really tried to use Windows full-time on a PC as computationally challenged as that, you'd probably pound a permanent groove into your desk from drumming your fingers impatiently.

What you'll *really* need...

If you use your computer a lot and you *hate* to wait, forget the minimum Windows requirements. You'll need a little more muscle under the hood if you expect your PC to keep up with your work. Here's Microsoft's recommended setup:

- A 486 or better CPU. There are at least eight different chips with 486 in the name; any of them are OK, as long as they zoom along at 33MHz or more.

- At least 8M of RAM, so you and Windows can do more than one thing at a time. (You can usually add new RAM in chunks of 4M at a time.)

- A video card and monitor (at least 15 inches) that can handle a screen resolution of 800×600 pixels.

- A hard disk that's at least 120M in size (preferably 200M or more). The Windows software most people use today chews up hard disk space faster than a starving student at an all-you-can-eat buffet.

I don't care what it costs. I want the fastest, coolest PC I can get!

The best PC you can use today to run Windows has these pieces inside:

- A Pentium CPU. Intel's Pentium is the Schwarzenegger of chips. At 100MHz and up, it's so hot, literally, that you can burn yourself if you touch the chip while the PC is running. (That's one more reason to keep the cover on the PC.)

- For most people, 8M of RAM is OK, but you'll want 16M if you do impressive processes like scanning color photos or publishing your own newsletter.

- If you're working with large files, like scanned photos, you'll need a big hard drive. At least 500M, or even a gigabyte, which is 1000 megabytes. (It sounds like a lot, but you'll be astounded at how fast it can fill up.)

- A Super VGA video card and a bigger monitor. The perfect size these days is 17 inches. Anything smaller doesn't let you see enough on your screen at once. Larger monitors (20 inches and up) cost thousands of dollars and tend to take over your entire desk.

4

Help! Fast Answers, Straight from the Source

● In this chapter:

- Where to start looking for help

- I know what I want to do, but how do I look it up?

- If the computer isn't working right, try looking here

- Help can serve up shortcuts and tips, too!

- I'm tired of looking this up every other day. Can't I print it out?

Sometimes you just need directions. Other times you need a search-and-rescue party . . . . ●>

T here are two ways to ask for help. There's "Excuse me. I
seem to be a bit turned around here. I wonder if you could
help me find my way back to the folder I was just in."

And then there's "HELP!!!!!"

No matter where you're lost, Windows has a built-in information system
that can give you the quick answer you need, when you need it.

Now what do I do?

That's the big question, isn't it? Windows does so many different things that
it's impossible to cover them all in a book like this one. In a weeklong
training course, you'd barely scratch the surface. In fact, even if you could
convince someone to pay you to become a Windows expert, it would be
months of full-time work before you figured it all out.

Fortunately, you don't need to convince your boss to rewrite your job
description. Because so many parts of Windows work the same way, it's
possible to figure a lot of things out by simply guessing what to do next.

The simple answer when you're not sure how something works is to ask for
help. Don't worry, there's plenty to go around.

How does Help work?

There's an extensive library of helpful reference material in Windows,
mostly stored in the Help folder inside the Windows folder. Although these
files are organized like books, they actually work more like videotapes.
Without a VCR to use as a player, your videotapes are just big hunks of
black plastic. Likewise, without a Help "player," your Help files are just so
much digital nonsense.

When you ask for help, Windows starts up its version of a VCR, running a
program called WINHELP.EXE. Then it pops in the tape, loading the most
appropriate volume for what you're trying to do right now. If you click on
the Start button and choose Help, you'll see the big file that gives you a
close-up view of everything in Windows.

Using Help: Windows' built-in instruction book

Open up Windows Help, and you'll see one of these three views. In Windows, Help works just like a shelf full of well-organized books.

*The **Contents** tab helps you see what main topics are covered in each Help file. This tab divides the Help "book" into sections, chapters, and individual pages and paragraphs.*

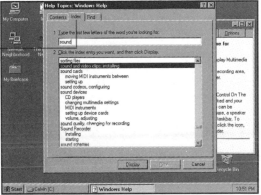

*Use the **Index** tab to find a specific section or page, and jump straight to it. This approach works best when you know exactly what you're looking for, and you're in a hurry.*

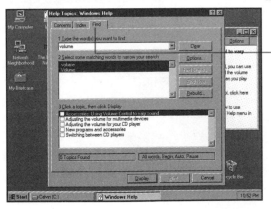

*The **Find** tab scans through every word of the Help book to help you find a particular word or phrase, no matter where it is, even if the author didn't think it was important enough to include in the table of contents or the index.*

TIP **It sounds strange, but there's even help for using Help. To get** more information, choose <u>H</u>elp from the Start menu. Double-click on How To, and then on Use Help to see the specifics.

How do I ask for help?

If you're on the bridge of the U.S.S. *Enterprise*, you can just say, "Computer!" Here on Earth, though, there are four ways to signal Windows that you need a little assistance

- Click the **Start button** and choose <u>H</u>elp from the menu. That opens the help system for all of Windows.

- Look on the **<u>H</u>elp menu** in most programs (Help is usually the last choice on the right). You'll probably open a help file created especially

What to do when you're not sure what to do next...

Most of the manuals that came with my software are covered with a thick layer of dust because the answers I need are usually easier to find with a couple of mouse clicks. There's no magic involved—just a little common sense. The next time you're feeling stuck, follow these suggestions to get unstuck in a hurry:

- Pull down all the menus, open all the dialog boxes, and push all the buttons. The feature you're looking for may be hidden underneath a button that says Advanced or Setup. Don't worry, you can't break anything just by looking. (But do pay attention to any warning labels you see!)

- Right-click everywhere. The Windows 95 shortcut menus are supposed to offer only the choices you need, when you need them. So try clicking on buttons, words, icons, and boxes. Maybe you'll get lucky.

- Press F1. For years, this has been the universal software Help signal, as recognizable as SOS or 911. It doesn't work everywhere in Windows, but it pays off often enough that it's worth a try when all else fails.

Every Windows program uses this built-in help system, so once you learn how to use it, you're well on your way toward being able to find Help in any program.

for that program. The last entry in the Help menu is typically About.... Choose this one to find out the name and version number of the program you're using right now.

- Click the **Help button**, if there is one. (You'll find them most often in dialog boxes.) In the Modem Properties dialog box, for example, the Help button takes you straight to the Modem Troubleshooting Wizard.

- Click the **Question mark button** in the top right corner of some dialog boxes (such as the one you see when you right-click on the desktop and choose Properties). The mouse pointer changes to a combined arrow-and-question mark. Aim that arrow at any part of the box and click for a pop-up explanation of what that piece of Windows really does.

Where am I now?

The best kind of help is the sort that's right there when you need it. In Windows, this is called **context-sensitive help**. It's a bit like having a Travelers' Aid kiosk on every street corner. When you use the main Windows Help system, it's like unrolling a map of the United States. Context-sensitive help gives you a detailed street map of the neighborhood you're standing in right now.

For example, let's say you're trying to coax more volume out of your expensive multimedia PC. You've found the Multimedia tab in the Control Panel window. Now what? If you need an explanation for any of the terms in the dialog box, just point to the label that has you baffled, then right-click. You'll see the words What's This? pop up. Click again to see an explanation like the one in figure 4.1.

There's a profound difference between context-sensitive help and the more general variety. Most of the time, Help takes you to the front of the book, where you have to start searching. But context-sensitive help looks around, tries to figure out where you might be stuck, then puts up detailed information about what you're doing right now.

Fig. 4.1
Can't figure out what
that button does?
Right-click anywhere
in a dialog box to get
"What's this?" help.
The information that
pops up is usually a
slightly more detailed
explanation than the
simple label.

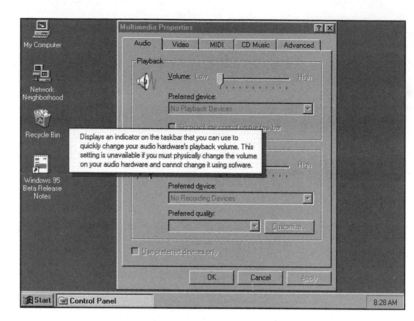

What are all these colors and buttons for?

Inside a Windows Help file, there are all sorts of secret passageways to extra information. When you see any of these special buttons or type treatments, you can click for more information, or jump directly to where you want to go.

- A **dotted-underlined word** means there's a definition waiting behind it; click on the word to pop up a definition (see fig. 4.2).

- A **Jump button** (a button with an arrow on it) means you can jump quickly to a particular folder or feature in Windows (see fig. 4.3).

- If there is related information for the topic, or a cross-referenced subject, you'll see a **plain button** like that shown in figure 4.3. Click on it for a list of other topics that may help you out.

- Some key topics have their own full-blown graphical displays, complete with animation (see fig. 4.4).

Fig. 4.2

You can pop up quick definitions of unfamiliar terms. On most computers, these links appear in green underlined text. When the pointer turns to a finger, it's OK to click.

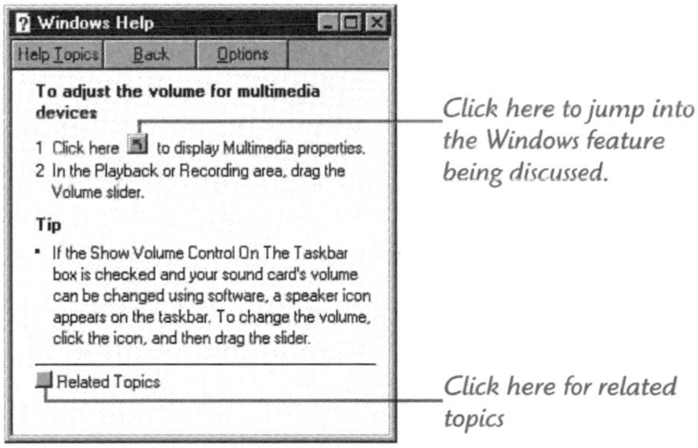

Fig. 4.3

Jump buttons let you open the dialog box or run the program you're reading about, with a single mouse click.

Click here to jump into the Windows feature being discussed.

Click here for related topics

Fig. 4.4

Other buttons and demos illustrate key tasks or point you to other parts of the Help system.

These buttons let you choose which topic you want to learn about.

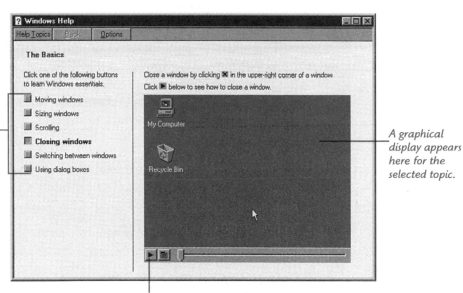

A graphical display appears here for the selected topic.

Some topics have animations. Click here to start the animation.

I can't remember how to...

Let's say you created a folder called "Hot! Income Tax Files," where you kept all of last year's financial records. It's April 16, and you've filed your tax return; now you want to rename the folder "Last Year's Tax Files" and copy it to a floppy disk, but you can't remember exactly how. Try these steps, and remember—you can follow the same general path to find the answers to any how-to question about Windows.

Start with the Table of Contents

The Windows Help file starts out with a handful of broad sections. By double-clicking on How To, then on Work with Files and Folders, we eventually drill down to a list of topics that includes Changing the name of a file or folder and Moving a file or folder. That sounds promising, doesn't it? But it's not the only way to get the answers.

 TIP **When you open a Help "book" for the first time, each section has** an icon to its left that looks like a closed book. Each time you double-click on a topic, the icon changes to an open book, and you'll see additional icons—for books and pages—just below it.

Try the Index next

Click on the Index tab and type the name of a word. Let's try **move**. You don't even need to type all the letters—as you hit each key, the selection bar in the Help list jumps to the first entry that begins with what you've typed so far. After three characters, you've reached moving, files or folders. When you double-click here, you get more choices, including an option to learn how to accomplish the same task by dragging and dropping.

Search tips

When you're having trouble finding the help you need, follow this list of handy tips:

- Try to think of synonyms. If "sound" doesn't work, maybe "audio" or "multimedia" will.

- Open a dialog box that looks like it might be related to your topic, then press F1 for context-sensitive help.

- Look for cross-references to similar topics. At the bottom of some Help windows, you'll see a button and label like the one in figure 4.5.

Fig. 4.5
When you see a button labeled Related Topics, click to see a list of similar topics.

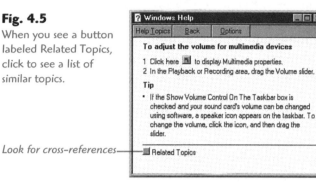

Look for cross-references ———

My computer isn't working the way it's supposed to...

There are two places to look: **Troubleshooting Tips** in the main Windows Help file, and **ReadMe files**, which are used extensively in Windows and Windows programs.

 Plain English, please!

Why are they called **ReadMe files**? It's a time-honored tradition in the software industry. The folks who made the manuals had to finish before the folks who made the program, and sometimes there were last-minute changes in the program that didn't match the printed manuals. A file called Readme (or README.TXT) was the answer, with last-minute changes noted here. **"**

TIP **Look for ReadMe files, not just for Windows but for everything.**
Try clicking the Start button and using Find Files to search for files anywhere on your hard drive that have the letters READ in their name.

There must be an easier way!

There usually is. Sometimes you find yourself doing the same thing over and over again, and it drives you crazy. For example, if you regularly send print jobs to a laser printer somewhere on your company's network, you'll understand how useful it can be to check your place in the print queue.

You *could* open My Computer, then open the Printers Folder, then open a window on the printer you want to check. But if you look in the Printing chapter of the Windows Help book, it suggests a faster, easier way: Drag the printer icon to your desktop and create a copy there. Now when you want to see whether your print job is done, you can just double-click on the icon.

Most of the Windows Help files have a Tips and Tricks section. Look here for other time-saving suggestions.

TIP   **How do you follow along with a complicated set of instructions?** Click the <u>K</u>eep Help On Top option (it appears whenever you press the Options button). When this feature is turned on, the Help instructions will "float" over whatever you're doing until you close the window or uncheck the Keep on Top option (see fig. 4.6).

Fig. 4.6
Help instructions "float" over your work.

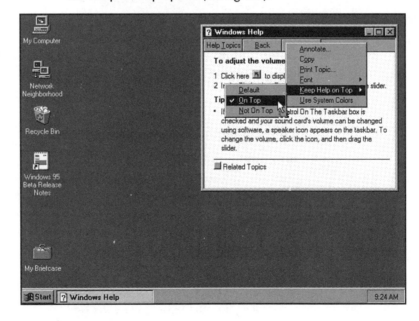

Q&A *I keep looking up the same things over and over. Isn't there an easier way to find the info I need repeatedly?*

Don't reinvent the wheel! When you learn something that isn't in Help, use **annotations** to save your comments. It's especially useful if someone else (like a PC support person at your company) modifies your system. Press the Options button, then choose Annotate. You'll see a small window where you can type a note to yourself or to anyone else who uses your PC.

Printing out those helpful hints

If you're having a hard time learning something, you can print out the help topic and keep it alongside your PC until you get the hang of it. When you see a particularly helpful Help screen, click the Options button and choose Print topic from the pop-up menu. If you'd rather incorporate the instructions into your own note, use the mouse to highlight the helpful material, then right-click and choose Copy. Now you can paste the copied material from the Windows Clipboard into your document or into a mail message.

Part II: Controlling Windows

5

Basic Mousing Around

● **In this chapter:**

- **Do I have to use a mouse? (Yes, but it's easy.)**

- **How do I point? Where do I click?**

- **Selecting objects**

- **And then there's drag-and-drop**

- **Opening windows with a double-click**

Bart Simpson's dad is probably a whiz with Windows. If you worked in the Springfield nuclear power plant, you would be, too . . . . ▶

When Homer Simpson has to handle radioactive materials, he stands behind a giant piece of safety glass. To move things around, he uses a remote-controlled robot arm. When he moves his hand to the right, the robot arm moves to the right. When he pushes a button, the robot's hand reaches down and grabs whatever's in front of it.

You do exactly the same thing (minus all the nasty radioactivity, of course) when you use a mouse with Windows. You can rearrange icons and folders and windows, drag them from one place to another, push buttons, and pick items off menus. The mouse is your remote control robotic arm for using Windows.

What It Looks Like	What It's Called	What It Does
	Plain old pointer	Windows is waiting for you to click something.
	Pointer with trails	Still waiting, but at least you can find the pointer.
	Pointers for resizing windows	Use these pointers to make a window bigger or smaller.
	Hourglass	Windows is working. You can move the pointer, but you can't do anything else.
	Pointer with hourglass	Windows is working, but you're free to do something else if you'd like.
	I-beam—insertion point	Type some letters or numbers here.
	No! pointer	Whatever you're dragging, you can't drop it here.
	Help pointers	Find more help about this item by clicking here.

Do I have to use a mouse?

Trying to use Windows without a mouse is like trying to drive your car backward, using only the rear-view mirror. You could probably do it, but it would take forever to get where you're going, and you'd have a horrible headache when you got there.

Mastering a mouse isn't that difficult, anyway. It may seem unnatural at first, but once you learn the basic techniques, you'll be able to move things around on your Windows desktop as easily as you shuffle papers on your real desktop.

The secret is to learn a handful of basic techniques that you'll use over and over in Windows, by themselves and in combination. Most of them are easy, especially after a little practice. We'll use Solitaire to run through some of the basic mouse techniques (see fig. 5.1).

Fig. 5.1

This may *seem* silly, but the Solitaire program is included with Windows for the express purpose of teaching users how to work with a mouse.

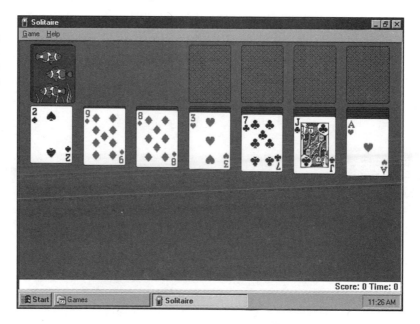

Start up Solitaire

To set up Solitaire just the way we want it, we'll use the mouse to get to the Games folder. There is an easier way, but the technique we'll use involves more work. The point is to learn these mouse techniques, so we'll go through the slower method first.

1 As you roll the mouse up, down, and around on your desk or mouse pad, the **mouse pointer** (often called just the **pointer**—it's the arrow you see on the screen) moves up, down, and around, too. Aim the pointer at the Start button in the lower left corner. Push the *right* mouse button, quickly, and release it. A very small menu will pop up.

2 Move the mouse pointer until the highlight bar covers the word Open, then press the *left* mouse button and release it (this is called **clicking** the button). After a brief delay, a window opens up, showing the Start menu in the title bar. Move the mouse pointer to the Programs icon, then click (press and release the left button) to select the icon.

Keep pointing at the Programs icon and click the *right* mouse button. Windows opens the Programs window. Now do the same trio of actions—point, select, and open—with the Accessories icon in the Programs window, and then with the Games icon in the Accessories window.

Point, select, act

You and your mouse will get along just fine if you remember the most fundamental principle of Windows: First you point, then you select, then you act.

Think of Windows as a furniture mover. You'll get great results if you say this: "See these chairs? This one, that one, and those two over there? I want them out of here." You point, you select, and you say the magic words. Blam. They're gone.

But what happens if you try it the other way around? You say, "I want you to move some chairs." With no further direction, the mover has no idea what to do next. Move them all? Just these three over here?

Repeat after me: first you point, then you select, then you act.

3 If you've pointed, selected, and clicked correctly, the contents of the Games folder should be laid out in a window on your screen, as seen in figure 5.2. Inside are icons for the games installed on your PC.

Fig. 5.2

How do you make this Games folder window appear? You point at the Games icon, click the right mouse button to pop up the shortcut menu, then click on Open.

4 Aim the mouse pointer at the Solitaire icon, and give the left mouse button two quick clicks, one right after another. (That's called a **double-click**.) If you double-clicked correctly, the Solitaire program will start up. If it didn't start up, try again.

TIP **Double-clicking can be tricky. Don't let the mouse move between** clicks, or Windows will interpret your actions as two single clicks instead of a double-click. If you have trouble keeping the mouse steady, try resting your wrist on the flat surface behind the mouse. Press gently—jab too hard at the button, and the whole mouse is likely to flinch from the shock. If you still can't get it, and you're ready to fling the mouse into the next room, just click the right mouse button and choose Open. Most of the time, that has the same effect as double-clicking.

Getting down to business with Solitaire

Before you can use Solitaire, you need to make sure it's set up correctly. Fortunately, you can use the mouse to do everything here, too.

Just below the Solitaire window's title bar you should see the word Game. Click there, move the mouse pointer to Options on the menu that drops down, and click again. A window filled with 3-D buttons and check boxes appears.

66 *Plain English, please!*

Pushing the right button is called **right-clicking**, but no one ever says "left-clicking." When you see the word **click** by itself, you can safely assume that you're supposed to push the left mouse button. 99

Click in the circle to the left of the Draw Three option, and make sure there's a check mark in the box labeled Outline dragging. (If it's empty, click on the box to add a check.) Click the OK button to close the Options window.

Pull down the Game menu again, and this time click on Deck. Click on any of the card designs you see, and watch as a fairly thick line appears around the pattern to show that you've selected it. (See fig. 5.3 for an example.) Pick the look you want for the back of the deck, and click OK.

Fig. 5.3

When you click a pattern, the pattern reverses color for as long as you hold down the mouse button.

My two favorite Solitaire decks are the two in the lower right corner. Watch carefully for the animated tricks in both: the sun above the palm tree occasionally shows his face (complete with Ray-Bans) and sticks out his tongue. In the other pattern, a stray ace slides up and down the card sharp's sleeve every so often. You also might like the robot, whose buttons and dials flash and move.

Q&A *I chose one of these patterns, but I never see the animations. What's wrong?*

Oops—forgot to tell you that this trick only works if you have the Timed Game option turned on. Click open the Game menu, select Options (getting good at this, aren't you?), and click Timed game. Click OK to start a new game with the timer on. Also note that you may need to drag the Solitaire window up and left a bit to see the timer in the bottom right corner. Dragging is covered a few pages from here. Stick around.

Really important mouse factoids

- The cord goes out the back, away from your hand. If you try to use your mouse the other way, the pointer will zig when you expect it to zag, and you'll get hopelessly confused.

- Your mouse has to be plugged into the back of your PC. If it suddenly stops working, follow the cord to the back of your PC and make sure it's firmly connected.

- As your mouse rolls around, it can pick up anything: dirt and dust, muffin crumbs, stray hairs, little bits of cheese. So clean it occasionally by turning it over, taking out the roller, and wiping off any junk.

- A mouse works a lot better if you use a **mouse pad** (a thin, soft, rubbery pad, often with a fairly slick surface, that you can run your mouse around on). You can get one for a few dollars at any computer store. Keep in mind that you need to keep the mouse pad pretty clean, too—or the mouse will pick up the crud off the mouse pad.

- If you run out of room on your mouse pad or your desk, pick up the mouse and move it to a better position. As long as the mouse is in the air, the pointer won't move. When you start rolling again, it'll pick up right where you left off.

- Most mice have just two buttons, but some have three. If yours has an extra button in the middle, you can safely ignore it—Windows only uses the left and right buttons.

Essential mouse techniques

In the course of starting Solitaire and setting it up, we did most of the basic tricks you can do with a mouse. Let's review the entire list right now.

Pointing

As you move the pointer around, it passes over different things. When you aim it at one thing in particular, that's pointing. It's just like moving your finger over the buttons on your VCR. Until you actually *push* one, nothing happens.

That's the way it is with Windows, too. Most of the time, nothing happens when you simply point. One exception is the help you get from the taskbar or from the toolbars in many Windows-based programs. Point to any button on the taskbar or toolbar, and just leave the arrow there for a few seconds. Then watch as a small label pops up to tell you what's really underneath that button. You didn't click—all you had to do was point.

Solitaire, on the other hand, is pretty dumb when it comes to the mouse. You can move the mouse pointer around all you want, pointing like crazy, but until you actually click one of the mouse buttons, absolutely nothing will happen.

Pixels and grids: what happens when your mouse scurries around?

There's nothing magic about your mouse. You roll it left and right, up or down, as roughly as you please, and the pointer slides across the screen in the proper direction. What's really happening?

The first mouse

Way back in the Jurassic era, the first computer mouse appeared.

OK, so it wasn't the Jurassic. It was 1967. But in computer terms, that might as well have been prehistoric days. Back then, a single computer took up an entire room. It cost a few thousand dollars just to use a computer for an hour. To program one, you had to punch holes in paper cards and feed huge stacks of them to the hungry machine. And there was no such thing as a *personal* computer. Entire universities had to share these incredibly expensive machines.

The father of the mouse was a visionary named Doug Engelbart. An engineer at the Stanford Research Institute, Engelbart dreamed up the idea of a mouse while working on a contract for

the U. S. Air Force. The first mouse wasn't much to look at. It was huge. It was made of wood. It had three buttons. And it had a long, boring name: "X-Y Position Indicator for a Display System."

It took more than 10 years before Engelbart's invention got its cute nickname. It took 17 years before it became popular. Engelbart was responsible for a long list of computer innovations that we take for granted today, including the ideas of windows and icons.

Today's mice are sleek and sophisticated, with the kind of lines you'll find on a Porsche or Ferrari. But anyone who's ever admired the simple engineering of a Ford Model T can appreciate the contribution Engelbart made to our working lives.

Let's start by looking at the **grid**. The Windows desktop is really just a precise arrangement of dots—normally, 640 dots from left to right, 480 dots from top to bottom. If you want to impress other people, you can call these dots by their technical name: **pixels**. Because they're so small, your eyes perceive the dots as icons and letters and other familiar things.

And then there's the **pointer**: it's really just a little picture of an arrow, an hourglass, or whatever Windows is set up to show you at the moment. It's made out of the same kind of dots as the rest of the screen.

Finally, there's the **roller ball**. When you slide the mouse across its pad, the little ball buried in the bottom of the mouse rolls around and turns a collection of gizmos inside the mouse. Its whole purpose is to send messages up the mouse cord, through the PC, and onto the screen. Every time one of those messages reaches the screen, Windows redraws the pointer picture so that the very tip of the arrow touches the specified dot on the screen. (The rest of the arrow? It's just there to help you spot that one all-important pixel.)

Give the mouse the gentlest possible push in the direction of the cord. "Move up one pixel!" is the message that flies up the wire. The pointer moves up, just barely. Push it a little farther. "Move up 10... no, 20 pixels!" Move it quickly from side to side and there'll be a flurry of messages. "Left 50 pixels! Right 80 pixels! Up 10! Left 10!" Fortunately, the mouse has limitless energy, so you can slide it all you want.

CAUTION   **When you hit the edge of the screen, Windows just ignores the** messages coming up the wire from the mouse. "Move up 80 more pixels? Sorry, I've reached the edge here. You'll have to head in another direction."

And when you click either mouse button, the mouse sends a special message up the wire. Windows checks its list of instructions to see what it's supposed to do when the pointer is poised over that pixel and it gets a click. If your aim is off even slightly, you might wind up doing something other than what you intended. That's why, when you aim the pointer anywhere on the screen, it's most important to concentrate on the tip of the arrow, not the arrow itself.

TIP **What do you do if the pointer seems to disappear every** time you turn your head? Make it bigger. Make it darker. Make it leave a trail so you can spot it the instant it moves. To do any or all of these things, double-click on My Computer, open the Control Panel folder, and double-click on the Mouse icon. Experiment with the options till you find the settings that work best for you.

Clicking (and its mirror image, right-clicking)

If you actually want to *do* something with whatever you're pointing at, you'll have to click it. Here's some practice. Point at the face-down deck of cards in the top left corner of the Solitaire window, and click. Each time you tap the mouse button, three cards flip off the deck and onto the face-up stack at the right.

In some cases, you'll have to double-click before anything happens. How do you know when to click and when to double-click? Just remember the difference between buttons and icons.

With buttons, a single click does the trick

It's easy to spot a **button**. Look for the 3-D effect, with a small shadow along the right side and the bottom. It takes a single click to work the following buttons:

- The Start menu

- Any open windows stored on the taskbar

- Minimize, Maximize, Restore, and Close buttons found at the right end of a window's title bar (see Chapter 2 for an explanation of what these do)

- The OK and Cancel buttons in dialog boxes, like the one holding the Solitaire options

With icons, it takes a double-click to do something

How can you spot an icon? Just look for a picture with a label underneath. These icons, for example, demand a double-click before they'll open into a window:

- My Computer and Network Neighborhood

- The Recycle Bin

- Every program, file, folder, or drive

TIP **Why do you have to double-click an icon? Because otherwise,** you'd constantly be opening windows and looking inside folders and starting up programs when you really didn't want to. Think of it this way: the first click tells Windows to get ready. If there's another click almost immediately, it opens the window. If not, Windows assumes you don't really want to open the window, and you're going to do something else instead.

What happens when I right-click?

Most of the time, right-clicking pops up a menu that's tailor-made for whatever you're pointing at. Whenever you're not sure what you can do with an icon, just right click it. The popup menu will tell you what's possible.

Q&A *I'm left-handed. Is there an easier way to use this mouse?*

 Windows lets you reverse your mouse settings, so that the right button does the jobs normally handled by the left button, and vice-versa. To switch mouse buttons, double-click on the Control Panel's Mouse icon and follow the instructions. It's a handy trick for left-handers. If you try it, though, remember to do a mental translation from now on: every time we talk about clicking and right-clicking, just reverse the directions.

Dragging-and-dropping

Before you can move something, you first have to pick it up. Back where Homer Simpson works, we'd pick up a container of some extremely dangerous substance by using the claws at the end of our remote-control arm. Well, the mouse works the same way. When you point at an icon and click the left mouse button, the claws clamp on just as though you had grabbed the icon in your hand (or paw, really, since you're using the mouse).

As long as you keep the button down, the claws stay clamped on and you can move the icon around. But you can only carry something around for so long before it starts to seem kind of, well, pointless. When you've dragged something far enough, you release the pressure on the mouse button, and it drops at the pointer's current location.

TIP   **Remember this sequence of events anytime you want to move** something from here to there. Point. Click and hold the left mouse button down. Drag the object. Let go of the mouse button to drop it.

Ready for some more work? Keep clicking on the Solitaire deck to turn over three cards at a time. When you see a card that can fit on one of your stacks below (a red 9 to go on top of a black 10, say), drag it down and drop it there. Because we turned on Solitaire's outline-dragging feature earlier, we can follow the process step-by-step.

Click on the card you want to move, and keep holding the mouse button down. As you move the card in the direction of the stack below, you'll see the card's outline appear (see fig. 5.4.) When you get close enough to drop it on the stack, the top card will turn dark to let you know it's OK to let go of the mouse button.

Fig. 5.4

Drag the red 9 onto the black 10. As long as you hold down the left mouse button, you can drag the card around. As soon as you let it go, though, it'll drop into place.

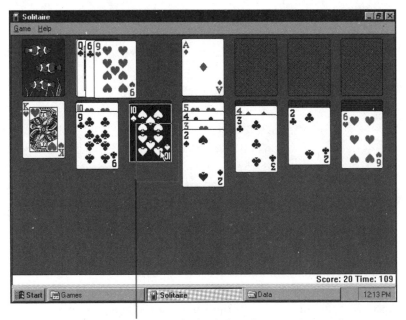

The outline may be hard to see in this book, but it's easy to distinguish on-screen.

TIP **If you try to drop the card on a stack where it won't work** according to the Solitaire rules, Windows just puts it back on the stack of cards that have been dealt. (You can't break the rules *that* easily.)

Dropping something on something else

Most of the time, you'll simply want to move an object from point A to point B. But, in special cases, you can drop it on top of something else and actually cause something to happen. Here are a few things you can do with this trick:

- **Drop an icon onto a folder** to move the icon into the folder.

- **Drop a file icon on a printer icon**; Windows will try to send the file straight to your printer.

- **Drop a program icon on the desktop** to create a special kind of icon called a **shortcut**, which you can use to start that program in a hurry. (More about shortcuts in Chapter 2.)

- **Drop a program icon on the Start menu**; Windows will add it to the top of the Start menu.

- **Drop a file icon onto a drive icon**; Windows will try to copy the file to that drive.

Right-dragging for total control

Here's something that's guaranteed to confuse everybody. When you drag a file onto a folder, what happens? That depends. If the file you're dragging and the folder you're dropping it onto are both on the hard drive in your computer, then the file will move. But if the folder is on another drive (like a file server on your network, or someone else's drive, or even a floppy disk drive on your own PC), then the file will be copied. Unless it's a program file, in which case…. Well, the rules are incredibly confusing. Fortunately, you don't need to memorize them; instead, use this foolproof alternative.

Whenever you want to move something, or copy something, or create a shortcut, click with the *right* mouse button and drag it. When you release the button, you'll see a list of choices like the one in figure 5.5. You can decide whether you want to move the file or make another copy of it—or cancel the whole thing.

Fig. 5.5
Windows lets you right-
drag just about
anything and drop it
just about anywhere.

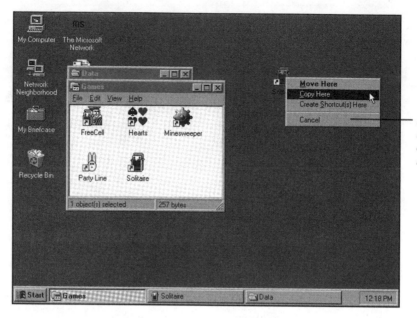

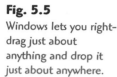

*Don't let go!
Pick an option
on this popup
menu first.*

Selecting objects

Up until now, we've been using the mouse to do one thing at a time: move an
icon or delete a file, say. But you can save time and energy by doing the
same thing with more than one object at once. Instead of moving a bunch of
files one by one, for example, you can pick out a group of icons and drag
them all to a new folder. It's just two steps:

1 The first step is to mark all the icons you want to work with.

2 The second step is to do something with whatever you selected.

Remember the example a few pages back about moving furniture? You point
out the ones you want, and the mover takes those. It would be even easier if
you had already labeled the furniture with "Take this," "Don't take this," etc.
This method works well with the mouse; you tag the objects you want to do
something with—it's called **selecting**.

How can you tell when you've selected something? Watch the way the
highlighting changes. Click on the taskbar button for the Games folder
window to bring it to the front, and let's try highlighting some icons.

• To select an icon, just click it.

- To select a group of adjacent icons, use the mouse pointer to "lasso" them. Imagine that the icons you want to select can be contained in a box. Point to one of the corners of that imaginary box, click the left mouse button, and hold it down as you begin to drag the outlines of the box. A dotted line appears as you drag, and each icon inside the box takes on a dark shading to show that you've selected it (see fig. 5.6). When you've successfully highlighted all the items, release the button.

Fig. 5.6

Icons inside the box take on a dark shading to show that you've successfully selected them. (I suppose you've noticed that I have a few more games than you do...)

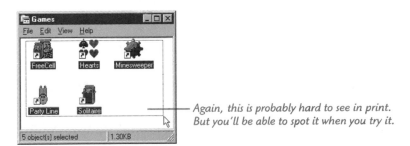

Again, this is probably hard to see in print. But you'll be able to spot it when you try it.

- To select a group of icons or items in a list when they're right next to one another, click on the first one, then hold down the Shift key and click on the last one. All the icons in between will be highlighted, too.

- To select a group of icons when they're not next to one another, click on the first one, then hold down the Ctrl key and click on the second, the third, the fourth, and so on.

TIP **Anytime you have to simultaneously hold down a key and click a mouse button, remember to press the keys first, then click.**

CAUTION **Be careful when double-clicking an icon, or you might** accidentally rename a file! Watch what happens when you click the name of an icon twice, slowly. The highlighting changes and Windows assumes you want to start typing a new name. To avoid this possibility, always aim at the picture, not the label. (Press Esc to quit renaming this time.) And practice double-clicking until you can do it flawlessly.

Opening a window by double-clicking

Double-clicking is just like pushing a button. It's the best way to open a window (although, as we've seen, it's not the only way). Double-click on an icon and something happens: programs start, folder windows open, a printer pops up a list of all the jobs it's waiting to do.

By now you've double-clicked on so many icons that you're probably an expert. But we're still working here, so find that Solitaire window and let's finish up.

Click on the deck of cards until you get to an ace. OK, now point at the ace and double-click. It should fly off the deck and onto one of the four stacks in the top right corner of the Solitaire window. Keep double-clicking as you play the game, to put the remaining cards of the same suit on top of the ace.

It's OK to cheat if you get stuck. Press the Ctrl, Alt, and Shift keys all at the same time, and hold them down while you click cards on the deck one at a time. Pretty cool, huh?

 TIP   **When you double-click, Windows expects that the clicks will come** one right after the other, as fast as lightning. But you can slow down the double-click rate so that Windows will wait a little longer for that second click. To retrain the mouse, open the Control Panel window and double-click on the Mouse icon. Slide the <u>D</u>ouble-click speed lever all the way to the left, and test the new settings by double-clicking the jack-in-the-box. There—isn't that better?

6

My Computer and Everything Inside It

● In this chapter:

- **What are all these things in My Computer?**

- **An ounce of backup is worth a pound of lost data**

- **Tell me about floppy disks**

- **What about CDs?**

Once you know how to search through the My Computer folder, you'll never again have to wonder what lurks in the dark depths of your computer's innards. . . . . ●

There are 6,537 separate data files on my computer's hard drive. If you were to print them all out and pile them onto my desk, they'd punch a hole right through the ceiling. (You know, sometimes it feels like I really *do* have that many pieces of paper on my desk.) Now, I'd never get any work done if I had to sift through a 10-foot-high stack of paper—or its computer equivalent—whenever I needed to find a letter. Instead, I use a logical filing system on my desktop and on my PC.

I don't just toss all those papers into one extra-extra-large filing cabinet. And I *don't* just throw all those data files into a single folder on my hard disk, either. In my office, all the paper goes into manila folders, and all the data files go into Windows folders. Folders with similar topics go into bigger folders, and I stash everything in my neatly alphabetized file drawers. So, no matter which desktop I'm dealing with, I can put my hands on the right file fast.

If you expect Windows to help you organize your work the same way, you have to understand two of its most important building blocks—drives and folders.

CAUTION
Formatting a hard drive is a job for a computer expert. Don't even *think* about doing it yourself unless you plan to install all your software, including Windows, from scratch. Fortunately, Windows makes it nearly impossible to accidentally format your C:drive.

Working with hard disks

Your disk drives work just like filing cabinets, and to keep your files organized you use the computer equivalent of manila folders. So far, so good. But just like the file cabinets in your office, you have to do a little prep work before you dump your data into folders.

Before you can use any disk—hard or floppy—it has to be formatted. You might have to format a floppy disk the first time you use it, but if your computer is running right now, your hard drive is formatted just fine, thank you. After formatting, the next challenge is to make sure there's enough free space on the disk, and that the files are organized properly.

Fast facts about disks

In your office, you have all sorts of storage spaces—everything from shoe boxes to file cabinets to closets. On your PC, you have all sorts of storage spaces, too, and each one works in its own unique way. Double-click on any drive icon, and it opens into a drive window. The right-click menus, on the other hand, pop up specific commands, like Eject for a CD, or Disconnect for a network drive.

Floppy disks
They don't hold much data, but they're portable. Your first floppy drive is A:, and a second drive is B:. Right-click here to format a disk or give it a descriptive label; drop a file on this icon to copy it to a floppy.

Shared volume
The outstretched hand appears whenever you tell Windows that it's OK for other people on your network to share one of your drives or folders.

Hard disk
Most of your everyday files go here. Your main hard disk is called C:. The right-click menu includes tools for making sure your files are stored safely.

Network drive
If there's a drive or a folder somewhere else on the network, you can tell Windows to give it a drive letter (but not A:, B:, or C:). Once you've done that, this icon appears.

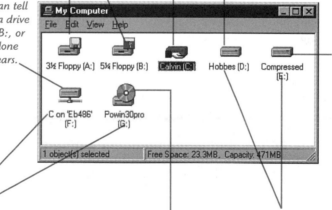

Compressed volume
It looks and acts just like a normal hard disk, but it's not. A special Windows program called DriveSpace works like a trash compactor to pack twice as many files as usual into this space.

Labels
In addition to its drive letter, every disk can have a plain-English name, also known as a label. Labels, which are strictly for informational purposes, can have as many as 11 characters, including spaces.

CD-ROM
By default, this window pops open automatically anytime you put in a new CD. Right-click to choose the Eject command from a menu (no, Windows won't put the CD back in its box). The commands on the popup menu will vary, depending on what type of CD it is (audio or data).

Drive letters
It's as easy as ABC. Every disk drive has a single letter, followed by a colon, for a name. Floppies are always A: and B:. Your main hard drive is always C:. If you have a second hard drive, it's probably D:. If there's a CD-ROM attached to your computer, it might be D: or E: or F: or anything up to Z:. Look in My Computer to see for yourself.

> ## Plain English, please!
>
> A blank, freshly manufactured disk is about as useful as a half-acre of dirt and weeds. **Formatting** prepares the magnetic surface of a disk so your PC can store data there, in much the same way that you'd pave the vacant lot and paint white lines so you could use it as a parking lot.

TIP   **You can take your choice of four different ways to arrange the** drives in the My Computer window. Right-click on any empty space and choose Arrange Icons from the popup menu. Now you can choose to sort the entries in the window by drive letter, type, size, or how much free space is available.

How much space do I have left?

Every time you save a file to a disk, it occupies some of the space on that disk, and sooner or later you'll use up all the empty space. Murphy's Law says you'll run out of hard disk space when you're rushing to beat a tough deadline. That's why you should keep a watchful eye on free disk space, especially if you're planning to install a new program. To see how much space is left on a disk:

1 Double-click to open My Computer.

2 Click on the icon for the drive you want to check. The total disk capacity and free space appear in the status bar at the bottom of the My Computer window. (If the status bar isn't visible, pull down the View menu and check Status Bar.)

3 To see a graphical display of free disk space, right-click, then choose Properties from the popup menu (see fig. 6.1).

4 As long as you're here, why not give your hard drive a friendly label? (My drives are named Calvin and Hobbes.)

> ## Plain English, please!
>
> Mega means million. So is a megabyte a million bytes? Not exactly. Your PC can only count in twos, so a **megabyte** is actually 2 to the 20th power, or 1,048,576 bytes. For anyone but an accountant, it's accurate enough to round off that precise number to an even million.

Fig. 6.1
Right-click on your
hard drive icon to see
at a glance how much
space is left.

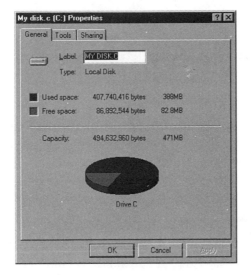

Whoops—I'm almost out of room!

It's one of the unpleasant realities of the universe, right up there with those laws that Newton and Murphy discovered. Sooner or later (usually sooner), you'll have more files than your hard disk can hold. If you've been checking your free disk space regularly, you'll get some advance warning. Otherwise, you'll just get a rude error message when you try to save a file. Either way, you have three choices:

- **Get a new hard disk.** That assumes you have a few hundred dollars to spare; you'll also need to find someone who'll install it for you. Ugh.

- **Clean some files off your hard disk.** The best solution to an overstuffed hard disk is to delete files you don't need. Of course, that's about as much fun as sorting your socks by color.

- **Stuff it.** I don't mean to be rude—really. Windows includes a program called DriveSpace that allows you to pack roughly twice as much data as normal into a typical hard disk.

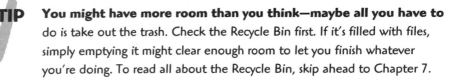 **You might have more room than you think—maybe all you have to** do is take out the trash. Check the Recycle Bin first. If it's filled with files, simply emptying it might clear enough room to let you finish whatever you're doing. To read all about the Recycle Bin, skip ahead to Chapter 7.

- Select Start, Find, Files and Folders and enter ***.BAK** in the Named box, then click Find Now. You'll see a list of all the backup files on your main hard drive! You can delete all of these safely to free up a little more space.

How does DriveSpace work? Well, imagine that your hard disk is a bag of potato chips. That bag doesn't feel heavy, but it sure takes up a lot of shelf space, thanks to all the air between the chips. DriveSpace squeezes the air—in this case, empty spaces and repetitious data—out of your files, then packs them tightly onto the disk. When you need to see a file, DriveSpace reaches into the compressed drive and quickly puts back the missing pieces before handing you the file. On most computers, the process happens so fast you won't even realize it's happening.

To compress your hard disk, follow these steps:

1 Start the DriveSpace program by using the Start menu: Follow the cascading menus from Programs to Accessories to System Tools. Click on DriveSpace.

2 Pick the drive you want to compress (probably C:) and then choose Drive, Compress. You'll see information about the proposed compression, as shown in figure 6.2.

To compress, or not to compress?

Some people just don't trust DriveSpace. I can't blame them. There's something almost magical about the way disk compression works, and it takes a giant leap of faith to trust Windows to stuff and unstuff your files safely and reliably.

Basically, DriveSpace takes all your files—hundreds or even thousands of them—and stuffs them into a single enormous file called something like DBLSPACE.001. The good news is you can get a few hundred megabytes of free disk space for

nothing. The bad news? If something happens to that file...

If you choose to use DriveSpace, be smart. Keep backup copies of your important data files, and store them in a safe place, preferably away from your computer.

Come to think of it, that's good advice even if you *don't* use disk compression.

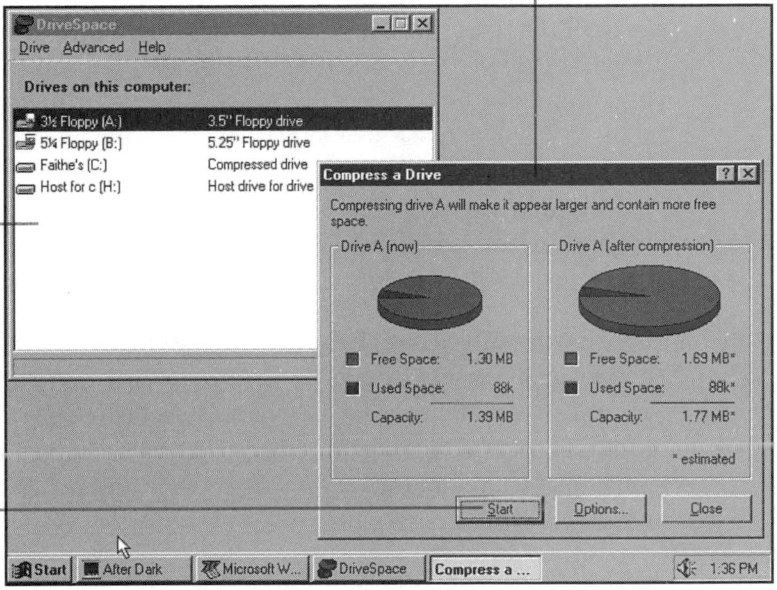

...and select Compress from the Drive menu.

Fig. 6.2
You can see what the results will be, before you actually do the compressing.

Pick the drive to compress...

Click here to start the compression.

3 Look in this dialog box for any warning messages. (For example, if you start with a big enough disk, you'll learn that DriveSpace can't handle a disk larger than 512M.) If everything looks OK, press Start.

4 DriveSpace goes through a lot of housekeeping and error-checking before it gets down to business, and the actual packing can take hours. To be safe, let DriveSpace do its work overnight.

66 *Plain English, please!*

A host drive is a confusing little bit of technotrivia that you may see after you use DriveSpace. If you've compressed your C: drive, you'll see two drive icons in My Computer. The C: drive looks the same as before, but the host drive (its drive letter is H: on my system, but yours may be different) contains a single bi-i-i-i-i-i-i-i-i-ig file, called a compressed volume file. That's where all your real files have been stuffed. No, DriveSpace didn't really create a second hard disk; this monkey business with drive letters is the only way Windows can keep track of things. Your best bet is to ignore the host drive completely. 99

Network drives are a little different

Most of the time, you'll probably store files on the hard disk in your own PC. If your office is on a local area network, though, you can also choose from other hard disks in other computers connected with yours by a network cable. Typically, these shared hard disks have names that you need to know before you can use them. On my company network, for example, the network administrator named all the file servers after Greek gods, so I save my work on a hard disk named Bacchus. A friend of mine works for a company that has three file servers—Larry, Moe, and Curly. Nyuk, nyuk.

Do network drives have to have drive letters like other drives? Not necessarily. You can always track down a file by typing its full name: `\\Curly\C\DATA\Letters`, for example. But some people find it easier to **map** a shared hard disk to an unused drive letter. In that case, you can work out a deal with Windows to go to that place on the network whenever you refer to a certain drive letter.

On your own computer, you can count on using C: (and maybe D:) most of the time. On networks, you'll typically find every letter from F: on up. If your network uses Novell NetWare as its operating system, you'll probably have an X:, Y:, and Z:, too.

To map a network drive to a drive letter, just find it in the Network Neighborhood, select the folder, and choose Map <u>N</u>etwork Drive from the popup menu. The dialog box that appears is deceptively simple: You pick a free drive letter from the list, click OK, and from now on, you can get to that place on the network by using the new drive letter.

> ❝ *Plain English, please!*
>
> A **file server** is a computer that's been set aside for people on the network to use for storing files. A **share** (also called a **volume**) is the name of the area that's available for network users to put files. To store files on a network drive, then, you'll need to enter its name as **\\server\share**. See figure 6.3 for an example. ❞

To disconnect a drive mapping and stop using that drive letter, right-click on My Computer and choose <u>D</u>isconnect Network Drive.

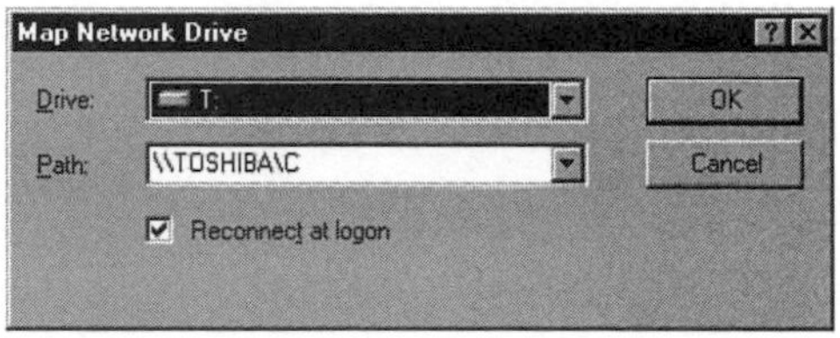

Fig. 6.3

The file server is called Toshiba, and the shared area is the entire hard drive, called C. Thanks to drive mapping, you can simply refer to this shared area as drive T:.

Disks can, and *do,* go bad

If you knew all the things that could go wrong with a hard disk, you'd probably never save a file again. Fortunately, Windows has a powerful tool designed to sniff out small problems on your hard disk and fix them before they become big problems. It's called **ScanDisk**, and everyone who uses a computer should use it at least once a month.

To start ScanDisk, open My Computer, and right-click on the icon for your hard disk. Choose Properties from the popup menu, then click on the tab labeled Tools. You'll see a page like the one in figure 6.4.

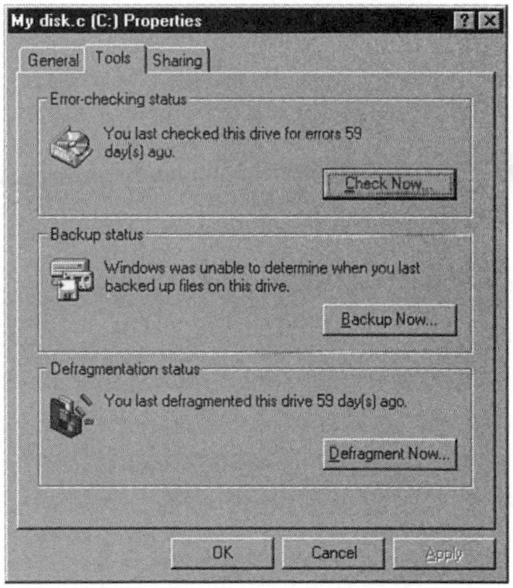

Fig. 6.4

Use ScanDisk to check your hard drive for problems. This powerful check-up program is just a right-click away.

What does ScanDisk do?

There are plenty of things that can go wrong on your hard disk. Here's what
ScanDisk looks for (and usually fixes):

- **Lost clusters.** A **cluster** is the smallest unit of space your hard disk
  recognizes. A **lost cluster** is like a single piece of a big jigsaw puzzle. It
  doesn't belong to a file, and by itself it's useless. A lost cluster is usually
  not a serious problem.

- **Cross-linked files.** Windows is trying to piece together all the clusters
  that make up a file, but somewhere along the line two files got
  scrambled together (remember *The Fly*?). ScanDisk can usually clean
  up the mess, but you may lose one or both files.

- **Illegal names, dates, and times.** It shouldn't be there, but somehow a
  file showed up on your disk with a name that includes an illegal character, or a date or time that doesn't make sense. These errors can usually
  be repaired without fuss.

- **Defects on the disk itself.** If there's a grease spot on a piece of paper,
  you can't write on it. Likewise, a defect on the sensitive surface of your
  hard disk can make it impossible for Windows to write data in that spot.
  ScanDisk marks that section as bad so Windows won't use it. If you
  have data in that spot, you may be able to recover it.

Q&A   *I always find errors when I check my hard drive with
ScanDisk. Is that bad?*

Maybe. If you constantly experience disk errors, you might have a hard disk
that's on the verge of failing, or there might be a bug in one of the
programs you use that's leaving a mess behind when you close it. Double-
click on the icon for the disk that's giving you troubles, and look for files
with names like FILE0000; ScanDisk creates those files as part of its
cleanup process. Try opening those files with WordPad. If you recognize the
data inside the files, you might be able to tell which program is causing the
disk problems.

How do I use ScanDisk?

Starting up ScanDisk is ridiculously simple. Just press the Check Now
button. You'll see the dialog box shown in figure 6.5.

Choose a drive to check. (You can check floppy
disks, too, but not CD-ROMs or network drives.)

Click here to tell ScanDisk to get to work.

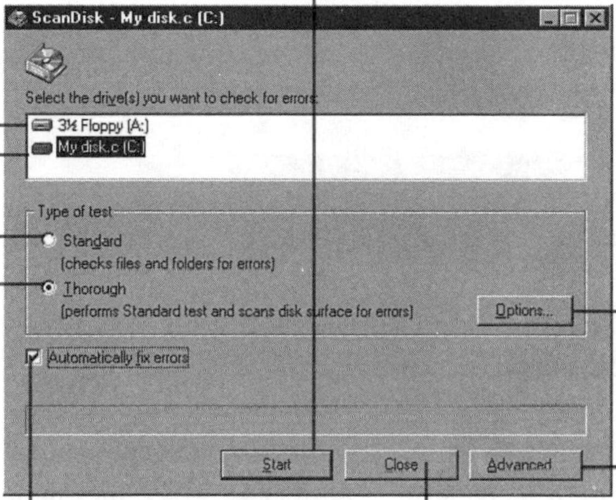

Fig. 6.5
Choose your disk-
checking options
carefully, or ScanDisk
may take hours to
finish its work.

How thoroughly do
you want to test your
drive? The Standard
option will be done
in a few minutes; a
Thorough test can
take hours.

Press either of these
buttons to choose from
a bunch of technical
options.

If you want ScanDisk to simply fix
any mistakes it finds, check here.
Leave this box unchecked and you
can review ScanDisk's suggestions
before it actually fixes anything.

Click here to close the
ScanDisk window.

TIP   **When you check the Automatically fix errors option, you give**
ScanDisk carte blanche to save lost clusters as files. After awhile, you might
end up with a disk filled with "recovered" files that don't have any real data
in them. Uncheck this box, and ScanDisk will ask you whether you want
those file fragments saved or not.

What's this Defragmenter thing?

Windows treats your hard disk like a dusty old warehouse filled with
cramped cardboard boxes. When you send in a big file for storage, the file
gets sliced into small clusters, and then each cluster gets stuffed into its own
box. Windows keeps a master list of which piece went where, so it can
reassemble the file later. That's fine most of the time, but it's not so good
when fragments of your file get scattered on parts of the hard disk that are
miles apart. This **fragmentation** can cause your whole system to slow
down while Windows scurries around putting a file together.

The solution? Use the built-in Windows Disk Defragmenter (see fig. 6.6). It sounds like science fiction, but it's really quite simple to use. To start it up, right-click on any drive, choose Properties, then select the Tools tab. The status window at the bottom of the dialog box will tell you how long it's been since you last used the defragmenter. Push the button labeled Defragment Now to start up the program.

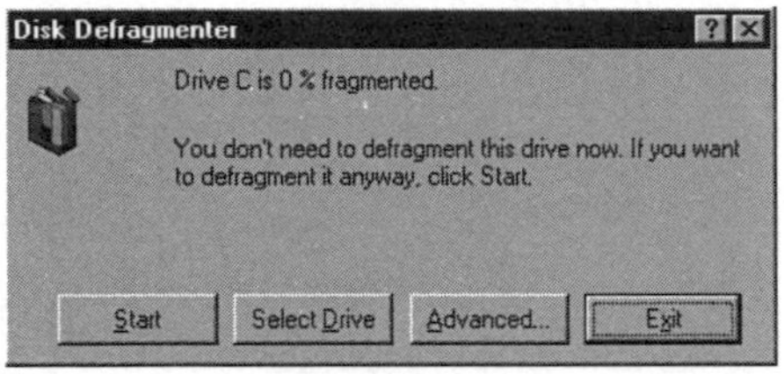

Fig. 6.6

Use the Disk Defragmenter to reorganize the contents of your hard disk so Windows can find files faster.

If you have more than one hard drive, you can select a different drive or ask Windows to check all your hard disks, one after the other. Click the Advanced button to see a hypnotizing (and very colorful) display as the Disk Defragmenter rearranges the contents of your hard disk.

TIP   **You don't have to wait while the Defragmenter does its work. You** can do other things, although you may notice that your computer seems to slow down under the extra workload.

I need to protect my precious files!

I don't like dental checkups. I hate waiting around while my car gets an oil change, too. But we do both those things, because if we don't do these simple tasks, the consequences are too unpleasant to imagine. Likewise, the data files on your hard disk will be a lot safer with a little preventive maintenance. What would you do if all your data files disappeared overnight? (After you stopped crying, I mean.) You could never reconstruct all that work from scratch.

The solution is to regularly back up your files to a safe place: to floppy disks, to a magnetic tape if you have a tape backup drive, or even to a network file server. Which strategy should you follow? It doesn't matter. Just pick one! To start the Backup program, right-click on a drive icon, choose Properties, then click the Backup Now button.

Back up those files!

To use the Windows Backup program, start by checking off the files you want backed up, then follow the wizard's instructions.

Press the Next Step button to move to a different dialog box, and then choose a location to store the backed-up files.

To restore a set of backed-up files, click the Restore tab and follow the directions.

To back up individual files, check the box next to each file name in the right-hand pane.

Check any of these boxes to select every file on the drive or folder.

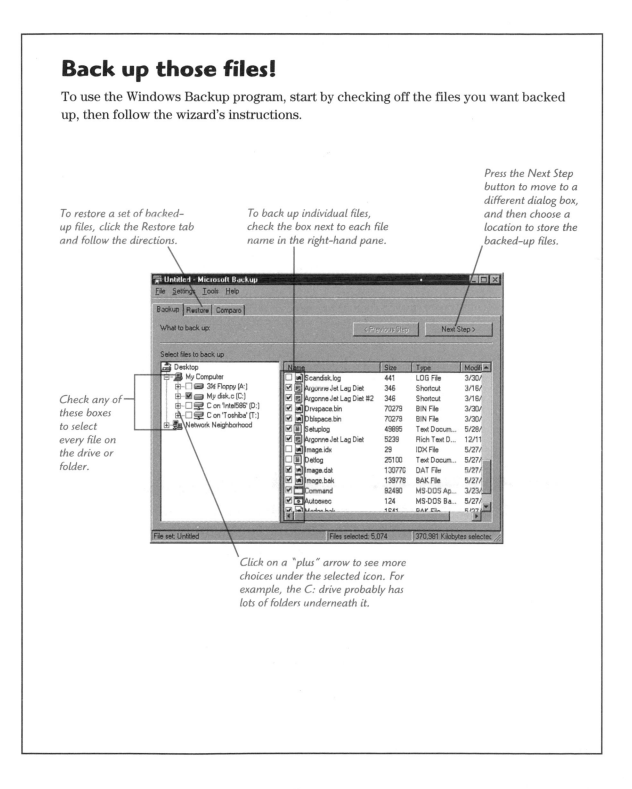

Click on a "plus" arrow to see more choices under the selected icon. For example, the C: drive probably has lots of folders underneath it.

Emergency disks... because you just never know

Another kind of backup is an emergency disk. You need an emergency disk, *just in case* something happens and Windows won't start up on your PC. If that happens, you just pop the emergency disk in your A: drive and turn the computer on. It's kind of like a secret back door to use when you're locked out of the main entrance.

To create an emergency disk, open Control Panel, choose the Add/Remove Programs dialog box, then select the Startup Disk tab and follow the instructions. Store your emergency disk in a safe place, against upcoming disasters.

Using floppy disks to move files around

Your hard drive probably has room for hundreds of megabytes worth of files (although if you're like me, you only have two or three megabytes of free space at any given time). Floppy disks hold far less; the most common size has a capacity of 1.44M. But the mere fact that they're small doesn't mean they're useless. Floppy disks come in handy when you need to share files with other people, when you want to take work home, or when you want to make backup copies of your irreplaceable data files.

How do I copy files to a floppy disk?

You can always use side-by-side folder windows to copy files from your hard disk to a floppy disk, but Windows gives you two better ways.

The easiest way? Point to the file you want to copy, select File, Send To, and then choose a destination to move files from your hard disk to your floppy disk drive.

If you regularly carry files around on floppies, put a shortcut to your floppy disk drive right on the desktop. Open My Computer, and drag the drive icon to the desktop. Windows will warn you that it plans to create a shortcut. Say yes. Now you can simply drag files out of other windows and drop them right on the floppy disk shortcut to copy them.

CAUTION **Remember: If you drag a program file with the left mouse button** and drop it onto a floppy, you'll end up with a copy. Use the *right* mouse button to drag files instead, and you can choose to move, copy, or create a shortcut of the file.

Why do I have to format floppies?

Before you can use a floppy disk for the first time, it has to be *formatted*—that is, Windows has to prepare the disk surface with a set of special markings that define where the data goes. Even after a disk has been formatted, you can reuse the disk-formatting tools to quickly erase all the files from it. To format a floppy disk, first make sure it's in the drive, then right-click on its icon in the My Computer window and choose Format underline. You'll see the dialog box shown in figure 6.7.

Fig. 6.7
Formatting floppies is simply a matter of filling in the blanks.

To reformat an already-formatted disk, choose the Quick option.

To format a new disk, choose the Full format option.

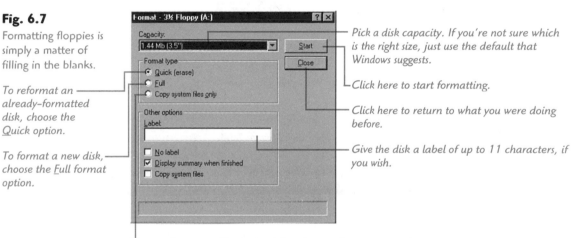

Pick a disk capacity. If you're not sure which is the right size, just use the default that Windows suggests.

Click here to start formatting.

Click here to return to what you were doing before.

Give the disk a label of up to 11 characters, if you wish.

To transfer system files to the disk without reformatting it, choose this option.

I want a copy of the whole disk

If you have a floppy disk full of files, it's easy to make an identical copy of the floppy. Put the original disk in your floppy drive, then right-click on the drive icon in the My Computer window. Choose Copy Disk from the popup menu, and follow the on-screen instructions, as in figure 6.8. You'll need a blank floppy for the copy, of course, but you don't need a second floppy drive. Windows is smart enough to tell you when it's time to remove the original disk and put in the new one.

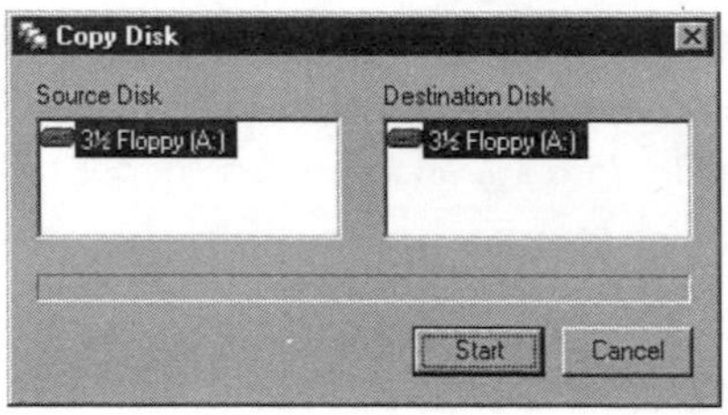

Fig. 6.8

To copy a floppy, right-click on the drive icon, select the drive types from this dialog box, and follow the on-screen instructions.

Copy Disk

Source Disk	Destination Disk
3½ Floppy (A:)	3½ Floppy (A:)

Start   Cancel

CAUTION   **If you're thinking of making copies of your Windows 95 disks so** a friend can use them, think again. Besides being illegal, immoral, and possibly fattening, it's also impossible. Windows disks use a highly compressed format that can't be copied, except with a special utility program.

Can I copy from a CD-ROM?

If you have a CD-ROM drive, you'll see its icon in the My Computer window. When it comes to CD-ROMs, you can do most of the same things you do with other types of drives—look at files, run programs, copy files from the CD to your hard disk. What can't you do with a CD-ROM? You can't add your own files to the disk. (The RO stands for Read Only, after all.) You can't delete files. You can't run ScanDisk or the Disk Defragmenter, either.

TIP   **For more information about how to work with CD-ROM disks,** look at Chapter 20.

7

Organizing Your Files and Keeping Them Neat

● **In this chapter:**

- **Getting around with the Windows Explorer**

- **Where can I put this file so I can find it again fast?**

- **Creating, renaming, moving, and deleting folders**

- **I know that file's out there some-where. How do I find it?**

- **Why you should *always* drag things around with the right mouse button**

- **Oops—I didn't mean to delete that file! Now what do I do?**

When you're buried under a mountain of paper, you grab manila folders and sort things out. Do the same with Windows to get those files on your hard disk under control . . . . ➢

Everything in your computer—every program, every document, every little scrap of information that Windows lets you save—winds up on your hard disk. If you have 6,000-plus files like me, how do you keep things straight? With the help of folders, Windows lets you keep things as neat as you want them to be.

Use folders to get organized in the first place. Make as many copies of your files as you like, and put them anywhere you want. After you've saved a bunch of files, tidy up by moving files from folder to folder. When your hard disk gets too cramped, reclaim real estate by deleting old files and folders you don't need anymore. Windows lets you clean up as much as you'd like, and it also gives you some tools in case you throw out too much. (Did you really mean to toss *those* files? Don't worry—you can probably find them in the Recycle Bin.)

In this chapter, we'll also look at the many ways you can find any file, anywhere, even when you can't for the life of you remember what you named it. If you can't figure out what's underneath that icon, you can always sneak a peek inside with the help of the built-in Quick Viewer.

How do I keep my files organized?

The first step is to open the root folder of your hard drive and create the main folders you'll use.

Double-click on a drive icon, and you'll go straight to the root folder.

66
Plain English, please!
When you double-click on a drive icon, you start out in a special folder called the **root**. If you think of your hard drive as a filing cabinet and each folder as one of its drawers, then the root folder acts like the frame that holds the drawers in place. The root folder has no name, just a backslash. Thus, to refer to the root of drive C:, you'd type **C:**. You can put files in the root folder if you'd like (and most people do), but the real purpose of this area is to hold the main folders you plan to use. 99

Windows does some of this filing and sorting for you. You don't have to look far to find examples of folders. After you get through installing Windows 95, you'll have a whole stack of folders—including, naturally, a Windows folder—stuffed with files and folders. (When I open my Windows folder, I can see 17 folders, and I know that there are eight more that Windows hides from me so I can't mess with them.) If I keep clicking, one of those sub-folders, System, has another *seven* folders inside it! Back in the root folder, there's a Program Files folder, a hidden Recycled folder, and a few more that are devoted exclusively to Windows tasks.

How do I use folders?

There's nothing complicated about folders. Used properly, they help you keep similar files together in a place where you can find them when you need them. If your bedroom were organized this way, you'd be able to track down a clean pair of socks in seconds, just by looking at storage areas inside of other storage areas: \bedroom\dresser\top drawer\box of underwear\ white socks. The socks are in the box, which in turn is in the drawer, which is ... well, you get the idea.

Windows lets you put folders inside of folders so they fall into the same sort of hierarchy. For example, you might create a folder called "1996 Budget"; then, inside that folder, you'd create additional folders called "P&L Statements," "Forecasts," and so on. Inside the "Sales Reports" folder, you might add a separate folder for each member of the sales staff.

For a graphic display of how this folder-in-a-folder routine works, just look at the outline-style Explorer view in figure 7.1.

 TIP **Do you think the Windows Desktop is something special? Nope,** it's just another folder. You might not recognize it as such, because the icons inside this folder are arranged differently from any other folder you'll see. Nonetheless, it acts just like a folder, as you can see if you open the Windows Explorer and look at it. (In the Explorer, you'll find the Desktop in the left-hand pane, at the very top of the tree—see fig. 7.1.)

Fig. 7.1

Use folders inside of other folders to keep your files organized. The Explorer view (left) lets you see the "tree" of folders; if you prefer, you can open a folder window (right) and look at only what's inside it.

Desktop ——

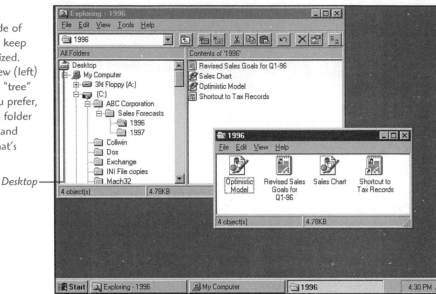

I want to create a new folder

Let's say you've just been promoted to sales manager. Congratulations! Now what are you going to do with all those sales forecasts that the folks in your department keep sending you via e-mail? For starters, open your C: drive and create a folder called `Sales Forecasts` in the root folder. You can throw all those sales forecasts in that folder if you'd like, or create a set of new folders, one for each of your salespeople, in that folder.

Sometimes you'll save files directly into these folders from your application programs. Other times, you'll get files from other people, and you'll need to do your filing after the fact. Either way, the technique is the same.

To create a new folder, just follow these steps:

1 Double-click on the My Computer icon and keep double-clicking on folders until you've opened the one where you want to create a new folder.

2 Right-click in any empty spot in this folder window and click on Ne<u>w</u>. Choose <u>F</u>older from the cascading menu (see fig. 7.2).

3 A new folder will appear, with a suitably generic label in place. To give it a more meaningful name, just start typing (see fig. 7.3).

Fig. 7.2
Right-click in any folder window to create a new folder from the popup menus.

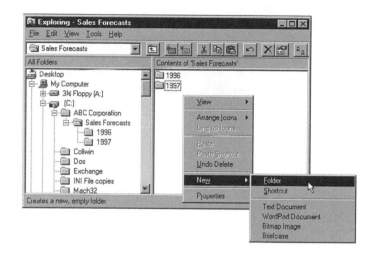

Fig. 7.3
The generic label New Folder isn't very helpful, is it? Just start typing to give it a more descriptive name.

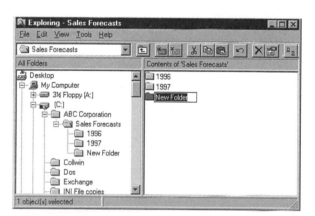

I want to get rid of a folder

It's easy to get rid of a folder. Just point at the folder, click once to select it, then right-click and choose <u>D</u>elete from the popup menu.

This desktop is too cluttered!

Whenever it's time to move or copy files from one place to another, you'll want to open two windows—one for the original location of the files in question, the other for the place where you want to move them. Trouble is, all that double-clicking can open a lot of windows on your screen, which makes it difficult to find the two you want to use. Before you can move or copy files, you need to sweep aside the clutter and arrange both folders on the screen so you can see them clearly. Here's how:

1 Minimize or close all open windows.

2 Open My Computer and double-click on the appropriate drive icon. Keep double-clicking on folders until you've opened the window where the files you want to move are stored.

TIP **Do you get a new window (and a bunch of unwanted clutter)** every time you double-click on a folder? It's easy to keep things neat and avoid window clutter. Open a window for My Computer (or any folder), and choose View, Options. On the dialog tab labeled Folder, make sure there's a dot next to the choice that reads Browse folders by using a single window, which changes as you open each folder. Click OK, and from that point on, whenever you open a new window, it will automatically close the previous window.

3 Open My Computer again, and double-click some more until you've opened a window on the folder where you want the files to end up.

4 Right-click on a blank spot on the taskbar, and choose Tile Horizontally or Tile Vertically, as shown in figure 7.4. Presto! Both windows will automatically zoom to fill half the available space, either one over the other (horizontal) or side-by-side (vertical).

Q&A *Whoops! I accidentally had three windows open when I chose the Tile command, and now all three windows are tiled on the screen. What do I do now?*

Right-click on the taskbar and choose Undo, then minimize the stray window and try again.

Fig. 7.4

Use one of the Tile commands to arrange these two windows on the desktop.

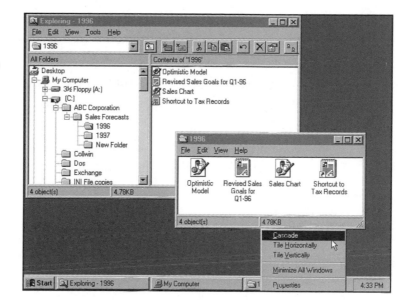

Moving files and folders around

As we saw in Chapter 5, you can use the mouse to drag just about anything from one place to another. Most of the time, that's how you'll move or copy files and folders. You could simply hold down the left mouse button and start dragging things around, but you'd be in for some very confusing times.

Dragging-and-dropping with the left mouse button, you see, has completely different effects, depending on what kind of object you're dragging and where you're dropping it. When you drag with the right mouse button, on the other hand, dragging-and-dropping always works the same way.

You never know what will happen when you use the left mouse button...

When you select an object, hold down the left mouse button, and drag, one of three things happens when you let go of the mouse button:

- **If you're moving to another folder on the same drive,** Windows will move the files to the destination folder. They no longer exist in their original location.

- **If you're moving to another folder on a different drive,** Windows will copy the files. You'll wind up with duplicate files—one in the original location and one in the destination folder.

- **If any of the files you're moving are programs,** Windows will create a **shortcut** in the destination folder. The file itself remains in the original folder.

Confused? You should be. Even certified Windows experts get befuddled sometimes by this now-you-see-it-now-you-don't nonsense. Fortunately, there's a better way: just hold down the *right* mouse button and drag. When you release the button to drop the object in its new location, you'll see a shortcut menu like the one in figure 7.5. *You* decide whether you want to move the file, copy it, or create a shortcut in the new location.

Fig. 7.5

When you hold down the right mouse button and drag an object—file, folder, whatever—you get to choose what happens next from this popup menu.

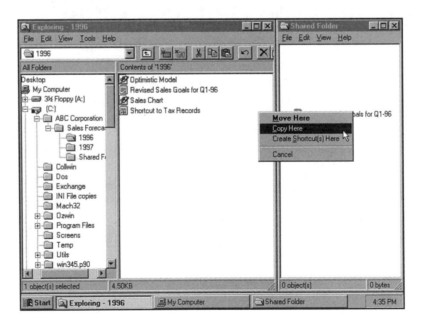

I don't *want* to drag all those icons around!

Some people never get used to the idea of dragging and dropping files. If that description fits you, use the other technique for moving and copying files. The trick is to *cut* or *copy* the original files, and *paste* them into their new home. You'll still need to open two folder windows: one for the folder that holds the files you want to move, the other for the destination folder. Once you've done that, it's a simple process:

1 Select the file or files from the original folder.

2 Right-click on one of the selected files to pop up a shortcut file menu.

3 Choose Copy if you want to leave the original files where they are and make identical copies in the destination folder. Choose Cut to delete the original files, essentially moving them to the new location.

4 Switch to the destination folder window, and right-click on an empty area. Choose Paste to finish the job.

I want to move a bunch of files

It's easy to select one file for moving or copying. Just point and click. But what happens when you want to move or copy or delete a whole bunch of files? You could handle each file by itself, but there's a much easier way to select a group of files.

- **To select every file or object in a folder,** look on the menu bar and choose Edit, Select All.

- **To select a group of files that are right next to one another,** use the mouse to select the first file in the group. Hold down the Shift key and then click on the last file in the group. Voilà! All the files between the two points are highlighted and ready for you to tell Windows what to do with them.

- **To select a large group of adjacent files,** use the mouse to draw an imaginary box around them. Pick one of the corners of this "box," hold down the left mouse button, and drag the selection to the opposite corner of the group you want to select. As you drag, you'll see the selected icons change color to let you know you were successful.

TIP **If you're having trouble selecting a group of files, try switching to** List view instead. The neat columnar display and smaller typeface make it easier to grab a flock of files.

- **To select a file here and a file there,** hold down the Ctrl key as you click on one file after another. Without that special keystroke, Windows won't let you select more than one thing at a time. With that help, though, you can select as many files as you want.

- **To actually move or copy the files** takes a little bit of practice. With a single file, it's easy— just watch the icon as it moves from one window to the other. When you've selected a group of files, though, the Windows pointer shows you a "ghosted" image as you drag. The outlines of the selected files let you know which files you successfully selected, but they also make it difficult to tell where you're supposed to drop the files. If you're confused, there's an easy way out: just keep your eye on the arrow pointer. When it's aimed directly at the destination folder or drive, the target changes color (as it has in fig. 7.6). When you see that signal, let go of the button. If it doesn't work right, right-click, choose <u>U</u>ndo Move or <u>U</u>ndo Copy, and try it again.

Fig. 7.6
Dragging a group of files (like the four in the top window) is easy, but where do you drop them? Keep your eye on the tip of the arrow in the bottom window.

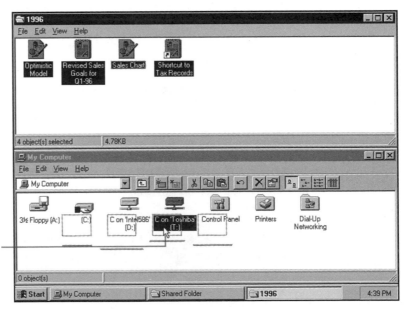

The ghostly image of the files you're dragging may be distracting. Ignore it and concentrate on where this pointer is aimed.

What happens when I try to copy a file with the same name?

Let's say you have a file called LETTER1 (everyone who uses computers eventually has a few files with dopey names like that). You want to make a copy of that file, so you right-click and choose Copy. Here's what happens when you choose Paste:

- If you make a copy in the same folder, your new file will be called Copy of LETTER1.

- If you point to another folder, and there isn't a file with that name there, you'll get another file called LETTER1.

- If you point to another folder, and there's already a file with that name, you'll see a dialog box like the one in figure 7.7.

Fig. 7.7
Windows won't allow
two files in the same
place with the same
name. Do you want to
replace the old file?

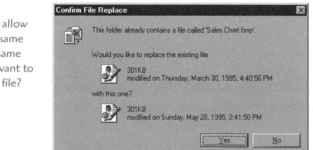

Using the Windows Explorer

For simple tasks, a simple folder window is usually sufficient. But there will be times when you want to do some major maintenance with your computer's file system—the PC equivalent of spring cleaning. For those days, you need a way to move files from folder to folder with just a few clicks. That's where the Windows Explorer comes in.

When you double-click on a drive or folder icon, you get a window filled with icons. When you right-click on an icon and choose Explore, though, you get a window with a split personality. On the right, it looks just like an ordinary folder window. On the left, you'll see an outline view that shows all the drives and folders on your desktop, your computer, and even other computers, if you're hooked up to a network.

The Windows Explorer, up close and personal

Use the Windows Explorer to do industrial-strength clean-up jobs with the files on your computer. The tree window on the left lets you move from folder to folder (and even to different computers on a network) with a minimum of mouse clicks. The window on the right acts like an ordinary folder window whose contents correspond to the icon you've selected on the left side.

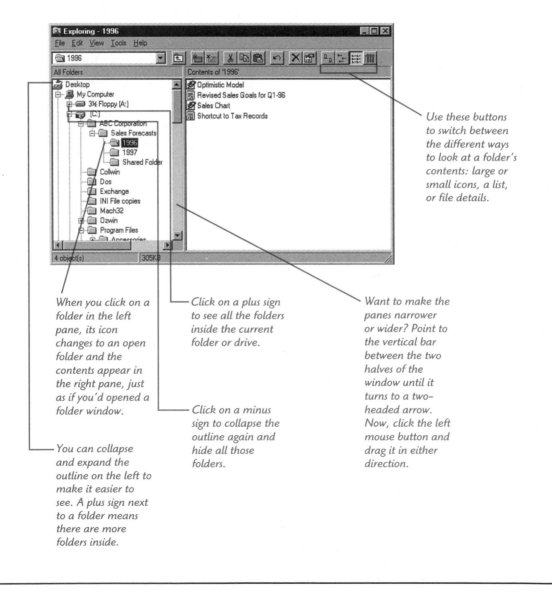

Use these buttons to switch between the different ways to look at a folder's contents: large or small icons, a list, or file details.

When you click on a folder in the left pane, its icon changes to an open folder and the contents appear in the right pane, just as if you'd opened a folder window.

Click on a plus sign to see all the folders inside the current folder or drive.

Want to make the panes narrower or wider? Point to the vertical bar between the two halves of the window until it turns to a two–headed arrow. Now, click the left mouse button and drag it in either direction.

Click on a minus sign to collapse the outline again and hide all those folders.

You can collapse and expand the outline on the left to make it easier to see. A plus sign next to a folder means there are more folders inside.

TIP   **No matter what kind of window you use, you can sort files in any** order you like. Choose <u>V</u>iew, <u>D</u>etails, and then sort the list by clicking the column headings. Click the headings again to sort in reverse order.

What's in that file? Use the Quick Viewer

One reason not to use names like LETTER1.DOC is that they don't tell you anything about what's in the file. It's especially confusing if Windows finds a bunch of files that share the same name but are stored in different folders. How do you tell what's inside? Try using the Quick Viewer. It works like an airport X-ray machine to peek inside the file and display its contents. The resulting display might not look exactly the way it would if you were to open the file with a fancy application, but it only takes a few seconds.

Point to the file you're curious about, and right-click. If Windows recognizes the file format, one of the choices available to you is <u>Q</u>uick View. Click to pop up a window like the one in figure 7.8, showing you the contents of the file.

Fig. 7.8
Use the Quick Viewer to peek inside a file without starting up the program that created it

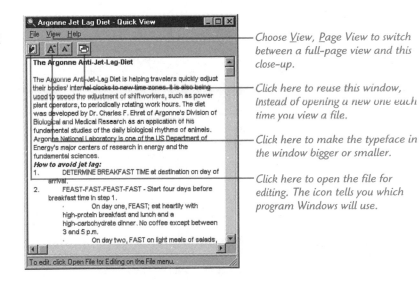

Choose <u>V</u>iew, <u>P</u>age View to switch between a full-page view and this close-up.

Click here to reuse this window, Instead of opening a new one each time you view a file.

Click here to make the typeface in the window bigger or smaller.

Click here to open the file for editing. The icon tells you which program Windows will use.

The foolproof way to find any file, anywhere, anytime

Like I said, there are 6,537 files on my hard drive. Give or take a few hundred. How do I find the one I need right now? It used to be that you had to open all the files and look through them to see which one had the data you were looking for. With Windows 95, though, you can search through an entire hard disk to find any file, any time—even if you only remember a tiny scrap of information about it.

To set the Windows bloodhound on the trail, click on the Start button and choose <u>F</u>ind, <u>F</u>iles or Folders. Use the Find Files command. You'll see a dialog box like the one in figure 7.9. What do you do next? That depends on how much you remember about the file in question.

Fig. 7.9
Can't remember where you put that file? Fill in the blanks in this dialog box to ask Windows to look for it.

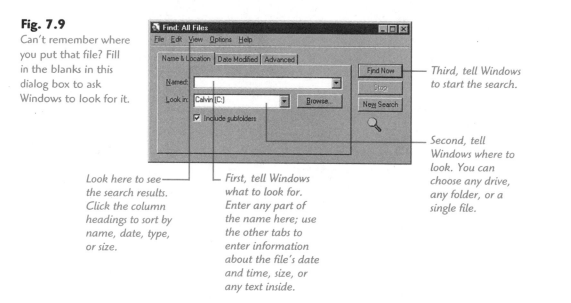

Third, tell Windows to start the search.

Second, tell Windows where to look. You can choose any drive, any folder, or a single file.

Look here to see the search results. Click the column headings to sort by name, date, type, or size.

First, tell Windows what to look for. Enter any part of the name here; use the other tabs to enter information about the file's date and time, size, or any text inside.

I think I remember part of the name

If you know a word (or even a few letters) that you used in the file name, enter it in the box labeled Named. Windows will search for those letters at any position within a file name. For example, if you enter **LET**, the search results windows will show Letter to the President and Collette's Report because both have those three letters somewhere within the name.

TIP **You can sort the search results in four different ways. Click on** the Name heading, for example, to sort by name, sorted in alphabetical (A-to-Z) order. Click again to sort in reverse (Z-to-A) order. The date, size, and folder options work the same way.

I don't remember the name, but I remember when I saved it last

If you're sure you last saved the file sometime in the past month, click on the Date Modified tab, and choose the option During the previous 1 month(s). You can also specify a range of dates here—for example, between March 15, 1995 and April 15, 1995.

I think I know which folder it's in

Then help Windows narrow down the search by specifying that folder (and only that folder) in the box labeled Look in. You can enter the folder name (**C:\Letters**) yourself, or click the Browse button to choose it from an Explorer-style list.

I remember a few words that were in it

Obviously, it won't do you much good to search for common words like "the," but if you remember a specific phrase, you can have Windows track down all files containing that phrase. If you're looking for a letter you sent to President Clinton, for example, click on the Advanced tab and enter **Clinton** in the box labeled Containing text. Then click the Find Now button to start searching.

Oops! The foolproof way to bring back a file you just deleted

Have you ever accidentally thrown away an important piece of paper? Uma Thurman's phone number, perhaps, or a sweepstakes check? If you really had won that publisher's sweepstakes, you'd root through old coffee grounds and eggshells to find that check. Fortunately, it's a lot less messy to recover lost files, thanks to the Windows Recycle Bin.

What happens when I delete a file?

There are several ways to delete a file, or a folder, or any combination of the two.

- From a folder window, select the icon or icons you want to delete, right-click, and choose <u>D</u>elete.

- Select the icon, then open the <u>F</u>ile menu and select <u>D</u>elete.

- Easier still, select it and press the Del key.

- If you can see the Recycle Bin on the desktop, you can also drag the selected files and/or folders and drop them on top of the icon. (I keep the Recycle Bin in the lower right corner of my screen just to make it easier to drag things there.)

No matter which way you choose, you'll see a dialog box like the one in figure 7.10. If you'd rather skip that extra step every time, right-click on the Recycle Bin, open its Properties sheet, and remove the check mark from the box labeled <u>D</u>isplay delete confirmation dialog.

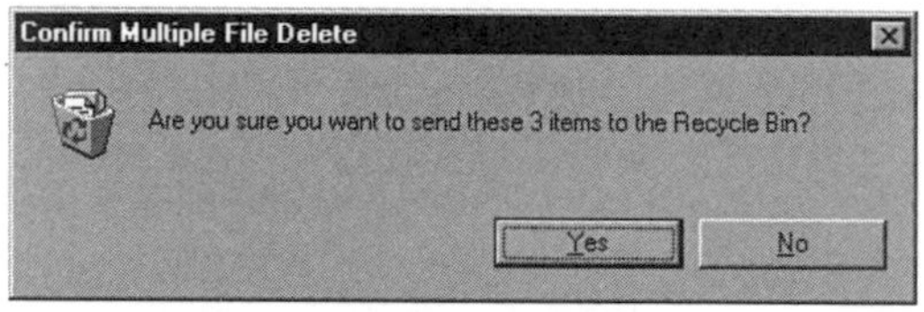

Fig. 7.10
Do you really want to delete these files? By default, Windows asks you to say OK every time you zap a file or folder.

Confirm Multiple File Delete	☒
Are you sure you want to send these 3 items to the Recycle Bin?	
<u>Y</u>es	N<u>o</u>

TIP **What if you're absolutely, positively certain you want to get rid of** an icon once and for all? Right-click on it, then hold down the Shift key as you choose <u>D</u>elete. When you use this trick, you'll bypass the Recycle Bin completely and simply vaporize the rascal.

How do I get my files back?

It's easy to tell when there's something in the trash—the Recycle Bin icon changes from empty to this full version. If you discover you need to resurrect a file you deleted earlier, double-click here. The window that opens up will look a lot like the one in figure 7.11. Select the files or folders you want to bring back, then choose <u>F</u>ile, <u>R</u>estore. Unzap! It's just as if the files never went away.

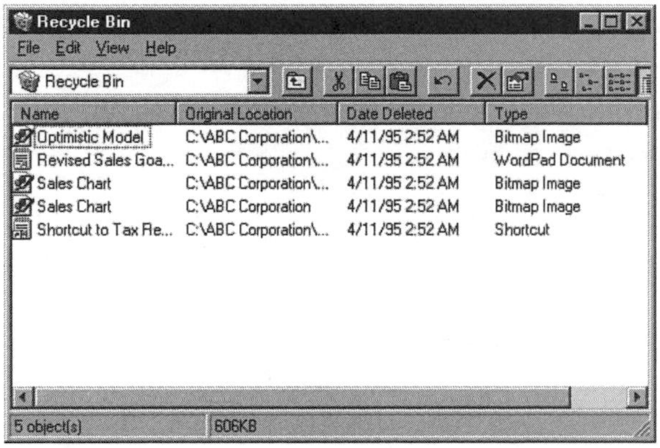

Fig. 7.11

To restore any of these deleted files, open the Recycle Bin and choose File, Restore from the menu.

What happens when the bin gets full?

The Recycle Bin isn't a bottomless pit. Sooner or later (probably sooner) you'll fill it up. When that happens, Windows automatically deletes files to make room for the freshly deleted ones. Of course, you can always tell Windows to take out the trash. Right-click on the Recycle Bin, then choose Empty Recycle Bin.

CAUTION When you're trying to make room on your hard disk to install a new program, the Recycle Bin can drive you crazy. You delete some old files thinking that you're clearing space. Instead of freeing up room, though, Windows just moves the deleted files to the Recycle Bin, where they still gobble up the same amount of space. The moral: when space is at a premium, always remember to empty the Recycle Bin.

How can I cut down the Recycle Bin's appetite?

If you're running tight on hard disk space, you might want to restrict the amount of space that Windows sets aside for the Recycle Bin. To adjust this setting, right-click on the Recycle Bin, choose Properties, and move the slider control left or right. Using the controls here, you can even turn off the Recycle Bin completely, although you can't remove its icon from your desktop. Beware, though—if you take this drastic step you lose the comforting ability to retrieve deleted files!

Using shortcuts

Sometimes a copy is better than the real thing. If you don't believe me, consider this scenario:

You, Ms. Sales Manager, have three rich and demanding customers. You keep each customer's sales records in a separate manila folder. You also have a product catalog the size of a phone book that you use, no matter which customer you're working with. If you make three copies of that catalog, and put one in each client folder, you've created a big problem the next time you revise your catalog. You have to remember to put a new copy in all three client folders, or you might wind up sending the wrong merchandise or charging the wrong price.

The solution is to store the catalog in its own folder, then store a note in each client folder that tells you where to find it. That's how shortcuts work. They act like little notes that tell Windows to find something stored elsewhere on the disk, or even on another computer, and open it—right now. Shortcuts use only a small amount of disk space, and they can point to just about anything, just about anywhere: programs, documents, printers and drives, even a location on The Microsoft Network.

How do I create a shortcut?

One of the most useful places to create a shortcut is right on the Windows desktop. For a program you use every day, like the Windows Calculator, why should you have to rummage through the Start menu? You don't want to move the program out of its home in the Windows folder, but you would like to be able to start it up by just double-clicking on an icon. Here's how:

- If you already know where the program is stored, just open its folder or highlight it in the Windows Explorer. Drag the icon using the right mouse button, then drop it onto the desktop, choosing Create Shortcut(s) Here from the menu that pops up.

TIP **When you drag-and-drop a program to create a shortcut,** Windows calls the new icon Shortcut to ... the program's original name. You can delete the two extra words if you like, or even completely rename the shortcut. Word, for example, takes up a lot less screen real estate than Shortcut to Microsoft Word for Windows.

- If you're not sure where the program is located, use the wizard. Right-click on the spot where you want the new shortcut to appear, and choose Ne<u>w</u>, <u>S</u>hortcut. In the first step (see fig. 7.12), you can browse through folders to find the program file; in the second step, you give your shortcut a name.

Fig. 7.12

The wizard lets you create a shortcut and name it in two easy steps.

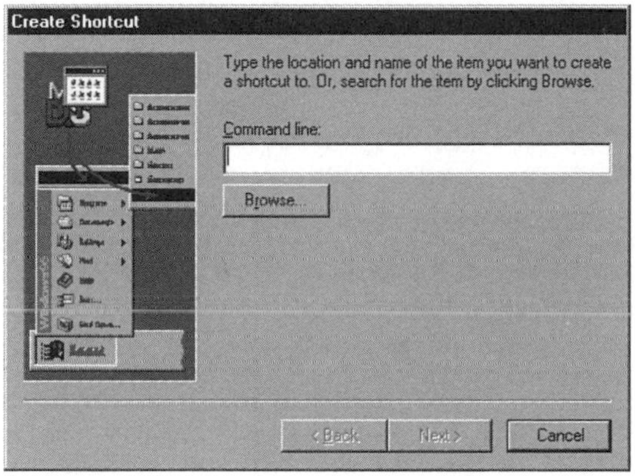

How do I use a shortcut?

Just double-click on it. Windows looks inside the icon, finds the shortcut note, and goes off to find the original file. If you've changed the name of the target file, or moved it to a new folder, it might take a few seconds.

Q&A   *My shortcut isn't working. What's wrong?*

Right-click on the shortcut icon, click P<u>r</u>operties, and look at what's in the box labeled Start in. You may have to tell Windows to start in a different folder—the one where your data files are stored, for example.

Why is this DOS shortcut different?

When you start a program that was designed to run under MS-DOS, Windows needs to rush around like a nervous headwaiter getting things ready first. All those details are stored in the program's Properties.

With the help of the DOS program properties (see fig. 7.13), you can control the amount of memory your DOS program gets, tell Windows whether to let it take over the whole screen or just run in a small window, and set dozens of technical options. Most of the time, you won't want to mess with these settings. If you have a DOS program that's giving you trouble, look in Chapter 11 for more details about how to get it working.

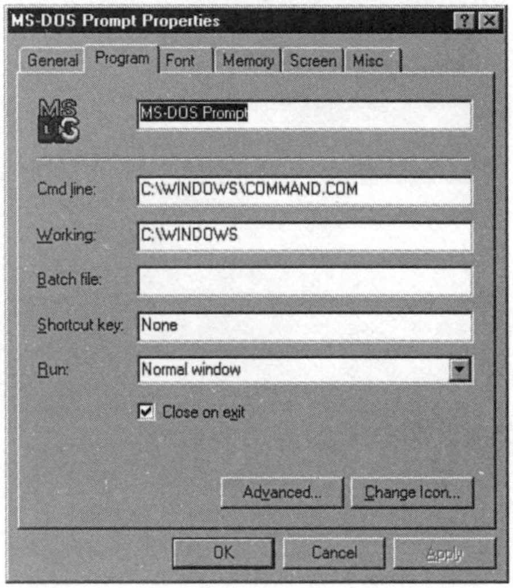

Fig. 7.13
DOS shortcuts are different. Look at all these confusing options!

MS-DOS Prompt Properties

General | Program | Font | Memory | Screen | Misc

MS-DOS Prompt

Cmd line: C:\WINDOWS\COMMAND.COM
Working: C:\WINDOWS
Batch file:
Shortcut key: None
Run: Normal window

☑ Close on exit

Advanced...   Change Icon...

OK   Cancel   Apply

8

Opening and Closing Windows

● In this chapter:

- The whats, wheres, and whys of windows

- How do I open a window?

- You can—and should—run more than one program at a time. Here's how

- Want that window out of the way? Minimize it!

- OK, I'm through with this window. Now what?

With a name like Windows 95, it only figures that the program's main building blocks are—you guessed it—windows . . . .

Windows (with a big W) uses lots of individual windows (with a small w) to hold all the different things you're trying to juggle at once. One window might contain a memo to your boss, while another one has a spreadsheet with the numbers you're supposed to put in that important memo. At the same time, you might have four or five folder windows open while you search for the memo you wrote *last* month. That's at least six windows already, and we haven't even counted that Solitaire game you've been playing while you thought no one was looking.

Sound complicated? It's not, really. Keeping track of five or ten windows and switching from one to another is no more difficult than zapping from CBS to NBC to HBO to the Home Shopping Network on your 123-channel cable TV system.

Of course, whether you're sitting in your living room or sitting in front of your PC, it helps to have a good remote control. And working with Windows' remote control is a snap, once you know which buttons to push.

So what exactly is a window, anyway?

Whenever you double-click on a folder, Windows draws a neat little rectangle on the screen and arranges the contents of the folder inside. That rectangle is a window. The same thing happens when you double-click on a program icon—the program opens in a window. Think of a window as an enclosed patch of land where your data can roam freely. The outside edges of the window, called **borders**, act like fences to keep the window's contents from wandering onto the desktop or into another window by accident.

What's in a window?

Windows are incredibly versatile spaces. You can move them around on the screen, arrange them side by side, make them bigger or smaller, or expand them to fill the entire screen. When you want to move a window out of the way, you can even stuff it into a box and store it (temporarily) on the taskbar at the bottom of the screen.

No matter what you do with a window, though, the contents always stay inside the window's borders.

Title bar
Each window has its own name badge to help you figure out what's inside. Double-click on any empty space here to maximize or restore the window.

Minimize button
You want the window out of sight, but you might need it again. Click here to stuff the entire window into a tiny box and store it on the taskbar.

Maximize button
Want to give one window your full attention? Click here to "explode" a window to full size, covering up everything on the screen except the taskbar. It changes to a Restore button after the window is maximized.

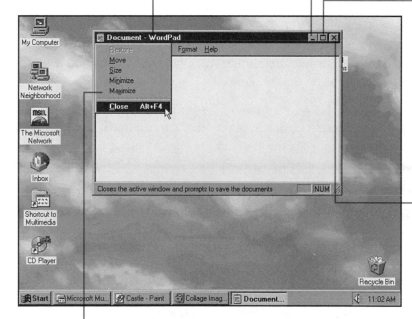

Close button
X marks the spot when it's time to put a window away for good. Click here to close a window.

Control menu
The one-stop shopping center for people who don't like to push buttons. Click the tiny icon just to the left of the window's label to make this list appear.

I want to start a program

Before we tackle the hard scenario—juggling a whole screen full of windows—let's try something simple: working with a single window.

1 First, make sure no programs are running. (You'll see any running programs in the taskbar.)

2 Click the Start button, and click on Programs.

3 Follow the cascading menu to the right, and click on Accessories to bring up yet another cascading menu.

4 Now, click on WordPad to start up Windows' built-in word processor.

You'll notice that it takes a few seconds before WordPad appears; that's because Windows has to go find the program on your hard drive and load it into your computer's memory.

When WordPad started up, it opened into a timid little window that only uses part of the screen. Hmmm, that's not exactly what we wanted, is it? We want to devote our full attention to WordPad, and we don't need to see any other distractions on the screen. So let's **maximize** WordPad.

Look at figure 7.1. See the three buttons at the far right of the WordPad window's title bar? The one in the center (it looks like a box with a thick border along the top) is the Maximize button. Click on that button and stand back as the WordPad window zooms out to take over the entire screen.

The buttons at the far right of the top of each window change, depending on whether you've maximized the window or not. The Maximize button is in the center of the bottom set; once the window's maximized, Windows puts the Restore button there instead (top set), so you can switch back to a window when you're ready.

That's much better, isn't it? The effect is just the same as if we'd clicked Channel 2 on our TV's remote control to watch David Letterman. The WordPad window now occupies the full screen, covering up everything except the taskbar down below.

Fig. 8.1
To enlarge a window so it takes up the entire screen, click on the Maximize button.

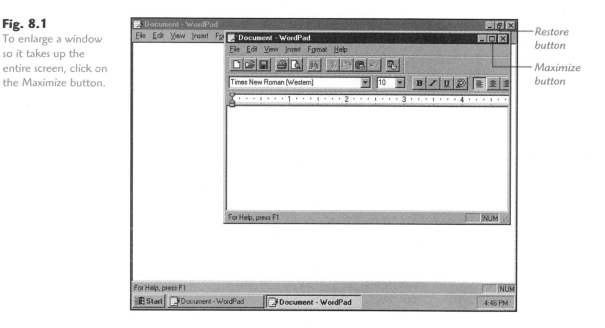

Restore button

Maximize button

When you **maximize** a window, it takes over the entire screen. As long as the window is maximized, there are a few things you can't do:

- You can't move the window around.

- You can't make it any bigger.

- You can't see its borders. For all intents and purposes, the edges of your monitor serve as the window's borders.

- You can't see anything on the desktop except the taskbar. If you want to open the My Computer window, you're out of luck until you figure out how to get this window out of the way (don't worry, it's not hard).

 TIP **Are those tiny buttons too small to hit without squinting? Make** the little suckers bigger:

1. Click the Start button and choose <u>S</u>ettings, <u>C</u>ontrol Panel.

 2. Double-click on the icon labeled Display.

3. Click on the tab labeled Appearance, and watch the contents of the window change. Aha! Now click on any of those pesky tiny buttons.

If the box labeled Item contains the words Caption Buttons, you succeeded; otherwise, try again.

4. Now click in the box labeled Size, then press the up and down arrows to make the buttons grow and shrink.

5. When you're happy with your new, extra-large buttons, click OK.

There are more goodies you can change to make Windows your own—check out Chapters 14 and 15 for details.

I want to start another program

To open a second window, we don't need to do anything with WordPad. Let's just leave it there, and use the Start menu to run Paint, Windows' built-in drawing program. Click the Programs menu, then Accessories, then Paint. Here, too, we'll have to wait a few seconds while Windows reads the Paint program from your hard drive and loads it into the computer's memory.

Just like WordPad did, Paint starts in a small window, which means we can still see Wordpad in the background. Since we don't want any distractions, let's click the Maximize button to zoom Paint to full size, too. Now it's occupying the entire screen, just as if we'd switched on Channel 4 to watch Jay Leno.

What happened to WordPad? Nothing. It's still there in the background, waiting patiently for us to pay attention to it again. But the only thing we can see besides Paint is the taskbar, just below the maximized Paint window. If we wanted to, we could start another program right now and begin multitasking. For now, though, let's stick with just two windows.

> 66 ***Plain English, please!***
>
> You can use Windows to do two, three, five, even twenty things—all at the same time—on your PC. Sometimes, one or more of the windows in the background are actually working, doing things like formatting a floppy disk, downloading a file from The Microsoft Network, or crunching a big batch of numbers. This frenzied, everything-happening-at-once activity is called **multitasking**. If the background windows are inactive, you're simply **task-switching**. 99

TIP **The taskbar is anchored to the bottom of the screen when you** first start Windows, but you can move it if you'd like. Aim the mouse pointer at the taskbar, click and hold the left mouse button, and then drag the taskbar to any side of the screen you'd like. It'll stick to the top, bottom, or either side.

I want to switch between two windows

Now that both programs are running, it's time to start zapping back and forth between them. For that, we'll need to use the taskbar.

3-D, without the funny glasses

How can you tell when a button on the taskbar (or anywhere else, for that matter) is "pushed"? The trick is to recognize some of the special effects that Windows uses to fake a three-dimensional look. And, unlike those cheesy 3-D science fiction movies that were popular in the '50s and '60s, you don't need special glasses to see them.

When you look carefully at the Maximize, Minimize, and Close buttons in any window, you'll notice a thin white line that runs along the left and top edges of each button, and a corresponding thin black line that runs on the right and bottom.

The effect of these matching lines is to create the illusion that the button is sitting on top of the title bar, catching rays from a light that shines from the top left-hand corner of the screen.

When you "push" a button, the lines reverse, with the left and top edges turning dark, and the bottom and right edges turning light. The image on the button's face also shifts slightly to the right. To your eye, which still thinks the imaginary light source is shining from the top left, it looks just as if the button is now depressed below the surface of the title bar.

Along the taskbar, the effect is more noticeable and a bit more dramatic, thanks to the lighter background behind the "pushed" button.

The taskbar works just like your TV's remote control. Each time you press a button on the remote control, the entire contents of the screen change. Click! There's David Letterman! Click! There's Jay Leno! Click! There's Dave again! Each time you click, one (and only one) program comes to the foreground, and everything else seems to disappear. You know you can switch between programs any time, but as long as Dave is on the screen there's no sign of Jay, and as long as WordPad is showing, there's no sign of Paint.

I want to switch between windows the fast way

There's an ultra-cool way to switch from one window to another without using the mouse or the taskbar. (In fact, it's so cool that the official Microsoft name for this little trick is **Coolswitch**.)

When you have more than one window open, hold down the Alt key and press the Tab key. Keep holding the Alt key down, but let your finger off the Tab key. A box will pop up in the center of the screen with the icons and labels for all your open windows (see fig. 8.2). To switch programs, just keep hitting the Tab key until the icon you're looking for is highlighted. Once you let go of the Alt key, the Coolswitch box will go away and your window will pop instantly into view.

Fig. 8.2
Bet your TV's remote control can't do this! Hold down Alt and press the Tab key repeatedly to zap between every window you have open.

Argonne Jet Lag Diet - WordPad

Can I move one window out of the way?

When you want to switch away from one window and start working on something else, Windows lets you set the first window aside temporarily. It's out of sight, but not out of memory. When you **minimize** a window, it's just as if you've taken the contents of that window, stuffed them into a box, and placed the box down on the taskbar. Everything in that window is still on call; you just need to push a button to bring it back.

Let's minimize both WordPad and Paint. To get Paint out of the way, push the Minimize button (it's the one with the small horizontal line along the button—the design is supposed to remind you of the taskbar). Do the same with WordPad.

Now press either button on the taskbar, and watch the same effect in reverse, as the window instantly zooms back up to its previous position.

What's the difference between minimizing and closing a window?

There's a critical distinction between minimizing a program and closing it. Remember how it took a few seconds for WordPad and Paint to load from the hard drive? In contrast, reloading either minimized application by pushing its taskbar button was nearly instantaneous.

When you **close** a window, you unload it from your computer's memory. In effect, you're telling it to go home and relax. If you decide you need it again, you'll have to wait while it wakes up, gets dressed, has a cup of coffee, and drives back to work. With a bigger program (like Microsoft Word or Excel, for example) it could take a minute or even longer for the program to go through all the rigmarole it requires to get up and running.

When you minimize a window, on the other hand, you leave it in memory. You're telling the program to go sit on the taskbar and take a quick coffee break. The next time you call, the program is still wide awake, fully dressed, and ready to get right back to work.

TIP **You've probably had it drilled into you since you were this high:**
Clean up after yourself. Well, don't do it here. As long as your computer has enough RAM, don't close programs—instead, get in the habit of minimizing them. You'll save time, and as long as you have enough memory you have nothing to lose. How do you know when you're running low on memory? If Windows tells you it's run out of memory or system resources, or if you hear the hard disk chugging away continually, and there's a long delay every time you try to switch between programs, it's time to close a few windows.

TIP **When you've got a lot of windows open, the buttons on the**
taskbar become unreadable. No problem—just point to any button and let the pointer sit there for a few seconds. Eventually, a little label called a ToolTip will pop up, telling you the full name of that button (see fig. 8.3 for an example). After the first tip appears, you can slide the pointer from button to button, and the remaining ToolTips will appear instantaneously.

Another fix for a full taskbar is to increase its height. Point to the top border of the taskbar, until you see a double-headed arrow. Then drag upward to make the taskbar tall enough for two rows of minimized programs.

Fig. 8.3
Let the mouse pointer sit on top of any button for a few seconds, until the ToolTip label pops up; now you can slide the pointer from side to side to see what's what.

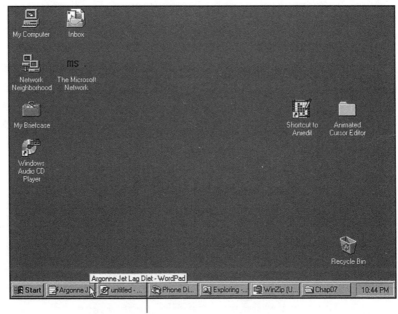

ToolTip label

How do I close a window?

When you're absolutely, positively sure you're all done with a window, it's OK to close it. To make it disappear, press the Close button, which is the one labeled with a big X. The X means "go away." All done. Cross it off your list.

You can't get into trouble by pressing the Close button. If you've got unsaved work in the window you're planning to zap, Windows will give you the opportunity to save it before it goes away.

If you prefer to use the keyboard instead of the mouse, you can almost always use the keyboard shortcut Alt+F4 to close a window, too.

TIP **There's another way to minimize, maximize, or close a window:** every window has a Control menu that you can pull down by clicking on the small icon at the far left of the title bar. Frankly, it's easier to use the buttons on the right side, but there is one time when it helps to know about the Control menu: If your mouse stops working, you can open the Control menu with Alt+spacebar.

CAUTION **There's one last way to close a window, but it's *strictly for emergencies*.** If a program just stops, with no explanation, you can shut it down by pressing the Ctrl, Alt, and Delete keys simultaneously, then choosing the name of the window from the popup list. It's a great way to get back to work when your program has failed, but the Ctrl+Alt+Delete should only be used as a last resort. Don't use it to close an application unless you're absolutely sure it's stopped working.

9

Moving Windows Around (and Moving Around in Windows)

● **In this chapter:**

- Resizing a window for a perfect fit

- Picking a window to work with

- Are there different types of windows?

- Taking a scroll with the scroll bar

- Cleaning up your window situation

Whoever said, "I don't do windows," wasn't a Windows 95 user. There are a mind-boggling number of things you can do to manipulate a window in Windows 95 . . . . ⊙

So far, we've been treating each window as if it were a television screen where we could watch only one program at a time. But, suppose we replace our tired old TV set with a state-of-the-art, 501-channel, fully fiber-optic on-ramp to the Information Superhighway. On the main screen, we might watch Jay Leno's monologue; but we'd use the picture-in-picture feature to keep an eye on Dave Letterman, so we could switch back when he gets to the Top 10 list. In fact, if we get a really hot model, we can put CNN, The Disney Channel, and MTV on the screen all at once, although even Larry King would have a hard time making sense of it all.

That's how Windows works when you really start to take advantage of its everything-at-once capabilities. You can shrink a window so it uses a fraction of the screen, leaving you a clear view of the desktop—and other windows—in the background. You can stack windows up like so many "While You Were Out" message slips, and shuffle through them just as easily. If a window's in the way, you can pick it up and move it somewhere else.

It's a great way to stay on top of all the demands of a typical working day. It's an even better way to get throughly lost on the desktop, unless you know the secret techniques for putting the right-sized window right where you want it.

How do I see what's behind this window?

The difference between maximizing and minimizing is an all-or-nothing proposition. A window either takes up the full screen or it's stuffed into one of those buttons on the taskbar. But, as you saw when you started up the WordPad and Paint programs, there *is* a middle ground between maximize and minimize. From either state, you can **restore** a program or folder to a window. As the name implies, restoring a window means putting it right back where it was before, in the exact same position and trimmed to the exact same size it was last time.

Unlike maximized applications, which hog every square inch of the screen, once a program has been restored to a window, you can resize it or move it around. You'd pay hundreds of dollars extra to get this feature on your TV set, but it's built right into Windows.

Windows hot spots

Title bar
Every window has a handle you can grab—this is it. Click anywhere on the title bar and drag the entire window to move it; let go of the left mouse button to drop it in its new location.

Maximize/Restore button
Zooms a window to take up the entire screen, or shrinks a maximized (full-screen) program or folder back to a window. The icon on this button changes, depending on whether the program or folder is maximized.

Window border
To make a window wider or narrower, taller or shorter, aim the tip of the mouse pointer at the edge of the window until the pointer changes into a two-headed arrow. Then click the left mouse button and drag the border; let go of the mouse button when the window is the right size.

Scroll bar
When there's more data inside the window than you can see at once, scroll bars appear. Grab the button in the center and drag down to move the contents of the window up; drag it up to shift the window's contents back down. The horizontal scroll bar works the same way, moving things from left to right.

Corner
Want to change a window's width and height with one smooth motion? Point to any corner, and watch the cursor change to a two-headed diagonal arrow; then drag the window to its new size.

How do I put a program or folder back into a window?

The way you restore a window depends on whether it's minimized or maximized at the moment.

If it's maximized—if you can't see anything else on the screen—look to the right of the title bar for the Restore button. It's supposed to look like two windows arranged one on top of the other, but I think it looks more like a Mr. Coffee machine. Look at figure 9.1 and judge for yourself.

Fig. 9.1

The Restore button. Click here to transform a maximized program or folder back into a window.

If WordPad isn't already open, start it up by using the Start button. Maximize the WordPad window, then push the Restore button to send it back into a window. Did you notice that the window returned to the exact size and position it was in when you started it up? Now press the Minimize button to temporarily stow WordPad on the taskbar.

Now that the WordPad window is off the main screen, there's no Restore button—but we can still make it return to a window with one swift click of the mouse. Aim the pointer at the WordPad button on the taskbar, and right-click. There, at the top of the popup menu, is the Restore command. Click on it, and WordPad snaps back into its familiar window on the desktop.

 TIP   **This is yet another illustration of a fundamental Windows 95** principle: When in doubt, right-click. You'll be amazed at the sheer number and variety of menus you'll see when you right-click on seemingly random objects like taskbar buttons, as shown in figure 9.2, and those little icons at the right of the taskbar!

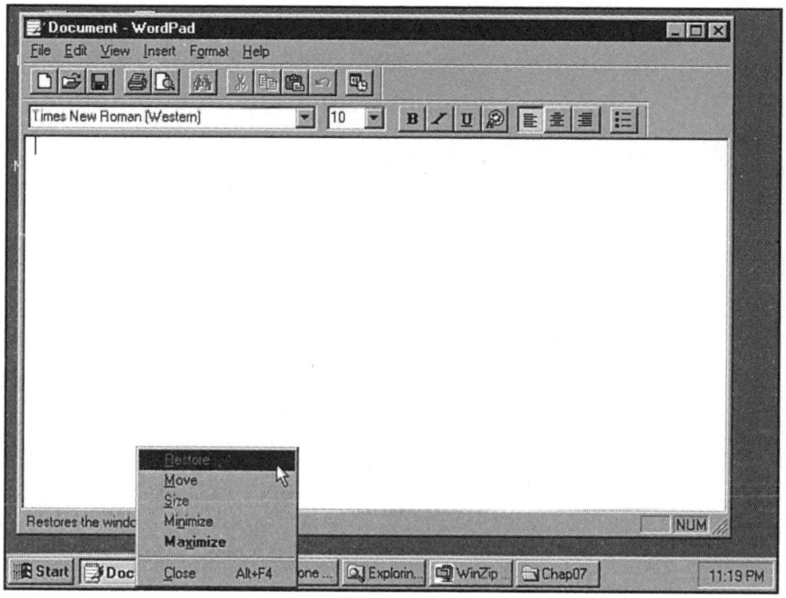

Fig. 9.2

Right-click on any taskbar button to display this shortcut menu. From here, with a single mouse click we can restore a program to a window, maximize it, or kiss it goodbye.

TIP When it's time to close a few windows, use this popup menu to quickly get rid of the ones you no longer need. Right-click on the window's taskbar button, and choose Close. Every time you use this popup menu, you extend the life of your mouse by one click.

How do I know which window I'm working with?

You can have hundreds of windows open simultaneously, but Windows can only focus on one window at a time. You use the mouse pointer like a spotlight to tell Windows which one you want to work with. No matter how many windows you can see on the screen, only the window you select can be in the foreground; all the rest stay in the background, waiting for their turn in the spotlight.

Windows uses the terms **active** and **inactive** to distinguish between a window in the foreground and one in the background. These terms are pretty unclear when you stop to think about it, though. When you click in a window, it doesn't suddenly become active. It just sits there, waiting for you to start typing or clicking. If you want something to happen, *you* have to do it! Harrumph...

Anyway, there are two cues you can use to tell which window's active. First, it won't be covered by any other window. Second, the title bar changes color. Unless you've fiddled with your desktop colors, Windows uses a dull gray for the title bar of a background (inactive) window, and bright blue for a foreground (active) window.

Why do some of my windows look different?

Most program or folder windows look and act alike, but you'll notice a big difference when you work with a window inside another window. These **document windows**, found in programs like Microsoft Word for Windows and WordPerfect for Windows, are generally pretty similar to program windows, but there are a few subtle differences. When you minimize a document window, for example, it doesn't plop down on the taskbar; instead, it shrinks into a miniature box, complete with its own Restore, Maximize, and Close buttons, at the bottom of the program window.

It doesn't matter what's inside—most windows work exactly the same way

- Most windows "remember" the size and shape they were in the last time you used them.

- Most windows remember their position on the desktop, too.

- It's easy to move a window almost completely off the screen. This is a little disturbing the first time you see it, but it's perfectly normal.

- Some windows can't be resized. The Windows Calculator, for example, is always the same size.

- A few special windows have an "Always on Top" option. Windows Help lets you do this, for example, so that you can follow step-by-step instructions in another window without losing your place. But most windows move meekly into the background when you click on another window.

TIP **With any window—even a window *inside* another window—there's** an easier way to maximize and restore. You don't need to hit that tiny button at the right of the title bar. Just aim anywhere in the title bar, and double-click to switch back and forth between a window and a maximized program.

Q&A *I accidentally made a window so small I can't see the menus any more. What do I do now?*

No problem. It may not look like a window, but it still acts like one. Aim the mouse pointer at any corner of the window until it turns to a diagonal, two-headed arrow. Now click the left mouse button and drag the window's borders out until the window is a more useful size.

This window is too big!

There are plenty of reasons why you might want to adjust the size of a window. The number-one reason is so you can see another window or the desktop. Unlike our picture-in-a-picture TV, you're not limited to a single size and shape, either: you can make one of these windows tall and narrow, or short and wide. It's up to you.

Resizing a window sounds easy, but it takes a little practice. Most people have trouble the first few times they try it. The secret? You have to hit the ultra-slim border *just right*—you'll know you've succeeded when the pointer turns into the two-headed arrow you use to resize the window. It's not easy. If your hand trembles ever so slightly, the pointer slips, and you have to start over again.

When you're aiming at a window's border, the tip of the arrow is the only part that counts. That end consists of one tiny dot, and you're trying to use that dot to hit a window border that's as thin as a piece of thread. If you're having trouble resizing windows, why not make the borders a little bigger? Right-click anywhere on the desktop, choose Properties from the popup menu, and when the Display Properties dialog box appears, click on the tab labeled Appearance. Click inside the box labeled Item, then type the letter **A**. The words Active Border should now be highlighted. Now click in the box labeled Size, and use the up arrow to increase the setting from a measly 1 to a wider 3 or 4. Click OK and try again. There—isn't that easier?

How small can I make a window?

The correct answer is "Ridiculously small." Just for fun, let's make the WordPad window as small as possible. Aim the mouse pointer at the window's lower right corner until it turns to a two-headed diagonal arrow. Now drag the window border up and to the left until there's nothing left but a title bar and a couple of buttons (see fig. 9.3). Well, that's pretty useless, isn't it?

Fig. 9.3
Click here, drag there. If you go too far when you're resizing a window, this is what you'll wind up with. Not very useful, is it?

How big can I make a window?

Let's try the other extreme instead. Grab the lower right corner of our microscopic Wordpad window, and drag the two-headed arrow as far as possible toward the lower right corner of the screen. Whoa! It looks almost like a maximized window, and it's nearly impossible to find the borders. This window isn't very useful, either.

What's the right size for a window?

When you're working with individual windows, follow the Goldilocks principle. The perfect window is not too big, and it's not too small. What's just right? Well, the window should be just big enough to show you what you need to see inside, yet small enough to let you see the rest of the desktop and any other windows you need to work with.

Grab the lower right corner of the WordPad window (if it's truly at the edge of the screen, you may only be able to see half of the two-headed arrow), and drag to the top left until the window is a reasonable size.

CAUTION Remember, some windows, like the Windows Calculator, are a fixed size and can't be resized.

I want this window out of the way

An active window will always cover up any windows underneath it. But you can move a window out of the way by using its built-in "handle"—the **title bar**. It's an easy, four-step process:

1 Click anywhere in the window you want to move to make sure it's in the foreground.

2 Click anywhere on the title bar, and hold down the left mouse button.

3 Drag the window wherever you like.

4 Let go of the mouse button to drop the window in its new location.

 Q&A *Hey! I can move the window off the screen! What's going on here?*

That's perfectly normal; in fact, it's a convenient way to take a quick look at the rest of the desktop without minimizing the window you're working with. If the window moves so far off the screen that you can't get it back, here's the secret fix: Hold down the Alt key and press the spacebar. That will pull down the window's Control menu. Press the letter **M** (for Move), and then use the arrow keys to slide the window back toward the main screen. When you can see enough of the title bar to grab, press Enter, and move the window using the mouse.

Help! My document won't fit in the window! Now what?

At the end of every television program, a list of credits appears on our super-duper state-of-the-art set. If David and Jay could handle their shows with a staff of 10 or 12 people, all those credits would fit on a single screen. In Hollywood, of course, even the guy who drives the catering truck gets his name in the closing credits. They could squeeze all the names onto one screen by printing them in type so small you'd need the Hubble Space Telescope to read it. Instead, the director displays the credits on a long list that rolls up from the bottom of the screen and disappears into the top as new lines force their way up from underneath.

Windows does exactly the same thing when there are more words or numbers or icons than you can see in a window. It's called a **scrolling list**, and you decide when and how to roll the credits.

How to scroll a document

Let's fill our WordPad window with more data than we can see at one time. Type a few words, press Enter, and repeat until you've forced a few lines off the top of the screen. As the first line disappears, you'll see a thin vertical bar appear along the right side of the window. There's an up arrow at the top of the bar, a down arrow at the bottom, and a square thingie in the middle, as shown in figure 9.4.

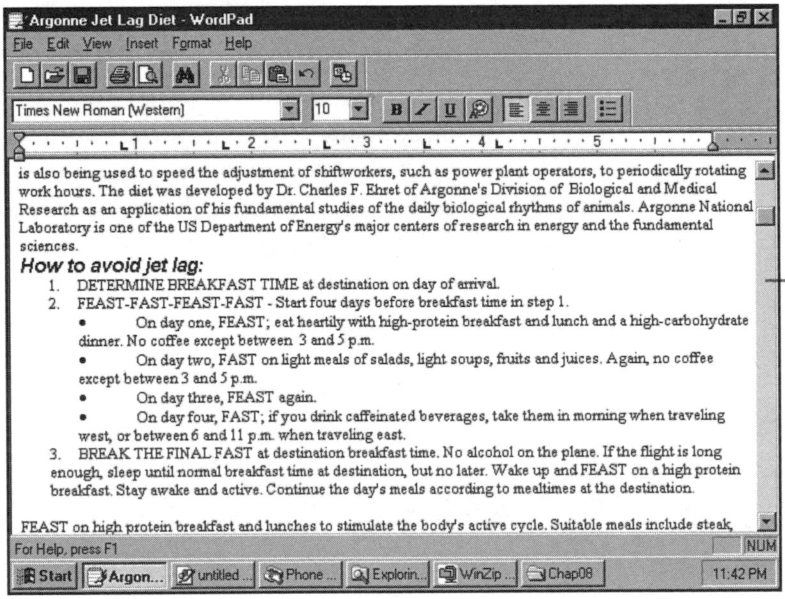

Fig. 9.4

When there's more in your document or folder than the window can hold, a vertical scroll bar appears along the right edge of the window. Grab the button in the middle of the scroll bar, and drag it up and down to see the window's full contents.

—Here's the scroll bar

Imagine that the contents of the window are printed on a long piece of paper, and that you can see a portion of it through the window. The square button in the middle of the scroll bar acts like a handle attached to the rope that pulls the piece of paper up and down, so you can see different sections of the paper. When the handle is up, you're seeing the top part of the paper. When it's down, you're seeing the bottom part.

When the scroll handle hits the top or the bottom of the scroll bar, you've gone as far as you can go. There's nothing more to see in the direction you've been scrolling.

TIP **You can move the scrolling list up and down in two other ways as** well: click the arrows at the top and bottom of the scroll bar. With each click, the list will move a short distance. To move in giant steps through the window, click in the middle of the scroll bar, above or below the handle. The contents of the window will jump a full screen at a time.

How much data is there?

The size of the scroll handle tells you how much (or how little) is hidden from view. The bigger the handle, the less there is in the rest of your window, and vice-versa. If you were looking at the file that contains this book, for example—all 90,000 words of it—you could probably scroll for a couple of hours, and the scroll handle would be as small as it gets. On the other hand, with a file that's just one line longer than your screen, you'd get a scroll bar with a jumbo-sized handle.

I can't see the right side of the screen, either

Scrolling a window horizontally is a little less common, but the principle is exactly the same. If the contents of your window stretch to the right or left, and your window isn't wide enough to show it all, a horizontal scroll bar will appear. Drag the handle to the left or right to pan through the entire window.

These windows are a mess!

Sooner or later, despite all the resizing, reshaping, moving, and manipulating, you'll wind up with too many windows on the screen. You can't concentrate, and you can't find *anything*. How do you clean up the mess? That depends on what you really want to do. In every case, the secret is to point to an empty space on the taskbar, and right-click. The popup menu that appears (see fig. 9.5) gives you three basic options, explained in just a second.

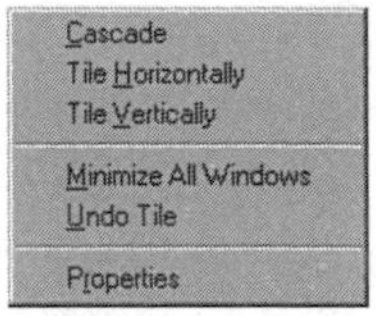

Fig. 9.5

Use the taskbar's popup menu to re-arrange windows with precision. Right-click on any free space in the taskbar to make it appear.

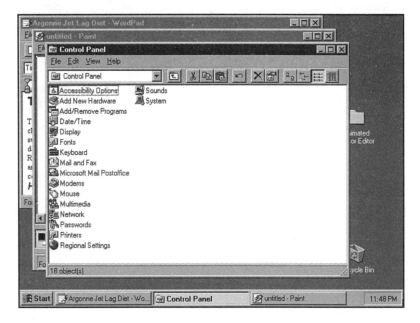

I want to focus on one window, but see all the rest

Then choose Cascade from the taskbar's popup menu. This option stacks all the windows one on top of the other (**cascades** them), fanned out like a poker hand, with just enough room to see the title bar and left edge of each window beneath the active window on top. (Fig. 9.6 shows an example of several cascaded windows.)

Fig. 9.6

The Cascade option lets you fan out every open window, like a poker hand.

I want to see several windows at one time

Then choose either of the **Tile** options from the taskbar's popup menu, and stack the open windows alongside one another. Tile Vertically resizes every open window, and lays them out edge-to-edge, side-by-side, as if you were laying tile on the kitchen floor. Tile Horizontally arranges the open windows, one on top of the other, as shown in figure 9.7. Either way, unless you have a jumbo monitor, you're best off trying this trick with two or three windows only; any more, and every window becomes too small to use comfortably.

Fig. 9.7

The Tile option arranges two or more windows alongside one another, either horizontally (as in this example) or vertically.

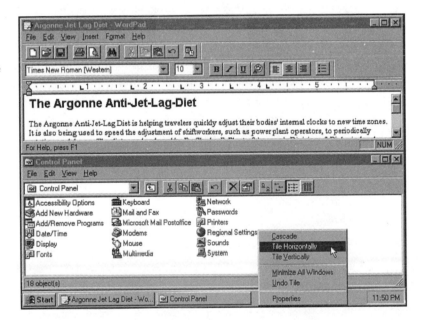

I want all these windows off my desktop. Now!

Then click on the Minimize All Windows menu choice, and watch each window shrink down onto the taskbar, one after another. When the job's all done, you're back at a sparkling clean desktop, with no annoying windows.

TIP

Want a little extra room on the screen? Then "hide" the taskbar.
Right-click in any empty space on the taskbar, and choose Properties from
the popup menu to give yourself a little extra room on the screen. Click on
the tab labeled Taskbar Options, and find the box that says Auto hide.
Click in the box to make a check mark appear, then click on OK to close
the dialog box. The taskbar disappears, giving you a little more working
room. To make it reappear, just bump the mouse pointer into the bottom
edge of the screen. Shazam! Up pops the taskbar.

CAUTION

Be careful you don't accidentally open two copies of the same
document! With some programs and most folders, when you click on the
icon and the window is already open, Windows just switches you to that
window. But other programs (including WordPad) let you open two or
more copies of the program, each in its own window. If you're not careful,
you can wind up editing the same file in two places. If you save the file in
the second window, you might accidentally overwrite the changes you made
in the first one. The only cure is to keep an eye on the taskbar and watch
out for duplicate windows.

10

Talking to Windows: Menus and Dialog Boxes

● **In this chapter:**

- Let's see a menu!

- Making your menu selections

- What are these symbols and marks on the menu?

- Providing more info with a dialog box

- What's with all the strange buttons and controls?

They may not be flashy, but menus and dialog boxes are your key to controlling Windows' every move . . . . >

Communicating with a computer is a tricky business. For all its speed and power, your PC is actually the strong, silent type: it has a limited vocabulary, it doesn't understand English, and you definitely can't talk to it. So how do you tell Windows exactly what you want to do—no ifs, ands, or buts? Simple. You ask Windows for a list of all the things your PC is capable of doing right now; then pick one.

These plain-English lists are called **menus**. After you make your selection from the list, Windows passes the instructions along to your PC in a way it's guaranteed to understand. If Windows needs more information—for example, if you ask it to save a file and it needs to know the file name—it will pop up a fill-in-the-blanks form called a **dialog box** to make the process a little easier.

Menus and dialog boxes are the most common ways to communicate with Windows and Windows applications. And here's the good news: They look and act the same, no matter where you are in Windows. Once you master a few simple concepts, you're well on your way to communicating with Windows.

What do I do with these menus?

A menu is simply a list of choices. You use menus all the time in your everyday life. When you drive up to the order window at MacDonald's, you pick your lunch from a menu. When you withdraw cash from your ATM, you touch a menu on the screen to tell the bank's computer to hand over a few $20 bills. Menus are always tailor-made to the circumstances: you can't get a burger and fries at the bank, and there's no way Ronald MacDonald will fork over forty bucks. The same is true of Windows menus: the actual choices you see will be different, depending on the kind of window you're working with; only the choices that make sense will be on the list.

When you choose something from a Windows menu, you're telling Windows you want it to do something. It might perform an action, or pop up a box asking you for more information. Or it might do nothing at all.

Mastering menus and deciphering dialog boxes

Menus and dialog boxes help you and Windows communicate without any misunderstandings.

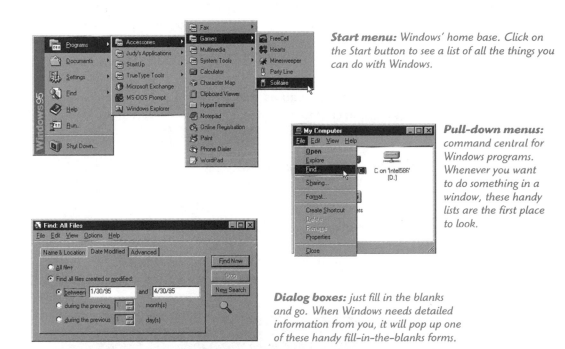

Start menu: *Windows' home base. Click on the Start button to see a list of all the things you can do with Windows.*

Pull-down menus: *command central for Windows programs. Whenever you want to do something in a window, these handy lists are the first place to look.*

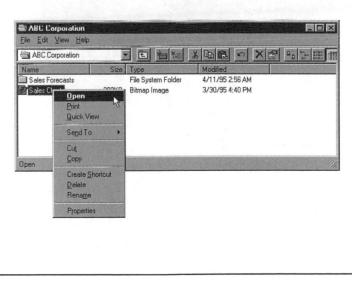

Dialog boxes: *just fill in the blanks and go. When Windows needs detailed information from you, it will pop up one of these handy fill-in-the-blanks forms.*

Pop-up menus: *quick shortcuts for common commands. Point to an item and right-click to get a list of options you're most likely to need for that particular item.*

The Start menu: click here to begin...

OK, you've wandered onto the Windows desktop and you're not exactly sure where to go next. When you want to know where you can go, it's time for a visit to the Start menu.

No other menu, anywhere else in Windows, is quite like this one. What's different? For one thing, you push a button to get to it; with other menus, you click on a word or an object. For another, the Start menu extends upward from the bottom of the screen, unlike other Windows menus, which follow a more conventional top-down organization. You'll also notice that the Start menu uses **cascading menus**, in which one menu choice leads to a brand-new menu (follow the small white arrowheads in fig. 10.1 to pick up the trail of cascading menus).

❝ *Plain English, please!*

Cascading menus get their name from the same effect you'll notice if you watch a waterfall as it rushes down a cliff. Each time the stream of water hits a rock, it splashes off in a new direction to form a new waterfall. If you can't remember what a cascading waterfall looks like, it's time to get up from that computer and take a vacation! ❞

Fig. 10.1

The Start menu is the first place to look when you're not sure where to go next. Cascading menus lead you automatically to other programs and other places in Windows.

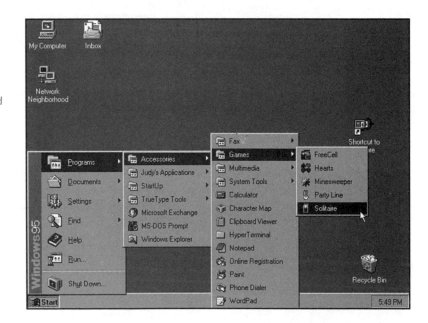

You'll use the Start menu every time you fire up Windows, but you'll use the two other kinds of menus—pull-downs and popups—much more often.

What do I do with these little arrows?

With cascading menus, one thing leads to another. When you rest your mouse pointer on a menu choice with one of those small black arrows, another menu pops out, usually to the right. Once you see the new menu, you're free to move your mouse pointer to one of the choices on that menu, where you may find even more cascading menus.

 TIP **Sometimes, menus cascade in a different direction than you** expect. If Windows sees that it's run out of room on the right side, it will pop up the new cascading menu to the left. If there's no room below, the new menu may shift up on your screen.

Suppose, for example, that you want to open WordPad so you can write a short report. Here's how it's done:

1 Click the Start button.

2 Move the mouse pointer to <u>P</u>rograms. When you do this, a **popout menu** cascades off to the right.

TIP **Cascading menus take a little getting used to. If you find that they** disappear before you can make your choice, try slowing down a little. When the menu appears to the right, move the cursor slowly, in a straight line, to the new menu. Now you can move up or down as fast as you like.

3 Move the mouse pointer to Accessories. When you do this, a second popout menu cascades off to the right, and displays the names and icons of all the Windows accessories.

4 Move the mouse pointer to the WordPad choice, and click once to open WordPad.

Pull-down menus: open-and-shut cases

Pull-down menus are *everywhere* in Windows. With a few rare exceptions, everything you can do in any Windows program is available underneath one of these main menu choices. (Sometimes your choices are buried under two or three cascading menus, but they're almost all in there somewhere.)

To find a pull-down menu, just look for the **menu bar,** right underneath a window's title bar. Think of the menu bar as a long curtain rod, with each individual menu hanging from it in a neat line. Each menu unrolls like an old-fashioned window shade to reveal the list of choices underneath (see fig. 10.2). Getting to a pull-down menu is easy: just point to one of the keywords on the menu bar, and click the left mouse button to unfurl it.

Generally, pull-down menus are **fixed**; that is, the available choices remain the same, no matter what you're doing in the program. Double-click on My Computer, for example, and you'll see the same menus—File, Edit, View, and Help—every time, without fail. Sometimes, however, the choices on a pull-down menu vary, depending on what you have selected or what kind of file is open.

Fig. 10.2

Everything you could possibly want to do in Windows, you can do from a pull-down menu. Use the File menu in the My Computer window, for example, to open or close a file, or even to find a file when you're not sure where you put it.

Q&A   *My mouse works, but I prefer the keyboard. How can I make menu choices without a mouse?*

Press the Alt key and the underlined letter of a menu name to open a menu or highlight a command. Press the down arrow to move the highlight down the list of commands in a menu. Press Enter to choose the command, or Esc to close a menu and say "Never mind, I don't want any of these."

Popup menus: shortcuts and settings

To uncover the last menu type, we'll have to go on the Windows version of a treasure hunt, because popup menus are literally hidden throughout Windows. Revealing these buried treasures doesn't take a pick and a shovel, though—just a click with the right mouse button (see fig. 10.3).

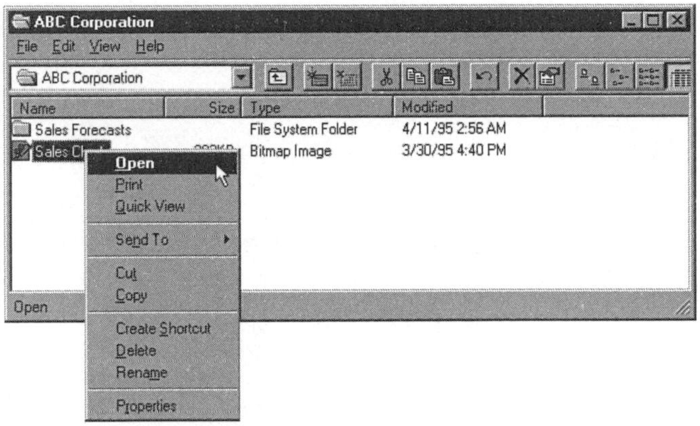

Fig. 10.3
Position the mouse pointer, click the right mouse button, and pop goes the menu. To pick a menu selection, point to your choice and click the left mouse button once.

```
ABC Corporation
File  Edit  View  Help

ABC Corporation

Name              Size  Type                Modified
Sales Forecasts         File System Folder  4/11/95 2:56 AM
Sales Ch...             Bitmap Image        3/30/95 4:40 PM
        Open
        Print
        Quick View

        Send To        ▶

        Cut
        Copy

        Create Shortcut
        Delete
        Rename

        Properties
Open
```

> **TIP** **Besides being hidden, popup menus are unlike pull-downs in** another way: the choices available from a popup menu change, depending on what you're pointing to. But you'll almost always see a choice called Properties, which will give you detailed information about whatever you're pointing to.

What can I do with popup menus?

You'll use popup menus for two main reasons: as shortcuts and to adjust the settings of nearly everything within Windows. The shortcut part is easy: when you click on the icon for your hard drive, notice how the first three choices on the popup menu are the same as the first three choices on the pull-down File menu. To adjust settings for a particular piece of hardware or a specific part of Windows, you'll use the Properties menu choice; you'll find references to these properties sheets nearly everywhere in this book.

I use the popup Properties menu all the time to make sure there's enough room on my hard disk before I copy a large file there. It's a simple process:

1 Double-click on the My Computer icon to open a window showing all the drives on your computer.

2 Point to the icon for your hard drive (drive C:), and click the right mouse button once.

3 Move the mouse pointer to Properties (at the very bottom of the menu), and click with the left button.

4 Check out the colorful pie chart Windows draws to show you how much of your hard disk has been used and how much is free. If you see only a tiny sliver of free space, it's time to put that disk on a diet!

5 Click the Cancel button to make the Properties sheet disappear.

> **TIP** **How do you know when a popup menu is available? You don't. So,** anytime you're not sure what to do, just point at something and click the right mouse button. Trust me: There's no way you can hurt your system just by popping up a menu, so click away.

Popup menus can be extremely useful, and sometimes the only way you'll find out about them is by accident. Suppose, for example, that you've been trying to find a file on your hard drive, and you've cluttered up the entire screen with stray windows. You'd like nothing more than to sweep them all out of the way in one motion. You don't know whether the taskbar has a popup menu, but you can find out by aiming the mouse pointer at the taskbar and clicking the right button. Yep, there's a popup menu, all right, and one of the choices is <u>M</u>inimize All Windows. Click there and voilà, your screen is clean again.

> **TIP** **I'm constantly amazed at the things I discover when I right-click** on some objects. For example, if you have a CD-ROM drive, you can right-click on its icon to eject the CD using a menu choice.

Selecting from the menu

Anything you can do in Windows, you can do with the help of a menu. It might not always be the fastest way, but it's guaranteed to work. If you're ever stumped at how to get a particular job done with a Windows program, your best bet is to look on every menu you can find—sooner or later, you'll find the command you're looking for.

Remember the basic principle of Windows: first select, then act. Before we can pick something from the menu, we have to point at it.

What are my choices?

Remember, pull-down menus work just like window shades. When you pull down the shade, it stays down. And when you click on a pull-down menu, the menu stays down, too, even if you lift your finger from the mouse button. That makes it easy to move from menu to menu searching for the right choice. Once you've found the menu choice you're looking for, just point at it and click again.

The whole point of pull-down menus is to make Windows easier to use, so it's reassuring to know that there are a few widely accepted conventions you can count on. The first two menu choices on the left are almost always File and Edit, and the last menu on the right is usually Help (see fig. 10.4). What's in-between is anyone's guess.

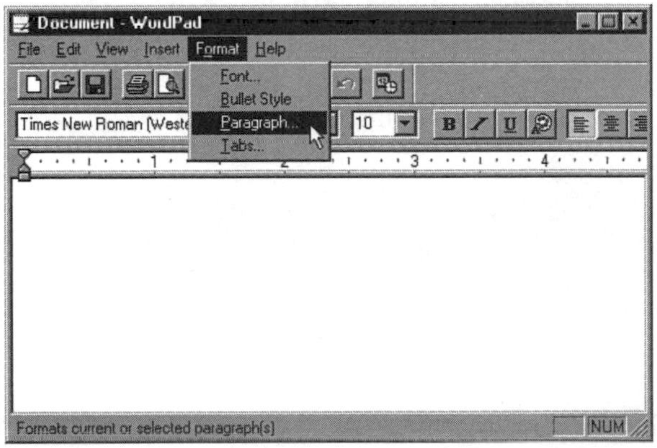

Fig. 10.4

Most Windows programs follow common conventions for the main menu. WordPad's main menu, for example, features the familiar File, Edit, and Help menus. Specialized menus like Format are displayed in the middle.

TIP You can almost always close a program by choosing E**x**it from the bottom of the File menu. You can almost always get information about a program by choosing Help, About.

How do I move to the next menu?

Notice how the mouse pointer is "sticky"—even when you take your finger off the mouse button, it keeps tracking through the menu choices. To see all the main menus, just move the pointer along the keywords in each menu bar.

Why don't some menu commands work?

Sometimes, choosing a menu item does something right away. If you choose File, Save, for example, and you've already given your file a name, a program like WordPad will simply save your most recent work using the existing file name, and return you to what you were doing.

But sometimes a menu choice does nothing at all. You can point and click 'til your finger falls off and nothing happens. What's going on? You've stumbled on a menu choice that's temporarily unavailable. Maybe you were working on a word processing document, and tried to use the Paste command without first cutting or copying something to the Clipboard.

Windows could simply remove the Paste choice from the Edit menu, but then you'd be left scratching your head. "I know it was there a minute ago," you'd say, as you scrambled through all the other pull-down menus to find the missing command. And you'd be right. So instead, Windows **grays out** the command (see fig. 10.5 for an example), to let you know that it's still there—it's just not available for you to use right now.

Fig. 10.5

When a menu choice is temporarily unavailable or inappropriate, it doesn't disappear from the menu. Instead, Windows "grays out" that choice so you'll know it isn't working right now.

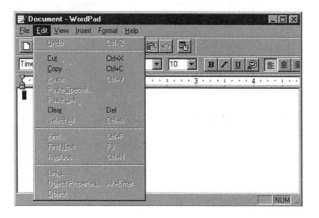

Q&A *I chose a command, but nothing seemed to happen. It wasn't grayed out, but it isn't working. What's up?*

Is there a check mark next to the command you think is not working? If there is, click the command again. Now is it doing what you expect?

Some commands are like on/off switches. A check mark means it's "on"; a lack of one means it's "off."

How do I get rid of this menu?

When you want to roll a window shade back up again, you've got to give it a snap. A Windows menu works in much the same way. If you decide you don't want to choose anything from the menu, just give a quick click anywhere in the window *except* on the title bar to make the menus roll up again.

Can we talk? Windows and dialog boxes

Sometimes, a simple menu choice isn't enough to get what you want. If you're sitting at that sidewalk cafe in the rue de Dialog and you ask the waiter to bring you *le Big Mac*, he'll know that you want a burger, but he won't know *how* you want it. Medium rare or burnt? Do you want lettuce and tomatoes? How about catsup? And would you care for some *pommes frites* on the side? Sigh .... Wouldn't it be convenient if you could just point to all your choices at once?

Well, that's precisely what Windows lets you do. Instead of bombarding you with one question after another, Windows puts together a simple fill-in-the-blanks form and hands it to you. You check a box here, pick an item off a list there, fill in the empty spaces, and hand it back by clicking the OK button. These interactive forms are called **dialog boxes**, and you'll use them constantly when you work in Windows.

Why do I have to deal with dialog boxes, anyway?

Windows is constantly asking you for more information. When you print a document, for example, you'll have to answer a few questions: Where's the printer? How many copies do you want? Do you want to skip any pages? What kind of paper? And so on.

Fortunately, you'll find the same kind of gizmos and widgets in all of Windows' dialog boxes.

For example, let's say you've just created a file using WordPad, Windows' built-in word processor, and now you want to save it. You get the ball rolling by doing the following:

1 Choose File, Save. Windows displays the Save As dialog box shown in figure 10.6.

Fig. 10.6

To save a file in WordPad, you use a dialog box to tell Windows exactly where and how you want it to store your work.

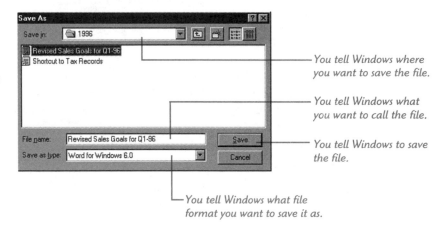

You tell Windows where you want to save the file.

You tell Windows what you want to call the file.

You tell Windows to save the file.

You tell Windows what file format you want to save it as.

2 Give the file a name.

3 Press OK if you want to save the file to the default directory.

The conversation can be as short and sweet as that, or you can get more elaborate: Which file format would you like to use? Which folder do you want to store the new document in? Windows will take its best guess, but you'll need to make the final decisions.

Dialog boxes look like program windows, but they behave a little differently. Generally, you can't resize dialog boxes, although you can move them around on the screen. And they're as persistent as a door-to-door salesman—in most cases, when a dialog box pops up on your screen, you've got to deal with it before you can do anything else.

TIP **Sometimes, a dialog box gets in the way of the very thing you** need to see to answer one of its questions. Although you can't resize dialog boxes, you *can* move them around the screen and out of the way. Put the mouse pointer on the title bar, click and hold down the left button, and drag the box to another location. That way, you can deal with those persistent questions without losing sight of your work.

Dialog boxes come in all shapes and sizes. Fortunately, they're made out of interchangeable parts, so once you learn to recognize the pieces, you'll know how to deal with any dialog box.

Different types of dialog boxes...

When you see a dialog box, odds are it popped up for one of three reasons:

- **Windows has a message for you.** It could be an error message ("I can't find that file"). Or it could be a more benign bit of information ("Congratulations! You've successfully installed WonderWord Pro! Please be sure to send in your registration card today!"). In any case, your only option when you see a message box is usually OK (although there might also be a Help or Details button to choose, which would provide more information about the message).

- **Windows wants you to make a choice.** If Windows were a close-up magician, it would ask you to pick a card—any card. You'll see this option when your choices are limited.

- **Windows needs more information.** Sometimes, *you* hold all the cards; for example, when you want to save a file, you can usually give it any name you'd like. In this case, Windows simply presents an empty box and says, "Type something here, please."

Dealing with dialog boxes

When you're faced with a new dialog box, don't panic—it may look different, but it works just like every other dialog box in Windows. Table 10.1 is your secret decoder ring.

Table 10.1 Dialog box controls and buttons

What's It Called?	What Does It Look Like?	What Do You Do with It?
Button. When you're done with a dialog box, your main choice will be the OK button. Other popular buttons include Cancel ("Oops! I didn't mean to open this dialog box!"), Help, and Close. If you see an ellipsis (...) following the label on a button, you can expect to see another dialog box if you press that button.	OK / Cancel	Press the OK button to send your input on to Windows. Press the Cancel button to back out without doing anything. Press Help if you're not sure what to do next.
Input box. When Windows doesn't know what to expect, it shows you an empty box.	New password:	Click inside the box and start typing.
Drop-down list. Sometimes, Windows knows what you want to do, but wants to make sure you can choose another option if you wish. In file boxes, for example, Windows assumes you'll want to use drive C:, but lets you pick a floppy drive or CD-ROM if you prefer. A drop-down list looks a lot like an input box, except that it offers you multiple choices.	Scheme: Marine (high color) / Marine (high color) / Plum (high color) / Pumpkin (large) / Rainy Day / Red, White, and Blue (VGA) / Rose / Rose (large) / Slate	Click on the arrow just to the right of the box to view the other choice on the list.
Scrolling list. When Windows is pretty certain that you'll want to pick one item from a long list, it uses a scrolling list. The scroll bars look and act just like the ones you'll find elsewhere in Windows.	Pattern: Bricks / Buttons / Cargo Net / Circuits / Cobblestones Edit Pattern...	Pick a file name from the list.
Check box. These tiny boxes come in handy when you need to make a simple yes-no decision. Sometimes a section of a dialog box will contain a number of check boxes arranged together.	☑ Password protected	Click the box to add a check mark; click again to remove the check mark.

What's It Called?	What Does It Look Like?	What Do You Do with It?
Radio button. Sorry, you can't get The Top 40 Countdown on your PC. But if you think of the button of an old-fashioned car radio, you'll understand how this button control works—and how it got its name. Since you can't listen to more than one station at a time, when you push one button, the one that had been depressed pops out. (The one that's currently "pushed" has a black mark inside the circle.)	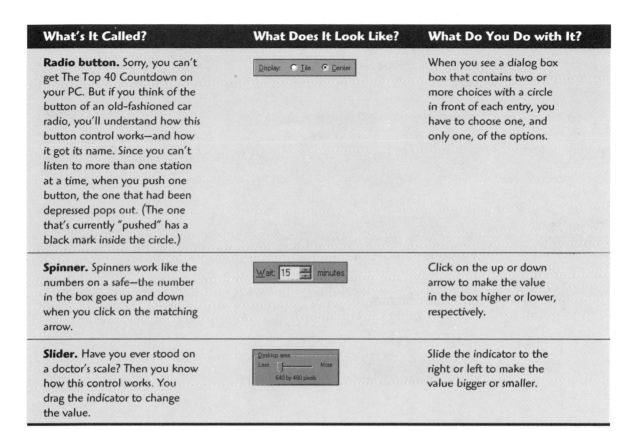	When you see a dialog box box that contains two or more choices with a circle in front of each entry, you have to choose one, and only one, of the options.
Spinner. Spinners work like the numbers on a safe—the number in the box goes up and down when you click on the matching arrow.		Click on the up or down arrow to make the value in the box higher or lower, respectively.
Slider. Have you ever stood on a doctor's scale? Then you know how this control works. You drag the indicator to change the value.		Slide the indicator to the right or left to make the value bigger or smaller.

Getting around in dialog boxes

If you've ever filled out a census form or taken part in an opinion poll, you'll feel right at home with dialog boxes. It's not a test; it's simply a convenient way for Windows to gather a lot of information in a very small space.

Most of the choices you'll make in a dialog box are simple and straightforward. Check boxes, for example, are easy—a check means yes, and a blank box means no. Radio buttons and drop-down lists are equally easy, as long as you're careful to click in the right place.

Scrolling lists can be trickier to work with, especially when they're used to keep track of files and folders. To see how to move through a scrolling list, right-click on any blank space on the Windows desktop and choose Properties. Click on the index tab labeled Background (you'll find it at the top of the box). You'll see the dialog box shown in figure 10.7. You'll see a matched pair of scrolling lists: one for patterns, the other for wallpaper. Use the up and down arrows to move through the lists. When you see an entry you like, click on it.

Fig. 10.7

Scroll through the list to select the background you want on your Windows desktop. You can use the arrow keys, the mouse, or the keyboard to move from one entry to the next.

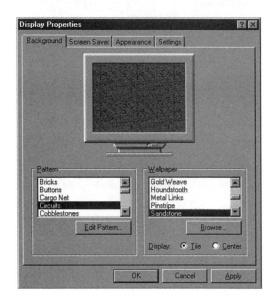

TIP

When a drop-down list or a scrolling list contains lots of files, there's a simple trick that lets you jump quickly through the list. Just press the first letter of the item you're looking for. For instance, if you're looking for a file named Sales Report, just press **S** to skip straight to the first entry that begins with that letter. In a long list, you can type the first few letters very quickly. In a folder window, for example, if you want to jump to the Sales Report file, you can type the letters **SAL** in quick succession; Windows will take you there.

It's easiest to work with the mouse, of course, but a few keys serve crucial functions when it comes to getting around in dialog boxes—especially crowded ones. The Tab key, for example, moves you from one section to the next, and the cursor keys (the up and down arrows) move between different options within each section. To set a check mark without using the mouse, just hit the spacebar.

TIP   **If a dialog box still has you stumped and leaves you speechless,** remember that you can press F1 (or the Help button, if there is one) for help written just for that dialog box. Help will pop up in its own box on-screen to explain what's in the dialog box and what you're supposed to do.

❝ *Plain English, please!*

When you get help that's specifically designed for the task or box you're working with at the moment, it's called context-sensitive help. Pressing F1 will get you context-sensitive help, no matter what you're up to. ❞

Q&A   *Hey—this dialog box won't let me do anything! What's up?*

It must be either inappropriate or impossible for Windows to do what's in that section of the dialog box. When that happens, you'll usually see that section grayed out.

The art of Windows

Who says all computer programmers are dull, soulless robots? OK, maybe some are, but there are also true artists who had a hand in making Windows what it is today. All those menus and dialog boxes and icons and wizards didn't just happen—each one was painstakingly created by one of many anonymous designers at Microsoft's headquarters in Washington State, USA.

If you could travel back in time to the late 1980s and see an early copy of Windows, you probably wouldn't recognize it. In those days, Windows was filled with crude, blocky, one-dimensional dialog boxes and menus that sometimes made no sense at all. Today, they're the software equivalent of those 10,000-year-old cave paintings scattered throughout northern Spain and southern France—interesting to look at, but truly primitive.

Somewhere along the line, someone decided that composition and balance had a place in computer software. History doesn't record who first came up with the idea of using different shades of gray to create the illusion of a three-dimensional dialog box. But he or she ought to get a medal.

OK? Cancel? You make the call

When you click OK, you're sending your message to Windows, and it's going to do exactly what you asked it to do. If you decide that's not what you want, you can back out gracefully by clicking the Cancel button that appears in many dialog boxes. If there's no Cancel button, you still may be able to back out by pressing the Esc key.

Q&A   *My mouse isn't working. How do I get around a dialog box without it?*

When you press the Tab key, you move forward to the next option in the tabbing order of a dialog box. As you move, the option that is currently chosen has a dotted line around it, or is highlighted. (Sometimes the highlight can be hard to see. If you're not sure which option is highlighted, press the Tab key repeatedly until you're sure where it's ended up.)

Press Shift+Tab to return to the previous option in the tabbing order. Press Enter to carry out the options you have chosen.

If one of the letters in a button or a label is underlined, you can use that letter to move directly to an option. Press Alt and the underlined letter at the same time. For example, to move to the File Name option in the above example, press Alt+N.

Part III: Working with Applications

11

Setting Up New Programs (DOS and Windows)

● In this chapter:

- Easy installation with the Add/Remove Programs Wizard

- Help! Windows is asking me technical questions!

- What to do when a program doesn't run right

- Tips and tricks for making DOS programs behave

You didn't buy Windows 95 just to play with the calculator—go get some programs to install! And the installation process is easy. . . . . ⊵

et's say it's your first day on a new job. Do you expect to get right to work? Of course not. First, you have to go through the new-employee orientation program. You'll meet the folks in the mail room, someone will issue you a phone number and a badge, and you'll pick up an armload of office supplies. After that, the boss will show you your new cubicle and your old computer (unless you landed a really great job, that is, in which case you'll get a corner office and a shiny new Pentium computer).

When you add a new application program to your PC, it has to go through a similar drill. First, it has to check in with Windows, and then it has to introduce itself to the other programs you use. It has to find a home folder, and it has to make a note of any special instructions that you give it. Sound like a lot of administrative overhead? It needn't be. A good installation program takes care of all those details behind the scenes.

How do I install a new Windows program?

The nice thing about Windows programs is that they all work pretty much alike, starting with the installation. Most of the time, setting up a new application is a simple point-and-click proposition. But you can speed up the process if you know how to add a new piece of Windows software to your system.

Start with Setup...

 These days, most software comes on floppy disks or CD-ROMs. The most popular way to get started is to put a disk in your drive and run a program called Setup. You could click on the Start button, choose Run, and type **A:\SETUP**. But there's a safer, easier way: click on the Start button, and choose Settings, Control Panel; then double-click on the Add/Remove Programs icon. You'll see a dialog box like the one in figure 11.1. Click the Install button, and follow the wizard's step-by-step instructions.

Fig. 11.1

Want to set up a new Windows program? Use the Add/Remove Programs utility in the Windows Control Panel.

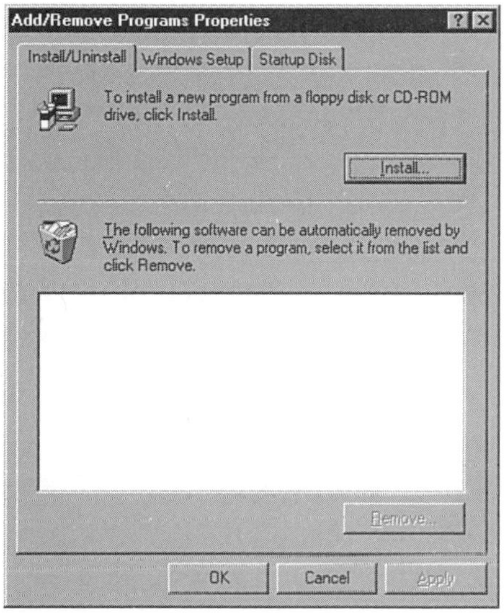

Answer a few questions...

Almost all Windows Setup programs ask the same questions over and over again: in which folder would you like the program files to be stored? Do you want to install all of the program or just some of it? Do you want to create a new group cascading out from the Programs entry on the Start menu? Once you've answered all the questions, you're ready for the tedious work of swapping disks. (Unless your software came on a CD-ROM, of course, in which case all you need to do is sit back and watch—once you see the Setup program start to copy files to your hard disk.)

> **TIP** ✓ **Just say yes! Windows and Windows programs that use SETUP will** almost always suggest the best place to store files. These preferences are called **defaults**, and you're less likely to get into trouble if you simply accept the defaults. If Microsoft Word for Windows wants to create a folder called C:\WINWORD, let it.

Make your preferences known...

Occasionally, the Windows Setup program will ask you some more detailed questions. For example, a word processor may ask you if you'd like to install its built-in grammar-checking module, or it may ask for your name and address so it can add that information automatically to your letters and envelopes. In some cases, the program will even order you to shut down

Windows and restart so that it can be sure that all the changes it made actually go into effect. Answer the questions as best you can, but don't worry about it too much. You can always run the Setup program again if you miss something urgent the first time around.

Try it!

If everything went well, the new program probably added itself to the Start menu. Select the program from the Start menu, click, and hold your breath. If it starts and runs properly, congratulations! You've successfully installed the new program.

Q&A *Windows told me that some of my files are out of date. What's that all about?*

When you use the Setup program that comes with some Windows programs (especially older ones), you may notice that a handful of them try to add files to the Windows\System folder on your computer. Now, if the files were from 1993 and you were using a version of Windows that you bought in 1992, this would probably be the right thing to do. But it's definitely a no-no to put those 1993 files in Windows 95.

Fortunately, Windows anticipates this possibility and keeps a safe copy of these essential files. If a Setup program wrongly replaces some system files, Windows will give you a chance to put the right ones back. Just say yes.

New software? It's not as easy as you think ...

Why does the Windows Setup program have to be so complicated? Why can't you just copy a bunch of files to your hard disk and get to work? Well, with a few programs you can, but those efficient little marvels are few and far between.

There are good reasons for using the official installation routine, not the least of which is consistency: you can be sure you won't miss an important step.

During Setup, you see, Windows typically stores the locations of program files, a description of the data files the application uses, and any special requests you might offer. By the time Setup is done, you may have files scattered all over your hard disk: besides the application's own folder, you can sometimes find new files in the Windows folder and in the place where you store your data.

If any of those pieces are missing, your new application probably won't work. And that's why it pays to follow the standard operating procedure, even if it seems a bit overcomplicated.

Why doesn't this program work right?

When is a Windows program not a Windows program? When it's an old Windows program that doesn't understand how to work with Windows 95, of course.

Now, there's nothing wrong with being old—sooner or later it happens to all of us. But the problem with Windows programs that were developed before Windows 95 came around is that they don't understand how to deal with long file names. If you use one of these older programs, any files you use with that program will be limited to eight characters and a three-character extension.

For a graphic example of the problem, look at figure 11.2. On the top is the up-to-date Windows 95 version of Notepad. Go ahead and open a file— it's not hard to tell what's inside each one. But now look at the old, pre-Windows 95 Notepad below. The same files show up with cryptic, confusing names like to-dol⁻1.txt. Is that your to-do list? Probably, but who can be sure?

Fig. 11.2

One great reason to insist on new Windows 95 versions of your programs. The new Notepad (above) shows you plain-English file names; the old version (below) keeps you guessing.

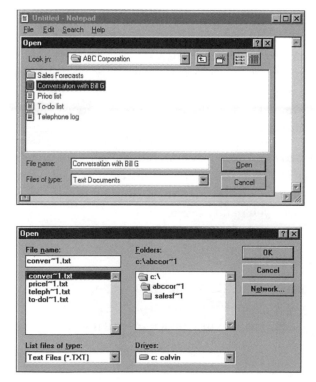

TIP **How can you be sure your software is up-to-date? One surefire** way is to look for the "Designed for Windows 95" logo on the box. When you see that logo, it means that Microsoft has certified that the program inside works just fine with Windows 95.

Q&A *I just added a new program, and now I can't find it. What should I do?*

Click on the Start button and choose Find, Files or Folders. In the box labeled Named, type part of the name you're looking for; click on the Advanced tab and, in the box labeled Of type, choose Application. Click the Find Now button, and if you're lucky your program will appear in the list below. If you still can't find it, choose View, Arrange Icons, by Date. The most recent files will float to the top, and your new program should be there. Once you find it, drag its icon onto the Start menu to add it to the top of the list.

It's not you, it's a bug!

When you walk into a computer superstore, you'll see aisle after aisle of Windows software. All told, you can take your choice of thousands of programs. Is that good news? Well, that depends. People have been writing Windows programs for years. Some are good programmers, some aren't. Some programs that worked just fine under the last version of Windows will do all sorts of screwy things when you try to use them with Windows 95.

If you've installed a program successfully but encounter odd things when you try to run it, don't assume you're doing something wrong. You could be looking at a **bug**—simply put, a mistake made by the program's creator. Sometimes you can work around bugs; other times you can't. But it helps to know what you're up against.

Here are a few of the puzzling symptoms you might see when you run into a bug in a program.

- Your system freezes up. You might be able to move the mouse, but nothing happens when you tap the keys or click the mouse button. The usual cure is to turn the PC off and then back on again. (You'll lose any unsaved work, unfortunately.)

- The picture on your monitor starts to act up. Windows might refuse to go away, or you'll see dark holes in the background. If you're lucky, you can save your work before you restart your computer.

- Everything begins to move at a glacial pace. When your PC gets reeeeeeeeaaaaaaaallllllll sllllooooooowwwwww like this, you might be moments away from losing all your work. Save what you can and prepare to restart your PC.

- You see a bright blue screen with a white error message on it. That generally means there was an error within Windows itself. If you're lucky, you can hit the Enter key and get back to work.

- You see a Windows dialog box, telling you your application has caused a general protection fault (see fig. 11.3). Click OK, and see if you can get back to work. You'll probably lose anything you haven't saved lately.

66 *Plain English, please!*

Protection? Is this some kind of racket? Nope. Windows is talking about memory. Every program you run should have its own chunk of memory that no other program can touch. If another program's data accidentally gets mixed into that space, there's no telling what can happen. But it's usually not good.

Imagine that all the data in your PC is being rushed from one place to another by messengers who run through the halls of your office building. Each time they return, they look in their inboxes for new packages. If a package that's supposed to go to the fourth floor winds up in the inbox for the second floor, both recipients will probably get hopelessly confused. Windows has some protection against this sort of thing happening, but it's not perfect. The moral? Save your data! 99

If your computer consistently acts up when you try to run one particular program, call the company that made the software and ask if they know about the problem. They might have a new, fixed version they can send you. If they don't, ask them when they're going to fix the bug.

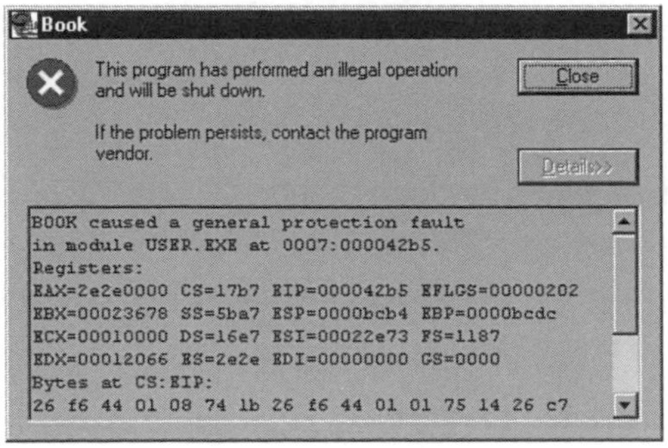

Fig. 11.3
Here's what a General
Protection Fault error
message looks like. It's
a warning that
something's gone
wrong, and displays
some techno-babble
for any programmer
who might be looking
over your shoulder.

TIP **What should you do if your computer crashes? Don't kick the**
computer; instead, close any open files (if you can) and restart your
computer. Before you start up another program, click on Start, Programs,
Accessories, System Tools, and run the ScanDisk program. This extra step will
make sure you don't have any serious problems that will get worse later.

What do I do with these old DOS programs?

Surprisingly, Windows finds it much easier to deal with old DOS programs,
the kind that don't use windows, icons, and—in some cases—even the
mouse. If you have one of these programs, the easiest way to set it up is to
drag it onto the Start button; to launch it, click on its entry in the Start menu.

Most DOS programs work just fine under Windows 95. But some, especially
games, need a bit of special treatment, and the first place to look when
you're having trouble is on its Properties sheet. Right-click on the program
icon, then choose Properties. You'll see a big, complicated set of sheets.

TIP **Windows stores all the technical details about how to run a DOS**
program in a **Program Information File** whose extension is the same as its
abbreviation—**PIF**. When you use the DOS Properties sheet, you're actually
making changes to this PIF.

Here's some hard-won advice on whether and when to mess with PIFs:

- If it ain't broke, don't fix it.

- Use context-sensitive help to learn what each item in the dialog box is.
  (See Chapter 4 for more details about help.)

Setting up a DOS program

If you absolutely must fiddle with DOS applications, here's where to look.

General

Strictly informational. There's almost nothing you can change here.

Font

Scroll through the list of fonts to make the text in the window bigger (and more readable) or smaller.

Program

If you have trouble starting the program, try setting the Working folder to be the same as the one the program is stored in. You can also click in the Shortcut key box and define a Ctrl+ or Alt+key combination that will pop up the program in a hurry.

Memory

Most of these options are strictly for propellerheads, but if your program is causing trouble, check the Protected box and try again.

Screen

Do you want the program to run in a window or puff up to fill the entire screen? You make the call. You can also have a DOS toolbar on a window, if you'd like.

Misc

More technical mumbo-jumbo, except for the Screen Saver check box. Some DOS programs freeze at the mere mention of screen savers. If your program is like that, uncheck the Allow screen saver box here.

- If you're having a lot of problems with DOS programs, start up the Windows 95 Help file and look on the Contents page for the MS-DOS Program Troubleshooter, as shown in figure 11.4 (you'll find it directly under the Troubleshooting topic).

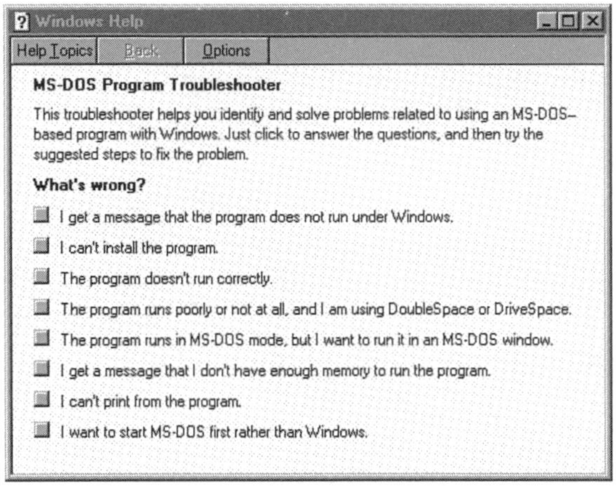

Fig. 11.4

Working out the kinks in an MS-DOS program. Windows can offer detailed help if you're having problems getting a DOS program to work properly.

How does Windows know what kind of file this is?

To start a program, you don't have to click on its icon. If you've found a file that was created by that program, you can double-click on that file's icon and launch the program instantly, with the file you clicked on already loaded.

How does it work? Well, Windows knows that every file on your PC has a first name and a last name. The first names have to be unique, but the last name (also known as the **file extension**) works just like your family name to identify a bunch of files that look and act somewhat alike. When you double-click on one of these files, Windows looks up its file type and says, "Oh, the .DOC extension means this is a document, and I need to use WordPad to open it."

Here are a few important facts about this whole process:

- File types are based on file extensions.

- Extensions have to be registered with Windows before your applications can automatically start up when you double-click on a document.

66 *Plain English, please!*

How does a file type get **registered**? When you first set up a program, it usually tells Windows which file types it can open and save. For instance, when you install Microsoft Word, it tells Windows to reserve the .RTF and .DOC extensions for its use. These extensions are "registered"—that is, added to a master list of extensions that Windows knows about. When you double-click on a data file to open it, Windows looks in this list to see which program to use. 99

- Registered extensions are usually hidden from you.

Why is this important? Because you can double-click a file and it will start up the program that recognizes it. You save time and effort because you don't have to start the program, then go looking for the file, then load it. Windows does it all in one smooth operation.

 Q&A *I have two files in the same folder with the same name. How can that be?*

They have the same first name, but their last names are different. One might be called WINDOWS.EXE, while the other is WINDOWS.INI. You can tell them apart in one of two ways: by the icon that the files use; or by right-clicking and looking on each file's Properties sheet to see its file type.

Working with file types isn't hard. Here's how to train Windows to open WordPad whenever you double-click on a file with the extension .LTR.

1 Use WordPad to create a file, and save it using any name you like, as long as the name ends with .LTR.

2 Open My Computer and navigate through the folders until you find the file you just created. Right-click on the file icon, and choose Open With from the popup menu. You'll see a dialog box like the one in figure 11.5.

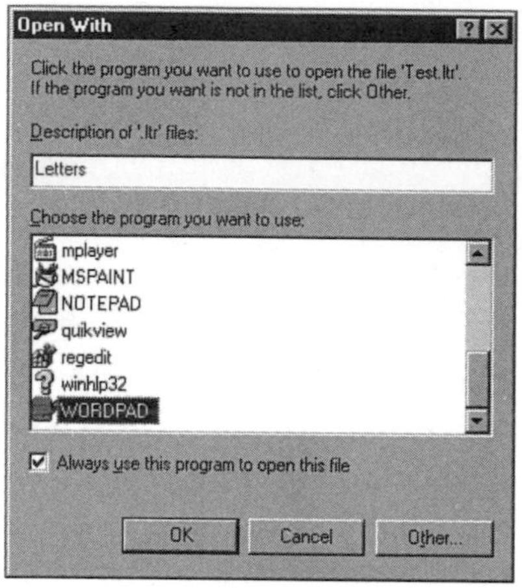

Fig. 11.5

Teaching Windows how to associate a file extension with an application.

3 Enter a description of the type of file. Then choose WORDPAD from the list of applications in the middle. (If the program you want to use isn't in this list, click the Other button.) Finally, make sure the box that reads Always use this program to open this file is checked. Click OK.

4 To make sure the extension was properly registered, open any folder window (My Computer works just fine) and choose View, Options. Click on the File Types tab. You'll see a dialog box like the one in figure 11.6. As you move the pointer through the list, the details below change to tell you about the file type and the application it's associated with. To change an existing entry, click the Edit button. To remove an entry completely, click on Remove.

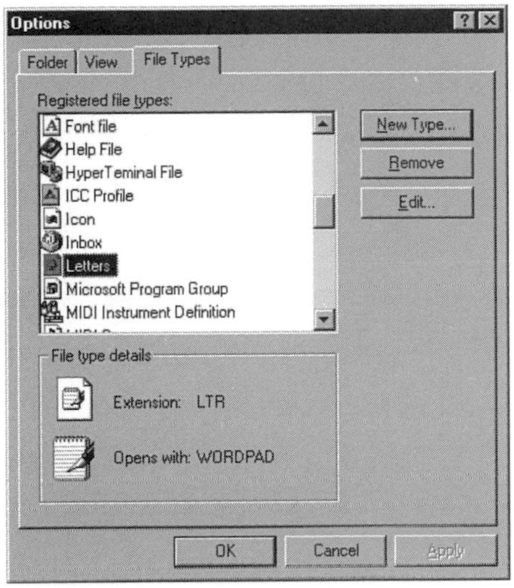

Fig. 11.6
Does this file go with
that program? Here's
where to find out.

>
>
> **Hold down the Shift key and then right-click on a file to see the**
> Op<u>e</u>n With menu instead of the <u>O</u>pen menu. This technique can come in
> very handy if you have two programs (like Microsoft Word and WordPad, for
> example) that you might want to use at different times to open up .DOC
> files. Only one of the applications can be associated with .DOC files, but
> the Op<u>e</u>n With menu lets you pick either one.

12

What Do All these Free Programs Do?

● **In this chapter:**

- How do I edit a simple text file?

- What can I do with WordPad?

- Not for artists only: creating a masterpiece with Paint

- Two ways to crunch numbers with the Windows Calculator

- Hearts, FreeCell, and MineSweeper: the other games

Write a letter, paint a picture, crunch some numbers, or waste some time. Windows has lots of tiny, free programs (and games). . . . . ➤

Windows is stuffed full of little programs designed to handle odd jobs. There's a Calculator and a Phone Dialer, a scratch pad for taking notes, and a word processor for writing letters. There's even a CD player that can coax music out of your multimedia PC.

In other chapters, we'll look at some of the more specialized accessories, like the ones that help you keep coworkers from getting annoyed about your CD's volume (Chapter 18), or the one that lets you create cool cover sheets for your outgoing faxes (Chapter 23).

In this chapter, though, we'll focus on the bread-and-butter mini-programs that help you keep track of words, numbers, and the occasional picture. We'll also look at the three games that complement Solitaire in Windows 95.

Field guide to the free accessories in Windows 95

Windows 95 is stuffed to the gills with programs that do all sorts of interesting odd jobs. Here's a quick rundown on what you can do with these free add-ins. To find the complete collection, click the Start button, choose Programs, and look in the Accessories folder.

Icon	Name	What It Does...
	Calculator	You won't want to use this ten-key calculator to figure your mortgage payments, but it's perfectly good for 2+2=4.
	CD Player	Play the *Lion King* soundtrack (or any audio CD) on a multimedia PC. This little program is surprisingly powerful and fun. See Chapter 20 for more information.
	Character Map	Pick a symbol, any symbol, from any font. Copy it to the Clipboard. Paste it into your document. Useful if you're trying to write in a language other than English.
	Clipboard Viewer	A small, simple program that lets you make sure what you cut or copy winds up on the Clipboard.
	FreeCell	A strategy-oriented solo card game. Highly addictive. You've been warned.

Icon	Name	What It Does...
♠♥♥♥	Hearts	The classic four-hand card game. Windows 95 lets you play against Bunny, Ben, and Michele. Or you can play real opponents on your own network.
	HyperTerminal	This easy-to-use communications program lets you dial up other PCs and online services. Useful enough for simple tasks. See Chapter 22 for more information.
	Minesweeper	A game of logic and strategy. Guess right and you win; guess wrong and—kaboom!—you lose.
	Notepad	This simple text editor is OK for jotting down a few words or sentences, but if you want your words to look good, you'll choose WordPad instead.
	Paint	For the Van Gogh in you. Use the shapes, text tools, different brushes, and spray cans to create colorful images.
	Phone Dialer	Speed-dial up to eight of your favorite phone numbers. Requires a modem. See Chapter 22 for more information.
	Solitaire	The original Windows time waster. Certified platinum: over 2 billion hours of productivity lost since 1990.
	Sound Recorder	If you've got a microphone and sound card, you've got a studio. See Chapter 18 for more information.
	WordPad	A surprisingly useful little word processor. Handles simple formatting, and it reads and writes files in the same format as Microsoft Word for Windows.

That program isn't on my PC!

I know, I know—some of the programs in that list aren't on your computer. So what happened? Do we have different versions of Windows 95?

Maybe. If your copy arrived on floppy disks instead of a CD-ROM, then you might not have everything on the list. But the more likely explanation is that the little programs you're looking for were never installed on your PC. Fortunately, we can take care of that in a flash.

Let's get serious for a second. The Typical option, when you install Windows 95, doesn't put the FreeCell, Hearts, and MineSweeper games on your system. What a horrifying oversight! To add these crucial missing pieces, first make sure you have your Windows 95 disks or CD-ROM. Then click on the Start button and choose Settings, Control Panel. Double-click on the icon labeled Add/Remove Programs, then click on the Windows Setup tab. The programs you're looking for are discreetly hidden; highlight the Accessories entry and click the Details button. You'll see a dialog box like the one in figure 12.1.

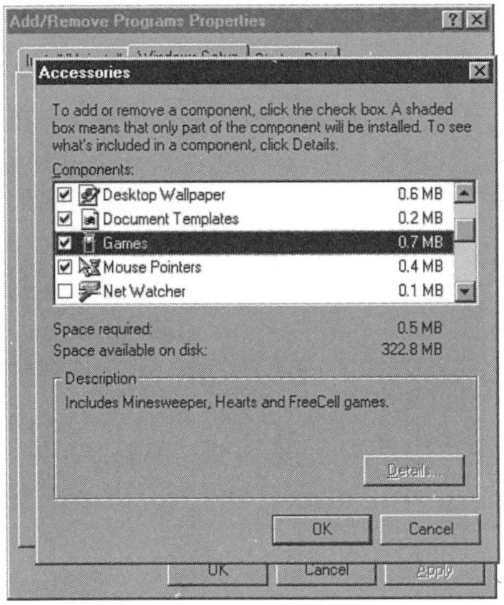

Fig. 12.1

Is there something missing from your PC? Use Control Panel to add these important Windows 95 programs.

Scroll through the list, and click in the empty box next to any item you want to add. (If the box is already checked, it means that piece is already installed on your computer.) After you've finished with the list, click OK twice to start the ball rolling. Windows may ask you to insert a specific disk; after it finishes chugging away, you can get back to, um, work.

CAUTION The Add/Remove Programs utility can be a little confusing until you learn how it works. A check mark means the item is already on your PC. If a box is empty, clicking to add the check mark tells Windows to add the program. Clicking to remove a check mark removes the program, too. Don't touch those check marks unless you want to take a program off your computer!

I need to jot down some notes

Windows includes a program that works just like the pad of scratch paper next to your telephone. It's called Notepad, and it's perfect for jotting down simple notes and lists (see fig. 12.2). It's easy to find, easy to use, and the files generally are smaller than the files your word processor creates, so you can save space on your hard disk.

Notepad has one big advantage over more powerful word processors—it's fast. On my PC, for example, I'll stare at the Windows hourglass for about 10 seconds while I wait for WordPad to start up. The Notepad window, on the other hand, opens up in a fraction of a second after I click its icon. You'll use Notepad all the time, especially for the little informational files (usually called something like README) that come with new software packages.

Fig. 12.2

Use Notepad to jot down simple notes and lists. The Word Wrap option makes sure your words fit neatly in the Notepad window.

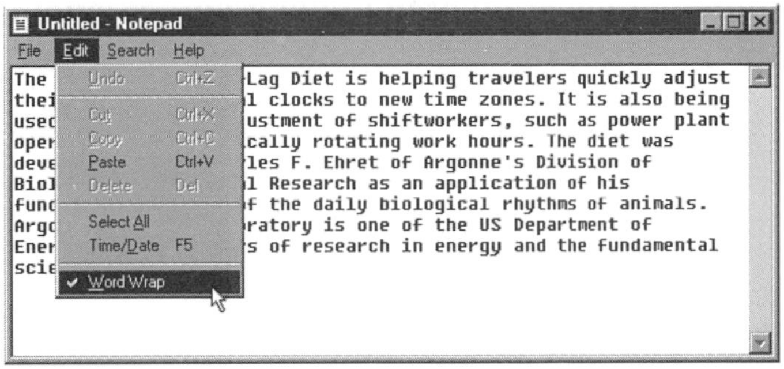

> **TIP** You can't use Notepad to open large files. But don't worry—if you select a file that's too big, Windows will pop up a gentle warning message and offer to let you use WordPad instead. That's the right choice to make.

I want to write a good-looking letter

You might jot down a phone number on any old scrap of paper, but if you're writing a letter to your boss, you'll probably want to use a businesslike piece of stationery. That's the difference between Notepad and WordPad. For more formal documents, where you want to make your words look good, you'll use Windows' built-in word processor, WordPad.

How can I make this document look great?

If you prefer, you can use WordPad as nothing more than a souped-up scratch pad. But its real strength is its ability to help you use different fonts and colors, and give you other word processing tricks to make your simple letters and reports get noticed. It can't do the tricks you might expect of a heavy-duty word processor like Microsoft Word or WordPerfect, but it's got enough oomph to produce a document like the one in figure 12.3.

Fig. 12.3

WordPad lets you choose different type styles, sizes, and colors—even add bullets to set off lists.

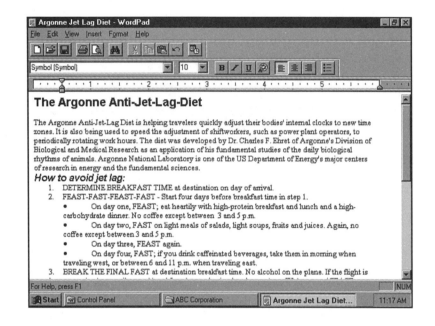

You can use WordPad's menus to apply special formats to the words you type, but it's easier just to use the tools on the bar at the top of the WordPad window.

Q&A *Most of my words are disappearing into the right side of the window. What's going on?*

You need to set the **word wrap** option. When you do that, WordPad puts up a solid wall along the right edge of the document; when the text gets there, it has to turn and run into the next line instead. Most of the time you'll wrap to the window so you can read your writing more easily, but sometimes you'll want to wrap to the ruler, especially when you want to see what your document will look like when printed.

WordPad tools

Use WordPad's collection of toolbars to make great-looking letters and short reports.

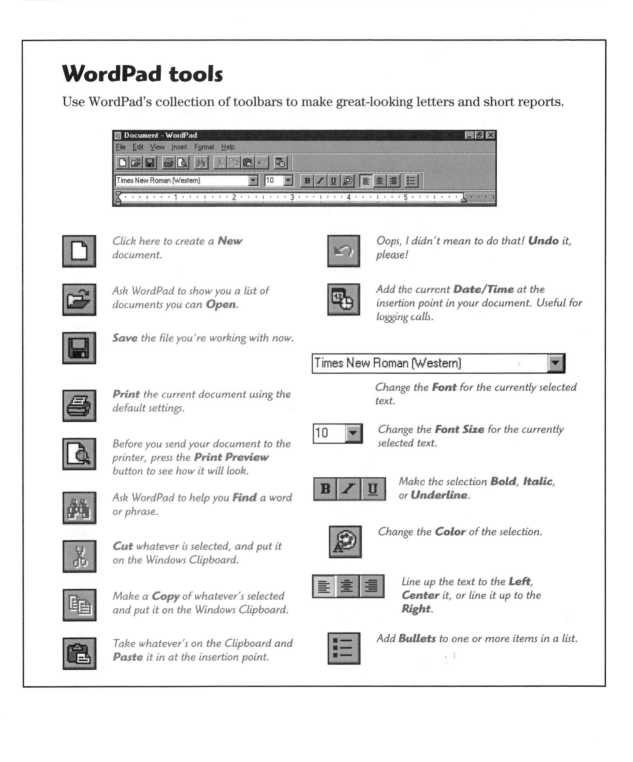

Click here to create a **New** document.

Ask WordPad to show you a list of documents you can **Open**.

Save the file you're working with now.

Print the current document using the default settings.

Before you send your document to the printer, press the **Print Preview** button to see how it will look.

Ask WordPad to help you **Find** a word or phrase.

Cut whatever is selected, and put it on the Windows Clipboard.

Make a **Copy** of whatever's selected and put it on the Windows Clipboard.

Take whatever's on the Clipboard and **Paste** it in at the insertion point.

Oops, I didn't mean to do that! **Undo** it, please!

Add the current **Date/Time** at the insertion point in your document. Useful for logging calls.

Change the **Font** for the currently selected text.

Change the **Font Size** for the currently selected text.

Make the selection **Bold**, *Italic*, or **Underline**.

Change the **Color** of the selection.

Line up the text to the **Left**, **Center** it, or line it up to the **Right**.

Add **Bullets** to one or more items in a list.

I'm ready to print now

To send a WordPad document directly to the printer, just click the Print button. Because I hate to waste paper, I usually go through one extra step, choosing <u>F</u>ile, Print Pre<u>v</u>iew to look at what Windows is planning to give me. To choose a different paper size or a different printer, select <u>F</u>ile, Page Set<u>u</u>p. To specify any special printing options (extra copies or only selected pages, for example) choose <u>F</u>ile, <u>P</u>rint.

How do I save this letter for later?

Most of the time, you can save a document for retrieval later. The technique is simple: Pull down the <u>F</u>ile menu, then click on <u>S</u>ave. If you haven't saved the current file already, Windows will ask you to give the file a name.

Which document type should I use?

You'll see the same dialog box whenever you choose <u>F</u>ile, <u>S</u>ave for a new document or <u>F</u>ile, Save <u>A</u>s to store a previously saved document under a new name (see fig. 12.4). Choose a folder in which to store the document, give it a name, and then click OK. The only important option in this dialog box is the file format, which you can specify using the drop-down list at the bottom of the dialog box.

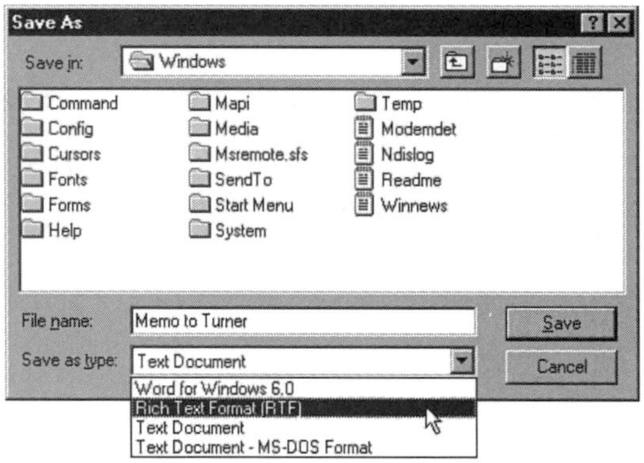

Fig. 12.4
Saving a file in Rich Text Format.

Save As		
Save in:	Windows	
Command	Mapi	Temp
Config	Media	Modemdet
Cursors	Msremote.sfs	Ndislog
Fonts	SendTo	Readme
Forms	Start Menu	Winnews
Help	System	

File name: Memo to Turner   [Save]

Save as type: Text Document   [Cancel]

- Word for Windows 6.0
- Rich Text Format (RTF)
- Text Document
- Text Document - MS-DOS Format

- Select **Word for Windows 6.0** if you want to see every last bit of formatting. This is the same file format that Microsoft Word and Microsoft Office use.

- Choose **Rich Text Format (RTF)** when you're not sure whether the person to whom you're sending the file can read a file in Word format.

RTF is a standard way for Windows word processors to exchange formatted documents.

- Select **Text Document** if you don't care about the formatting—and simply want to save the letters, numbers, and other characters in your file. This is the right choice when you're working with DOS batch files and system files.

- Select **Text Document—MS-DOS format** when you expect non-Windows users will also use the file.

I want to create a picture

If you have any artistic talent at all (unlike me) you'll want to try the Paint program.

OK, its drawing tools aren't sophisticated enough to turn you into another Michelangelo, but there's certainly enough to help you create a simple sketch to use in a letter or report. To launch the Paint program, click on the Start button and follow the cascading menus from Programs to Accessories. The Paint window consists of an image area, plus a color palette and a tool box.

How do these tools work?

All of the drawing tools in Paint work the same way. Click on the tool button to pick up the tool (the mouse pointer will usually change shape to show you what you can do right now). If there are any options available for the tool, you can select them from the bottom of the tool bar. For example, the Magnifier gives you a choice of four different zoom levels, from actual size to eight times normal, while the Line tool lets you select one of four thicknesses. Finally, click and drag to use the tool (most allow you to do something slightly different with the right mouse button).

How do I work with colors?

If you've ever seen the Hollywood portrayal of a great artist (Charlton Heston as Michelangelo, for example), you know that every painter uses a **palette** to mix colors for use on the canvas. When you use Paint, your palette of colors appears at the bottom of the screen. You can choose from as many colors as your hardware will let you see—literally millions, if you have a really good video adapter—but you can only work with two colors at a time—one for the foreground and one for the background.

The Paint tool box

The tool box contains your brushes, pens, and other drawing implements.

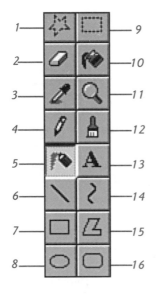

5   *Airbrush sprays the foreground color onto the area.*

6   *Line creates a straight line.*

7   *Rectangle creates a rectangle.*

8   *Ellipse creates ellipses.*

9   *Select is like Free-form select, except the selection is always a perfect rectangle.*

10   *Fill with color fills any enclosed area with the foreground color.*

11   *Magnifier zooms in for a closer look at an area of the drawing.*

1   *Free-form select marks an area to cut, copy, or move.*

2   *Eraser/Color eraser replaces whatever's there with the background color or the foreground color.*

3   *Pick color "picks up" a new foreground color or background color.*

4   *Pencil lets you draw freehand.*

12   *Brush is like the Pencil but more flexible.*

13   *Text lets you select a font and other text attributes.*

14   *Curve is like Line but with extra points.*

15   *Polygon lets you create as many odd sides as you want.*

16   *Rounded rectangle—Exactly like a rectangle, except for the rounded corners.*

To change the default colors temporarily, click on the appropriate square in the color palette. Use the left mouse button to change the foreground color; the right button controls the background. Watch as the two squares at the left edge of the palette change to show you which colors are active right now. Remember, these colors affect everything you do—from drawing a line to creating colorful boxes and circles. Always check the colors before you use any of the Paint tools.

TIP **You can anchor the toolbox and color palette to any edge of the** Paint window, or you can drag either one so it floats in the window. To drag the color palette, point to any empty space just above the little color squares. Moving the toolbox is trickier: you have to double-click on the little area beneath the tools without releasing the mouse button after the second click. When you do it correctly, you'll see a thick, shaded box appear around the box, signaling you that it's ready to be moved. To snap either piece back into position, drag it to the edge and watch it go.

How do I add text to a drawing?

I sometimes use Paint to create combinations of text and graphics that I can insert into reports to help mark the beginning of a new section. You can, too. Our goal is to create a graphic that looks like figure 12.5.

1 Start by clicking the Text tool, then click and drag to define a rectangle where you want your letters to appear. When you release the mouse button, the insertion point (a thin vertical line) will appear.

2 Choose a typeface, size, and any text attributes such as bold or italic. If you don't see the Text Toolbar, choose View, Text Toolbar choice to make it visible.

3 Start typing. Don't worry if your text doesn't fit perfectly in the box. When you're through typing, you can use the sizing handles on each corner and in the center of each edge to stretch the text box to fit the type.

4 When you're satisfied with the look of the text, it's time to add a border. First, click the Line tool and select a line thickness. In this case, we'll use the third choice. Next, click the Rounded Rectangle tool; make sure the top shape is chosen in the area at the bottom of the tool box.

Fig. 12.5
Use Paint's Text and Rounded Rectangle tools to create this graphic for use in a report.

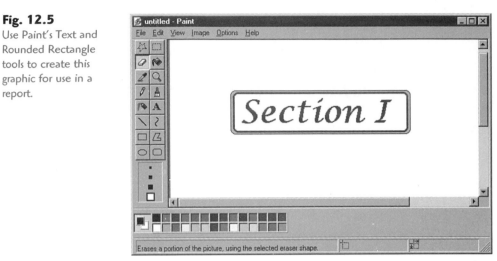

5 Click on a spot just above and to the left of the type where you want the border to begin, then drag the shape to the right and down to complete it. Release when you reach the lower right corner. (You could hold down the Shift key as you drag to create a perfect square. Use the same trick with the Ellipse tool for a perfect circle, or with the Line tool for a perfect horizontal or vertical line.)

6 To create the interesting 3-D effect, go back to the Line tool and choose the thinnest line, then click on the Rounded Rectangle tool and draw another border around the original shape. It might take several tries to get it just right; use Undo if you want to start over.

 TIP **If you don't like the results of anything you do in Paint, use** Edit, Undo immediately. Don't be afraid to experiment a little: Paint lets you undo the last three things you did.

7 To add the 3-D shading between the inner and outer border, use the Fill With Color tool. Click on the gray square in the palette, then on the Fill With Color tool. The cursor will change to a bucket with a dribble of paint coming out. Aim the end of that dribble at a spot between the borders. (If you can't see it clearly, use the Magnifier tool to zoom in closer.) Click to fill in the color.

8 Finally, save the image you've just created. You could just choose File, Save, but there's a much more efficient way to make sure you just save the portion you want. Click the Select tool, and use the right mouse button to drag a rectangle around the graphic. When you release the button, a shortcut menu will pop up. Choose Copy To; Paint will let you choose a location and a name for your graphic.

I need to add up some numbers

Windows includes a handy accessory you can pop up whenever you need to crunch a few numbers. I use the Windows Calculator every month to help when I reconcile my checking statement, but it can do much more than that.

You can view the Windows Calculator in either of two modes, as shown in figure 12.6.

- By default, it acts like a ten-key adding machine. You can use the numbers on the keyboard or click the buttons using the mouse. Use the Edit menu to copy and paste numbers to and from the Calculator.

Fig. 12.6

Simple or scientific? The two faces of the Windows calculator. If you know what all those buttons are for, you're a full-fledged rocket scientist.

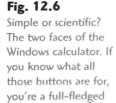

- If you want to do scientific and statistical calculations, you can switch the Calculator into genius mode by choosing View, Scientific. I don't have much use for these functions, but if you do, you can get instant help on how to use them by right-clicking on any button. To return to the simple view, choose View, Standard.

I just want to relax!

Who says Windows 95 is all work? Your boss might not want you to know about them, but Windows includes a collection of four cool games. We've already seen and worked with Solitaire at length. Now it's time to look at the other three games.

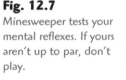

TIP   **If you have the CD version of Windows 95, there's also an** arcade-style game called Hover. You'll find it in the Hover folder on the CD.

Minesweeper

The object of the game is to clear away every square on the screen without stepping on a mine. It's tougher than it looks! Each time you click on a square, you'll see either a bomb or you'll clear one or more squares and reveal some numbers. Click on a bomb, and the game is over; the numbers tell you how many bombs are adjacent to that square. When you're sure you know where a bomb is hidden, right-click to mark the square with a flag. Click both buttons simultaneously to clear all the squares around the one you're pointing to. Figure 12.7 shows a game I just lost. (Notice the unhappy face just above the playing area? Click that button to start a new game.)

Fig. 12.7

Minesweeper tests your mental reflexes. If yours aren't up to par, don't play.

—*Click here to start over.*

Hearts

In my college days, I used to spend days at a time playing this game instead of studying. Now you can play against the computer and goof off just as though you were back in school! Or you can convince from one to three other people on your network to play with you.

To play against the computer, click on the Hearts menu choice, then check the radio button labeled I want to be dealer, and click OK. Choose Game, New Game to start. For a summary of the rules and some tips on best playing strategies, look in on-line Help. Figure 12.8 shows a game I'm playing with three computer opponents.

Fig. 12.8

The point of the classic four-player card game called Hearts is to avoid taking hearts or the Queen of Spades.

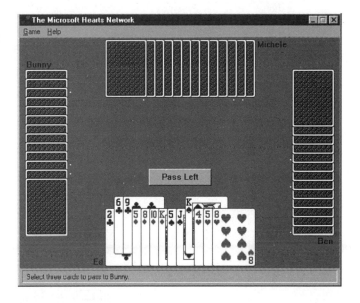

FreeCell

Bored with Solitaire? This is another solo game that uses one deck of cards. The object of the game is to move all the cards into the four home cells at the top right, each in a stack of its own suit, starting with the ace. You shuffle cards from stack to stack on the bottom, using alternating colors in descending order (a black queen on a red king, for example, or a red 7 on a black 8). The four cells at the top left are the free cells, where you can temporarily store cards while you move others around. Figure 12.9 shows a game in progress.

Supposedly, it's possible to win every game of FreeCell. For complete rules and strategy tips, use the <u>H</u>elp menu. Bet you can't play just one game!

Fig. 12.9

Once you've mastered Solitaire, check out the nearly endless display of possibilities in FreeCell, the other solo card game.

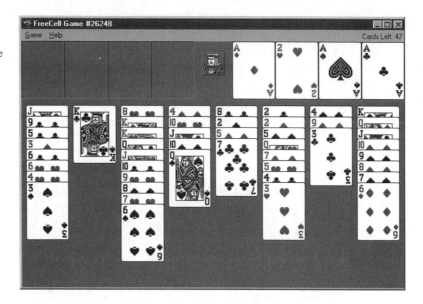

13

Using Windows to Tie It All Together

● In this chapter:

- Easy sharing with the old cut-and-paste routine

- Special tricks for cutting and pasting in a DOS program

- What's so special about Paste Special?

- Linking, embedding, and other sophisticated tricks

With Windows, you can combine text, graphics, charts, tables—whatever—into magnificent, attention-getting documents. . . . . ▷

When you're ready for a great meal at a great restaurant, you certainly don't expect that just one person will prepare the whole thing. There's a crew of assistant chefs who slice, dice, and chop all the different ingredients. The vegetables are over there, the meat and seafood are over here, and the pastry chef is in a world of her own. If the master chef is running things right, though, all those pieces come together to form a perfect presentation on your plate.

Windows lets you work the same way. You might have a formatted report in your word processor, a set of charts and pictures in your graphics program, and a stack of numbers in a spreadsheet program. When it's time to blend all the ingredients into one good-looking document, Windows makes it easy. The secret? Learning how to cut, copy, and paste.

Cut, copy, and paste: the easy way to move things around

When you want to take a little data from here and put it over there, the technique is the same, no matter where you are in Windows. It doesn't matter whether you're moving between two different places in the same window or between two completely different applications—thanks to Windows, you'll always follow exactly the same procedure.

If you managed a warehouse, you'd probably carry around a clipboard, big enough to securely hold a few sheets of letter-sized paper. To manage the process of transferring data, Windows uses a similar holding area called the **Clipboard**. As you move from place to place in Windows, the Clipboard stays discreetly alongside you. Most of the time, you don't even notice that it's there. When you want to move something from one place to another, though, it's right at your fingertips: You pick up the thing you want to move and fasten it to the Clipboard. Whatever's on the Clipboard stays there as you move to your next destination. When you're ready to set the copied object down in its new home, just unfasten it, and put it where you want it.

Using the Clipboard to cut, copy, and paste is simple, as long as you remember the universal rule of Windows: first you select, then you act:

1 Select the thing you want to copy or move. It could be anything: a word or sentence, a few cells from a spreadsheet, some or all of a picture. Use the technique that works for the application you're in. For example, in WordPad, hold down the left mouse button as you drag across the words you want to highlight.

2 Right-click on the highlighted section, and click on the <u>E</u>dit menu; then choose Cu<u>t</u> or <u>C</u>opy as shown in figure 13.1. (If your application doesn't use popup menus, look for <u>E</u>dit on the pull-down menus.) Windows takes a snapshot of whatever is highlighted and places it in the Clipboard. If you chose <u>C</u>opy, your document remains just as it was; if you chose Cu<u>t</u>, whatever was highlighted is now gone.

3 Move the mouse to the place where you want to paste the copied material. This could be in the same document, or in a completely different document in another application. Click to be sure the insertion point is where you want it to be.

4 Pull down the <u>E</u>dit menu and choose <u>P</u>aste. Whatever is on the Clipboard will appear at the insertion point.

Fig. 13.1

To put the selection from this WordPad document onto the Clipboard, use the right mouse button to pop up this menu. Use the same menu to paste it into its new location.

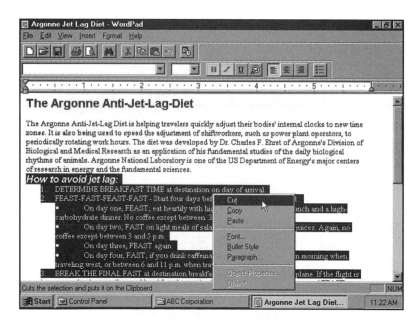

CAUTION   **The Clipboard can only hold one thing at a time. If you've copied** or cut something, it will wipe out anything that's currently being stored on the Clipboard. That's why, if you're shuffling a lot of data around, it's always a good idea to paste it into its new home *immediately* after you've cut or copied it to the Clipboard.

What happens when I paste data?

When you paste something from the Clipboard, Windows tries to figure out the most appropriate action to take with the specific type of data you've put there. It's easiest when the type of data is exactly the same, and less predictable when the data types are very different. Here's a sampling of what you can expect:

- **Words and numbers** usually move easily from one place to another. The formatting may or may not survive the trip, though. For example, if you copy a fat bold headline from a Wordpad document and paste it into a Notepad file, the words appear, but the bold attribute disappears.

- **Pictures** can move from one place to another in a variety of formats. Most of them are simple bitmaps, which means you have to paste them in at exactly the same size and shape as the original, unless you want them to be distorted.

> ❝ *Plain English, please!*
>
> A bitmap image is one that consists of different-colored dots (bits) that the eye sees as a single image. Bitmaps are useful for simple tasks, but they can get ugly when you try to change the size or shape of the image. For those kinds of tasks, graphics artists use sophisticated formats that tell Windows how to draw the picture, no matter what size and shape it takes. The Windows Paint program uses only bitmaps. ❞

- You can even use the Cut, Copy, and Paste commands to move **files** from one place to another. Open My Computer and keep double-clicking until you reach the folder window that contains the file or files you want to move. Highlight one or more files, right-click, and choose Cut or Copy from the popup menu. Now you can move to another folder window, right-click, and use the Paste command to insert the files in that folder.

Can I cut and copy with a DOS program?

It's easiest to move things between Windows programs, but there's a special set of procedures for copying text to and from MS-DOS programs. Here's how:

1 Open your MS-DOS program in a window. If it opens in full-screen mode (where it takes over the entire screen, with no taskbar, no title bar—no evidence of Windows anywhere), force it into a window by holding down the Alt key while you press Enter.

2 Click on the icon at the far left edge of the DOS program's title bar to unfurl a pull-down menu. (See fig. 13.2 for an example.)

3 Highlight the Edit command.

4 To copy part or all of the screen, choose Mark. This switches the mouse into marker mode, which allows you to swipe it across any portion of the DOS screen to highlight a rectangle. When you've marked the section you want to copy, press Enter. Whatever you marked is now available on the Windows Clipboard, and you can paste it anywhere you want.

5 To paste text from the Clipboard into your DOS program, make sure the insertion point is at the right spot in your DOS screen. Next, use the same pull-down menu to choose Edit, Paste.

Fig. 13.2
Run any DOS application in a window and you can cut, copy, and paste text between it and Windows applications.

What's so special about Paste Special?

When you highlight part of a document and right-click on it, you'll almost always see the same three choices: Cut, Copy, and Paste. But in most programs, when you use the pull-down Edit menu, you'll see a fourth option as well: Paste Special. What's so special?

The plain old Paste command acts instantly. But when you choose Paste Special, Windows waits for more instructions from you before it actually inserts the contents of the Clipboard. The options it presents to you are context-sensitive, with different options, depending on what you've selected.

Why would you want to do this? It's a good way to save time if you want to choose a different format for whatever you're pasting, or if you want to get rid of any formatting completely. For example, you might want to copy some text from a WordPad report, then paste it into a letter. If you used Paste, the text you added to the letter would retain the formatting of the report text. To make the newly pasted text blend in properly, you'd have to fuss with fonts and margins.

Instead, copy the section to the Clipboard as usual, then move to the second document and Select Edit, Paste Special. You'll see four choices, as shown in figure 13.3.

Fig. 13.3

When you use Edit, Paste Special, you have more control over how the words on the Clipboard wind up in their destination.

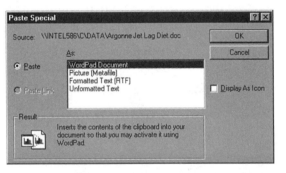

There are two options you'll use most often. The first is Rich Text, which lets you transfer the words and the formatting together. The other useful option, Unformatted Text, simply pastes in the words, which then pick up whatever format is already in the document.

 TIP **Are you tired of constantly shifting your hands between the** keyboard and the mouse? Try these universal shortcuts instead: Ctrl+C copies the current selection to the Clipboard; Ctrl+X cuts it; Ctrl+V pastes the contents of the Clipboard to the current insertion point.

All about OLE

You can't pick up a new Windows program without hearing the term **OLE** (it's generally pronounced *oh-lay*, like the shout you hear at the *corrida*, although you can also refer to it by spelling out the letters). What's it all about? OLE stands for **Object Linking and Embedding,** which is an extremely technical term for the act of working with two types of data in one place.

You've already seen how copy-and-paste (or cut-and-paste) works. When you select some data and paste it into a different document, it becomes part of the second document. You can make changes to the original document from which it came, but those changes won't be reflected in the fragment that you pasted somewhere else. If you make a lot of changes, you could spend the rest of your life re-copying and re-pasting the same data!

Linking and embedding are two ways to avoid doing all that rework. I'll talk about each of them in detail, later in this chapter. For now, it's sufficient to know that when you link two documents, or when you embed information from one document in another, Windows stores information about the *connection* between the two documents. This technique lets you edit information in an original document and guarantees that your changes will show up wherever there's a reference to this document.

Sounds cool, doesn't it? Coolness has its cost, though. Using OLE drags down the performance of your computer, especially if you don't have very much RAM (figure you'll need 16M of RAM if you want to think about doing anything truly interesting with OLE).

CAUTION **If you have only 4M of RAM, don't try to use OLE. If it works at all, it'll be creepy–crawler slow. Even with 8M, extensive OLE use can be an exercise in frustration. If you plan to use OLE extensively, you'll need a powerful computer.**

Using different types of data in one file

Let's say you've written a report in WordPad. You know what you want to say, but you need to add a drawing to make it easy for your co-workers to see what you're talking about. So you fire up the Windows 95 Paint program and create your own work of art. Those are two completely different kinds of data. Can you really mix words and pictures together?

Yes, you can. In fact, you have several choices for ways to mix and match different types of data in a single document.

You can **paste** the picture into your document, with or without formatting. You can **embed** the picture in the document. Or you can **link** the picture to the document. The technique you choose will dictate what you can do with the document later.

What's the difference between pasting, linking, and embedding? To understand the distinction, let's imagine that we're in a fancy restaurant—the kind where there's more silverware in front of your plate than you'll use at home in an entire month. You've asked the waiter to bring you some oil-and-vinegar dressing for your salad. Instead of going into the kitchen, though, he goes into the back office and uses his Microsoft Salad Dressing for Windows 95 software. What happens next?

I want these two kinds of data mixed into one document

Our waiter could just pour a little bit of oil into a big bottle of vinegar and bring the whole bottle to the table. He might have to shake things up to get it to look good, but for all practical purposes, you see one big bottle of salad dressing in a bottle labeled "Vinegar." (If our waiter is smart, he'll relabel the bottle "Oil-and-vinegar" before he brings it to our table.)

In Windows terms, that's exactly what happens when you simply paste one type of data into a document that contains another type of data—for example, when you insert a picture into a WordPad document. The data that you're pasting (the oil) gets added to the original document (the vinegar) in a format that the original document can recognize. For all practical purposes, the drawings and words mix together to form a single document that you can use without any big fuss. The label on the outside says that it's a WordPad document, but you know there's a drawing mixed in with it. Most importantly, there's no easy way to take the pasted picture back out, any more than you could extract that oil from the vinegar and start all over again.

I want two kinds of data to travel together without being mixed

Let's say that our waiter isn't certain how much oil you want with that vinegar. So, instead of mixing it up for you he brings two bottles to the table—a large bottle of vinegar and a small one filled with oil. He doesn't want the two bottles to get separated, so he fastens the smaller bottle to the side of the larger bottle and brings it to the table. You can see what's in each bottle without any work at all, but to put the dressing on your salad, you have to open each bottle separately.

In Windows terms, the big bottle is the **container**, the smaller bottle attached to it is the **embedded object**, and the complete package is called a **compound document**. The second document is literally stored right alongside the first so that the two types of data never mix. When you embed one piece of data in a file that contains another kind of data, they're not mixed together, so you can edit either one separately. Just as you could replace the olive oil with canola oil, you could change the picture without having to start all over.

Even though they travel together and can be looked at together, the data types in a compound document (words and pictures in the case of our document, oil and vinegar in the case of the salad) remain completely separate. If someone across the table asks you for the salad dressing, you hand them the complete package. Likewise, if you send your two-in-one document to someone else, you don't have to worry about them getting separated.

I want to use two kinds of data together, but store them separately

OK, let's say this restaurant is fancy, but not very well-stocked. There are dozens of bottles of vinegar, but there's only one bottle of oil. Attached to the big bottle of vinegar, there's a picture of the bottle of oil, along with a note that tells you to ask the waiter when you want some oil. Just ask, and the waiter will bring it from the pantry anytime you want to add dressing to your salad, stand there while you use it, and return it to the pantry when you're done.

Why on earth would you want to do something this complicated with your data? Well, imagine that the picture is your company's logo. If you insert a separate copy of the logo into all your documents, you'll have to go back and change each document separately if your company logo changes. A better solution is to keep the logo art in a central file and include instructions for finding the **linked object**—in this case, the logo file stored on the company network.

Links always contain both a picture and a set of instructions for finding the original. So if you send a file with the linked logo to someone else, she can see what the logo looks like. She can even print it out. But if she wants to change the logo, her application will have to follow the instructions in the link to find the original logo and the application that created it.

How do I recognize an embedded or linked object?

Most of the time, when you've inserted one object into another, you won't even notice a difference. The one time you will notice it is if you click on the embedded object. When you do, you'll see a dark line that forms a box around the object. In each corner, and in the middle of each side of this box, you'll see black squares called **sizing handles**. (See fig. 13.4 for an example.) You can drag these handles in any direction to change the size and shape of the object.

Fig. 13.4

The dark box and square handles around this object are your visual cues that this is an embedded object. Right-click on it for more information about what it is and what you can do with it.

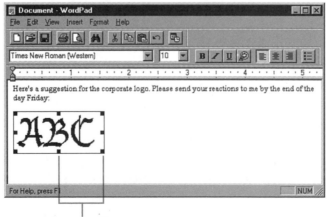

Sizing handles

What am I supposed to do with an embedded object?

To select an embedded or linked object, just click it. Like any object anywhere in Windows, the best way to find out more information about what it is and what you can do with it is to right-click it.

If you've embedded or linked an object from one program into a document created by another program, you don't necessarily have to do anything special with it.

- To **view** the document, just open it. All the information you need to see is already there, so you'll see exactly what you expect to see.

- To **print** the document, just choose the print command as you normally would.

- To **edit** the inserted object, right-click on it, then choose the appropriate command from the bottom of the menu. (See fig. 13.5 for an example of what you might see.) You can also change any of the options for an inserted object by using this menu.

Fig. 13.5

Right-click an embedded object, and choose Properties to see what you can do with it. The same popup menu also includes the option to edit the picture.

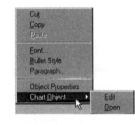

> **TIP** Remember, the menus that pop up when you right-click on an object change to reflect what Windows can do with that object. So, if you're not sure what an object is, use the right mouse button!

Do I really need to worry about OLE?

Most of the time, you don't really need to be concerned about how you're cutting and pasting between two different places. Windows looks at the different types of data you're trying to mix together, makes a few assumptions about what you probably want to do, and then takes care of the details.

When you're not sure what will happen, try the <u>P</u>aste command first. If you're not satisfied with the results, undo what you just did and try again with Paste <u>S</u>pecial.

 Q&A *I pasted something into a document, and now there's a box around it. What's that all about?*

Congratulations! You just embedded one document inside another without even realizing it. If that's not what you wanted to do, you'll have to tell Windows to do the paste differently. Go to the <u>E</u>dit menu and choose Paste <u>S</u>pecial. This time, you'll see a dialog box with a list of the options available to you. As you highlight each option in the list, look in the Results area at the bottom of the dialog box to see what will happen, then choose the one that matches what you want.

Part IV: Making Windows Work the Way You Do

14

Changing the Way Windows Looks

In this chapter:

- **I can't see all the windows I need at the same time!**

- **Want to put your favorite picture on the desktop? Here's how**

- **This screen is boring**

- **Keep other people from snooping when you go to lunch**

- **Help—I can't find my mouse pointer!**

I want my Windows desktop to be just as comfortable and personal as my office. Don't you? Fortunately, Windows lets you do just that. . . . . >

Your office probably started out looking just like mine: white walls, a cork-covered bulletin board, an empty desk, and some bookshelves— oh, yes, a computer, too. Pretty boring, huh? That's why I've added all sorts of personal touches to the environment. Step into my office and you'll find family pictures, a couple of Dilbert cartoons, a wall calendar, a bunch of framed pictures (I'm partial to racehorses), and a coffee mug that says, "You want it WHEN?????"

It's no problem to personalize your Windows environment, just as you can redecorate your office to make it more comfortable. Replace that boring green background with your favorite picture, change the colors and fonts, even shrink the whole display so you can see more details at once. With a few notable exceptions, these changes don't have much of an impact on productivity. They're strictly for fun and visual relief.

Put more data on the desktop— here's how...

How much do you want to see on the screen at one time? Well, how sharp is your eyesight? When you installed Windows, it most likely came up using the normal video settings, where everything on the screen is big and easy to see. If you have the right combination of video card and monitor, though, you can change the resolution (Windows calls it the **desktop area**) and put more pixels on the screen. Is this the right option for you? You'll have to make a trade-off between your eyesight and the convenience of seeing more of your work on the screen.

❝❝ *Plain English, please!*

Pixels are the small dots of color that make up the image on your screen, and **resolution** is simply a fancy term for the number of dots that Windows displays on a single screen. Resolution is usually expressed as a measurement—when we refer to 640×480 resolution (pronounce it six-forty-by-four-eighty), that means a display with room for 640 dots from side to side, and 480 dots from top to bottom. Increasing the resolution while using the same monitor means that everything on the screen appears smaller, and so you can see more words, numbers, pictures...whatever data you're working with. ❞❞

Decorating the desktop

Does this screen look familiar? Windows 95 lets you personalize practically every part of the workspace, just for fun.

*You can adjust the **colors** for every part of the Window environment, from the desktop background to the labels under each icon.*

***Wallpaper** consists of graphic images that fill all or part of the desktop.*

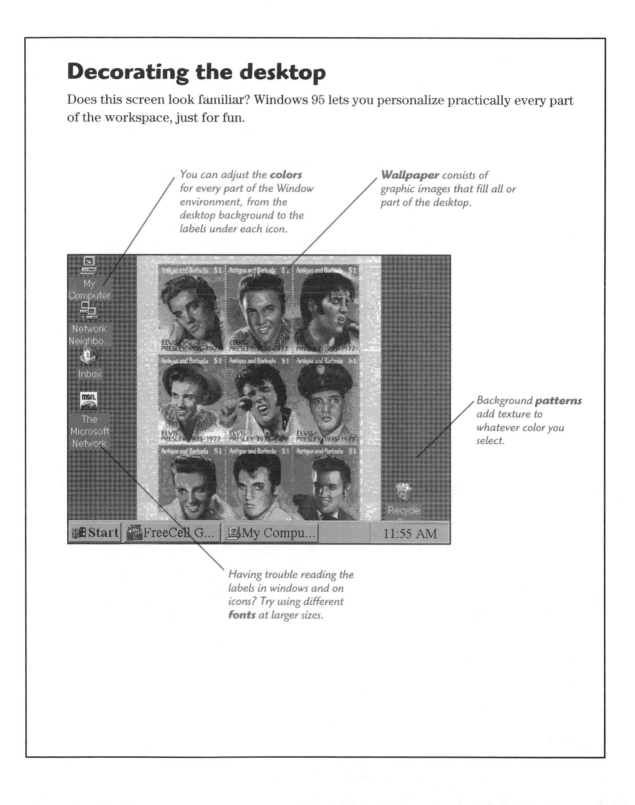

*Background **patterns** add texture to whatever color you select.*

*Having trouble reading the labels in windows and on icons? Try using different **fonts** at larger sizes.*

If your hardware allows it, you can change the screen **resolution** (to see more details on the screen at once) and the **color palette** (to make photographic images look more realistic).

You can also tell Windows to use a **screen saver** that puts something else on the screen if you haven't touched a key or used the mouse for a while.

What happens when I change resolution?

If you've ever looked through the viewfinder of a camera, you understand everything you need to know about screen resolution. Let's say you're taking a group photograph at a family reunion. The photograph you get back from the Fotomat is always the same size (just as your computer screen stays a constant size) but, depending on where you stood, the image on the photo might be very different.

Stand close to the group and look through the camera—you can only get two or three people in the picture. Take a step back and Uncle Bill shows up in the frame, but everyone looks a little smaller. Go back a few more steps, and you can squeeze in everyone in the family, including all those cousins and even the family dog, but you'll need a magnifying glass to tell whether that's Uncle Bill or Aunt Hillary in the back row.

Each time you increase the resolution of your Windows screen, it's exactly like stepping back to get more into the picture. Eventually, the image will be so small that it won't be usable. See figure 14.1 for a graphic illustration of how much more room you have on-screen when you increase the display resolution.

Table 14.1 describes the four most common choices of screen resolution.

Table 14.1 The four most common screen resolutions, in plain English

Number of Pixels	How It Looks	Use this Setting if You...
640×480	Normal	...have average eyesight and work with ordinary documents or games.
800×600	Wide angle	...regularly cut and paste information between two applications.
1024×768	Extra–wide angle	...have a big monitor, and regularly have lots of windows open at once.
1280×1024	View from the Space Shuttle	...have a *really* big monitor, and the eyesight of a red-tailed hawk.

Fig. 14.1

If your eyesight is 20/20, you can make everything on the Windows desktop smaller—and see more on the screen.

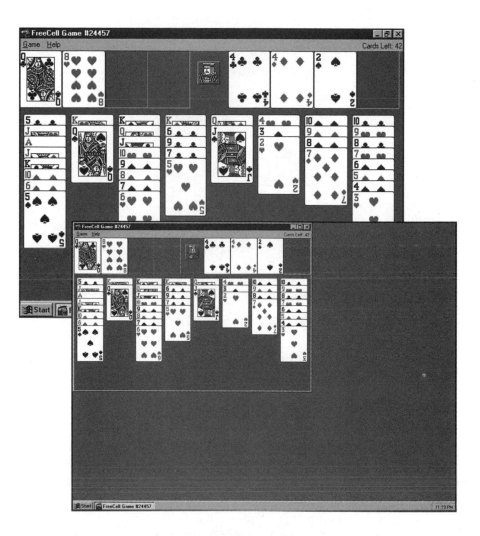

How to adjust the screen resolution

Right-click on any empty spot on the desktop, and choose P<u>r</u>operties. Click on the Settings tab (see fig. 14.2) to reveal all the controls for adjusting the image size and number of colors you can see at once.

CAUTION **Be very careful with the button labeled Change Display Type!**

If you specify the wrong monitor type, you could end up sending a signal to the monitor that causes some of its innards to *literally* go up in a puff of smoke. Thanks to Plug and Play, Windows will probably set up the monitor correctly. Unless you're sure you know what you're doing, don't touch this button.

Fig. 14.2

Use this dialog box to adjust the settings for your screen.

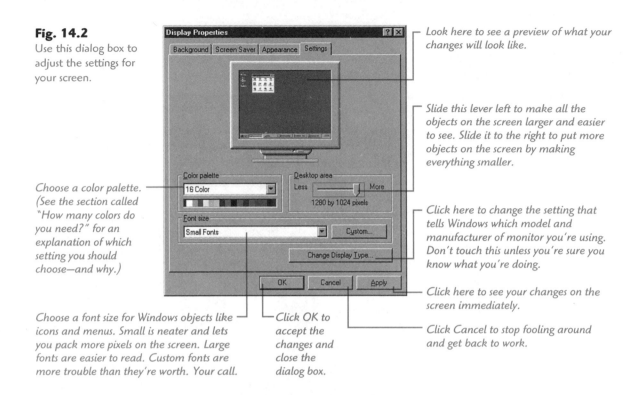

Look here to see a preview of what your changes will look like.

Slide this lever left to make all the objects on the screen larger and easier to see. Slide it to the right to put more objects on the screen by making everything smaller.

Choose a color palette. (See the section called "How many colors do you need?" for an explanation of which setting you should choose—and why.)

Click here to change the setting that tells Windows which model and manufacturer of monitor you're using. Don't touch this unless you're sure you know what you're doing.

Click here to see your changes on the screen immediately.

Choose a font size for Windows objects like icons and menus. Small is neater and lets you pack more pixels on the screen. Large fonts are easier to read. Custom fonts are more trouble than they're worth. Your call.

Click OK to accept the changes and close the dialog box.

Click Cancel to stop fooling around and get back to work.

How many colors do you need?

Setting the Windows color palette is like shopping for paint to redo your living room. At the lowest setting in the Display properties sheet, you get your choice of **16 colors** that can appear on the screen at once. That's like doing the walls, the trim, and all the furniture and decorations using only the colors on the sale shelf at the Sherman-Williams store. It's not a heck of a lot of choices, but you can probably find something you'll like.

When you boost the level to **256 colors,** you can take your choice of any combination of colors from the ready-mixed selection in the paint store. In practice, since you're doing the walls and the trim and the furniture and decorations, that means tens of thousands of combinations. Surely you'll find *something* you like in there.

If you have an expensive video card and monitor, you can boost the color resolution to **High Color** (65,536 colors) or even **True Color** (16.7 million colors). That's the equivalent of bringing in your own swatches of color and asking the paint store to match them molecule for molecule.

Why not choose the highest number? Because it slows down your screen. It's as if Windows has to search through the entire list of colors and calculate all those bits for every dot on the screen; that uses a tremendous amount of computing power. And while Windows is getting a headache sorting through all those colors, it can't do anything else.

For most of us, 256 colors is about right. It offers enough color options to look good most of the time, but not so many that Windows will neglect the rest of its work while it's sorting through the color palette.

Besides, can you *really* put 16.7 million colors on the screen? Do they all have names? (Hey, the Crayola Company had to use strange names like Burnt Umber when they got up to 64 crayons, so what could they possibly come up with for the box with 16.7 million crayons inside?) The only time you'll really want to use lots of colors is when you're working with **digital images** (like the photographs found on Photo CDs); then you'll appreciate the smoother, sharper, more realistic images. For most day-to-day work, 256 is puh-lenty of colors.

Q&A *When I changed the resolution, the color palette changed, too!*

Your video card doesn't have enough memory on it to handle all those colors at all resolutions. If you want to see photos in True Color, you may have to choose the smallest desktop area—640×480. If you want to pack more pixels on the screen—at 1024×768, for example—you'll have to settle for fewer colors.

Decking the walls

I don't like wallpaper. If I bought a new house, and discovered that the kitchen walls had been covered with quaint country scenes, I'd spend days scraping it off and repainting. Fortunately, changing the wallpaper in Windows doesn't require a belt sander. Just right-click on the Desktop, choose Properties, click the Display tab, and you can redecorate in a few seconds (see fig. 14.3).

Fig. 14.3
Use the Display
Properties sheet
to change the
background pattern.

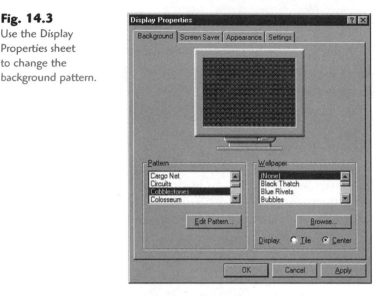

Wallpaper? Patterns? What's the difference?

When it's time to redecorate your Windows desktop, you have the same choices you have in your house. You can use a single color for the background, just as you might paint the walls canary yellow. Or you can add artwork—images or patterns—to make the background more interesting.

Windows gives you two choices for images. Background **patterns** are simple, repeating arrangements of black pixels that create a design when viewed together—like a fancy tile pattern for a kitchen countertop or floor.

Wallpaper, on the other hand, is an actual graphic image, such as a photograph or drawing, that covers up the background color you've chosen. You can center a single image on your desktop, just as you would hang a large painting on the living room wall; or you can choose a smaller image and let Windows duplicate it to cover the entire surface of the desktop.

Wallpaper is always a separate image file, stored in a format that Windows can recognize. Typically, this is the **bitmap image format**.

CAUTION **Wallpaper and background patterns can make your screen look as** sophisticated as the Museum of Modern Art, but they can also make it difficult or impossible to see icons on the desktop. If you choose an intricate wallpaper pattern, be prepared to squint.

I want a nice, clean screen...

That's easy. Just make sure that (None) is selected in both list boxes. You'll see a plain background with only the colors you've selected—no patterns or pictures.

I want to break up this boring color

Then use one of the Windows background patterns. These work just like a decorative pattern on a kitchen tile. The base color of the tile may be different, but the pattern itself is always black. Choose a pattern from the list, then look in the preview screen above to see what it will look like. Or you can take a close-up look at the pattern (and even make changes to it) by clicking on the Edit Pattern button. When you do, you'll see a dialog box like the one in figure 14.4.

Fig. 14.4
Click the Edit Pattern button to create your own desktop look.

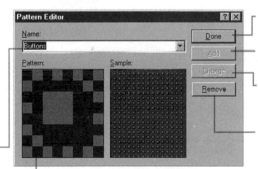

Click here when you're through editing patterns.

Click here to add the new pattern to the list.

Click here to replace the existing pattern with the one you just changed.

Click here to delete the pattern from the list. Zap, it's gone!

Enter a new name here. If you don't, Windows assumes you want to replace the existing pattern.

Each big block is a pixel. Click once to turn the pixel to black; click again to restore it to the default background color.

Q&A *I selected a pattern and clicked OK, but I don't see it.*

Make sure that you don't have any wallpaper selected. To clear the selection, highlight the (None) entry in the wallpaper list. Wallpaper always covers up the desktop pattern, which covers up the background color.

I want to see the big picture...

When you have a favorite image stored in the right format, why not use it as the Windows wallpaper? If the image is big enough to take over the screen, then check the <u>C</u>enter option in the Wallpaper box. Windows will neatly position the image so it's perfectly centered on your screen, as in figure 14.5.

Fig. 14.5
When you ask Windows to center an image as wallpaper, it positions it right smack in the center of the screen. If the image is smaller than your desktop area, you'll see some of the background color and pattern as well.

Some people like to use an image that's slightly smaller than the full screen, as shown in this figure. That way, they can arrange desktop icons like My Computer and the Recycle Bin without having to squint to pick them out against the background image.

The tiled look: bricks and boxes

Take your favorite postage stamp, put it in a frame measuring two feet on each side, and hang it on your living room wall. What happens? The stamp practically disappears, of course. The same thing happens if you take a small bitmap image, just 20 or 30 pixels on each side, and try centering it on your screen. The tiny image is overwhelmed by that big desktop.

To make the framed image stand out on your wall, you could use an entire sheet of stamps instead of just one. You can do the same with a bitmap wallpaper image. When you check the <u>T</u>ile option, Windows copies your original image and uses the copies to fill the entire screen, as shown in figure 14.6. The repetition makes a much better visual impact, because the image gets to fill a proper amount of space.

Fig. 14.6

A small image can look lonely when it's centered on the screen (top). Choose the Tile option, though, and Windows will repeat the image as many times as it takes to fill the screen (bottom).

TIP When you're experimenting with different desktop options, use the Apply button instead of the OK button. That way, you can check out different looks without constantly clicking to reopen the Display properties box.

Where to find wallpaper

If you're looking for wallpaper, you can find interesting images just about anywhere. Windows comes with some of its own, including my personal favorites, Gold Weave and Sandstone, which look great as tiled backgrounds. For a pretty full-screen image, check out the Clouds file. All three, plus a lot more, can be found in the Windows folder.

TIP   Can't find the wallpaper files? You probably didn't install them.
To put them on your hard disk, you've got to go through the following
tedious steps. Click the Start button, choose Settings, and click the Add/
Remove Programs icon. Select the Windows Setup tab, highlight Accessories,
click the Details button, and (finally!) check the Desktop Wallpaper box.
Click OK to copy the desktop wallpaper to your hard disk.

You can find other images, everything from animals to space shots, in art
and photo collections available from a variety of sources: on CD-ROMs, from
online services like CompuServe and The Microsoft Network, or even from
the Internet. (That's where I discovered those hip Elvis postage stamps.)

You can even make your own wallpaper, if you have a little artistic talent
and the Windows Paint program. (See Chapter 12 for more information on
how Paint works.) After you've created and saved the Paint image, look on
the File menu for the two Set as wallpaper options.

Redoing the color (and font) schemes

The Windows default colors are pretty boring. Dark green. Blue. White.
Yawn. It's almost as bad as a model house, which is designed to be safe and
bland so as not to offend anyone.

Want a different look and feel? A purple background? Lime-green title bars?
Red letters? Hey, it's your computer. You can use any colors you like, and
you can even replace the fonts Windows uses for the labels on icons and
folders.

Windows comes with a predefined collection of desktop arrangements,
with different coordinated colors and fonts. These collections are called
schemes, and you can find them in the Display properties dialog box. If you
find a scheme that has some elements you like, use it as the base for your
own desktop. Start with the ready-made choices, then add your own options
and save the edited scheme under a new name of your choosing, as shown in
figure 14.7.

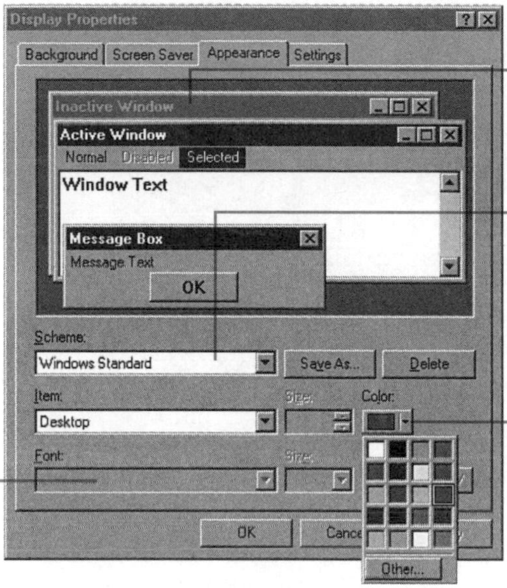

Fig. 14.7
As you work, watch the example screen change to reflect how your options will look. If you're not happy with the way it's turning out, just click the Cancel button and start over.

Pick a part of Windows that you would like to see displayed in a different color or with a bigger, bolder font.

Give the collection of visual effects a name, called a **scheme**. Next time you want your desktop to adopt this look, don't redo all that work; just select the scheme.

Click here to pull down the color list—the small box filled with color squares. Choose a size and a color, where appropriate.

Choose a label font, where appropriate. Remember to specify size and attributes (bold, italic, color) for any fonts.

TIP If you're not sure what a part of the desktop is called, look in the preview window. All the parts of this window are "live;" if you click on the menu bar here, for example, it selects the Menu option in the Item list below so you can adjust its size, color, and associated font.

Where did all my colors go?

It doesn't matter how many colors you've told Windows you want to use. When you pull down the color list in the Display Properties sheet, you only see 20. What happened to the others? Well, you'll have to mix them by yourself. Here's how:

1 Pull down the Color control, and click the Other button. Right off the bat, you get an expanded list of 48 colors to choose from (see fig. 14.8 for an example).

2 Still can't find the right one? Click one of the empty squares in the section labeled Custom Colors; this is where you'll store the new color you're about to create.

Fig. 14.8
Don't see the precise color you're looking for? Use the Custom colors dialog box to mix it yourself.

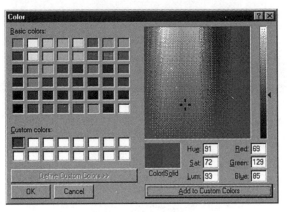

3 Use the controls at the right to pick your color. Move the black **cross hairs** from side to side in the color matrix to shift along the spectrum from red to yellow to green and blue, and so on. Moving the cross hairs up and down changes the intensity of the color.

4 Having trouble seeing any colors? You might need to adjust the amount of black or white in the image. Drag the slider at the right down to add more black; push it up to add white. Stay somewhere in the middle, though; if you go all the way to the top or bottom all your color will disappear.

5 Preview your color in the box just below the color matrix. When you're happy with the look, click the button labeled <u>A</u>dd to Custom Colors, then click OK to exit.

I can't read these labels!

Then change the font size. The normal size for window titles, for example, is 8 point. Try bumping it up to 9 or 10 points to make those labels more readable. (Don't know a point from a pixel? See Chapter 17 for more details about fonts.)

These buttons are too small!

You won't find a setting for adjusting the Minimize, Maximize, and Close buttons. But you can adjust their size just the same: when you change the size of the type in the Active and Inactive Title Bars, the size of the buttons changes, too. To make the buttons bigger, just make the Title Bar font bigger.

Oops—that's *ugly.* How do I get it back to normal?

Don't like that purple and lime-green after all? I don't blame you… Open the Display properties sheet and choose one of the predefined schemes stored there instead. You can always get back to normal by choosing Windows Standard from the list of schemes on the Appearance page.

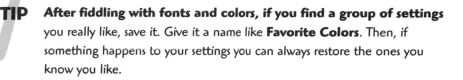

TIP **After fiddling with fonts and colors, if you find a group of settings** you really like, save it. Give it a name like **Favorite Colors**. Then, if something happens to your settings you can always restore the ones you know you like.

CAUTION **If you accidentally make the background color and the foreground** color the same somewhere in Windows, you won't be able to see what you're doing. To fix it, just go to the Desktop and restore the Windows Standard scheme.

Installing a screen saver

Computer old-timers will tell you that screen savers are necessary to prevent characters from "burning in" to your monitor. That used to be true, but it isn't any more. Still, there are two reasons to use a screen saver: for fun or for privacy.

The concept behind a **screen saver** is simple. When you tell Windows to use a screen saver, it starts a timer each time you tap a key or click a mouse button. When a predetermined amount of time passes without any action, Windows replaces whatever's on the screen with the screen-saver image, usually something that moves.

My favorite screen saver is one called Bezier, which draws fancy looping geometric shapes called **Bezier curves** on the screen. To install it, click the Screen Saver tab in the Display Properties sheet, as shown in figure 14.9.

Fig. 14.9
See this screen saver?
You're getting sleepy,
very sleepy....

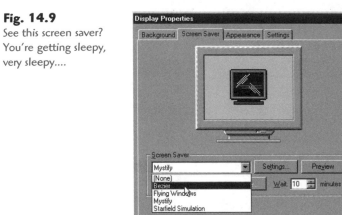

The following table describes what the options do; as usual, the sample screen shows how the various settings will look after you choose OK.

Table 14.2 Screen Saver Options

Choose this Option...	...and then Adjust this Screen Saver Setting
Screen Saver	Pick the screen saver you want from this list.
Settings	Set preferences here—for example, how fast the image moves and which colors it uses.
Password protected	Enter an optional password here. Once the screen saver kicks in, you'll have to enter this password before you can get back to work. This feature is handy if you want to be able to walk away from your desk without worrying about snoopy coworkers.
Wait	Tells Windows how long you want it to wait before turning on the screen saver. The default setting of 1 minute is a little quick. Try 5 or 10 minutes for starters.
Preview	Click to see a full-screen demonstration of the screen saver in action.
Energy saving features of monitor	The Energy Star section lets you tell Windows to shut down your monitor (saving power) after a certain length of time. (This option is only available for monitors that support this feature.)

Fine-tuning the mouse

Most people don't realize that you can also change the mouse pointers that come with Windows. And that's just one of the changes that are possible. If you sometimes have trouble picking out the pointer on your screen, double-click on the Mouse icon in the Control Panel. You'll see a sheet like the one in figure 14.10.

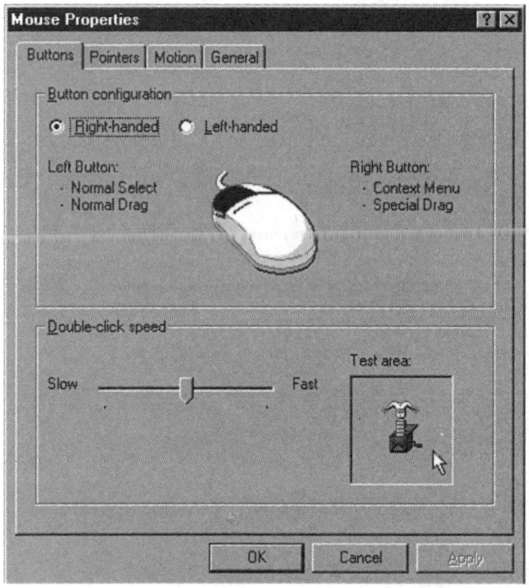

Fig. 14.10

Master your mouse! Windows lets you adjust all sorts of mouse options to make it easier for you to find that pesky pointer.

These are some of the options available:

- **If you're a lefty...** Click on the Buttons tab and tell Windows you want to switch the functions of the left and right mouse buttons.

- **If you have trouble double-clicking...** Tell Windows to be more patient. Look for the Double-click speed control on the Buttons tab. Move the slider to the left to make Windows less sensitive, then test the new double-click rate on the Jack-in-the-box at the right.

- **If you think the mouse pointer is too small...** Pick a new pointer scheme from the list. The Windows Standard variety includes large and extra large sizes.

- **If the pointer is moving too fast or too slow...** Click on the Motion tab and slide the Pointer speed control in the appropriate direction.

- **If you sometimes lose track of the mouse pointer...** Try adjusting the Pointer trail settings on the Motion tab. This option is especially useful on notebook computers.

Changing the date and time

Not every PC keeps perfect time. If you notice that the time on the taskbar isn't quite right, reset it. Right-click on the time display and choose Adjust Date/Time. You'll see the sheet shown in figure 14.11. Enter a new date or time, if necessary, and Windows will reset the system clock as well as the display.

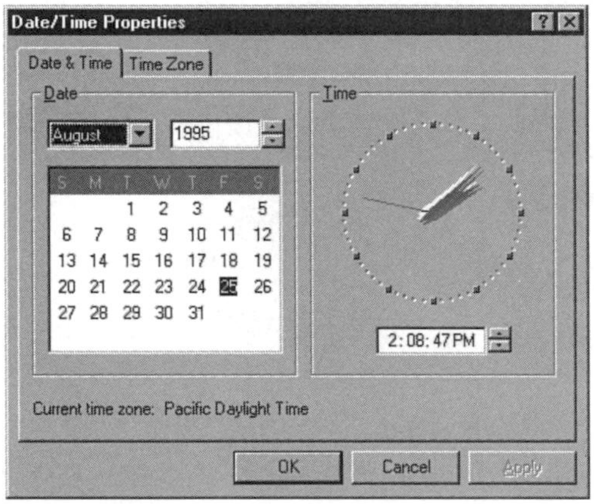

Fig. 14.11
The Windows clock lets you reset the system date or time without a lot of fuss.

![Date/Time Properties dialog box with Date & Time and Time Zone tabs. Date section shows August 1995 calendar with 25 highlighted. Time section shows an analog clock and 2:08:47 PM. Current time zone: Pacific Daylight Time. OK, Cancel, and Apply buttons.]

Why does Windows care what time zone you're in? That can be important if you dial into a network that's in another time zone, or if you send e-mail out over the Internet, where it might be received by someone in Afghanistan. As long as both computers know about time zones, they'll be able to keep track of which file or message came first.

TIP **If your PC loses track of the right time at an alarming rate,** try this trick: drag a shortcut of the Date/Time icon from the Control Panel into the Startup folder. That way, every time you turn on your PC, you'll get a chance to reset the clock.

15

Putting Your Favorite Things Where You Want Them

● In this chapter:

- **Tell Windows exactly what to do with your data files**

- **Start menu a mess? Reorganize it!**

- **Make the taskbar bigger—or make it disappear**

- **How to whip up new documents from scratch**

- **Give your desktop a productivity makeover**

Just as there's more than one right way to organize your kitchen, there are plenty of smart ways to organize your Windows desktop to make yourself more productive . . . . . ❯

How you use your computer is a matter of personal preference, in much the same way that cooking shows off your individual style. Do you lay out all the cast-iron pots and stainless steel mixing bowls before you start preparing that gourmet dinner? Or do you clean and chop every ingredient first, *then* go looking for the utensils? Or do you call Pizza Man to have a pizza delivered?

Everyone has a different style of working, and Windows is nothing if not flexible. In this chapter, I'll show you how to rearrange the programs you use most often and how to group your working documents into efficient folders. In short, how to organize things so you can find them with as little fuss as possible.

It's important to know your working style

Where do you start? Well, it helps if you know how you prefer to work. Do you tend to create a bunch of new documents, work with them for a few minutes or hours, then move on? Or do you work with the same set of documents for days or weeks at a time? It also helps to know how you can use Windows to keep your programs and documents close at hand.

How should you organize your work with Windows? Which techniques will make you most productive? That depends on whether you prefer to start with documents or with the programs that create them. From the two choices below, pick the statement that best describes the way you work, then read the guidelines that follow.

- I know which *program* I want to start with…

  Every program on your hard disk has an **executable file.** When you double-click on this file, your program starts. Your organizational challenge is to find the program, start it up, and then use the program's <u>F</u>ile menu to create a new document or look for one you've already used. The trouble is, these executable files are scattered all over your hard disk, and you don't want to go searching for them every time you want to start a program.

> ## ❝❝ *Plain English, please!*
>
> An **executable file** is one that starts (or executes) a program when you double-click it. WordPad and Paint are executable files; so are Solitaire and Minesweeper. Contrast these files with simple **containers**, such as the My Computer window or any folder, and **documents** that require you to open a separate program to view or edit them. ❞❞

- I know which *document* I want to start with...

  What's in a **document file**? Well, all your data is there—words, numbers, pictures, and so on. The file has a name that, presumably, describes the contents. There's also information in the file that tells Windows about the program that created that data file. Once you find the document, just double-click on it, and trust that Windows can figure out which program it needs to run to start the file. Here's the problem: if you've organized your hard disk into a collection of folders inside folders inside more folders, you could spend your whole day just searching for documents.

Windows knows your (file) type

When you double-click on a file, Windows has to make some fast decisions. What kind of file is it? Which program created it? Is that program running right now? If not, where is it?

To answer all those questions, Windows maintains a list of **file types**, with each entry containing three pieces of information: a friendly name, a file extension, and the name of the program Windows should start up when you want to use that kind of file.

Let's look at what happens after you create a file with Notepad. (Make sure to give it a long file name like Important Notepad Document.) Open a folder window, right-click on the name of the file you just created, and inspect its properties. You'll see plenty of information about its file type. Just below its icon, after the word Type, you'll see the words Text Document. That's the friendly name.

Now look a few lines lower on the properties sheet, next to the entry for the MS-DOS name. You'll see a clipped-off version of your long file name that ends in a period followed by three letters. In this case, those three letters are TXT, which is the file extension that Windows tacks onto the end of every file classified as a Text Document.

Those little three-character stragglers are annoying and confusing most of the time, so Windows hides them from you by default. But it doesn't actually get rid of them because that's how it knows to use Notepad to open these files. To see where that **association** between the file type and program is stored, open a folder window, choose View, Options, and click on the File Types tab. Scroll through the list until you get to the entry called Text Document. You'll see a box like the one in figure 15.1.

Fig. 15.1

When you double-click on a file, Windows looks in this list to see what it's supposed to do next.

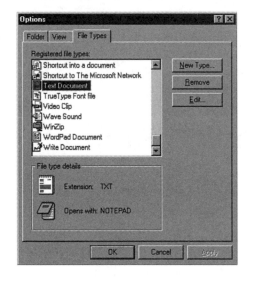

When you double-click on a file in a folder, Windows checks its list of File Types to see what it's supposed to do next. If it knows how to handle that file type, it starts the program and loads the file. If it doesn't know how to handle the file type, it asks you what to do (see fig. 15.2).

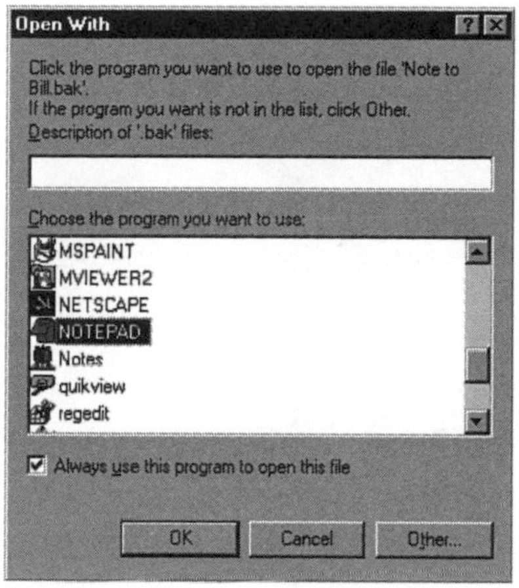

Fig. 15.2

When you double-click on a file and Windows doesn't know what to do with it, Windows asks you for help. Just pick a program from the pop-up list, and you're in business.

Open With   ? ✕

Click the program you want to use to open the file 'Note to Bill.bak'.
If the program you want is not in the list, click Other.
Description of '.bak' files:

Choose the program you want to use:

- MSPAINT
- MVIEWER2
- NETSCAPE
- NOTEPAD
- Notes
- quikview
- regedit

☑ Always use this program to open this file

| OK | Cancel | Other... |

 Q&A *My program isn't in the list that Windows offered me. What do I do now?*

Click the button labeled Other and find the icon for the program you want to use. Click Open to add that program to the list. Then click OK to associate it with the file you want to edit.

Add a shortcut to get to what you need

Instead of forcing you to search for programs and documents all over your hard disk, Windows lets you create shortcuts to both. A **shortcut**, as we saw in Chapter 7, is a special sort of icon that contains instructions that tell Windows exactly where it can find a particular file. And because you can create more than one shortcut for any file, you can have the best of both worlds. Keep your hard disk organized the way you want it, then use shortcuts to temporarily pull together groups of programs and documents into one convenient location.

When you right-click on a shortcut and choose Properties, you'll see a dialog box like the one in figure 15.3. Notice that the name of the shortcut doesn't have to match the name of the file it points to. That makes it easy to label a shortcut with a descriptive name (like Working Copy of Sales Chart) without changing the original file name (Sales Chart).

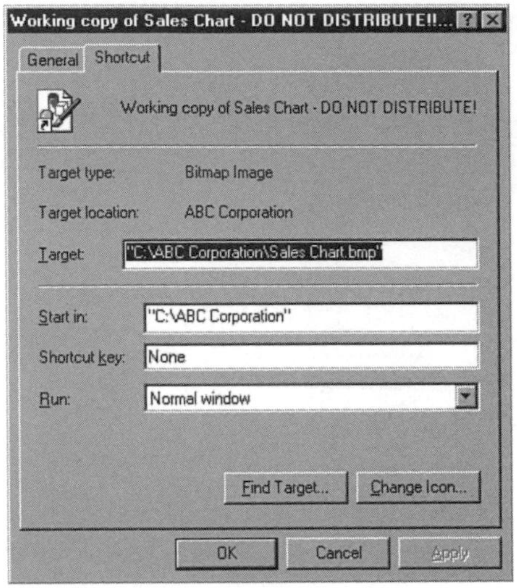

Fig. 15.3

Shortcuts are incredibly useful tools for getting and staying organized.

You can use shortcuts just about anywhere in Windows. They're particularly useful in these places:

- **To add a shortcut to the Start menu...** just drag a file and drop it on the Start button.

- **To put a shortcut on the desktop...** use the right mouse button, drag one or more files out of a folder and onto the desktop, then choose Create Shortcut(s) Here from the popup menu shown in figure 15.4.

- **To add a shortcut to a folder...** right-click on one or more files, and choose Copy. Then point to an empty space in the new folder, right-click, and choose Paste Shortcut.

- **You can even put a shortcut inside an e-mail message...** just create the shortcut in a folder, and drag it into your new message window.

TIP **Shortcuts can come from anywhere, not just your hard drive. If** you've found a location on The Microsoft Network that you like, you can create a shortcut to that location and put it on your desktop. You can also drag a file or folder from a shared folder on another networked computer or file server, and make a shortcut out of it. Don't worry—Windows can keep track of where everything came from.

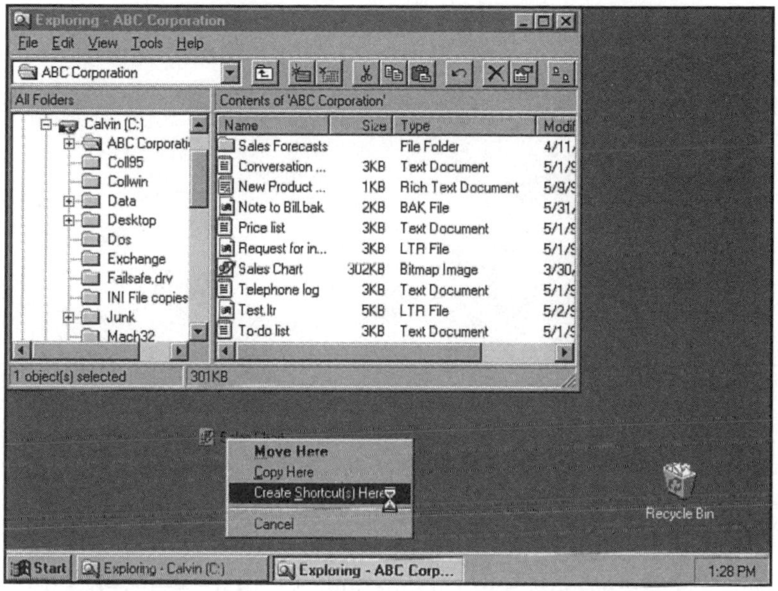

Fig. 15.4
Use the right mouse button to drag a file out of its folder and onto the desktop as a shortcut.

You can even add shortcuts to the Start menu

All your programs should be available in the cascading menus that pop out from the Start menu. But for programs you use every day, that "click, wait, click, wait, click" routine can get pretty annoying. For those programs, why not create shortcuts at the top of the Start menu?

Adding an icon to the Start menu

Putting your favorite icon at the top of the Start menu couldn't be easier. Just open the folder that contains the file you want to add, drag the icon out of the folder, and drop it right smack on top of the Start button. If you drag WordPad from the Accessories folder onto the Start button, for example, it creates an instant shortcut that shows up at the top of the Start menu, as shown in figure 15.5.

Fig. 15.5

Drag icons out of any folder and drop them onto the Start button, but don't get carried away! Five is enough.

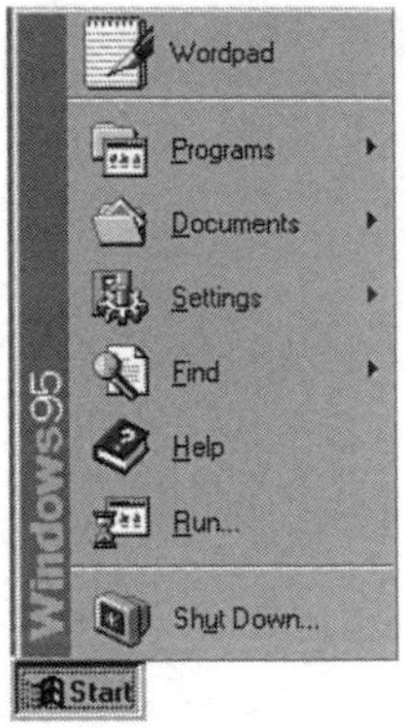

My Start menu is a mess!

Over time, as you add new pieces of software to your system, the Programs section of your Start menu will start to get cluttered. It seems like every program insists on creating its own folder, even if it's only going to put one or two icons in it.

To cut through the clutter, put the programs you use every day at the top of your Start menu, while putting others you use regularly a click away inside the Programs folder. Finally, reorganize all those folders into a smaller number of folders, consolidating and renaming where appropriate. (I've put all my CD-ROM icons into a single folder, for example.) It's easy enough: Just right-click on the taskbar, choose Properties, and then click on the Start Menu Programs tab.

- Click the Add button to call up a special version of the Create Shortcut Wizard that automatically adds a new entry to the Start menu's Programs list.

- Click the Remove button to bring up a special box that lets you instantly zap a shortcut or folder from anywhere in the Start menu's Programs list.

- Click the Advanced button to call up a special version of the Windows Explorer that lets you manage all the folders and icons in the Programs area of the Start menu (see fig. 15.6).

Fig. 15.6
To move a shortcut or folder, make sure the icon you want to move is visible in the right pane and the folder you want to move it to is visible in the left pane. Then drag the icon and drop it on the new location.

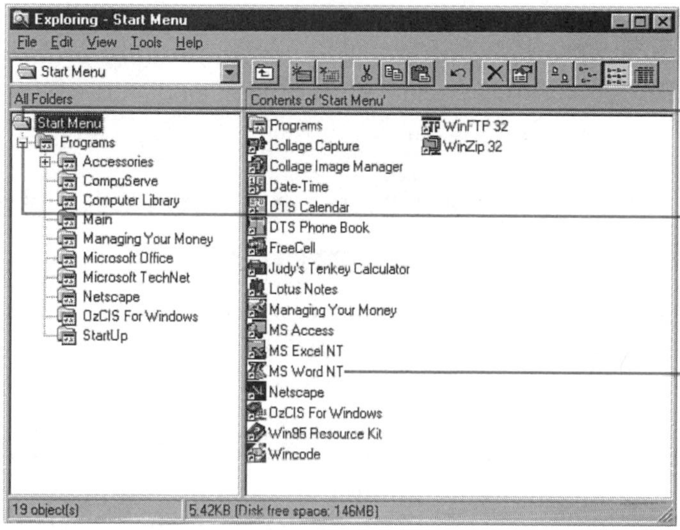

Click on any folder name in the left pane, and you'll see its contents in the right pane, just as if you had opened a folder window.

To see folders inside of other folders, click on the plus sign to the left of any icon in the left pane.

To rename a shortcut or a folder, click on its name in the right pane and start typing. To delete an object, highlight the entry and press Delete.

How can I get this program off the Start menu?

The Start menu is just another folder that's found inside the Windows folder. To delete a shortcut, you can just right-click on the Start button and choose Open; rename, move, and delete icons in the Start menu folder window, just as you would in any other folder. The easier way, though, is to right-click on the taskbar, choose Properties, and then click on the Start Menu Programs tab. The Remove button gets rid of unwanted shortcuts without any fuss.

Now, organize your Start menu to make it efficient

Now that you know how the Programs folder on the Start menu works, what should you do with it? Try these organizational strategies.

Put your top five programs on top

The Windows setup program puts all your programs into folders that you can access by clicking the Programs choice. For the programs you use every day, why go through that extra clicking? Pick the five programs you use most often, and drop them onto the Start menu to put them closer at hand. Why five? Well, OK, maybe six or seven, but any more than that and the top of the Start menu will run out of room at the top of the screen (unless you've set your display to run at a higher resolution).

Reorganize the rest of your shortcuts in the Programs menu

Consolidate all those little groups into a handful of folders. Take the programs you use once a week and move them straight into the Programs folder; that way they're only one cascading menu away instead of two.

> **TIP** **Use lots of shortcuts!** There's no law that says you can only have one shortcut for any program or document. If you have a favorite program, scatter shortcuts anyplace where you might want to get to it.

Put a Favorite Places folder on the Start menu

Do you constantly find yourself going to the same places and doing the same things? I have a few folders that fit that definition, so I've created a special folder filled with shortcuts for each of them. To create your own Favorite Places folder, open the Start menu folder (it's inside the Windows folder) and right-click on any empty space. Choose New, Folder, and immediately type in the folder name you want to use. Now, open a folder window for drive C: and right-drag the folder icons you use most often into the new folder. Choose the Create Shortcut(s) Here option, and you're done.

Make your Start menu a little leaner

For some reason, Windows insists on using big, clunky icons on the Start menu. That's fine until you start adding your own entries to the Start menu. Oops—you're bumping into the top of the screen! To streamline the Start menu, open the taskbar Properties dialog box, and put a check mark in the box labeled Show small icons in Start menu. See figure 15.7 for a before-and-after comparison.

Fig. 15.7
With the default Large Icons, the Start menu rapidly runs out of room. Turn on the Small Icons option and it slims down in a hurry.

Working directly with documents

The most natural way to get work done with your PC is just to pick up a document and start typing. After all, the alternative—starting up a program—is a little like picking up a frying pan and then trying to decide what to cook. If you constantly find yourself working with the same documents, Windows gives you plenty of ways to quickly pick up where you left off before.

I just worked with that document yesterday!

Whenever you create a new document or open one you saved previously, Windows adds an entry on its built-in document-tracking list. To open one of the 15 documents you've used most recently, just click the Start button and choose Documents. A list of names like the one in figure 15.8 will cascade out from the Start menu.

Fig. 15.8
To resume working
with one of the
documents on this list,
just click its choice on
the menu. Windows
will launch the pro-
gram and load the file
for you.

Q&A *I know I worked with a file this morning, but it's not on
the Documents menu. What did I do wrong?*

Nothing, probably. Windows can only keep track of files that are opened
from a folder window, from the Windows Explorer, or from a program that
was designed for Windows 95. If you use the File menu to open or save a
document with an older Windows application, it won't be added to the
Documents menu.

The Documents menu doesn't go on forever, of course. There's a limit of 15.
After you've filled the list, Windows kicks the oldest one off to make room
for any new entries.

TIP To clear the Documents menu, open the taskbar Properties dialog
box, and click on the Start Menu Programs tab. In the bottom half of the
dialog box that pops up, you'll see a section devoted to the Documents
menu. Click the Clear button to empty the list and start with a clean slate.

Cooking up new documents from scratch

Some people like to whip up an angel food cake without Betty Crocker's
help. And when it comes to computers, some people like to create new files
without any help from application programs. If that's your style, Windows

has a feature you'll love. As long as Windows knows how to create the file type you're looking for, a new document is just a few clicks away. All you have to do is use the New button in any folder—or even on the desktop.

Let's say you're talking with your best client on the phone. You've gotten past the pleasantries, and now it's time to get down to business, which means you need to take some notes. Right-click on any empty spot on the desktop, and choose New, Text Document. Windows instantly adds a new icon to your desktop, with the (boring) default name, New Text Document (see fig. 15.9).

Fig. 15.9

Right-click on the desktop and click New to create a NotePad document from scratch. Rename it now or wait until later.

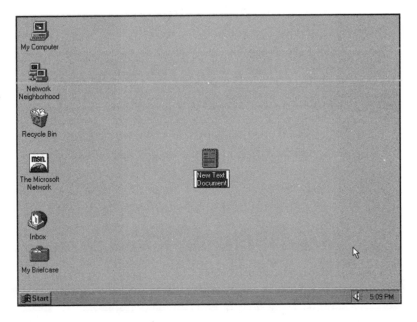

Just start typing to give the new document a new name; it's already highlighted for you. Press Enter to make the new name permanent. Press Enter again (or double-click) to start NotePad and load the new document. Now you can begin entering your notes.

When you're finished, save the document just as you normally would. You can leave it on the desktop if you like, or you can move it to another folder by using the right-click shortcut menus and the Cut and Paste commands.

Making the taskbar mind its manners

If you've gotten into the habit of right-clicking on everything in Windows, you've probably already discovered that there are a pack of options for the taskbar as well. That's right—because the taskbar is just another Windows object, it has properties that you can inspect (and change) with a quick click.

Here's a sampling of what you can do.

Hide it, if you like...

Some people, especially those with smaller monitors, don't like having the taskbar take up any space at all at the bottom of the screen. If that's you, no problem—right-click the taskbar, choose Properties, and check the Auto hide box. From now on, the taskbar will turn to a thin gray line at the edge of the screen whenever you have any windows open.

To make it pop up again, just slide your mouse pointer to the edge of the screen where the taskbar normally appears. (That's usually the bottom, but if you've moved the taskbar to another side, as we'll talk about in a few pages, you'll have to adjust accordingly.) As soon as the mouse pointer bumps the edge of the screen, the taskbar will pop up.

Make it bigger, if you prefer...

Normally, the taskbar is tall enough to hold one row of buttons—no more, no less. But if you regularly open lots of windows and don't mind losing a chunk of the screen, you can make it taller:

1 Aim the mouse pointer at the top of the taskbar until it turns into a two-headed arrow.

2 Grab the edge of the taskbar and drag it up. You can keep dragging until the taskbar takes over about half the screen, but you'll be better off starting with two rows, as shown in figure 15.10.

Fig. 15.10

Not enough room on the taskbar? Grab its upper edge and drag upward to make it bigger. This example has room for two rows of buttons, but you can keep dragging till it takes over half the screen.

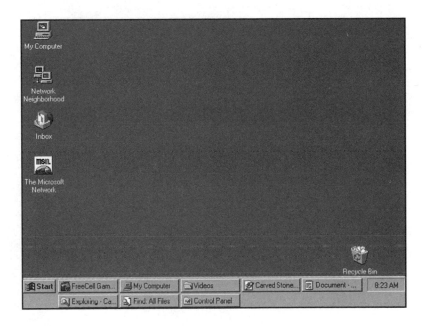

> ## ❓ Q&A *My taskbar disappeared, and the Auto hide option isn't checked. Where did it go?*
>
> You might have accidentally dragged the taskbar down instead of up, so that it's set to be zero buttons high. To put it back to normal, aim the mouse pointer at the very bottom of the screen (or to the side where you've moved the taskbar) until it turns to a two-headed arrow, then drag the pointer up slightly. The taskbar will pop back into position.

Move it, if you want to...

The taskbar is "sticky"—it fastens itself to the bottom of the screen like a refrigerator magnet. If you don't like it at the bottom of the screen, though, you can stick it to any of the four edges of the screen. Just aim the mouse pointer at any empty spot on the taskbar, click, then drag it up to the top of the screen and watch it fasten itself there; your new taskbar will look like the one in figure 15.11.

Fig. 15.11
Don't like the taskbar
at the bottom of the
screen? Drag it to
either edge of the
screen or to the top
(as in this example),
and it will "stick" to
the nearest edge.

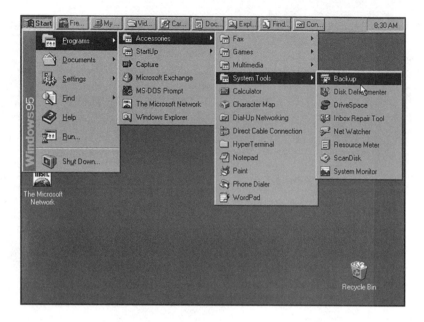

There are actually good reasons to leave the taskbar on the bottom of the
screen. When it's positioned on either side, it's nearly impossible to read
the labels on the buttons. And when it's fastened to the top edge, its menus
end up where I expect my other program's pull-down menus to be. But it's
your computer, and if you want your taskbar somewhere else, that's your
privilege.

TIP **Some older Windows programs don't communicate well with the**
taskbar. The result? Part of a crucial screen or dialog box may be hidden
behind the taskbar. If you use an application that displays this behavior, try
hiding the taskbar so it stays out of your way.

Give your desktop a makeover

Windows puts a few things on the desktop, whether you want them there or
not. My Computer, the Recycle Bin, The Microsoft Network, and the Network Neighborhood—you can't get them off the desktop with dynamite. But
that still leaves plenty of room on the desktop for the things you use every
day. When they're on the desktop, you can get to them with a click or two
(see fig. 15.12).

Fig. 15.12

The desktop makeover: You might not want to clutter your desktop with all these shortcuts, but a few are certain to fit comfortably into your working style.

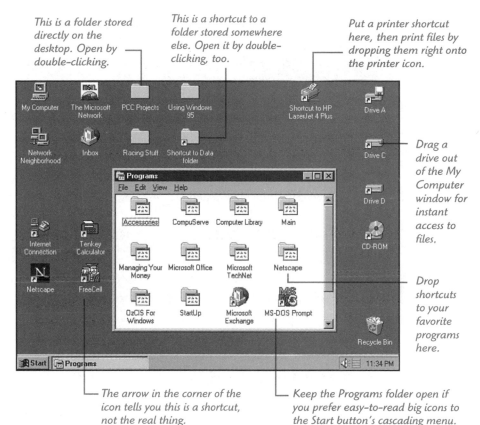

This is a folder stored directly on the desktop. Open by double-clicking.

This is a shortcut to a folder stored somewhere else. Open it by double-clicking, too.

Put a printer shortcut here, then print files by dropping them right onto the printer icon.

Drag a drive out of the My Computer window for instant access to files.

Drop shortcuts to your favorite programs here.

The arrow in the corner of the icon tells you this is a shortcut, not the real thing.

Keep the Programs folder open if you prefer easy-to-read big icons to the Start button's cascading menu.

Just try to count how many times you click the mouse button every day. A few hundred? Easily. If you keep up with that pace (which isn't all that frantic, really) your mouse fingers will click more than 50,000 times a year. Whew! Interested in a few finger-saving shortcuts? One unbeatable way to let your fingers do a little resting is to put a few strategically selected shortcuts on the desktop.

Drop a drive on the desktop

On my desktop, I have shortcuts that take me straight to two hard drives, a floppy drive, a CD-ROM reader, and a hard drive on another computer across the network. To copy a file, I drop it on the floppy drive icon. I can also poke around on any hard drive without having to detour through the My Computer folder.

It's easy to add these shortcuts to your desktop. Just open the My Computer window and drag one or more drive icons onto the desktop. Windows will protest. You cannot copy or move this item to this location, it will say, Do you want to create a shortcut to the item instead? Yep, that's *exactly* what you want to do. Say yes, and all you need to do is rearrange the icons to your liking.

Put a printer icon there, too

Maybe you need this, maybe you don't. If your print jobs go halfway across the building to a popular networked printer, it's a must-have. With a shortcut to that printer on the desktop, you're never more than a double-click away from checking your place in the laser printer line.

Add shortcuts to your favorite programs

There are a few programs that I use every single day, without exception. For those greatest hits, I want instant access, regardless of where I happen to click. I've created shortcuts to my top three programs so I can launch them with a double-click.

Add shortcuts to your favorite folders, for that matter

I don't know about you, but I tend to store most of my stuff in a few special places, and they're not all that easy to get to. My Letters folder, for example, is buried five folders beneath My Computer. I don't want to move those files, but I do want to get to them without 10 mouse clicks. The solution? I right-dragged the icon for the Letters folder onto the desktop and told Windows to create a shortcut. Now, when I want to look through Letters, I just double-click.

Fill a new folder with your favorite shortcuts

At any given time, I might be juggling work for three different clients. The files for all these projects are scattered on every corner of my hard drive. There's no need to move them around, though. Instead, I create a separate folder for each client, put it on the desktop, and fill it with shortcuts to the files I want to access when I'm working on a project for that client. I can have multiple shortcuts to the same document, too, which is a useful way to make sure I can always get to the master copy of documents I share across projects.

Here's a simple illustration of how you can use this technique to save time and energy. Let's say you have two big clients whose happiness is Job One on your job description. You've got letters, memos, and e-mail about their business stored all over your hard disk. Your company also keeps an online price list stored on a network file server so everyone in the company can get to it quickly.

To make sure you don't lose track of any details, create a folder for each client right on the desktop. Then, make sure your price list is handy, no matter which folder you're using.

1 Find an empty space on the desktop, right-click, then choose New, Folder. Give the folder a name, and repeat the process for the second client.

2 Drag shortcuts for all your letters and memos into these folders, or move the documents themselves here.

3 Open the Network Neighborhood, and find the price list on the file server. Select the icon, right-click, then choose Copy.

4 Switch back to one of the folders on the desktop, right-click on an empty space, and choose Paste Shortcut. Repeat for the second folder.

Now, no matter where you're working, you'll never be more than a couple of clicks from that all-important document.

Keep the Programs folder open

Do you hate the cascading menus that fly out of the Start menu every time you click on Programs? Do you miss the Windows Program Manager? Then you might appreciate this shortcut. It doesn't look or act exactly like the old Program Manager, but the large icons and labels are easier to see than those tiny ones on the Start menu. With the Programs folder open on the desktop, you can always get to it with one click on the taskbar.

Give your folders a new look

When you first open up a folder, you get great big icons with nice readable labels. My Computer, for example, starts out this way. The default view is fine most of the time, but there are specific instances when you'll want to change the look of one or more folders.

The secret to quickly changing views is to turn on the toolbar in your folder window. Choose <u>V</u>iew, <u>T</u>oolbar, then look for the set of four buttons at the far right edge of the toolbar. (You can also accomplish the same end by using the pull-down <u>V</u>iew menu.)

CAUTION If you've turned your desktop into a work of art, with every icon positioned exactly where you want it, DON'T use any of the Arrange Icons options that pop up when you right-click on the Desktop!

I want to see more icons in each window

 Try the Small Icons view or the List view. They're nearly identical; the only difference is that the Small Icon view arranges everything in rows, from left to right, while the List view arranges things in columns, from top to bottom. Who thinks of these things?

I want to see as much information as possible

 Then you'll want to use the Details view. The advantage here is you can quickly sort a list by clicking on the label at the top of the column.

 TIP In Details view, you can sort by date or size with a single click. Just click on the word Modified to sort by date. Click on Size to reorder the files by size, from smallest to biggest.

I want those big icons back!

 Large icons are easier to see, and their labels are easier to read, too. For windows where you don't have a lot of objects, the Large Icons view is just fine.

Part V: Out of the PC, Onto the Page: Printing and Fonts

16

Printing Perfect Pages

● **In this chapter:**

- I have a new printer—now what?

- Which port should I use?

- How do I know this printer is working right?

- Why printing sometimes takes forever

- Using Windows to share your printer

The whole point of having a computer is to get a printed copy of your work, right? Otherwise, how will non–computer people appreciate you? . . . . **>**

The screen is a great place to create and edit documents, but when it's time to share them with others, you don't want to lug your monitor all over the office. PCs and printers go together like ham and eggs, as long as they're set up correctly. And one of the most important jobs Windows does is to make sure that you can capture your work on paper for other people to see.

It's not a small job, either. With the right software, you can print some pretty complex documents—filled with fancy fonts, eye-grabbing graphics, and all manner of lines and boxes. If your printer and Windows don't have perfect communication, there's no telling what will wind up on the page.

Best of all, you don't have to have your own printer, because Windows lets two or more people share a printer over a network. You might not be able to justify an expensive color printer for one person, but it starts to make a lot more sense when ten people can share it.

Why do I need to worry about printing?

As long as you set up your printer properly and keep it filled with paper and toner, you shouldn't ever have to think about it. But it helps if you have a basic understanding of how Windows works with a printer.

The goal of printing, of course, is to be perfectly **WYSIWYG**—which is pronounced *whizzy-wig* and means What You See Is What You Get. Here's how it works:

After you get your screen looking just right, you tell Windows to print the job. Right away, it looks to see that you have a printer hooked up; then it looks for the driver for that printer.

> ❝ ***Plain English, please!***
>
> This printer isn't a car, so why does it have a driver? Ahem. A driver is a special piece of software that lets your computer talk intelligently with a piece of hardware. In this case the printer driver acts like a PC-to-printer dictionary for Windows. Your PC is filled with drivers; fortunately, you rarely have to think about them. ❞

Inside the Printers folder

All the printer settings are gathered in one folder; to find it, choose <u>S</u>ettings on the Start menu.

*Click here to set up a **new printer**. The icon reminds you that adding a new printer is as easy as tearing a new sheet of paper from a scratch pad.*

*If you've hooked up to a **network printer**, you'll see this cable underneath its icon.*

*You can spot a **shared printer** by the outstretched hand underneath it.*

*Yep, as far as Windows is concerned, the **fax** capabilities in Windows are just like a printer.*

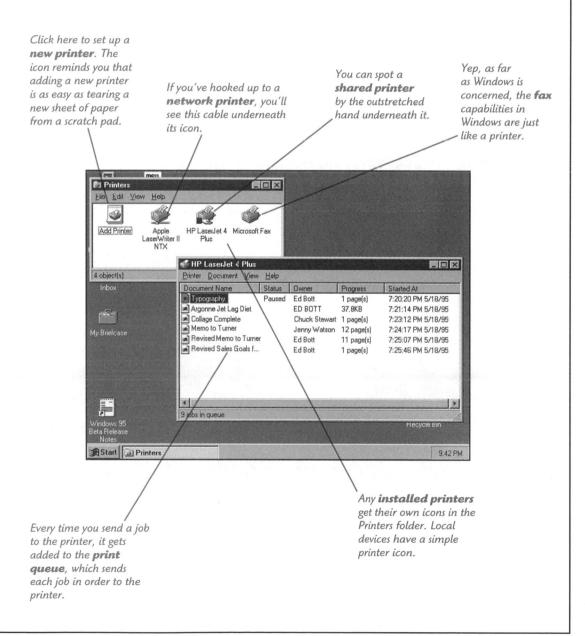

*Every time you send a job to the printer, it gets added to the **print queue**, which sends each job in order to the printer.*

*Any **installed printers** get their own icons in the Printers folder. Local devices have a simple printer icon.*

With the right driver, Windows can tell your printer exactly which fonts to use, where all the graphics go, and just how to draw those lines and boxes. If your printer has any fonts of its own installed, Windows has to decide whether to use those fonts or substitute the ones that are in your document. As it works, Windows creates a full description of the document, one page at a time, in a language your printer can understand.

This all happens very fast, which is good news for your speedy PC, but lousy news for your printer, which actually has a lot of physical work to do while it handles the paper. There's no way the printer can keep up with the PC, so Windows puts the job in a special holding area called a **print queue,** and dribbles it out, a little bit at a time, to the printer.

Installing a new printer

When you set up a new printer, you're really installing special driver software that tells Windows exactly how to turn What You See into What You Get. Fortunately, setting up a new printer ranges from easy to ridiculously easy.

My printer just installed itself

The ridiculously easy way to set up a printer is to make sure you have a Plug and Play printer. In that case, all you have to do is connect the printer cable to your PC and turn on the power to the printer. The next time you start Windows, it will detect the addition of the printer (you'll see a message box like the one in fig. 16.1), and then automatically configure it for you.

Fig. 16.1
If you have a Plug and Play printer like any recent Hewlett-Packard LaserJet, Windows will handle all the details of installing and configuring it.

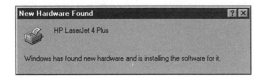

I guess I don't have a Plug and Play printer. Now what?

No Plug and Play? No problem. Use the Add Printer Wizard instead (see fig. 16.2). To get to it, click the Add Printer icon in the Printers folder. Follow the instructions, and pay particular attention to the last step, where you have the chance to do two things on one screen:

- Give the printer a **friendly name**. You can call it Zonker or Big Red, if you like, but it might be more useful to add a descriptive name, like "Apple LaserWriter, Art Dept."

- Tell Windows whether you want to make this the **default printer**. Say yes here, and Windows will automatically send all your print jobs to this printer unless you go out of your way to choose another printer.

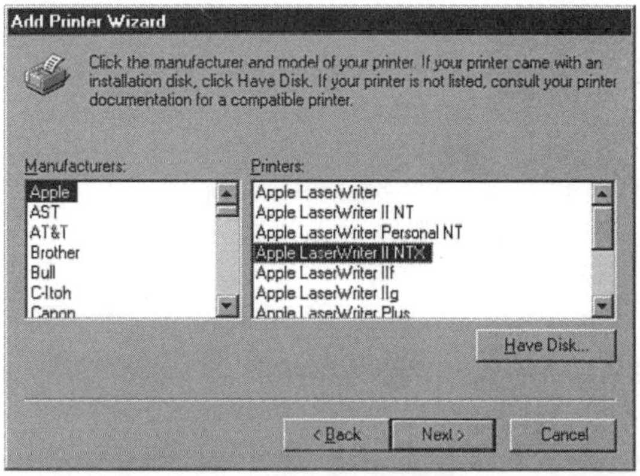

Fig. 16.2

If you don't have a Plug and Play printer, use the Add Printer Wizard to pick your printer's model from this list.

Which port should I use?

A **port** is the socket on the back of your computer where you plug in the cable that goes to your printer. You have your choice of **parallel ports** (or **printer ports**) and **serial ports** (or **communication ports**). Except in very rare cases, the correct choice is a parallel port, usually the one called **LPT1**. Make sure you have the correct printer cable, then connect it securely to the printer and the back of the PC.

TIP   **If you look in the list of ports, you may see Microsoft Fax listed**
as a printer, hooked up to the FAX: port. That's not a mistake. As far as
Windows is concerned, any fax machine is just a special printer, even if it's
halfway around the world. It puts images on paper, just like any printer, and
the telephone line acts just like a ve-e-e-e-e-e-e-ery long version of a
printer cable.

How do I know my printer is installed correctly?

When you first install a new printer, Windows offers to print a test page for
you (see fig. 16.3). Just say yes! This is the best way to make sure that the
printer works correctly. Later, if you have any problems, come here and
print another test page to determine whether the problem is with your
printer or your application.

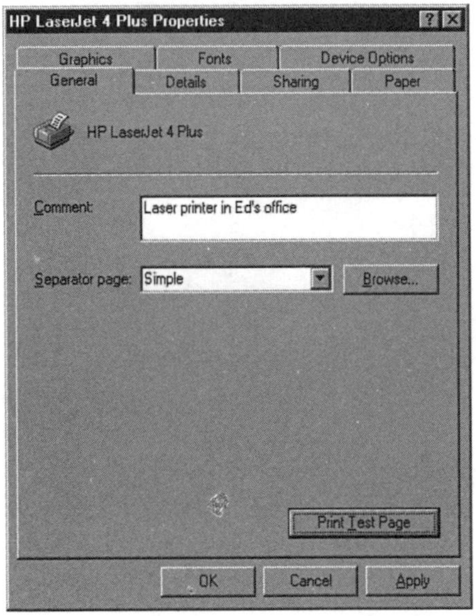

Fig. 16.3
Is your printer hooked
up correctly? To find
out, right-click on its
icon in the Printers
folder, choose
Properties, then click
the Print Test Page
button.

Can my printer do any special tricks?

Hey, this isn't the Late Show with David Letterman. No Stupid Printer
Tricks, please!

But it's true that every printer is different, and you may find that your printer is capable of doing some Smart Printer Tricks. The best way to find out is to right-click on the printer icon and look around. What will you find? Lots of properties, as the dialog box in figure 16.4 shows.

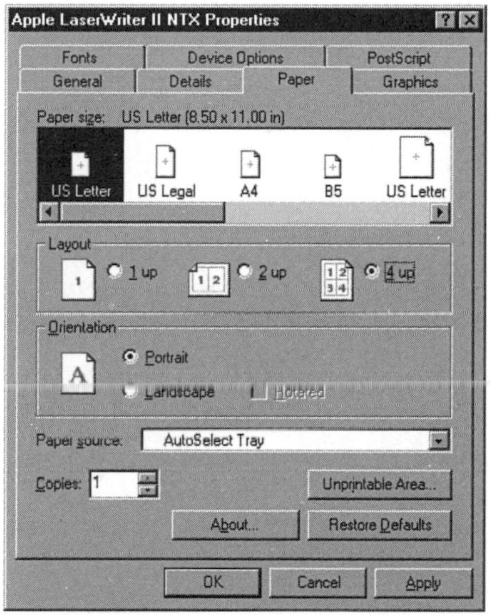

Fig. 16.4

If you have a PostScript printer and 20-20 eyesight, you can cut your paper bill by shrinking long documents so that four pages fit on a single sheet.

You'll find all the routine information about your printer here—its name, port, and location, for example. But, depending on the kind of printer, you may also find some surprises.

- Ignore the technical mumbo-jumbo, like `Aggressive printer memory tracking`. (Are they serious?)

- There's an option to print a special sheet of paper called a **separator page** at the start of each new job, so you don't have to guess who printed what.

- You can shrink the entire page, which lets you put more than one page on each sheet of paper in some cases; with PostScript printers, for example, you can choose 2 up and 4 up printing. (See fig. 16.4.)

- You'll even find **color options** here, if you have a printer that produces color output.

❝ *Plain English, please!*
If you look in the printer properties sheet, you'll see references to the **enhanced metafile format,** sometimes abbreviated as **EMF.** That's the ten-dollar name for the temporary file that Windows creates and then sends to your printer. A very small number of printers can't handle EMFs. **❞**

OK, I'm ready to print!

Eventually, you get everything looking just the way you want it on your screen, complete with fonts and lines and boxes and margins and pie charts and pictures of your vacation. Of course, you want everything to look exactly the same on the paper as it did on the screen. What do you do now?

PostScript or LaserJet?

When you buy a new printer, you can choose from literally thousands of different models. But eventually it all comes down to a single choice: Do you want to use the PostScript language? Or will you be more comfortable with the Hewlett-Packard language?

No, you don't have to actually learn either language to use one of these printers. The Windows printer drivers take care of these translations for you. But there are differences between the two types of printers.

PostScript is the most common language among people who do desktop publishing. If anyone you know uses an Apple Macintosh, chances are it's hooked up to an Apple LaserWriter, the best known PostScript printer. It's not super fast, but a PostScript printer lets you print complex graphics with beautiful results. If you plan to make your own newsletters, this is your choice.

The Hewlett-Packard Page Control Language (PCL) is the way that LaserJets and most ink-jet printers talk to Windows. The graphics aren't as good-looking as the ones that come out of a PostScript printer, but these printers are fast and can handle just about any job you can throw at them.

There's a third standard, too, for old, noisy dot-matrix printers, but these are becoming less common.

Most printers, no matter who manufactured them, use one or both of these languages. If you can't find your printer on the official list of Windows 95 drivers, look at the printer manual and see whether it emulates one of these printers. If it does, you can choose the Apple LaserWriter II NT or the Hewlett-Packard LaserJet III and be very happy with the results.

With most applications, you can just choose File, Print, or click the Print button. When you do, you'll see a dialog box like the one in figure 16.5, taken from WordPad.

Fig. 16.5
Choose File, Print; most applications will show you a dialog box like this one.

Tell Windows which pages you want to print—all? some? just one?

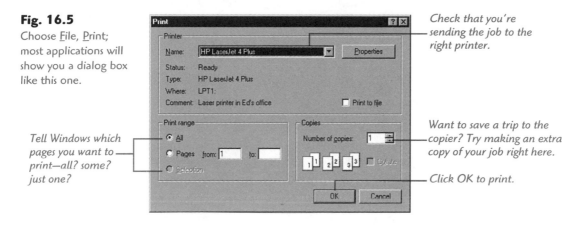

Check that you're sending the job to the right printer.

Want to save a trip to the copier? Try making an extra copy of your job right here.

Click OK to print.

> **TIP** **Many programs offer a Print Preview option. If the program from** which you're trying to print gives you this choice, take advantage of it. You can quickly look at what Windows thinks it's going to send to the printer. If it doesn't look the way you expect it to look, fix the problem before you've wasted paper (and time) printing it out the wrong way.

> **CAUTION** **Old Windows programs don't use the same dialog boxes as new** ones written especially for Windows 95, so with these programs you may not be able to set up your pages and printers completely. If this is the case, you probably need to contact the company that made the program and ask them if they have a new version designed for Windows 95.

What happens when I click the Print button?

When you tell Windows to print (either by choosing a menu item or clicking a button) it starts a complicated process that would make a rocket scientist proud. And something can go wrong at any of these steps.

What Windows Does	What Can Go Wrong	How to Fix It
Matches up fonts. With non-TrueType fonts, you need both a screen font and printer font. Windows uses the screen font to show you how the document will look, and the printer font to print it.	The fonts you see on the screen don't match the ones on the printed pages.	Replace the fonts that aren't printing with TrueType fonts.
Converts graphics on the screen into dot patterns that your printer can print.	Graphics are missing or don't look right.	The printer may need more memory to handle complex graphics. Try printing at a lower resolution.
Looks to see whether you've issued any special instructions, like extra copies or two-sided printing.	You asked for two-sided printing, but nothing happened.	This feature is only available on some printers when a special hardware option is installed.
Sends the job to the print queue at the right speed.	Pages are missing, especially sections with graphics, because the printer can't keep up with the PC.	Check the printer properties and increase the timeout setting so that Windows waits longer for the printer to finish.

66 *Plain English Please!*

A print queue is a line that your print jobs wait in. Your print jobs stack up like 747s waiting to land at O'Hare Airport. When print jobs are coming from every direction, Windows makes like an air traffic controller, and keeps each job in a holding pattern until the printer is ready, then it waves the next job through and lets each job in turn make a safe final approach to the printer. The process of doling out print jobs at just the right speed is called **spooling**. 99

Q&A *My fonts are all messed up. What went wrong?*

You chose a non–TrueType font that isn't available on your printer. (For more information about TrueType fonts, skip to the next chapter.) When that happens, Windows looks around for the next available match and tries to print it. If its best guess isn't good enough for you, choose a new font, preferably one with the TT (TrueType) symbol next to it.

My page came out sideways!

You wanted zig, but Windows set up the printer for zag. It happens, because Windows has two settings for each piece of paper. With standard American 8-1/2 by 11-inch paper, you can print in **portrait** mode (with the long edge going from top to bottom, the way letters typically are printed) or in **landscape** mode, which is what happens when you give that same piece of paper a quarter turn, so the long edge runs from left to right.

Changing orientation between portrait and landscape is easy with new Windows applications (including Paint and WordPad). Just choose File, Page Setup to see a dialog box like the one in figure 16.6. Can't remember which is portrait and which is landscape? Just click the appropriate button and the graphic at the top of the box shifts to give you the answer.

Fig. 16.6
Choose File, Page Setup to pick a new paper type and orientation. The graphic at the top reminds you that landscape is sideways.

Why is this print job taking so long?

When you print to a shared printer, especially a slow one like a color printer, you sometimes have to wait in line while other jobs work their way through the printer. But sometimes delays are caused by hardware problems: the printer might be out of paper, jammed, or just not turned on. (Don't laugh—it happens.) You won't know exactly why your print job is moving like rush hour traffic on an L.A. freeway unless you check your place in the print queue.

Did I say freeway? Actually, the print queue is more like a one-lane highway. When four or five people try to print at once, only one job gets to actually go to the printer. The others have to slow down, line up single file, and wait their turns. If you tell Windows to pause one of the jobs, it's just as if you've put on your emergency brake in the fast lane. Everything comes screeching to a halt until the stalled job gets moving again.

Double-click on the printer icon in the Printers folder and you'll see a list of all the jobs waiting to be printed, including yours (see fig. 16.7).

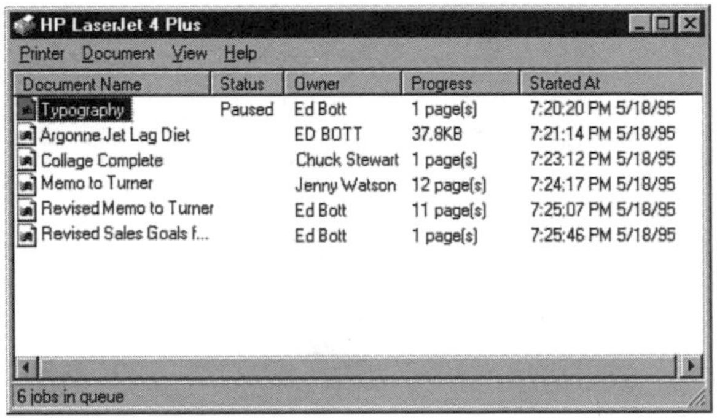

Fig. 16.7

There's a traffic jam here, because the top document is paused.

HP LaserJet 4 Plus				
Document Name	**Status**	**Owner**	**Progress**	**Started At**
Typography	Paused	Ed Bott	1 page(s)	7:20:20 PM 5/18/95
Argonne Jet Lag Diet		ED BOTT	37.8KB	7:21:14 PM 5/18/95
Collage Complete		Chuck Stewart	1 page(s)	7:23:12 PM 5/18/95
Memo to Turner		Jenny Watson	12 page(s)	7:24:17 PM 5/18/95
Revised Memo to Turner		Ed Bott	11 page(s)	7:25:07 PM 5/18/95
Revised Sales Goals f...		Ed Bott	1 page(s)	7:25:46 PM 5/18/95

6 jobs in queue

Here's what you need to know about print queues:

- Windows works its way through the list from top to bottom.

- If there are any problems with the printer, you'll see an informative message in the window's title bar.

- The first column shows the document title and (sometimes) which program printed it.

- To see whether there's a problem with one of the documents, look in the second column to check its status. Out of paper and Paper jam are among the common errors you'll see here.

- The next column shows who sent the job to the printer.

- How far along is this job? Some programs report progress in pages; others use bytes. If you see Now printing page 3 of 457, you can probably guess that it'll be a while before your print job emerges.

- Who was there first? Every job's starting time shows up here.

> **TIP**   **Every time you send a job to the printer, Windows puts a tiny** printer icon into the notification area at the right of the taskbar. To see all the jobs that are waiting in the queue, double-click on this icon.

Oops—I didn't mean to print that!

Sooner or later, it happens to everyone: You send a big job (40 pages? 100? 400?) to the printer, and the instant you finish clicking the Print button, you realize that you left out a paragraph on page 1. You could just let the printer chew through all those pages, then throw everything away and start over. But if you're quick enough, you can jump in right now and stop everything.

You have to be quick, though, because you can only cancel a print job if the job is still in the queue. Open the printer window, select the job, right-click, and choose Cancel Printing from the shortcut menu (see fig. 16.8). If you don't want to kill the job, but just want to stop it temporarily, choose Pause Printing instead.

Fig. 16.8

To kill a print job, open the printer window, select the job, right-click, and choose Cancel.

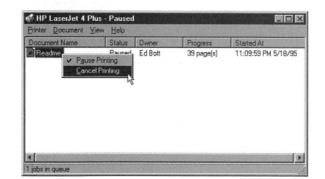

TIP **Want to make sure you can always see where you stand in the line** for the printer? Add the printer icon to your StartUp folder. First, open the Printers folder. Then use the <u>F</u>ind command on the Start menu to search for and open your StartUp folder. Drag the printer icon from the Printers folder into the StartUp folder and restart Windows. Now, every time you start up Windows, the printer window will open automatically. All you have to do is click its taskbar button to look at the queue or cancel a print job.

When you have to share: printing on a network

What makes printing on a network different? Not much, except that you'll probably have to walk down the hall to get your job instead of reaching a few feet away from your desk. If you have a network set up, you can hook up a printer to any PC and share it among everyone on the network. Here's how.

Setting up your system to use a network printer

If there's a printer out there that you want to use, it's easy to get connected. If your network administrator or another Windows user has given you the rights to use the printer, you just need to find its icon, point, and print. Here are step-by-step instructions:

1 Browse through the Network Neighborhood until you find the printer's icon.

2 Select the printer icon, and right-click to pop up the shortcut menu.

3 Choose Install to add the printer driver to your PC, and then follow the Wizard's instructions. Windows may ask you for the Windows 95 disks or CD to finish the installation process.

4 Now, you can print to this printer just as if it were hooked up to your own computer.

Sharing your printer with someone else

Before you can let other people use your printer, you have to agree to share it with them. Here's how:

Click the Start button and choose Settings, Printers to open the Printers folder. Right-click on the printer you want to let other people use, and choose Sharing. You'll see a dialog box like the one in figure 16.9.

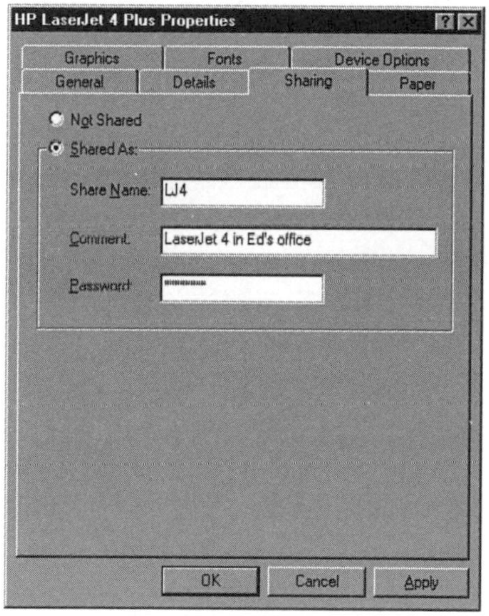

Fig. 16.9
Before you can let others send jobs to your printer, you have to tell Windows it's OK to share it with others. Right-click on the printer's icon and choose Sharing to pop up this dialog box.

HP LaserJet 4 Plus Properties

| Graphics | Fonts | | Device Options |
| General | Details | Sharing | Paper |

○ Not Shared
● Shared As:

Share Name: LJ4

Comment: LaserJet 4 in Ed's office

Password: ********

OK   Cancel   Apply

Q&A *My printer is installed correctly, but I can't find the Sharing command on the shortcut menu. Where did it go?*

You need to add File and Printer Sharing services. Open the Network folder in Control Panel, click the Add button, and choose Service. Click Add again. Highlight Microsoft and choose the File and Print sharing entry that matches your network. Click OK, and follow the instructions. You'll need to restart your computer before the changes will take effect.

- Give the printer a **name**. You'll use this name plus the computer's name to identify it.

- Attach a **comment**, if you like. The right description here can help others figure out exactly where this printer is and what it's used for.

- Enter a **password** here if you don't want Bob in Accounting sending his 200-page spreadsheets to your printer.

Click OK, and Windows adds a little outstretched hand to the bottom of the printer's icon. Now, other people can share your printer, although you can restrict access by only letting a small group have the password.

TIP **If you want your assistant to be able to send jobs to your laser** printer but you really hate the idea of having other people share it, hide it! When Windows asks you to give the share a name, add a dollar sign to the end—**LaserJet4$**, for example. When Windows sees the dollar sign, it knows to hide the printer in the Network Neighborhood on other machines. Anyone who knows the secret name can still hook up to the printer by typing it in, but no one will be able to browse through the network and see it.

How do I tell which print job belongs to me?

You can tell Windows to add a **separator page** every time it starts a new print job. It wastes one sheet of paper for each job you send to the printer, but in a big office it can be the only way to make sure your print jobs don't wind up on someone else's desk by mistake.

TIP **You can only control the option for separator pages if the printer** is attached directly to your computer. If you want Windows to print a special page to help you spot the beginning of each new document you print on a shared printer, you'll have to ask the owner of the PC the printer is hooked up to.

To turn this feature on, right-click on the printer's icon, and look on the General properties tab.

Choose a **Simple** separator for a big, easy-to-read, no-nonsense page that contains the document's name, who sent it, and when it was printed.

A **Full** separator page lets you add a graphic instead, but it doesn't give you any clue who printed the job.

Rushing a print job

There's a special variant of Murphy's Law that applies to shared printers. Let's say you're late for a meeting where you're supposed to present the sales results for the last quarter. You've sent the job to the printer, but it's not coming out. You check the print queue and discover that Bob in Accounting has 27 big jobs stacked up, and it might be hours before they all finish printing.

What do you do? Hey—it's time to cut in line in front of Bob. (Don't worry, he'll probably understand.)

1 Open the Printers folder.

2 Double-click the icon for the printer where your print job is waiting.

3 Select your print job and drag it to the top of the list. Voilà! You're now next in line.

The printer's jammed!

It used to be that troubleshooting a network printer meant walking down the hall to see whether it's jammed. That's still necessary with older printers, but new Plug and Play printers can actually send messages back to your PC (like the one in fig. 16.10). In that case, you can call someone whose office is a little closer to the printer and ask them to fill it with paper.

Fig. 16.10
Some printers, like this HP LaserJet, can actually let you know when they're having problems.

My printer isn't hooked up. What do I do?

Most of the time, you'll want to click the Print button and send your work straight to the nearest laser printer. There are times, though, when you want Windows to print your jobs even though the printer isn't ready right now.

- You might be on an airplane, miles from the nearest printer.

- There could be a problem with your network printer, but you'd like to keep working while it's being repaired.

- Maybe you have a series of long documents to print, and you just don't want to keep getting up to retrieve them from the laser printer.

In any of these cases, you use a feature called **deferred printing** to tell Windows to go ahead and print, but store the jobs in a queue right on your hard disk. Later, when Windows notices that the printer is available, it will offer to print the jobs for you.

How do I turn on deferred printing?

If Windows can't find the printer you specify, it will hold your work in a queue until both you and the printer are ready. How you work this way depends on whether the printer is normally attached to your PC, or whether you connect to it across the network.

- To defer printing to a local printer that is functioning properly, right-click on the printer's icon, and choose Pause Printing.

- To store up print jobs on a notebook PC that's not connected to a printer right now, right-click on the printer's icon, and choose Work Offline. You'll see the printer icon fade away to indicate that you've turned it off temporarily.

OK, I'm back. How do I print these stored jobs?

You shouldn't need to do anything. When Windows senses that the printer is available again, it will usually offer to print and store jobs for you. You'll see a dialog box like the one in figure 16.11.

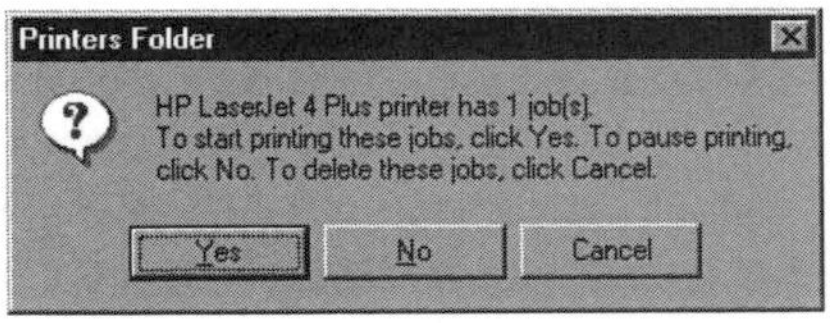

Fig. 16.11

When you get back to the office and reconnect your notebook PC to the network, Windows offers to print any jobs you previously deferred.

Printers Folder

HP LaserJet 4 Plus printer has 1 job(s).
To start printing these jobs, click Yes. To pause printing, click No. To delete these jobs, click Cancel.

[Yes]   [No]   [Cancel]

Of course, you can always force the issue, too, especially if you just decided to defer printing while you churned out a big stack of work. To tell Windows you want to use the printer, just right-click on its icon, and click <u>W</u>ork Offline again. When the check mark disappears, you're back in business.

17

Making Text Stand Out with Fonts

● **In this chapter:**

- ● **Font? Typeface? Point size? What's that all about?**

- ● **You can use fonts to help make text easier to read**

- ● **I bought some new fonts. What do I do now?**

- ● **How do I keep track of which font is which?**

- ● **I need to add special characters to my documents**

Need just the right look for that special document? Windows 95 makes it easy to see which fonts you have to choose from . . . . ▶

Pick up any newspaper or magazine—or, for that matter, this book. Pay no attention to the words for now; instead, just look at the way those words are arranged on the page. You'll see a mixture of large and small letters, big bold headlines and tiny footnotes, maybe even some fancy script that would be right at home on a wedding invitation.

If the designer was on the ball, those words aren't just randomly arranged on the page. Instead, the size and shape and placement of the letters have been carefully chosen to help guide your eye to the most important parts of the page. The big bold headlines signal the start of a new section, while the body of each story is displayed in type that's large enough that you can see it without squinting.

You don't need to be a high-paid designer to perform the same typographic magic with your documents. Windows has all the tools you need to create documents that look like they were done by a desktop publishing genius. Each of those different typographic styles is called a **font**, and once you learn how fonts work, you're ready to put together your own front page.

What is a font, anyway, and why should I care?

Imagine how confusing the world would be if everyone dressed exactly alike. How would you tell the policeman from the butcher or the auto mechanic from the baseball umpire? That's why, over the years, we've come up with uniforms that help us see at a glance what people do for a living. The cop has a blue uniform, the butcher a white smock; the mechanic is dressed in greasy overalls, while the umpire is wearing a chest protector. Underneath all those outfits, of course, they're just people.

The words and letters you use in your documents operate exactly the same way. Letters, numbers, and characters all start as basic shapes—a capital A always looks like a tepee with a crossbar, for example—but you, as the type designer, can blow up a letter or shrink it, dress it in dark colors, or give it a fancy costume.

There's more to a font than just a pretty (type)face

There's plenty of technical jargon in every font, but it doesn't have to be confusing. The **font** is the complete description, including all these attributes.

The **typeface** *is a name that describes the overall shape and detailed features of a set of characters. Times New Roman and Arial are the two most-used typefaces, because they come with Windows.*

Typography - WordPad

File Edit View Insert Format Help

Times New Roman
Arial
Courier New

This is 12 point type

72 points

This is regular.
This is Italic.
This is Bold.
This is Bold Italic.

Serif? Or Sans Serif?

Start | Control Panel | Windows | Typography - WordPad | 7:50 AM

Attributes *(also known as effects) include bold, where each letter is thicker and darker; and italic, where each letter is slanted a bit to the right.*

The **size** *of a font is usually measured in* **points**. *For example, the letters in this paragraph are about 9 point, while a big newspaper headline in 72-point letters would be one inch high.*

Sans serif *typefaces have smooth lines and corners.* **Serif** *typefaces, on the other hand, have little decorations on the corners.*

For a quick illustration of how different typefaces can represent the same shapes, look at the letters in figure 17.1. In every case, you can easily recognize the basic shape, but these examples illustrate the nearly infinite number of ways you can draw those same characters so that they have some personality.

Fig. 17.1

The letters are the same, but the look is completely different. Different fonts can give your words some personality.

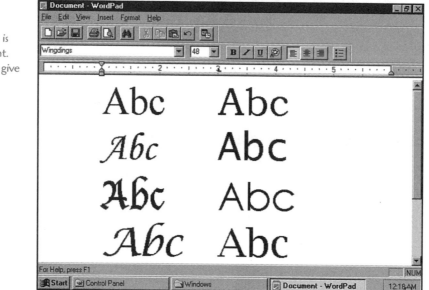

What can I do with fonts?

Every time you press a key—the letter A, let's say—on your computer's keyboard, it sends a message to Windows: "Hey! I'm sending up an *A*—put it on the screen!" The trouble is, because that letter has no uniform, you have no way of telling what it's supposed to do. So before Windows puts it on the screen, it looks for your instructions as to how you want it displayed.

- For a banner headline on a newspaper, you would probably use thick, dark letters with no fancy frills.

- For a wedding invitation, on the other hand, you might choose a script typeface that looks like it was written by hand.

- For the fine print at the bottom of a contract, use the thinnest, smallest type imaginable, so that only lawyers and bald eagles can read it without a magnifying glass.

In all three cases, the basic shapes of the letters are the same—you can tell the difference between a capital A and a small b, right?—but the thickness of the lines, the decorations on the corners of each letter, the slant of the letters, and so on are all different.

How do I tell Windows which font to use?

Most Windows programs that use text let you specify the exact look you want for those words. You can simply make a word a bit bigger, or you can change everything about it, so that it takes on a completely different look. With most applications, you'll find the font choices grouped under a menu call Format.

> ## 66 *Plain English, please!*
>
> **Formatting** is a catch-all word for the way you tell Windows exactly how you want a document to look when it's printed. The name of the font determines one type of formatting; other kinds of formatting define the spaces around and between the words. Is there extra space between lines? How much room do you want for the page margins? 99

To specify a font in WordPad, for example, choose Format, Font. You'll see a dialog box like the one in figure 17.2.

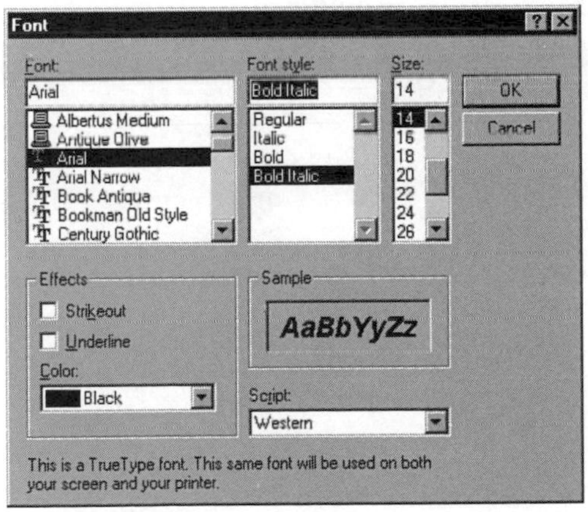

Fig. 17.2
Give your words and letters a little personality by adjusting the formatting of each character. This is how WordPad arranges your Font options.

Q&A *I changed the font formatting, but my document still looks the same. What happened?*

If you chose formatting without having any text selected, you won't see the results until you type some new characters. Windows adds the formatting information at the insertion point, so it affects whatever you type from that point on. If you wanted to format the existing document, go back and try it again, but this time select the text you want to see changed.

What's TrueType?

Johannes Gutenberg (who invented the printing press) would be amazed if he could see what's happened to type since the days he was carving pieces of wood into letters. For the past few years, Windows has included a bit of technological wizardry called **TrueType** that lets anyone work with typography in ways that used to be reserved exclusively for professional typesetters.

Why is TrueType cool? Because What You See on the screen is really What You Get out of the printer. If that doesn't seem like such a big deal, consider the alternative: From Gutenberg's day until as recently as 30 years ago, when you wanted to typeset your company's annual report, you had to pay a printer to pick pieces of hot metal type out of a humongous drawer and arrange them in heavy racks. Every different size, weight, and typeface had its own drawer full of metal.

Now that's a lot of metal, so it's not surprising that most typesetters, even if they had a huge selection of typefaces, only offered a limited

selection of sizes. "You want 24 point? Sorry, we have 18 and 36—pick one."

TrueType gets rid of all that metal and substitutes some mental gymnastics instead. Each typeface is stored in your computer as a set of instructions that Windows uses to draw a letter on the screen. These instructions are completely **scalable**, so they work at every size from 4 points to 128 points. When you ask for 24 point Times New Roman, Windows first reads the instructions for putting that letter on the screen. Then it gets out its internal calculator and figures out how big to make each line and serif on each letter.

TrueType fonts can scale up to humongously big sizes without using up extra space on your hard disk. They can be rotated at any angle, so you can do clever typographic tricks for logos and things. And best of all, they work on any printer that works with Windows, so you can be certain that what will come out of the printer will be what you expect.

To give your text a makeover, follow these steps. (Make sure you have some text selected first!)

1 Choose a typeface (WordPad calls this the font). In this example, you get a handy preview area that shows you what the typeface looks like.

2 Pick an attribute (WordPad calls them **styles**). Some typefaces offer four or more styles, while others give you only two to choose from.

3 Set the size. As a rule of thumb, 10 or 12 points is appropriate for body text, while headlines can be as big as Windows will allow you to make them.

4 If you want any special effects attached to the text, like strikeout or underline formatting, this is the place to check. It's also where you can specify a color. (Please, no lime green on fluorescent pink!)

5 Ignore the Script box unless you're using a special keyboard designed to produce foreign characters.

Which fonts do I get with Windows 95?

Windows is incredibly stingy with fonts. When you first install Windows, you get just a handful of fonts. The TrueType fonts include Arial, Times New Roman, and Courier New (which looks like an old-fashioned typewriter). You also get a couple of useful fonts that include interesting and sometimes strange characters that you can use in headlines, or as bullets for the beginning of each item in a list. The Symbol font includes a few boring examples, but the font called WingDings has the best little surprises of all (see fig. 17.3).

You can simply switch to the WingDings font, start typing, and see what you get. But the faster way, as we'll see shortly, is to use the built-in Windows Character Map applet instead.

Fig. 17.3
When you choose the WingDings font and start typing, your letters turn into these strange and interesting symbols instead.

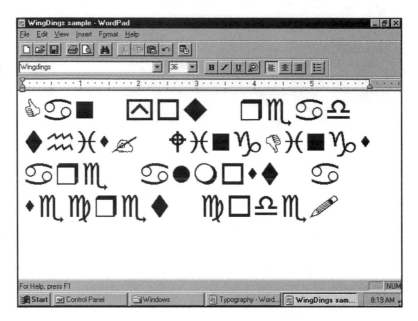

What are those other fonts? And why do they look so ugly at 23 points?

When you look in the Fonts folder, you'll see two different types of icons. One has a blue and gray TT for a label. The other has a big red A for an icon.

It's easy to figure out that the ones with TT on the label are TrueType fonts. The others are called **raster** fonts. What's the difference? Let's try blowing up a few letters from each and see what happens (see fig. 17.4).

Yuck. The problem with the raster fonts is that they're not scalable the way TrueType fonts are. Instead, they're specifically designed to look good on the screen at a small number of sizes.

Think of how a photograph works and you'll see the difference. TrueType fonts work like a photographic negative. When you ask Windows to blow up a TrueType font, it goes back to the original, and creates a new image just for that size. All the features are crisp and clear. When you blow up a raster font, though, it's like enlarging a photograph from a newspaper. As it gets larger, you begin seeing the dots instead of the picture.

Fig. 17.4
TrueType fonts (top) keep their nice, smooth edges as they get larger. Raster fonts (bottom) look great at some sizes, but get downright ugly when they're blown up.

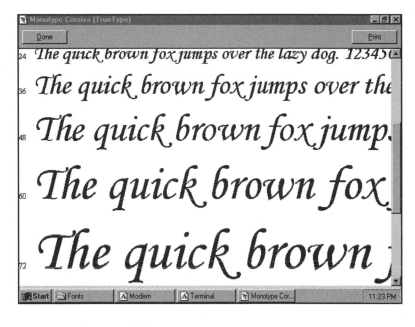

Windows includes five raster fonts: Courier, MS Sans Serif, MS Serif, Small, and Symbol. These raster fonts are useful because they work quickly and look good on-screen. But they won't necessarily look good when they come out of the printer, especially when you use them at sizes other than what they're designed for.

TIP   **You can tell Windows that you don't want to see those ugly raster** fonts anymore. In the Control Panel, open the Fonts folder and choose <u>V</u>iew, <u>O</u>ptions. On the last tab, there's a check box that tells Windows to show you only TrueType fonts.

Font management

The best part about the way Windows works with fonts is that you don't really need to think about them unless you want to. Windows does the work of managing fonts, and whenever you use a Windows program, you automatically have access to all those fonts.

In fact, the only time you need to open the Fonts folder is when you want to add a new font, remove one, or figure out just what the heck that font looks like anyway.

How do I add a new font?

Some Windows programs automatically add new fonts to your system as part of their installation. You can also buy fonts or download them from online collections like the ones on CompuServe or The Microsoft Network. When you have a new font (or a bunch of them), and you want to start using them in Windows, here's what to do:

1 Open the Control Panel and double-click on the Fonts icon to open the Fonts folder.

2 Choose <u>F</u>ile, <u>I</u>nstall New Font. You'll see the dialog box shown in figure 17.5.

Fig. 17.5
When you open the Fonts folder and choose <u>F</u>ile, <u>I</u>nstall New Font, you'll see this dialog box.

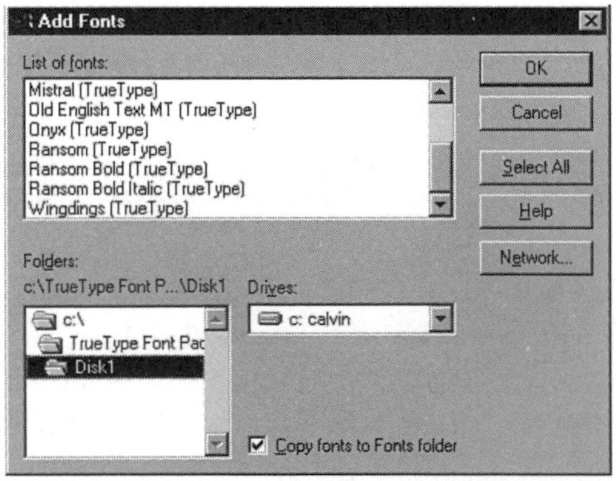

3 Browse through drives and folders until you find the one that contains the fonts you want to add. If the new fonts came on a floppy disk, for example, select A: here.

4 Select the fonts you want to add from the list of fonts. (If you have a disk full of fonts, save time by clicking the Select All button.)

5 Make sure to check the box labeled Copy fonts to Fonts folder. That way, Windows will let you use those fonts next time you need them.

6 Click OK. Your hard drive will whir for a while, and when it's done your new fonts are installed.

TIP **There used to be a limit to the number of fonts you could install** under Windows. No more. Now, as long as you have room on your hard disk, you can have a thousand fonts or more. Of course, you might have trouble keeping track of them all, but that's a different story...

I wonder what *that* font looks like?

OK, so you've installed a few hundred fonts, and now you're working on a new WordPad document. You know the typeface you want is out there, but you can't remember whether it's Marlett or Algerian or Braggadocio Bold. How can you pick the right one?

Well, if your application offers a preview window like the one in WordPad, it's easy: Just pick the font name in the dialog box, and you can see a small sample of the typeface. If your application isn't so considerate, or you want to see a larger preview, try looking at the entire font.

In the Control Panel, open the Fonts folder and double-click on the font you're curious about. You'll see a box like the one in figure 17.6.

You get all sorts of interesting information when you open a font this way:

- Who made the font?
- What does each letter look like?
- How does this font look at different sizes?

Fig. 17.6
Double–click on a font icon for a detailed preview of what it looks like at a variety of sizes.

To see what this font looks like on paper, just click the Print button and Windows will send a detailed type sample to your printer.

To close the dialog box and get back to work, click the Done button.

That's *almost* the right font...

What happens if you know the right font is there, but you can't remember its name? If you can find a font that's close to the one you want, Windows will find other fonts that are similar in characteristics.

To track down a font this way, open the Fonts folder and right-click on an empty space in the window. From the popup menu, choose View, List Fonts by Similarity. This looks a little like the Details view you'll see in other folders, but this window's a little different, as figure 17.7 shows.

To use this view, simply choose the font you want to match in the list box at the top of the window. When you do, Windows will instantly re-sort the fonts in your list, and tell you whether they're very similar, fairly similar, or not similar at all. Double-click on the entries at the top of the list to see if you've found the right one.

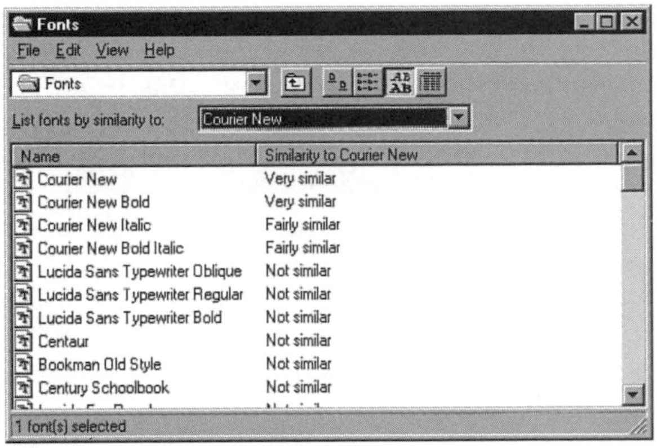

Fig. 17.7
Can't find that font? If
you can find one that's
close to what you
want, Windows will sort
the rest of your fonts
by similarity.

I want to use a special character

There's more to life than letters and numbers. If you want to use one of those fancy WingDings characters to insert a Flying Fickle Finger of Fate before every important paragraph in your report, you have two choices.

The hard way is to memorize the secret Windows code for that character. For the finger WingDing, you can simply choose the WingDings font and type a capital **F**. That's fine if you want to memorize that detail. But you don't need to.

The easy way is to use the Windows Character Map applet. If you installed this program, you'll find it on the Start menu under Accessories. When you fire it up, you'll see a window like the one in figure 17.8.

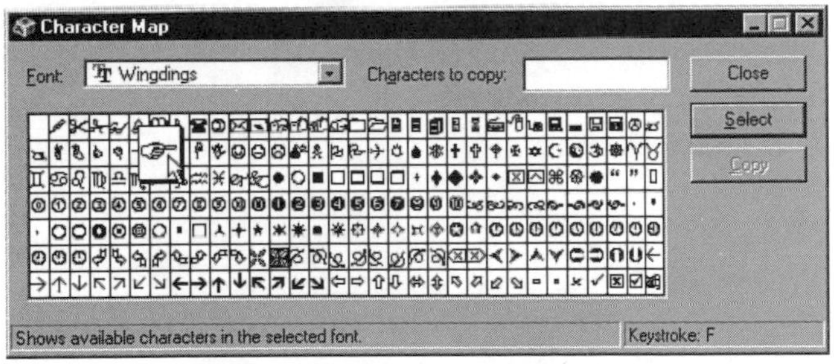

Fig. 17.8
The Character Map
window.

TIP **If the Character Map applet isn't available on your menu,** you'll have to install it from the original Windows disks. Open Control Panel, choose Add/Remove Programs, and use the Windows Setup program to add this accessory.

The Character Map accessory is fairly easy to use.

1 Pick the typeface you want to use from the list box at the top. In this case, we'll choose WingDings.

2 Pick a character from the following list. Can't see those tiny characters? Point to any one of them, click the left mouse button, and hold it down as you slide the pointer across.

3 When you find the character you like, double-click to add it to the Characters to copy box at the top right. Continue adding as many characters as you like.

4 Click the Copy button to copy your selected characters to the Windows Clipboard.

5 Click Close to return to your application, and use the Paste command to insert the characters into your document.

I have too many fonts!

Confused by all those fonts? Get rid of some. Deleting a font is as easy as right-clicking and choosing Delete.

CAUTION It's OK to delete fonts you've added, but don't delete any of the raster fonts that come with your system, like MS Sans Serif and MS Serif. All sorts of programs depend on them. Likewise, don't delete the Times New Roman, Arial, or Courier TrueType fonts.

Using fonts the smart way

Design experts have a clever phrase for documents that use too many fonts. That's called **ransom-note typography**, because the results look like what kidnappers produce when they chop letters out of a newspaper and paste them on the page.

It's not hard to avoid ransom-note typography. Just follow these simple rules:

- Try not to use more than four fonts on a page. If you do, your readers will get confused.

- Pick a serif face for headlines and a sans serif face for body type, or vice versa. The contrast helps readers easily see which is which.

- Use a simple typeface for body text. Intricate fonts are harder to read, especially at small sizes.

- Make sure there's a noticeable difference between different levels of information. If your headlines are 18 points and the subheads are 14 point, readers might not notice the distinction. Try 24 point and 14 point instead.

- If you really want to produce a ransom note, look for a Microsoft TrueType font called Ransom, which actually produces the silly look you're trying to avoid. It's fun for invitations and notes with friends, although you won't want to use it for a memo to the boss.

Part VI: Lights, Camera, Action: Multimedia and More Fun

18

The Amazing, Talking, Singing, Exploding PC

● In this chapter:

- *Multimedia?* What is it, anyway?

- How to coax sound out of your PC

- Adding sound to your startup (and other system events)

- This thing is too loud!

- Use the Windows sounds—or record your own

- What about video?

The personal computer may have started life in a gray flannel suit, but it can do more than crunch numbers and fiddle with fonts. . . . . ●

I f your computer has the right hardware, it can handle just about anything your senses can recognize—from simple sound bites to CD- quality songs, from full-size, symphony-style orchestrations to full-motion Hollywood-style video.

If you ever tried to get a multimedia game or CD-ROM to work with the previous version of Windows, you're probably still recovering from the experience. Coaxing sound and video out of a PC running Windows 3.1 was a hit-or-miss experience, and keeping everything running wasn't all that much fun, either.

Fortunately, Windows 95 is much better than its predecessor at handling demanding jobs like playing sound and video clips. In fact, if your multimedia PC is relatively new, chances are that your most pressing multimedia challenge will be figuring out how to turn down the volume.

What is multimedia, anyway?

That's a good question.... The funny thing about multimedia is that no two people can agree on exactly what it is. But most of us know it when we see or hear it. Generally, here's what you can expect to find when talk turns to **multimedia**:

- **Digital audio**—play back CD-quality sound, and even record your own.

- **Full-motion video**—not as sharp as what you're used to seeing on your TV, but good enough for even some demanding applications.

- **Hypermedia links**, like those found on the Internet's World Wide Web, where you click on buttons, pictures, and other "hot spots" to make multimedia events happen.

- Software to keep sound and pictures properly synchronized.

- More software to let you *edit* multimedia data files—snipping the relevant 10 seconds out of a 2-minute sound clip, for example.

TIP **Data files for some of these multimedia types are huge.**
A 10-second sound clip, for example, might take up a healthy 100K of disk space, while a single four-minute music video file could consume more than 40 megabytes of disk space! That's why CD-ROMs (which can hold more than 600M) are so widely used for multimedia software.

Setting up a sound card

If you're lucky, your PC left the factory with its own sound card, and you never had to wrestle to snap it into a slot inside the PC. But upgrading your old PC for multimedia is no longer an exercise in torture.

 TIP **For step-by-step details on how to add a new piece of hardware,** like a sound card, see Chapter 3.

Squeezing speech and melodies out of a sound card is a four-step process.

Step 1: plug in the card

If you're queasy about the prospect of taking the cover off your computer, stop right here. If that's the way you feel, turn the computer over to an upgrade expert.

CAUTION **There's enough voltage inside your PC to knock you out cold—** or worse. So never, ever try to replace or repair anything inside your PC unless you've turned off the power first.

Step 2: introduce the card to Windows

This should happen automatically with a Plug and Play sound card. With others, you may need to tell Windows to go looking for the new device. Either way, you'll need a disk from the sound card's manufacturer if you don't see the name of the card in the Windows Add New Hardware Wizard list.

Step 3: set everything up

 Add a volume control to the taskbar if you wish; otherwise there are very few options. Double-click on the Multimedia icon in the Windows Control Panel to pop up the full set of controls, as shown in figure 18.1. For example, this is the place to tell Windows how you prefer to record sounds. Radio Quality doesn't sound as good as CD Quality, but the files are much smaller. You'll have to balance the sensitivity of your ears against the free space on your hard disk to decide which setting is right for you.

Step 4: begin annoying everyone within earshot

You'll find plenty of sample sounds and videos in the Media folder (but only if you have the CD-ROM version of Windows). Many of them are associated with particular sets of system sounds, but there are a few surprises (including a small collection of Beethoven and Mozart tunes) if you look deeply enough.

Using sound

With a sound card and a pair of speakers, you can make a mighty racket. And there are two different forms that Windows sounds can take. Before you start clicking, though, let's explain the difference between the competing sound standards.

- **Wave-form audio sounds** are simple recordings, just like the ones you make on a portable cassette player. If you hold a microphone up to the TV speaker when the Simpsons are on TV, for example, you can record a file that consists of Homer saying "Doh!" Wave files typically have the extension .WAV.

- **MIDI sequences**, on the other hand, behave more like sheet music than cassette tapes. Where a wave file always sounds the same when you play it back, a MIDI file will play back differently, depending on which instruments are in your MIDI "orchestra." (By the way, you pronounce MIDI this way: *mid-ee*.) Typically, MIDI files carry the .MID extension.

66 *Plain English, please!*

MIDI? WAV? Excuse me? **MIDI** is an acronym that stands for **Musical Instrument Digital Interface**. The name comes from the digital definitions of different "instruments" in a MIDI orchestra. **Wave-form audio**, on the other hand, is simply a descriptive name for the file format. 99

MIDI files are much more compact than wave files, typically compressing down by as much as 30 times. But wave files sound better. In most applications, you'll find MIDI used for background music, while wave files are used for speech and vocal music. And as you probably guessed, you can find a wealth of extra information about audio files by right-clicking and poking around in the Properties sheets, as in figure 18.2.

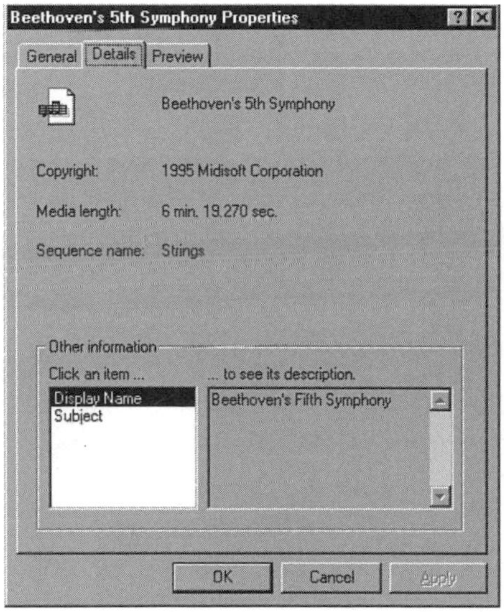

Fig. 18.2

What's in that MIDI file? Just right-click to see all the details. The properties sheet even contains a Preview tab from which you can play a media file without running Media Player.

So what can I *do* with these sounds?

You can embed sound clips in mail and in reports, but the most common use of sound clips today is to make your computer beep and tweet in clever, distinctive ways. Windows lets you control this process by associating sound files with distinctive Windows events. There are dozens of Windows events that you can embellish with sounds. Here are some suggestions:

System Event	Sound
Start Windows	Robin Williams bellowing, "Good morning, Vietnam!!!!"
Empty Recycle Bin	*Star Trek* transporter room noises
Program Error	HAL (the psycho computer in *2001: A Space Odyssey*) saying, "I'm sorry, Dave. I'm afraid I can't do that."
Exit Windows	Arnold Schwarzenegger snarling, "I'll be back!"

TIP **A sound clip is just another data file, so it's easy to send it to** someone else. Just open a folder window containing the sound file, and drag it into a document or a mail message. As long as the recipient has a sound card, he or she can simply double-click the embedded sound icon to hear your message.

Using the Sounds icon in Control Panel, you can tell Windows you want it to play your favorite *Star Trek* sound every time a window opens. If you can find the clip, Windows can make the association. Here's how it works:

1 Double-click on the Control Panel Sounds icon to see the dialog box shown in figure 18.3.

2 On this computer, Windows plays something called The Microsoft Sound every time it starts up.

3 Not sure what you'll hear when you play that file? Click the VCR-style Play button in the Preview box to quickly listen.

4 To change the sound, just pick a different file from the drop-down list (the topmost entry is None). Use the Browse button to search other folders for interesting sound clips.

5 Click OK to apply the new sound to your desktop.

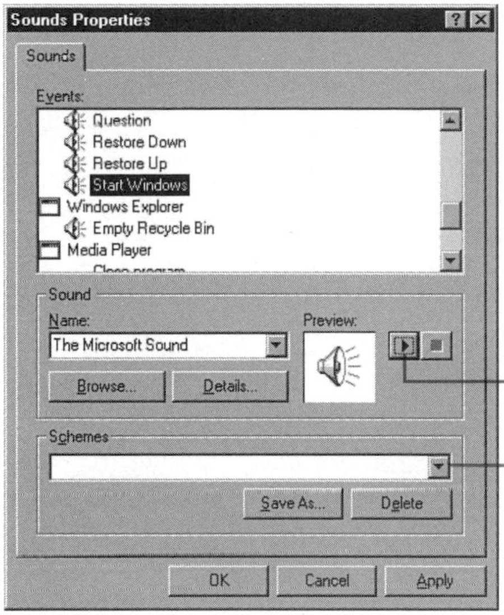

Fig. 18.3
Match the sound with the Windows event to personalize your working environment.

Click here to play the selected sound

Click here to display a different sound scheme

CAUTION **Sounds can drive you crazy! It may seem hip right now to have** Homer Simpson saying "Doh!" every time you see a dialog box, but how funny will it sound the 1000th time? Really, a few sounds go a long way.

Like that mix of sounds? Save them!

In the bottom of the Sounds dialog box, you may have noticed a section called Schemes. Windows includes a handful of ready-made **sound schemes**, loosely organized around themes like Robots and the Jungle. But you can make your own just as easily. Let's say you've finished tinkering with the sounds. Maybe you've downloaded a few megabytes of clips from your favorite movies. You've matched the sounds you want to hear more often with your favorite system events. How do you save it?

Simple. Just open the Sounds dialog box, click Save As, then type the name under which you want to save your killer sounds.

 TIP **You can remove or change sounds for a single event in a scheme** you like.... I've done that with the Utopia theme, in which I like almost all the system sounds except the whoosh that blasts out of the speakers every time a menu pulls down. After attaching No Sound to the menu pull-down event, I like the results much more.

Hey, turn it down!

When the guy in the next cubicle begins to complain, it's time to adjust the volume control. On most PCs with modern sound cards, you'll have a Volume Control icon (a tiny speaker) on the right side of the taskbar, in the notification area. To use this volume control, point at the icon and click.

In fact, this simple volume control offers one of Windows' best multimedia features—an instant mute button. To shut off all sounds in a flash, click on the taskbar volume control, then check the Mute button, as shown in figure 18.4.

Fig. 18.4

Just like the mute button on your TV, this option lets you answer the telephone and actually hear what the caller is saying.

Windows also has a more sophisticated volume control that you can access by simply double-clicking on the taskbar icon for the volume control. With the help of this applet, you can adjust the sound for every different kind of incoming and outgoing data type! (See fig. 18.5 for this small wonder.)

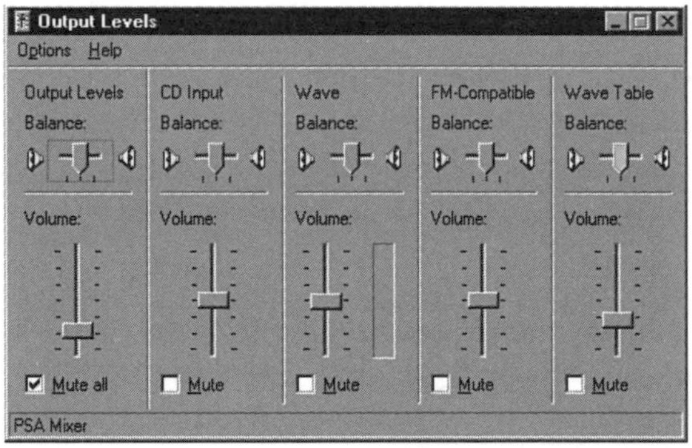

Fig. 18.5

I like my CDs and wave files to be just right: not too loud, not too soft. If your tastes run differently, adjust the volume controls accordingly.

What to do with all those multimedia files

Assuming you upgraded to Windows 95 with the CD-ROM version, you should have an entire folder full of sound and video files. (Look in the Windows folder for another folder called Media, and use the Start menu

Find, Files or Folders command to search for Wave Sounds, Video Clips, and other fun multimedia files.)

By default, Windows associates those files with its own all-purpose playback device called Media Player. To find it, follow the cascading menus from the Start menu through Programs and Accessories, ending up in the Multimedia folder. This simple applet may look like a 98-pound weakling, but it can kick sand in the face of multimedia applications twice its size and weight.

What does Media Player do?

It provides a **common interface** for all sorts of media files, including sound and video.

Properties and options change to match the type of file. For example, you can tell Windows to let video clips take over the entire screen when they play, or you can specify that they run in a small window instead.

It lets you **cut-and-paste** data to and from any application that supports Object Linking and Embedding (OLE). Is that important? Mark my words: Within two years you'll be storing voice clips inside mail messages on your computer, and you won't be able to tell where voice mail ends and e-mail begins!

The Media Player uses controls that are remarkably like those found on your CD player or VCR at home. Table 18.1 shows the buttons in the Media Player window; see figure 18.6 and follow along.

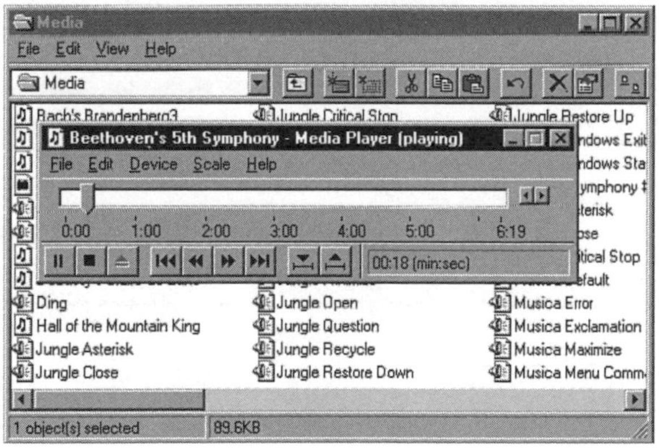

Fig. 18.6

Want to play a snippet of sound or a video clip? Use Windows' built-in Media Player, which changes personality to match the data you feed it.

Table 18.1   Media Player Buttons

What the Button Looks Like	What It Does
▶	**Play** starts a clip. (If you double-click on a media file, however, it begins playing instantly.)
❙❙	**Pause** temporarily stops playing. (When you click the Play button, it changes to Pause. When you click Pause, it changes back to Play.)
■	**Stop** instantly shuts down the media file you're playing.
▲	**Eject** applies to CDs only, physically ejecting the CD on drives that allow this command.
❙◀◀	**Previous Mark** skips back to a spot you marked previously.
◀◀	**Rewind** lets you move backward through a video or sound clip.
▶▶	Click the **Fast Forward** button to jump ahead a few seconds. You can also drag the slider to rewind or fast forward the clip visually.
▶▶❙	**Next Mark** jumps ahead to the next spot you've selected.
▼	**Start Selection** puts a "begin here" mark in the current file.
▲	**End Selection** tells Windows where your selection ends. Once you've marked a beginning and an end, you can copy the selected area to the Windows Clipboard and paste it into a new file.
[slider 0:00 1:00 2:00 3:00 4:00 5:00 6:18]	The **scale** lets you quickly move around in a lengthy media clip by simply dragging the slider control.

Play it again, Sam!

You want to reuse a media file? No problem. Choose Edit, Options, and you can automatically rewind a clip when it reaches the end; that way, all you have to do is push the Play button. Or, in the same Options dialog box (shown in fig. 18.7), check the Auto Repeat box to make sure the background music continues to play until you say, "Enough already!"

Fig. 18.7

Want to have a continuous sound or video background for your next electronic slide show? Open a MIDI sequence file or video clip and check the Auto Repeat box.

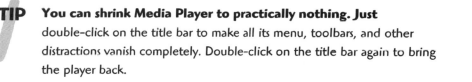

> **TIP** **You can shrink Media Player to practically nothing. Just** double-click on the title bar to make all its menu, toolbars, and other distractions vanish completely. Double-click on the title bar again to bring the player back.

Recording your own sounds with Sound Recorder

Most modern sound cards include a microphone and a jack on the back of the card, so that you can record your own voice memos or interesting sounds. To take advantage of this technology, follow the Start menu through Programs and Accessories to the Multimedia folder; you'll find the Sound Recorder applet there (it's illustrated in fig. 18.8).

Recording a sound couldn't be simpler:

1 Open the Sound Recorder applet.

2 Click the red, round Record button to start recording. You'll get a chance to give your recording a meaningful name later.

3 Click the Stop button when you've said your piece.

4 Use the Effects menu to tinker with the quality of the sound.

5 Click OK when you're satisfied with the new sound.

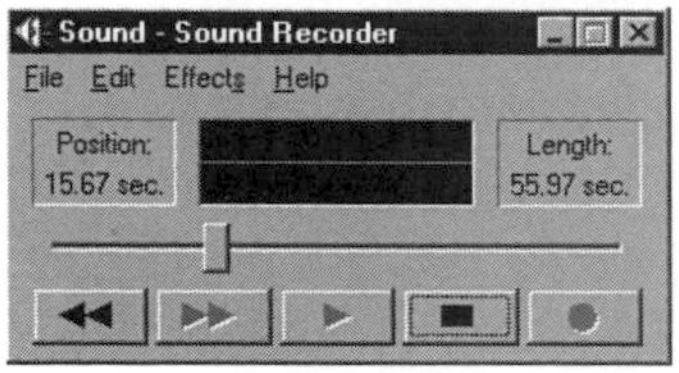

Fig. 18.8
Record your own
sounds and use them in
other documents. All
you need is a sound
card and a micro-
phone, plus this mini-
program.

Q&A *My sounds don't sound right. Most are tinny, and some won't play at all.*

You probably have an old 8-bit sound card. That's an older low-end card that handles some (but not all) sound files. It might be time to think about getting a new 16-bit sound card—or better yet, a Plug and Play card.

Video for Windows

A lot of video clips get played automatically as part of a program. Microsoft's nifty encyclopedia, *Encarta 95*, for example (shown in fig. 18.9), has dozens of video clips and sound files. You don't need to use Media Player in those cases. Instead, the program does the work.

Fig. 18.9
Most of the video clips
you'll find will be on
CD-ROMs like this
one, Microsoft's award-
winning *Encarta*
encyclopedia.

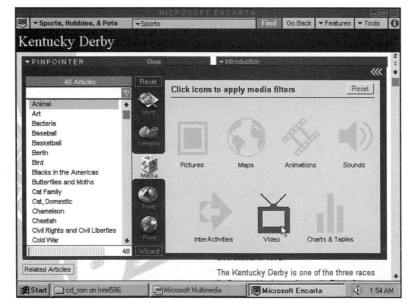

But what do you do when you just want to look at a video file? For Microsoft Video for Windows files (they have the extension .AVI) Media Player is perfect. For starters, choose Device, Properties to tell Windows whether you want the video to stretch to fit the entire screen, or whether you can settle for a small window (see fig. 18.10). You'll get a sharper picture in a smaller window, but you may choose to settle for some fuzziness so that people standing a few feet away can see the clip more easily.

Fig. 18.10

You probably won't be happy viewing most video clips at full-screen resolution. To make the image larger, try moving up a little at a time.

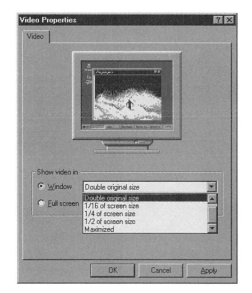

There's an amazing amount of technobabble associated with multimedia. Behind the scenes, Windows has to deal with codecs, for example, which are compression-decompression routines that take those enormous video files and make them a little less huge. There are frame rates and sampling rates and audio formats and...well, you get the idea.

Most of the time, you'll find video clips on CD-ROMs (try browsing through the Windows 95 CD, for example, to see which videos are included). You may find that some CD-ROMs don't use Media Player; instead, they depend on a different application to play back video. The most popular is Apple's QuickTime for Windows. You won't find it listed in the Windows Help files, but the basic principles for this player (and others like it) are the same.

Q&A *Why does this video look so jerky?*

You don't have enough hardware. Video is incredibly demanding, hardware-wise. If you don't have a fast CD-ROM and a Pentium, you can expect to see some problems with your video. What kind? Dropped frames, jerky motion, sound that doesn't keep up with the picture. There's no real cure, unfortunately, short of getting a new PC.

19

Mobile Computing: Taking Your Show On the Road

● In this chapter:

- **What are these PC Card slots for?**

- **He's dead, Jim—monitoring your notebook battery's vital signs**

- **How to dock your notebook**

- **Use the Briefcase to keep files in sync**

Planning to run Windows on a portable PC? You'll have to learn a few special techniques—things don't always work the way you expect. . . . . ❯

U nlike desktop PCs, notebook computers are not all the same. Notebook PCs are more like snowflakes (no two notebooks are exactly alike). Besides the obvious differences in size and shape, there are subtle differences in the way the keyboard is laid out, how the mouse works, and what happens when you start running on batteries instead of AC power.

Because notebook computers are so different, it's impossible to offer too much specific advice for making them work properly. But there are four areas where you'll find specific features of Windows 95 that were devised exclusively for notebook use.

 TIP **One of the four Windows setup options is designed especially for** portable computers. If you have a notebook, make sure you choose this option when you set up Windows, so that all the right files are copied to your notebook. And if you didn't (because you didn't know then what you know now)? Find those Windows disks and run Setup again. Windows is smart enough to add just the pieces you need.

Making sense of your PC Card slots

The engineers who design portable computers go to a lot of trouble to make them as small and light as possible. So it's no surprise that inside a notebook PC, actual physical space is a rare and precious commodity. On your desktop computer, you can add all sorts of useful devices by plugging them into add-in slots. Notebooks use add-in slots, too, but they're considerably smaller, and they work differently.

These slots go by two names—**PCMCIA** (the old name) and **PC Card** (the newer version). Your notebook computer probably has at least one and maybe two PC Card slots, usually located on one or both sides. The PC Cards themselves are about the size of a credit card, and come in varying thicknesses. In all cases, they're designed to be small enough to fit in a shirt pocket.

> **⁶⁶ *Plain English, please!***
>
> PCMCIA (to pronounce it, just rattle off the letters, one after another) originally stood for the industry association that developed the PC Card standard, the **Personal Computer Memory Card Interface Association**. But anyone who had to remember this tongue-twister knows what it must *really* stand for: *People Can't Memorize Computer Industry Acronyms...* **⁹⁹**

What kind of devices can be packed onto a PC Card? You name it. I've seen modems (the most popular choice by far), network interface cards, and hard drives ranging up to 300M in size. There are connectors for portable CD-ROM drives, sound cards that hook into external speakers, and even digital cameras that let your $3000 computer do what a $300 camera can do.

Here's what you need to know about PC Cards.

- Like many kinds of hardware in Windows, *they need software drivers.* **To check that your PC Card driver is properly installed,** right-click on My Computer and choose Properties. Click on the Performance page, and you'll see a screen like the one in figure 19.1. If Windows says that a 32-bit PC Card driver is installed, you're in business. If not, your notebook computer is running more slowly than it should—it's time to call the manufacturers and ask them when their Windows 95 drivers will be ready.

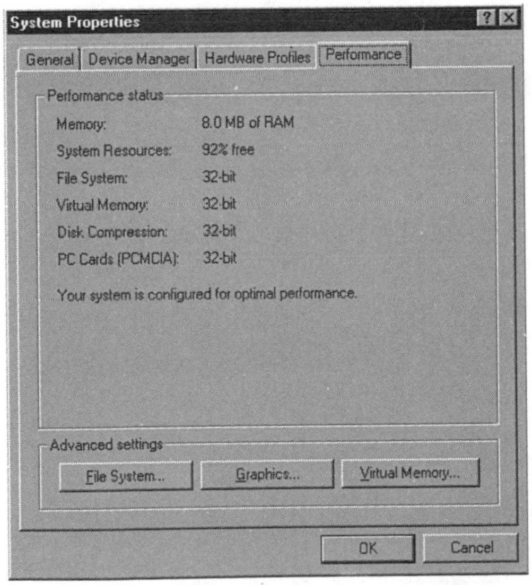

Fig. 19.1

Burrow under the My Computer icon to see whether your notebook PC's PC Card driver is correctly installed. (On this notebook, everything's just fine.)

- **To use a PC Card**, just insert it firmly into the slot. (You may also need to fuss with specialized cables if you're using a device like a modem or network adapter.) Windows uses the Plug and Play features to detect that you've added a new device, and the installation process is automatic.

- **To remove a PC Card,** you first have to tell Windows you're planning to remove it. Why? Because some programs may depend on that card, and it's Windows' job to notify them in advance before you slice the lifeline. To give Windows proper notice, use the PC Card icon on the taskbar. Double-click to pop up a full-sized window (like the one in fig. 19.2), which lets you adjust all the settings for each device, or just click on the icon to pop up a quick list of cards that can be removed (see fig. 19.3).

Fig. 19.2
Double-click for a full-sized window, complete with options, or...

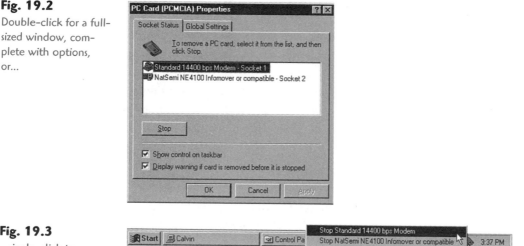

Fig. 19.3
...single-click to pop up a shortcut menu.

How long will this battery last?

On your desktop PC, you rarely think about power, but it's a huge issue with notebook PCs. When you're flying from Los Angeles to New York, and you absolutely, positively must have your work finished by the time the plane touches down, you'll want Windows' help to squeeze every last ounce of life from your notebook's internal batteries.

Every notebook maker gives you its own power-management utilities, usually found under a Power icon in the Windows Control Panel. Once you've set all the options to the ones you like, you'll want to keep an eye on your battery gauge, just as you keep an eye on your car's fuel gauge. Once again, the trick is to look on the notification area at the right side of the taskbar.

When your notebook is plugged in, you'll see an icon that looks like a power plug there. Pull the plug, and the icon changes to a battery with gauge. How can you tell how much juice is left? Two ways:

- The easy way is to simply let the mouse pointer sit over the battery icon. After a few seconds, you'll see a tool tip telling you how much longer Windows thinks your battery will last.

- The harder (but more informative) way is to double-click on the same icon, where you'll see a dialog box.

What do I do with this docking station?

Some notebooks come with an optional accessory called a **docking station**. It's a slick idea: when you're on the road, you use whatever is installed in your PC and its PC Card slots. But when you get back to the office, you slip the notebook into the docking station and it automatically hooks up to your company network, to a desktop CD-ROM drive, even to a separate full-sized monitor and keyboard.

Every time you switch between "notebook in the docking station" and "notebook on its own," Windows does a quick check of the environment to see what has changed. Should the desktop be set to a new size to take advantage of the bigger monitor? Are there any application programs using data on the network that need a chance to save their files before exiting? To make sure Windows has enough notice to handle these changes gracefully, always follow the notebook maker's instructions for docking and undocking. Typically, this means:

- Put the notebook into its suspended mode before inserting it into the docking station.

- Use the computer's "eject" button (either on the screen or on the docking station) to remove the notebook. Don't just start disconnecting wires!

You shouldn't have to do anything to set up a docking station properly, because all those details are designed to be handled by the Windows Plug and Play feature.

Bringing it all home (and then to the office)

Some people use a notebook PC as their one and only PC. If that's you, skip this section. But what if you have a notebook *and* a desktop PC? How do you make sure that the files you've worked with on the desktop PC are the same ones you take on the road? Well, you have two options.

The hard way: use a floppy disk

The old-fashioned technique for moving files from one place to another is to do it in two steps: copy the files from the first machine onto a floppy disk, then stick that disk into the second machine and copy the same files to the other hard disk.

Besides being slow and cumbersome, this technique has plenty of room for error. You have to be extra careful that you never accidentally replace the new file you just edited with the older file on the other machine. Murphy's Law says you'll only do this when the file you're working with is valuable and irreplaceable (at least that's the way it works for me).

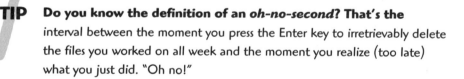

TIP Do you know the definition of an *oh-no-second*? That's the interval between the moment you press the Enter key to irretrievably delete the files you worked on all week and the moment you realize (too late) what you just did. "Oh no!"

The one-button way: use the Briefcase

Windows 95 has a special utility designed just for notebook users. It's called the **Briefcase**, and it works much like a smart version of the fancy leather briefcase you use to carry paperwork to and from the office. Here's how it works:

You tell Windows to create a special briefcase folder on your notebook PC, and then you drag data files from your desktop PC into the Briefcase. Every time you're ready to leave on a trip, you ask Windows to rummage through the Briefcase and compare its contents with the originals. If it finds different versions of the same file, it offers to replace the older version with the newer one. If it finds files you've created in either place since you last updated the Briefcase, it offers to create them in the other location as well. And if it notices that you've deleted files in one place, it asks if you want to delete them in the other location as well.

Set up your Briefcase

If you installed Windows using the Portable option, you should already have a Briefcase right on the Windows desktop, right-alongside the My Computer icon. To add a new Briefcase after the fact, just click on the desktop and choose Ne<u>w</u>, Briefcase. The first time you open this window, you'll see the Welcome message (shown in fig. 19.4). Follow these instructions to get started.

Fig. 19.4

Can't remember how a Briefcase works? Don't worry—the first time you use a new Briefcase, you'll see this helpful message.

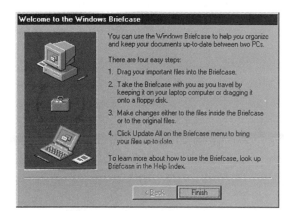

Keeping the Briefcase in sync with the original

Once you've copied the files from your desktop to the notebook Briefcase, work with them by opening the Briefcase and double-clicking on the files you want to edit. Windows knows where the original is located, and whether the two files are up-to-date. If you want to quickly check on the status of your files, just open the Briefcase and choose <u>V</u>iew, <u>D</u>etails. You'll see all the extra information in a window like the one shown in figure 19.5.

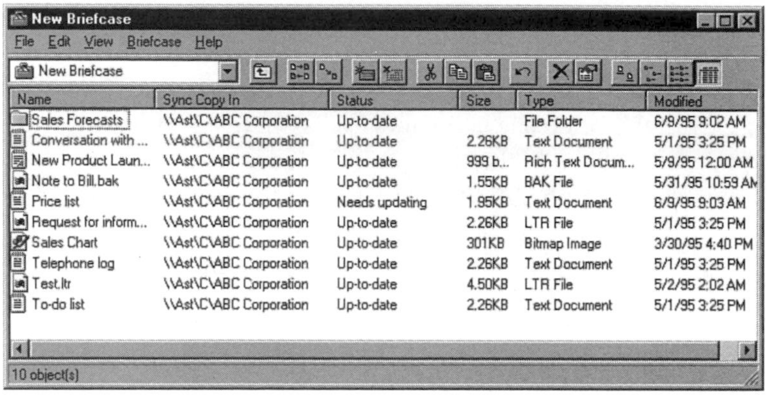

Fig. 19.5

The Status column tells you all you need to know about the files in the Briefcase. Click on the column heading to bring all the "needs updating" files together.

To tell Windows you want your files updated, choose Briefcase, Update All. (If you just want to update a file or two, highlight those entries and use Update Selection, instead.) Windows will compare dates, times, and sizes of each file in the original location and in the Briefcase, then show you what it found in a window like the one shown in figure 19.6. The name and status of the original files appears on the left; the information for the Briefcase copy is on the right.

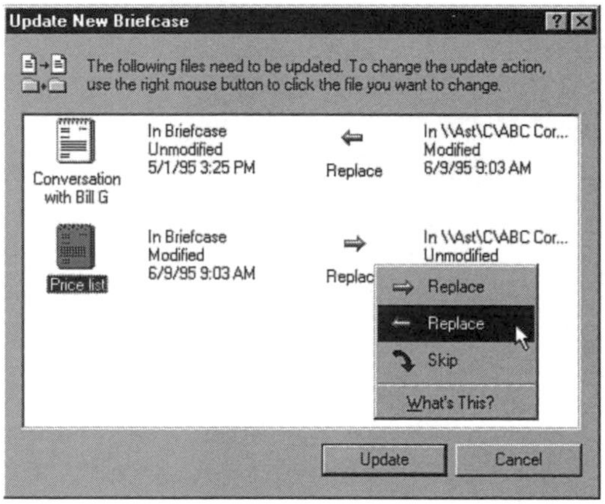

Fig. 19.6

When you're ready to compare the Briefcase files against the originals, choose Update All. You can override the suggested updates by right–clicking.

After it's finished its check, Windows offers to replace older files with newer versions, in either direction. If it sees that both files have changed, Windows offers to Skip the exchange. You can override either action by right-clicking on the action icon and choosing a different action. When you're ready to bring the Briefcase up-to-date, click the Update button.

CAUTION   **Make sure that the system clock on each PC is set correctly. The** Briefcase uses date and time stamps to decide which direction your files should move. If the date is incorrect, you might accidentally replace a newer file with an older one.

20

CD-ROMs

● In this chapter:

- **What is a CD-ROM, anyway?**

- **Getting your CD-ROM installed**

- **You can even play music CDs on your computer**

- **Giving your CD-ROM a drive letter**

- **The CD started playing by itself—what gives?**

It looks like something that would hold Pavarotti or Pearl Jam. It holds as much data as two regular hard disks. What is it?. . . . . ▶

'm talking about CD-ROMs, of course. If you bought your PC anytime in the last year or two, chances are it just came with a special drive designed to read these shiny disks. If your PC doesn't have one, you're missing out on a world of cool stuff and some genuine time-saving features.

What is a CD-ROM, anyway?

As far as Windows is concerned, a CD-ROM is just another way to store and retrieve data. As far as we're concerned, though, a CD-ROM is a special kind of compact disc—it looks exactly like the musical variety, but works exclusively with PCs. So what makes these discs different from the ones with music on them?

- The acronym stands for **C**ompact **D**isc, **R**ead-**O**nly **M**emory. As the name implies, you can only read data from a CD-ROM disc—you can't use it to store your own files.

- You need a special CD player to read the data from a CD-ROM disc. (Sorry, your Walkman can't do the job.)

- CD-ROMs hold a lot of data. You would need about 450 floppy disks to match the capacity of a CD-ROM, and a single CD-ROM can hold more data than most hard drives.

- Compared to floppy disks, a CD-ROM is practically indestructible.

- Compared to hard drives, a CD-ROM reader is relatively slow. When you ask a CD-ROM reader to track down a few bits of data, it takes about 20 times as long as a hard drive, on average.

- There's no limit to the number of CD-ROMs you can keep in your collection—simply load the proper disc into the CD-ROM player when you want to use it.

66 *Plain English, please!*

Is it **disc** or **disk**? That depends. Virtually all of the storage devices that you normally associate with a computer end in **K**—hard disk, floppy disk, optical disk, and so on. But because CD–ROMs evolved from the audio industry, they follow a different standard spelling—compact disc. 99

CD-ROMs are very useful

CD-ROMs are perfect for passing around big programs—like Windows 95—and big data files, like games and collections of video clips. Two or three years ago, you had to have the sleuthing abilities of Sherlock Holmes to hunt down a CD-ROM. Today you can find them practically anywhere.

Just because they use a different storage system, though, there's no reason to treat this software any differently. Software on CD-ROMs is licensed like the kind you get on floppies, and making unauthorized copies is equally illegal.

Here are a few of the things you can do with your CD-ROMs.

Install a new program

These days, buying a new program on floppy disks is like buying the stripped-down model of a new car. Yes, it'll get you where you want to go, but you won't get any of the optional features, like power windows and cup holders.

The same is true of software, and the best example is Windows 95 itself. You *can* get a version of Windows 95 that comes on 14 floppy disks. Of course, the only way Microsoft managed to squeeze this big program onto so few disks was by leaving out a lot of the fun stuff that comes standard on the CD version. Other programs are even bigger—Microsoft Office, a collection of three or four big application programs, uses more than 40 floppy disks! If you've ever installed one of these monster programs, you know how tiring it can get: Please insert disk 37 into drive A: and click OK...

You probably have better things to do with your time, which is why it's always a good idea to choose software that comes on CD-ROMs whenever you have the option. If you have a new CD, open the Windows Control Panel and let the Add/Remove Programs Wizard automatically search your CD for a setup file. If it finds one, it offers to install the software for you, as you can see in figure 20.1.

Fig. 20.1

What could be easier? Well, actually, there *is* an easier way, called Autoplay—but we'll get to that in a minute.

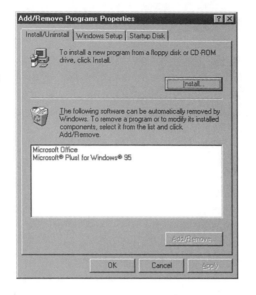

Play a multimedia game or a video clip

Why would you want to use a CD-ROM for fun and games? Because video files are huge—a three-minute music video, for example, can take up nearly 30 megabytes of hard disk space. (See fig. 20.2 for a graphic example.) At that rate, one or two cool games like *Myst* and *The Seventh Guest*, which depend on video for their special effects, would take over your hard drive faster than a swarm of termites chomping through a log cabin.

Fig. 20.2

This video clip from *Interview with the Vampire* runs only two-and-a-half minutes but it gobbles up more than 20M of disk space. That's fine for the Windows 95 CD-ROM, where we found this clip, but you wouldn't want to use your hard disk this way.

Play a music CD

Yes, there's a big difference between music CDs and CD-ROMs. Put a CD-ROM in a typical music CD player and nothing will happen. But I'll bet you didn't know you can put a music CD in a CD-ROM player and get results!

If your sound card and CD-ROM reader are properly connected, you can slip in a music CD and have it play through your computer's speakers. It's an easy and convenient way to have some relaxing (or energetic) background music while you work.

How do you coax tunes from your computer? On most multimedia PCs, it happens automatically. When you insert a music CD, Windows senses the new disc and automatically launches the CD Player program. If that doesn't work, you can start the CD Player yourself by clicking the Start button and following the menus from Programs to Accessories to Multimedia. When you start the CD Player miniprogram, you'll see a screen like the one in figure 20.3.

Fig. 20.3

Use the Windows CD Player to turn your PC into a giant Walkman, temporarily.

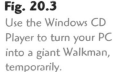

Use the toolbar for one-click access

Like most Windows programs, the CD Player has its own toolbar, which gives you one-click access to the functions you'll want to use most often. It also has a status bar at the bottom of the window and an elapsed-time indicator smack in the middle. If any of these pieces aren't visible, look under the View menu for the commands to turn them on.

Here's what the CD Player toolbar lets you do:

- Create and edit a **play list** that includes the artist, title, and songs on the CD.

- Display the **track time elapsed**—how long the current song has been playing.

- Display the **track time remaining**—how long before the current song ends.

- Show the **disc time remaining**—how much longer before the entire disc will reach the end.

- Play the songs on the CD in **random order**.

- Play **continuously**—when the disc reaches the end, start over again.

- Play just the **song intros**—a snippet of 10 seconds or so from the beginning of each song. Handy when trying to find that song whose name you just can't remember.

TIP Can't remember what any of the CD Player controls do? Look for the ToolTips. Let the mouse pointer rest over any button, including the play controls to the right of the elapsed-time display, and a helpful label will pop up to tell you what the button does.

Build your own playlist

One of the coolest features in the Windows 95 CD Player is its ability to keep track of the details of every music CD in your collection, including the artist's name, the title of the CD, and the names of each song on the disc. Unfortunately, it's not automatic—you have to enter the information yourself. But you only have to do it once. Each time you insert a music CD, Windows scans the disc for a special identification code, then looks in the list of titles you've entered. When it finds a match, it puts up a list like the one in figure 20.4.

Fig. 20.4

You can drag titles from the right window to the left to create a custom playlist of just the songs you want to hear, in just the order you want to hear them.

Building your own playlist is a snap. Choose D̲isc, Edit Play L̲ist from the pull-down menus, then follow these steps:

- **To add information about a new CD...** press the Tab key to move from field to field. Use the CD's liner notes to enter the title and artist's name, then start entering the titles of each track. After you've entered a song title, just press Enter to move to the next entry.

- **To change CD information you've already entered...** click on the appropriate field and start typing. Click on the song titles in the right window to correct a typing mistake.

- **To move from track to track...** use the VCR-style buttons to play, pause, or skip to a different track.

- **To play songs in a specific order...** click the Edit Play List button at the far left of the toolbar, then drag the titles from the A̲vailable Tracks window on the right and drop them in the Play List window on the left. Click the C̲lear All button to start from scratch.

- **To turn down the volume...** choose V̲iew, V̲olume Control. You'll have to use the pull-down menus—no toolbar button here.

- **To eject the CD...** click the Eject button at the bottom right of the CD controls.

Where does Windows keep all the information about music CDs that you type in? You'll find it in your Windows folder, in a little file called CDPLAYER.INI. If you've painstakingly entered lots of information about the CDs in your collection, it's a good idea to make a backup copy of this file. That way, if anything ever happens to it you can simply restore your backup instead of retyping all those entries.

Q&A *The CD Player program says it's playing just fine, but I don't hear any music. What's wrong?*

You need to make a special connection between your CD player and your sound card before you can hear the sound from a music CD. If you have an external CD-ROM reader—one that sits on your desktop outside your PC—there will be a cable that runs from the back of the CD reader to a jack on the sound card. Internal CD-ROM players—those that are installed directly in your computer's case—use a special wire that is connected inside the PC. Talk to the company that sold you your PC for details on how your drive works.

Run programs (okay, slowly)

You can actually run some programs directly from a CD-ROM. Most of the time, you won't want to. Why? Because running a program this way makes a turtle race look like a flying finish at the Indy 500. Even the fastest CD-ROM reader crawls compared to your hard disk.

Some programs will give you the option of setting up to run directly from the CD-ROM. Most of the time, you should just say no. There are two exceptions:

- When you're so pressed for space that you literally don't have enough room to install the program.

- When you just want to try out the new program, and you're not concerned with actually getting any real work done. If you don't like the program, pop out the CD-ROM and send it back; you haven't cluttered up your hard disk. If you do like it, though, go back and install it properly on your hard disk.

Setting up a CD-ROM

Setting up a CD-ROM is either very easy or practically impossible. Most of the time, assuming you have a relatively new, relatively popular CD-ROM drive, you can just plug the drive into its controller board; Windows will recognize it automatically, install any necessary driver software, and let you start using it.

 What happens if your CD-ROM doesn't work? Try forcing Windows to install the drive. Look in the Windows Control Panel and double-click on the Add New Hardware icon. Follow the wizard's prompts and let Windows search for the device. If it finds the drive, you're in business. If it can't find the drive, go one more screen and look for your drive's name in the section labeled CD-ROM controllers.

Still not there? Then it's time to get professional help, preferably from the place that sold you the CD-ROM reader in the first place.

Which drive letter does your CD-ROM get?

As I noted in Chapter 6, every drive in your system uses a letter of the alphabet, followed by a colon, for its name. Your first floppy drive is always A:, your main hard drive is always C:, and so on. Which letter gets assigned to your CD-ROM? That depends. Windows usually takes the next available letter, but that isn't always D:. If you have two hard drives, for example, or if you've used DriveSpace disk-compression, or if you're on a network and you've assigned drive letters to various folders on different file servers, your next available drive letter could be anything between E: and Z:. And it could change from one day to the next, depending on your network setup.

That can play havoc with programs that expect to see the same drive letter every time you start them up. So Windows lets you permanently assign a drive letter to your CD. On my system, for example, I've set the CD-ROM reader up so it always appears as drive E:. Here's how:

1 Right-click on My Computer and choose Properties. The System Properties sheet will pop up.

2 Click on the Device Manager tab to bring that page to the front.

3 Look on the list of hardware for the CD-ROM category, and click on the small plus sign to its left. Highlight the name of the CD-ROM reader and click the Properties button. You'll see a display like the one shown in figure 20.5.

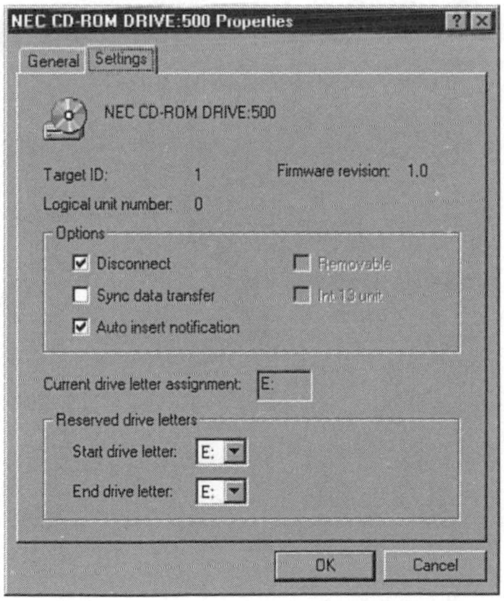

Fig. 20.5

Use the Windows Device Manager to make sure that your CD-ROM always uses the same drive letter. In this example, we've told Windows to reserve E: for the CD-ROM.

NEC CD-ROM DRIVE:500 Properties

General | Settings

NEC CD-ROM DRIVE:500

Target ID: 1   Firmware revision: 1.0
Logical unit number: 0

Options
☑ Disconnect   ☐ Removable
☐ Sync data transfer ☐ Int 13 unit
☑ Auto insert notification

Current drive letter assignment: E:

Reserved drive letters
Start drive letter: E:
End drive letter: E:

OK   Cancel

4 Choose the drive letter you want to reserve (in this case E:) in both boxes. Why is there a start and a finish? If you have a CD-ROM changer that holds multiple discs, you might need to reserve more than one letter to accommodate all those discs. You big spender, you.

5 Restart your computer and look in the My Computer folder to make sure Windows recognized the changed drive letter.

Hey, that CD's playing itself!

If you slip a CD-ROM in your CD-ROM reader and your computer instantly starts up a program, don't get spooked—that's just a feature called **AutoPlay**.

The idea is that some CD-ROMs—especially games and educational software—should act just like a video cassette or a music CD instead of a disk filled with files and folders. AutoPlay discs have a couple of extra files that Windows looks for every time it notices you've changed CDs. If it finds those files, it launches its main program automatically.

If you purchased the CD-ROM version of Windows 95, you can see AutoPlay in action. Just slip the disc into your drive, and (assuming you've already installed Windows) you'll see a screen like the one in figure 20.6.

Fig. 20.6

Whenever you insert this disc into the CD-ROM reader, Windows automatically starts up this program.

TIP **What if you don't want your AutoPlay CD to start** automatically? Hold down the Shift key as you insert the CD-ROM, and Windows will ignore the AutoPlay instructions. Now you can open the My Computer window, right-click on the CD-ROM icon, and use other options like <u>O</u>pen to see the files on the CD-ROM.

In search of cool CD-ROMs

Wondering what you can do with a CD-ROM? Well, besides Windows 95, there are literally thousands of titles you can put in a CD-ROM drive to jazz up your computer. Picking a few at random means leaving out some excellent CD-ROMs, so don't take these as recommendations but rather as starting points.

One of my favorite CD-ROMs is *Star Trek: The Next Generation Technical Manual*, which includes full plans for the Starship *Enterprise*. A must for Trekkers.

I read Stephen Hawking's book, *A Brief History of Time*, and was thoroughly lost in the dense discussions of relativity and space-time

continuums. Then I saw this CD-ROM, and now I know why the universe is expanding.

Microsoft's *Cinemania '95* is an amazing collection of movie reviews, film clips, biographies, etc., that no movie buff should be without.

Bookshelf '95 is an encyclopedia, thesaurus, dictionary, atlas, and more, all in one. Perfect for students, business people, and anyone who's curious about the world around them.

And then there's *Myst*, which is the strangest, most mysterious game you'll ever see. Even if you don't like games, you might like this spooky, eerie, mysterious adventure.

Part VII: Communicating with the Rest of the World

21

Working with Other Computers

● In this chapter:

- **What's a network, anyway?**

- **Why you might have to type a password when you start Windows**

- **Safely share files and printers with other people**

- **How to connect to a file server**

Think networking is difficult to understand? Think again. After all, it's just sharing . . . . ▶

In the office, you probably share documents all the time. So how can you send your version of a file to someone else for her comments? One way is to copy your file to a floppy disk, stick it in a manila envelope, put it in your out-basket, and wait a few days for the revisions to work their way back to you. Not a very practical solution, is it? Wouldn't it make more sense if you could somehow hook your computers together so you could both see the same file anytime?

That's the idea behind computer **networks**. With the help of a little bit of extra hardware (and a lot of wire), you can extend the reach of your computer to share files, folders, and printers—instantly. Computer networks can stretch around the world, or they can be as small as two PCs sitting side by side on the same table. No matter how big or small your network is, you can work with it easily, once you learn the basics.

Network basics

In general, networks help you get more out of the hardware you own, and they also let you keep your data locked up by assigning passwords and defining permissions so that only the right people can get to it. There are slightly different techniques for sharing (and securing) files and printers on different kinds of networks.

Nearly every kind of network lets you share files on a central computer called a **file server**. As long as you know the name of the file server, and your **network administrator** (the person who runs your network) has set up the network to allow you to access it, you can read and write files on folders on the file server. Depending on the kind of network your company uses, you may also belong to a **workgroup**—a (usually) smaller assortment of users on the network. A bank, for example, might choose to create workgroups called Admin, Mortgage, and Collections.

❝ *Plain English, please!*

You'll sometimes hear people refer to their network as a LAN or WAN. What's that all about? **LAN** stands for **Local Area Network**. As the name implies, a LAN is usually concentrated in a single location, and most of the machines are connected with wires. A **WAN**, which is short for **Wide Area Network**, includes two or more LANs, usually joined together by high-speed telephone lines. In big companies, it's not surprising to see WANs that tie together people on three different continents. ❞

The same is true for printers. Instead of buying an expensive laser printer for every employee, your company can hook up one printer to a network and let everyone in the department use it anytime.

On some networks, you can let other people share a folder on your own computer's hard drive so you can both get to the files anytime. And Windows even includes a game called **Hearts**, which lets you fool around with your coworkers instead of getting work done.

How do networks work?

If you've ever used interoffice mail, you already know the fundamental principles behind computer networking. When you want to send a printed report to someone else, you slip it into an envelope, write the recipient's name on the To: line, put your own name on the From: line, and put it in your outbox. The next time the mailroom guy passes by on his rounds, he picks up the envelope and delivers it.

Your company's computer network handles files in much the same way. Each PC on the network uses a piece of software called a **network client** to chop files into small pieces called **packets**. The client software on the sending end stuffs these packets into the electronic equivalent of manila envelopes, and adds the To and From information, plus details about how to put the file back together; the client on the receiving end opens all the envelopes and reassembles the pieces into a file that looks just like the one that was sent. (This all happens quickly and invisibly, of course.)

Every computer on the network has a plug-in card called a **network adapter**. It's easy to spot the adapter—that's where the network cable is plugged into your PC. It functions something like a combination in- and out-basket, since every packet that comes into or out of the computer has to go through this little piece of hardware.

For your computer to successfully send envelopes full of information across the network, it has to use the same **protocol** as the rest of the computers on the network. No, it has nothing to do with which fork you use at the embassy; a protocol is simply the language that your network speaks. Protocols generally have tongue-twisting acronyms like IPX/SPX or TCP/IP instead of plain-English names.

Finally, your network may allow you to add **services** such as file and printer sharing. With the right service installed on your networked computer, for example, you can give someone else permission to send documents through his network adapter, across the cable, into your network adapter, and ultimately to your printer or onto your hard drive. Needless to say, you'll want to think carefully about the consequences before you let someone share your PC or printer!

TIP **Some of the techniques described in this chapter won't work on** your network. It all depends on how much trust the person who set up your network had in you and your fellow workers. If you work for the CIA, security will surely be a lot tighter than if you work for a real estate agency.

What's in the Network Neighborhood?

 If you're connected to a network, you'll find an extra icon on your Windows desktop. Just as My Computer contains everything that's inside your personal PC, the Network Neighborhood is filled with icons representing everything your computer is connected to. Figure 21.1 is a representation of what I see when I double-click on this icon.

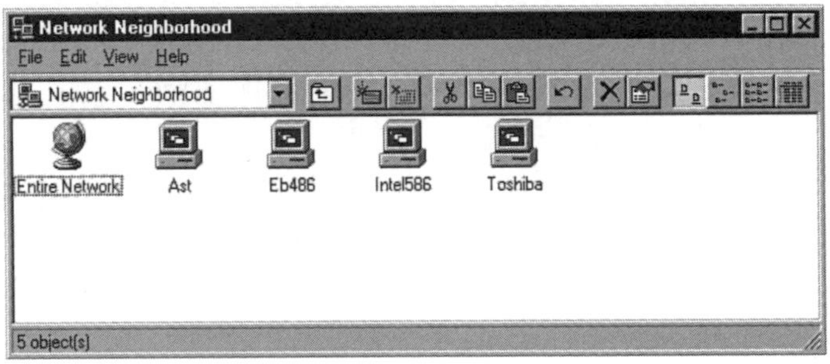

Fig. 21.1

You and your immediate neighbors show up in the Network Neighborhood. If you want to see everything that's available on your network, double-click on the Entire Network icon.

Here's what you'll find inside:

- An icon for the Entire Network. Double-click here to see all the resources (printers, shared folders, file servers, and so on) in all the workgroups on your network.

- Other computers in your local workgroup (they have to be running Windows 95 or a compatible version of Windows, such as Windows for Workgroups 3.11).

- File servers, such as those on a NetWare or Windows NT network.

> 66 *Plain English, please!*
>
> **NetWare** is a network operating system sold by Novell Corp. of Salt Lake City, Utah. If your company has a network today, chances are it's running NetWare because this is the market leader by a wide margin. **Microsoft Windows NT** is a version of Windows that is specifically designed for advanced computer networks. It's nowhere near as easy to use as Windows 95, but it's much more secure—a fact that would be important if you wanted to keep your company's data safe. 99

Every PC across the network gets its own icon in the Network Neighborhood. Dig a little deeper and you can see whether the owner of that PC has put the Windows equivalent of a "Share Me" sign on any of his folders or printers. For example, if Bob in Accounting wants you to look over this month's payroll report, he could put the report in a folder, call it `Payroll Reports`, and tell Windows that it's OK if you look at it. Now, when you explore the icon for Bob's PC in the Network Neighborhood, you'll see that shared folder as well.

CAUTION **Be prepared to wait when you double-click on the Entire Network icon.** If you're part of a big network, it can take a few minutes, literally, for Windows to track down all those pieces and build the list of icons to show you.

Getting started with Windows on your network

If you're on a network, you log on to the network automatically every time you turn on your PC and start Windows. There are a variety of Windows log-in screens, depending on which kind of network your company uses. (See fig. 21.2 for an example of one such dialog box.)

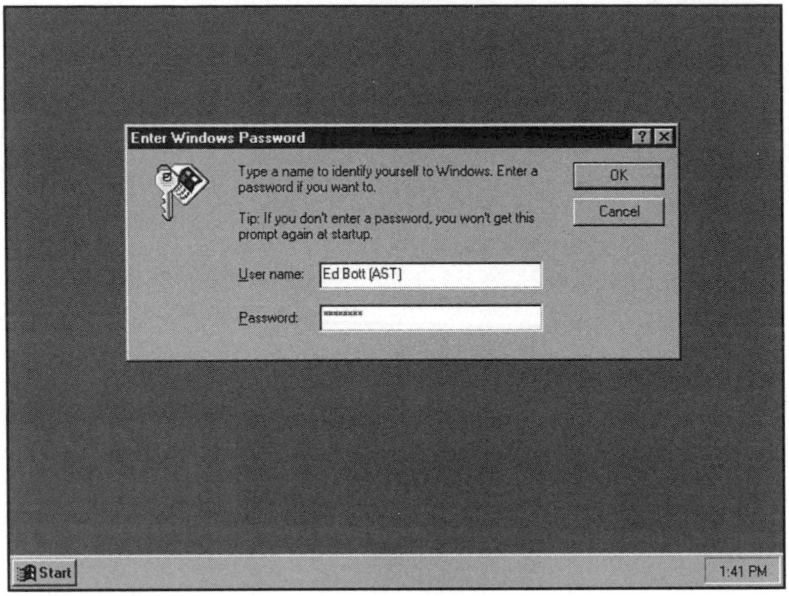

Fig. 21.2

Every time you turn
on your computer,
Windows asks you to
log in by entering your
user name and
password.

Why do I have to log in?

Logging in does two things. The process sends your user name and password to any file servers on your network so that you can have access to files stored there. It also tells Windows how you like your desktop arranged. In some companies, network administrators set up a PC so that more than one person can use it. In this case, you can have different icons on your Windows desktop than someone else who uses your PC.

Q&A   *Help! I forgot my password!*

Call your network administrator. It takes special management tools to erase your old password and give you a new one when you've forgotten the original password. Why the runaround? Well, the whole point of passwords is to offer security. If you forget your password, there's no way Windows can tell that it's really *you* instead of some snoop trying to steal your files.

Hate your password? Change it!

You can change your Windows password by double-clicking the Passwords icon in the Control Panel. Windows will ask you to enter your original password (to prove you are who you say you are), and then enter the new password. If you want to change your password for another network, such as NetWare or Windows NT, use the Change Other Passwords button in the same dialog box.

How does Windows know who I am?

Easy. You (or whoever set you up on the network) entered some information in a dialog box like the one in figure 21.3.

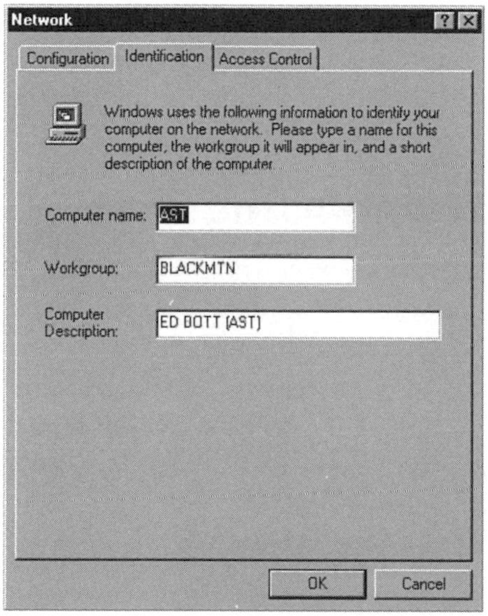

Fig. 21.3

Name, rank, and serial number? The Network properties dialog box lets you tell Windows your computer's name, the name of your workgroup, and a description of your computer.

You already entered your **user name** when you logged on to the network. (The user name is usually some variant of your first and last name, although it can be any name or sequence of nonsense, if you prefer.) Windows uses this information to identify your network rights and desktop preferences.

Your computer also has a name that other people need to use when they connect to any folders or printers you've set up for sharing. To change your computer name, right-click on the Network Neighborhood icon and choose Properties. Click the Identification tab and enter the new name. The next time you start your PC, you'll see a different name for your computer in the Network Neighborhood.

Why one name for you and one for your computer? Well, there's no reason why two or more people can't use one computer, with different mailboxes and desktops and other personal preferences. But no matter who's using the computer, its resources will always remain the same. Identifying users by user name guarantees that mail will get to the right place. Identifying computers by computer name makes it easy for anyone who wants to share a resource to find it quickly.

How to use the files on a file server

To use files on your own computer, you double-click on the My Computer icon. To use files on another computer, you have to go through one extra step.

The easy way: browse through the Network Neighborhood

Just as on your own computer, you can open or save files on any computer to which you're networked—just point and click. Start in the Network Neighborhood, double-clicking on the name of the computer you want to use, and then work your way through the shared folders until you find the place and name you want. You can even do this using the File Open and File Save As dialog boxes when you save a document, as shown in figure 21.4.

Fig. 21.4

Use the drop-down list in the File Open and File Save As dialog boxes to work with a file on another computer somewhere in the Network Neighborhood.

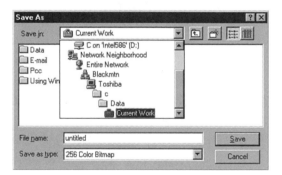

The hard way: map to a drive letter

On your own computer, you're used to referring to disk drives by letter, such as A: and C:, for your main floppy and hard drives. With some programs, drive letters are the only way to use files; these programs (mostly older DOS and Windows programs) won't let you point and click your way through the Network Neighborhood. Instead, you have to fool Windows into using a drive letter for one of these shared folders. The process is called **drive mapping**—as the phrase suggests, you're creating a "map" of network locations, each one labeled with a drive letter, that Windows can refer to when you use one of the mapped drive letters. Here's how:

Browse through the Network Neighborhood until you reach the folder you want to use. Right-click on the shared folder, and choose <u>M</u>ap Network Drive. (Fig. 21.5 shows the dialog box.) Notice that the computer name and folder name are already filled in. You'll see a slightly different version of the same dialog box if you right-click on the My Computer icon, and choose the <u>M</u>ap Network Drive command.)

Fig. 21.5
Use this dialog box to tell Windows where in the Network Neighborhood to look when you use a specific drive letter.

Click OK to tell Windows about the mapping. The mapped drive (E:, for example) will appear in the My Computer folder.

Check the Reconnect at logon box if you want to make the drive-letter mapping permanent; leave this box empty if you just want to use this folder one time.

Pick a drive letter from the drop-down list.

What do all those slashes mean?

The complicated strings of text in the drive-mapping boxes are called **UNC names**. Just as you can refer to locations on your computer with a drive letter, a colon, a backslash, and a folder name, you can refer to locations on another computer by typing its full name. A UNC name starts with two backslashes, followed by the computer name, another backslash, the name of the shared folder or volume, another backslash, and so on.

Here's how it works. Let's say your company has a file server named Calvin, on which the network administrator has defined a shared folder named Hobbes. Hobbes in turn contains a folder called Letters. You can get to the Letters folder (in a File Save As dialog box, say) by typing its full UNC name:

`\\Calvin\Hobbes\Letters`

> **❝ Plain English, please!**
> UNC means **Universal Naming Convention**. That's a fancy designation
> for an agreement between different network software makers. UNC names
> allow you to connect to any file server, even when you don't know exactly
> what kind of network operating system the file server is using. **❞**

Share information (and your printer, too!) with other people

When you're working in an office as part of a team, you'll find plenty of
productive ways to use Windows' built-in sharing features. On a Windows
network, you can set aside a portion of your hard drive (or all of it, for that
matter) as a sort of lending library. Anyone else on the network can stop by
and browse through the contents at his or her leisure.

If security's an issue, you can have Windows assign a librarian to monitor
the shared area and demand some ID, in the form of a password, before
letting a stranger in. Windows lets you share printers and CD-ROM drives,
too.

You might share your entire hard drive with a trusted administrative assistant; that way, every time either of you wanted to use the files on your hard
disk, they'd be right there. Or you could give a coworker the rights to look at
just one folder filled with documents you're collaborating on. The documents themselves remain on your hard disk while Windows' messengers
shuttle them across the network wire on demand.

Can I share a folder?

To share files with others on your network, follow these steps:

1 To share an entire drive, right-click on the icon for the drive you want in
the My Computer window. To share a folder, right-click on the folder
icon. Choose Sharing from the shortcut menu. You'll see a sheet like the
one in figure 21.6.

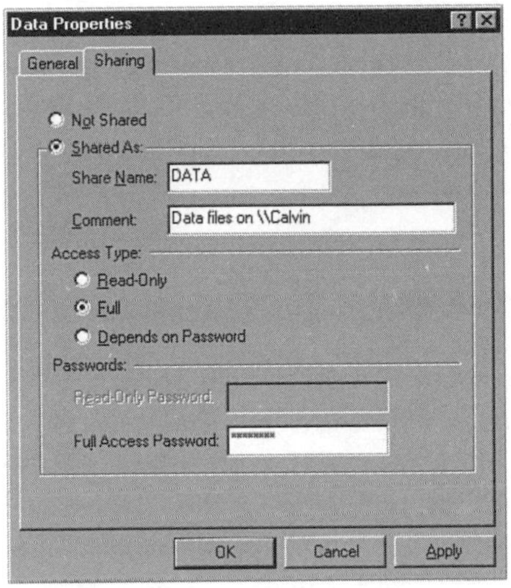

Fig. 21.6

Right–click on a drive or folder and choose Sharing to reveal this sheet.

Data Properties

General | Sharing

○ Not Shared
◉ Shared As:
    Share Name: DATA
    Comment: Data files on \\Calvin
    Access Type:
        ○ Read-Only
        ◉ Full
        ○ Depends on Password
    Passwords:
        Read-Only Password:
        Full Access Password: ********

OK | Cancel | Apply

2 Check the Shared As button, and give the shared drive or folder a name. You can call it anything, but it helps to use a descriptive name, since this is the name other people will see when they browse through the Network Neighborhood.

3 Choose whether you want to allow others to simply read files on your hard drive, or whether it's OK for them to edit and delete files, or create new ones.

4 If you want to restrict access to the shared folder, assign a password. You can have separate passwords for read-only access and full access, so that different people have different levels of access to your files. (**Read-only**, as the name implies, means that other users can open the files stored there, but they can't create new ones or change the ones that are already there. For that, a network user needs **full access**.)

5 Click OK to make the changes effective. Note the hand that appears under the folder or drive icon to indicate that it is shared.

To share a printer, open the My Computer folder, double-click on the Printers icon, highlight the name of a printer, and follow the same steps.

When you browse through the Network Neighborhood and double-click on the icon for a PC, you'll see an icon for each shared folder and printer that's available. To open the shared folder, just double-click. If the owner of that computer has assigned a password, you'll have to enter it here before you can see what's available.

Hearts: using the network to waste time

If you and three coworkers want to take a break at the same time, Windows offers a fun version of the classic card game Hearts that you can play over the network. To start a game of Hearts (or join one that's already in progress) click the Start button, and follow the cascading menus through Programs, Accessories, and Games. Never played Hearts before? It's easy to learn. Just choose Help, Help Topics, and look for the section called Playing Hearts.

Hearts is a four-handed game (although Windows is perfectly willing to provide up to three of its own players, if you can't get a foursome together). The object of the game is to end up with the lowest score possible after 13 rounds of one card per player. When possible, every player has to follow the suit of the first card played; if you can't follow suit, you can dump a heart (worth one point) or the Queen of Spades (worth—shudder—13 points). Sound simple? It's a surprisingly complex game, with all sorts of strategic twists and turns, and it's perfect for whiling away the hours when you should be working.

There's also an odd mini-program called **Party Line** (also found in the Games folder) that lets you exchange one-line messages with coworkers who are also running the Party Line program. The point of the program is to start rumors. After you've clicked on the program icon, a thin one-line window will appear at the top of your screen. Click on the rabbit ears at the left of the title bar and choose Start a rumor to send a message to everyone else's PC. They'll see a display like the one in figure 21.7.

Fig. 21.7

What's the office buzz? Use Party Line to send anonymous messages to anyone who's tuned in. Click the rabbit ears to start a rumor or see the history.

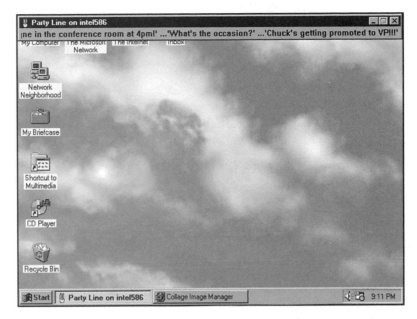

22

Adding a Modem (and Setting It Up)

● In this chapter:

- **How to install a new modem**

- **My modem is too noisy!**

- **Why does Windows want to know where I'm calling from?**

- **Use HyperTerminal to get connected online**

- **Windows can even dial the phone for you!**

Communicating via modem sometimes feels like magic. When it works, it's wonderful! When it doesn't, you need this chapter. . . . . ⊙

Whenever you use your computer and a modem to make a call, you're basically passing a big bucket of electronic bits from one place to another over a wire. Of course, it doesn't feel like that to you—or to the person on the other end of the wire. As far as the two of you are concerned, you just sent (or received) a piece of electronic mail, or a fax, or a file, or a page full of information from the Internet.

We can't cover every communications nuance in this chapter, but we will get through the important first steps: installing a modem, making a connection to another modem somewhere in cyberspace, dialing your phone, and figuring out why things don't always work the way they should.

What's a modem, and what's it good for?

A **modem** (pronounce it *moe*-dem) is a specialized piece of hardware that converts data from digital form—bits and bytes on your hard disk or your computer's memory—into analog form, that high-pitched warbling sound you hear when two modems meet. What sounds like horrible screeching is actually the very precise language that two modems use to transfer information back and forth.

With the right software, you can use your modem to exchange just about any form of information. Depending on what you're trying to accomplish, the communications part may work in the **background**, shuffling data into and out of your computer while you work on something else. Or it may run as a **terminal program**—a sort of all-purpose communications window in which you type commands to make the computer do what you want.

> ## ❝ *Plain English, please!*
>
> Why are they called **modems**? The **mo** is short for modulate (pronounce it mahd-juh–late), which is the process of converting the digital data on your PC into analog sound patterns that can travel over a telephone wire. The **dem**, as you might have guessed, is short for demodulate (same as before, but add dee on the front), which is the process of reassembling the sounds into bits at the other end of the line. Put it together and you get mo(dulator)-dem(odulator), an extremely formal term for the nearly magical devices that convert data between digital and analog forms. ❞

Here's a partial list of some of the things you can do with a modem and a phone line:

- Send e-mail to just about anyone, just about anywhere (and get fast answers), through a variety of commercial services and academic or government connections.

- Send and receive faxes without ever touching a piece of paper.

- Connect two PCs together and share files (or even print a 30-page document on a printer that's 3,000 miles away).

- Dial your telephone and keep a log of your phone calls.

- Connect to an online service like CompuServe or The Microsoft Network.

- Browse through the Internet's vast collections of data in search of information or entertainment.

More Plug and Play: how to install a modem

Windows 95 doesn't recognize every modem ever made, but sometimes it feels that way. Thanks to the Plug and Play hardware detection, Windows can automatically install any of several hundred types of modems.

When you add a new modem to your computer, the best strategy is to let Windows figure out on its own what brand it is. Most of the time, Windows will get it right, and most of the time, the process won't take that long. To let Windows take a stab at it, follow these steps:

1 Plug the modem into your PC, and make sure both are powered up and ready to go.

2 Connect your telephone line to the modem.

 3 Double-click on the Modems icon in the Windows Control Panel, and click the Add button in the dialog box that appears.

The Install New Modem Wizard (shown in fig. 22.1) pops up. Follow the instructions, and you should be done within a few clicks.

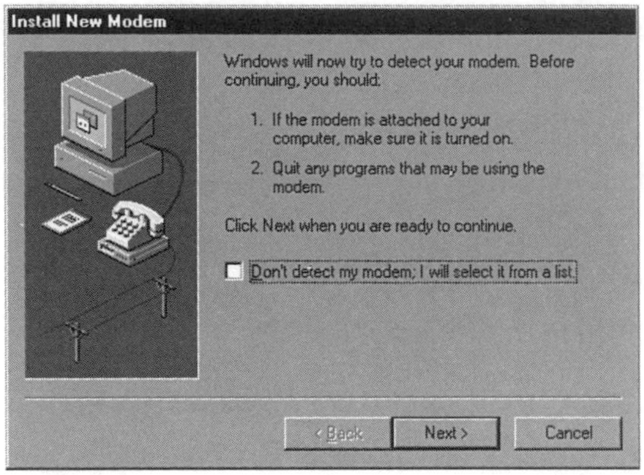

Fig. 22.1

The Install New Modem Wizard walks you through the process of introducing a new modem to Windows.

What does the Wizard do when it installs a new modem?

- It stores the set of commands your modem recognizes, so that Windows can use them to talk with other modems.

- It tells Windows which port you've used—in other words, where on the back of your PC you've plugged in the modem. (For more information about the different types of ports on your PC, refer to Chapter 16.) On most computers, your modem will use one of two serial ports, COM1 or COM2.

- It tells Windows how many bits of information your modem can handle per second.

As long as Windows successfully detected your modem, it should have filled in all these entries correctly.

TIP **Should you get an internal modem that sits inside your PC? Or are** you better off with an **external modem**, which plugs into the back of your PC and sits on your desktop? The internal species cost less and save space. External modems are easier to turn off when you run into troubles, and they give you a cool set of blinking lights and LED displays to watch as you connect. Personally, I prefer external modems, but you can't go wrong with either choice.

Changing your modem setup

You may never need to adjust the settings Windows uses to communicate with your modem. But if you start to encounter problems, the way to tinker with the modem properties is the same way you fuss with the properties of any Windows object. First you have to find its icon: Open Control Panel and double-click on the Modems folder. The window that opens will probably look something like the one in figure 22.2.

Fig. 22.2
Whenever you install a modem, Windows adds it to the Modems folder, where you can adjust its settings later with a single click.

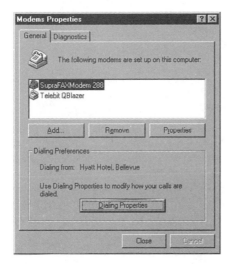

Never overlook the obvious when your equipment isn't working

I once mobilized an entire technical support department to diagnose a serious communication problem. It turned out that I, um, well... OK, I had forgotten to connect the modem to my phone line. (The tech support guy had a good sense of humor, fortunately.) I learned that day to always check the obvious. Before you ask for help, ask yourself these questions:

- Is the modem plugged in?

- Is the power turned on?

- Is the modem connected to the phone line?

- Have I checked the connections carefully? Any loose wires?

- Is my modem dialing the right phone number?

Oh, and this advice applies to more than just modems. Try running through an equivalent checklist any time you have a problem with your PC or printer. Unless, of course, you **like** having a tech support expert tell you to turn on the power before you call next time.

Talking to the hardware

Highlight the modem you want to reconfigure, then click the button labeled P̲roperties. That should pop up the Modem Properties sheet for that specific modem, with the General tab highlighted, as shown in figure 22.3.

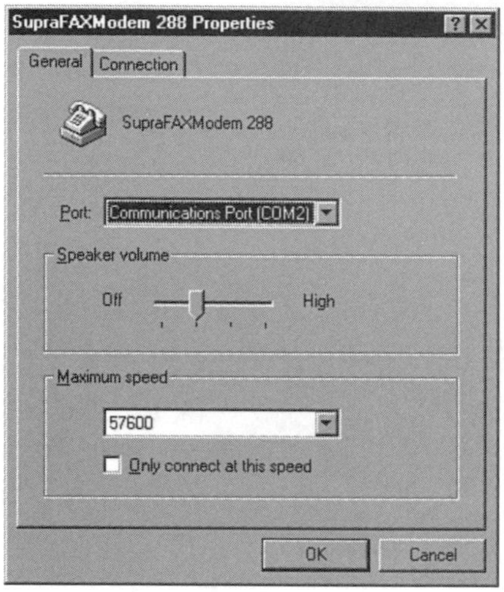

Fig. 22.3

Use the Modem Properties sheet to tell Windows you've plugged the modem into a different port.

Which port should you use? Windows almost always gets this right, but if it can't figure out the puzzle, you'll have to fill in the blanks. Most of the time, you'll plug a modem into a serial port with the label COM1 or COM2. If your PC has two ports, there's a good chance your mouse is plugged into the other serial port.

What speed should you select? Again, you should trust Windows' judgment most of the time. You can usually set this number as high as it will go and count on the communication software to set the correct number on the fly.

And what's that sliding control labeled S̲peaker volume? I'm glad you asked…

That screeching is driving me crazy!

Almost every modem has a speaker that you can turn on and off. You can also control its volume. For some people, the sound is like fingernails on a chalkboard, but I like to leave the speaker on at its lowest volume until I'm connected to the modem on the other end of the line, then turn it off completely. Here's how to adjust the volume for your modem:

- **To turn the volume down...** slide the pointer to the left. The highest volume is at the right, and each tick to the left cuts the noise level considerably.

- **To shut the speaker off completely...** slide that pointer all the way to the left. You may discover that you also have to fuss with a dialog box in your communications software to make this change permanent. If you use Dial-Up Networking connections, you can set a different speaker volume for each one.

Making connections

After you've successfully set up the hardware part of your modem, it's sometimes necessary to configure the software side so that other modems can understand your modem when it starts squalling. Click the Connection tab of the Properties sheet for the modem you're using to see which options are available (see fig. 22.4).

Fig. 22.4

Here's where you adjust the fine points of your online connection.

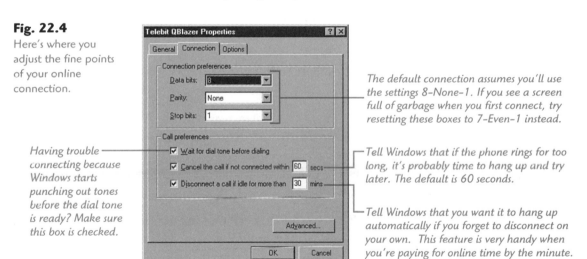

The default connection assumes you'll use the settings 8–None–1. If you see a screen full of garbage when you first connect, try resetting these boxes to 7–Even–1 instead.

Having trouble connecting because Windows starts punching out tones before the dial tone is ready? Make sure this box is checked.

Tell Windows that if the phone rings for too long, it's probably time to hang up and try later. The default is 60 seconds.

Tell Windows that you want it to hang up automatically if you forget to disconnect on your own. This feature is very handy when you're paying for online time by the minute.

CAUTION **What should you do with that button labeled A<u>d</u>vanced? Ignore it.** Most of the options there will thoroughly scramble your attempts to communicate with the outside world. Don't mess with these settings unless a modem expert tells you to. And even then, tread carefully.

Why does Windows care where you are?

In communications, just as in real estate, location is everything. Does the phone at your office work the same as the one at home? Probably not. And what about hotels? If you're in the office, you might need to dial 9 to get an outside line. At some hotels, you dial 8 to access long-distance lines. At home, you just dial the number. Windows lets you define and save different locations as part of your communication profile. When you move from one location to another, just let Windows know, and it will handle the dialing details flawlessly.

Dialing for data with HyperTerminal

Once you've got the modem properly configured and all the settings just so, it's time to connect to the outside world. You may have a communications program that automatically hooks up to an online service. (The software programs for America Online and CompuServe do this, for example.) But you can also use a terminal program to control the remote computer directly. This procedure is always more difficult because you actually have to type commands at a prompt. But for some systems, it's the only option for getting connected.

HyperTerminal is a Windows 95 replacement for the old Terminal program that came with Windows 3.x. To use HyperTerminal, you create and save a connection document that contains all the settings for the number you want to call. Later, you just double-click on the icon for your connection to dial up again. Here's how it works.

 To open the HyperTerminal folder, click on the Start button and follow the cascading menus from Programs to Accessories, then open the Hyper-Terminal folder. See the icon labeled Hypertrm? Double-click here to create a new document with all the information you need to connect to another computer.

The process couldn't be simpler. Give your connection a name, and pick an icon from the list that the setup wizard offers.

Next, enter an area code and a phone number for the connection, and tell Windows which modem you expect to use.

How to set up a new location

To switch locations, double-click on the Modems icon in Control Panel, then click the button labeled Dialing Properties. You'll see a dialog box much like this one. Set up the location as desired. Then click OK to save your changes, Cancel to back out without saving.

The drop–down list contains all the locations you've defined. Click New to begin a brand-new location; click Remove to get rid of a location you don't plan to use again.

Enter the area code and country of the location. Windows will compare these items against the numbers in your address book to decide whether to treat a call as local or long distance.

Want to charge the call to a telephone credit card instead of the phone you're using? Check this box and follow the instructions.

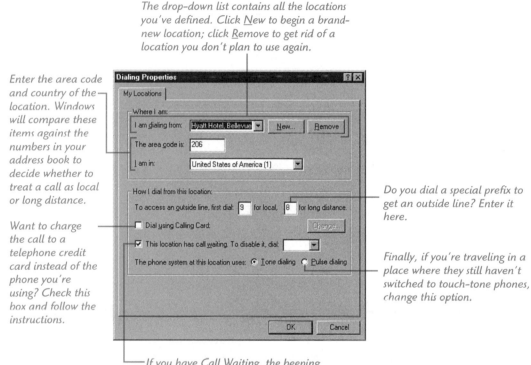

Do you dial a special prefix to get an outside line? Enter it here.

Finally, if you're traveling in a place where they still haven't switched to touch–tone phones, change this option.

*If you have Call Waiting, the beeping tones can thoroughly befuddle a modem. Check here to disable call waiting. On many phone systems, you can punch *70 to turn off this feature.*

You're finished. HyperTerminal assumes you're ready to dial right now and pops up the dialog box shown in figure 22.5. Pick a new location if you need to, then click the Dial button to establish your connection.

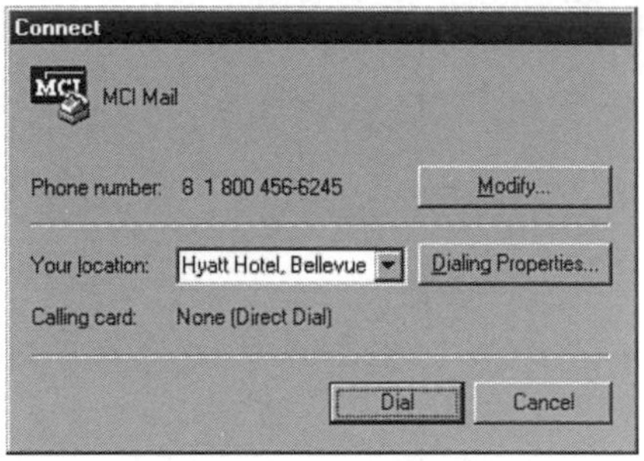

Fig. 22.5
Use a HyperTerminal connection to dial into another computer or an online service. You can tell Windows to use a different location so you don't have to worry about dialing the right numbers first.

There isn't enough space here to cover all the things you can do with HyperTerminal. For that, you should check out the online help files. But here's a sample of some things worth trying:

- Every time you make a connection, the program saves the data that passed by on your screen. As long as you save the connection, you can open it again and review the text from the last session.

- To make a connection or disconnect immediately, use the icons on the HyperTerminal toolbar.

- You can send and receive files of all sorts when you've connected to another modem. Pull down the Transfer menu, and look for the Send File and Receive File options.

TIP **How do you know you've successfully established a connection?** Look in the notification area, right next to the clock on the right of the taskbar. You'll see a small modem icon with two lights that blink on and off to indicate that data is going back and forth. Double-click on the icon to pop up a big window with more information about the current connection.

Setting up the Windows Phone Dialer

Thanks to one last Windows accessory, you can actually use your modem as a sort of personal assistant to place phone calls for you. Here's how. (Of course, this only works if your phone and modem are properly hooked together.) Make sure there's a phone line running from your wall jack to the line jack of your modem, and another wire running between your telephone and the phone jack on your modem.

 Look in the Accessories folder for the Phone Dialer icon (if it's not there, you may have to install it using your original Windows disks or CD-ROM). Click to pop up a window like the one in figure 22.6.

Fig. 22.6

The Windows Phone Dialer uses your modem to place phone calls. Once you hear the ringing phone, it's OK to pick up the line and prepare to start talking.

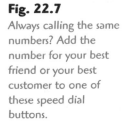

To dial a number, click in the box at the top left and enter your number. You can also click on the keypad buttons to enter the phone number.

When you hear the phone ringing, pick up the receiver and prepare to start talking.

To program one of the Speed dial buttons at right, just click on the button and fill in the dialog box shown in figure 22.7. Add a name and telephone number, then click one of the $\underline{S}$ave options. Now you can dial that number simply by clicking the Speed dial button.

Fig. 22.7

Always calling the same numbers? Add the number for your best friend or your best customer to one of these speed dial buttons.

Q&A *I programmed a speed dial button, but I got it wrong. How do I start over?*

Choose $\underline{E}$dit, $\underline{S}$peed Dial, then click the button you want to change.

This @%&#!! modem doesn't work!

Murphy has a special book of "Murphy's laws" reserved just for modems and communications issues. It's a thick book, too. The best starting place for fixing modem problems is the Windows online help system. Search for `Troubleshooting` and find the page shown in figure 22.8. Virtually all the tough modem problems are explained well here, with helpful step-by-step instructions.

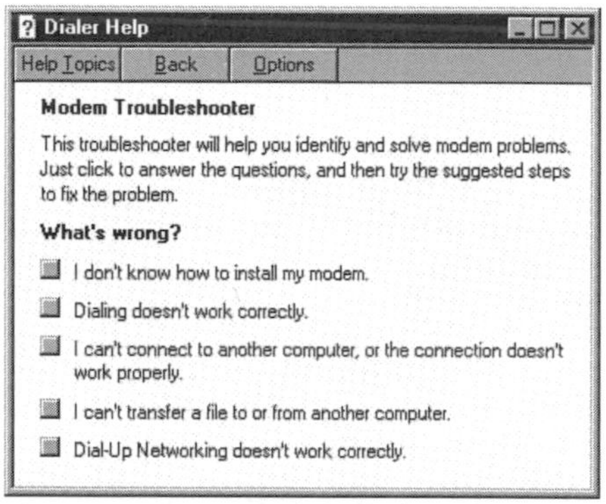

Fig. 22.8
Use the Windows online help to track down trouble with your modem.

How fast is fast enough?

If you were sending nothing but one-line messages to the people on your electronic mailing list, you probably wouldn't care how fast your modem is. But when you start sending around complicated messages with attached files, you soon discover that time really is money. If you can send twice as many bits across the wire every minute, you can send the same file in half the time.

Modem speeds are a moving target, but today the fastest conventional (analog) modems transmit data at a maximum speed of 28800 bits per second, or **bps**. The previous generation of modems, many of them still sold today, operate at half that speed, or 14400 bps. Still older models work at 9600 bps. (Some people use the term **baud** to refer to bits per second. They're wrong, but it's a technical detail more than anything else.)

For most jobs, a modem that runs at 14400 bps (just say "fourteen-four" if you want to impress other people as a computer expert) is sufficient. If you intend to browse the World Wide Web or transmit other large graphics and sound files, you'll want a 28800 bps modem (just say "twenty-eight-eight").

Want to go faster than that? Sorry, no can do—at least not with this technology. You'll have to switch to a different telephone standard called ISDN (Integrated Services Digital Network). But that's a topic for another book. For now, just stick with POTS (Plain Old Telephone Service).

23

Sending and Receiving E-Mail and Faxes

● **In this chapter:**

- Sending a message to someone you love (or hate)

- Reading and organizing the messages you get from others

- Faxing off a quick note

- Creating elaborate faxes out of documents

- It's for you! Receiving a fax with your computer

With Windows 95 mail and fax services, you can keep in touch with people the high-tech way! You may never need to visit the post office again . . . .

Windows provides an all-in-one program to make sure you stay intouch with anyone in the outside world— especially if he or she also uses Windows. Microsoft Exchange lets you send and retrieve electronic mail and faxes, as well as keep track of names, addresses, and other important information for friends, family, and business contacts.

You can say just about anything in e-mail, from a simple "Hello" to a long explanation of why fourth-quarter expenses went through the roof. (But before you send your first e-mail, look over the essentials of e-mail etiquette later in this chapter.) As long as you have a fax modem, you can even use Exchange to send and receive faxes.

E-mail essentials

If you understand how the postman gets mail and packages to your door, you've already mastered the basic concepts of electronic mail. You create messages, add attachments, fill out an envelope, and drop it in the Exchange mailbox, where the Windows postal agent picks it up at the same time it drops off any mail that other people have sent to you. Best of all, you don't have to lick a single stamp!

Where do I start?

 Before you can use Exchange, you have to set it up on your PC. If it isn't installed on your system, use the Add/Remove Programs icon in Control Panel to add it to your system. Windows includes a wizard to help you set up Exchange the first time.

 If you want to change any of the Exchange options, double-click on the Mail and Fax icon in Control Panel to pop up the Settings dialog box for Exchange. To change any of the options, click an item in the list and then click the Properties button. You'll see a sheet like the one in figure 23.1.

Some of the options are self-explanatory, but most of them are technical and absolutely baffling. If you're not sure how to configure Exchange, ask your network administrator for help, if you're on a network. (If you're not on a network, most of the really difficult settings don't apply to you anyway.)

A guided tour of the Inbox on the desktop

E-mail to anywhere: use Microsoft Exchange to send and receive mail and faxes—not just on a local network, but anywhere in the world.

Toolbar
One-click access to frequently used mail functions. Push the button to create a new message, reply to mail, manage your Address Book, and more. Exchange lets you add new buttons or delete existing ones.

Column headings
Click on any heading to sort your messages. Click again to sort in reverse order.

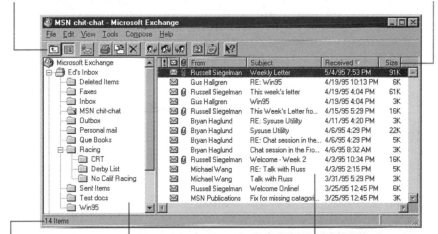

Status bar
Look here for helpful messages about the current task.

Folder list
Organize your messages, faxes, and even files into folders. You can add as many new folders as you like, and even put folders inside other folders.

Message window
The contents of the selected folder show up here. The default view shows the message title, sender's name, and other details, but you can create as many different views as you like. For example, you can group all your messages by sender or by subject.

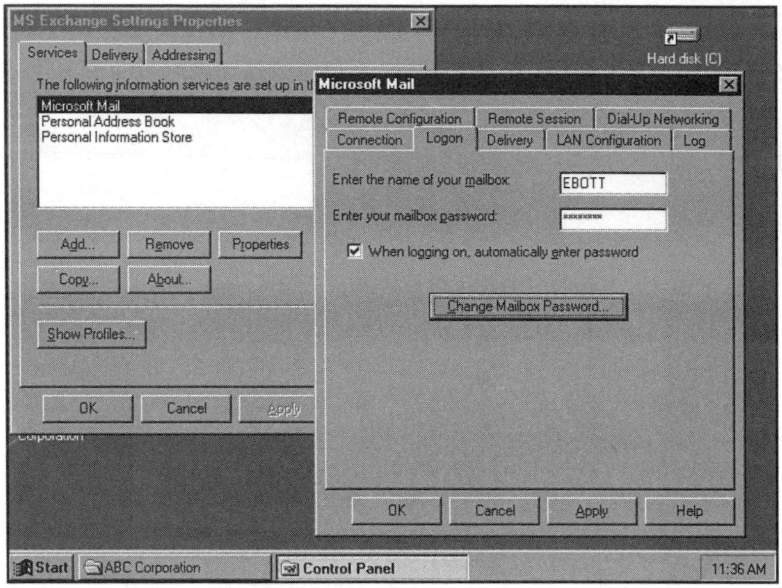

Fig. 23.1
Double-click on the Mail and Fax icon in Control Panel to pop up this configuration dialog box, then click Properties to see more details about each item. Confused by all these options? Ask your network administrator to make sure you're set up correctly.

What can I do with Exchange?

After Exchange is successfully installed on your PC, just click on the Inbox icon on your desktop or choose Microsoft Exchange from the Programs section of the Start menu. Once the Exchange window opens, you can do one of four things:

- **Send a simple message** as e-mail. It might be the electronic equivalent of a postcard ("Having a wonderful time. Wish you were online.") or as heavy as a package from the IRS. You can send it just about anywhere: to someone on your local network, if you're on one—or to a friend using The Microsoft Network, CompuServe, or the Internet.

- **Send a fax**. To send an Exchange fax, you'll need a modem that has fax capabilities built in, and the person on the other end of the connection needs a fax machine or a fax modem.

- **Send a file** (or a whole bunch of files) as an e-mail attachment. The attachment might be a file you've created with a word processor or a spreadsheet; all the recipient has to do is double-click on its icon to see (and edit) the file.

> ## 66 *Plain English, please!*
>
> An **attachment** is a file that rides along with an e-mail message, just as you sometimes receive a package with a letter taped to the outside. Almost all mail systems can exchange attachments with each other these days, thanks to the standardization of mailing methods. (You don't really need to know about all the standards, but in case someone asks you, Microsoft Exchange is "MIME-compatible." That's a standard.)
>
> Attachments are tricky things—if the person on the other end of the mail connection is using a mail program other than Microsoft Exchange, there's no guarantee the standard attachment-handling formats will work. The package might get lost or damaged in transit. If you plan to exchange an important attachment with someone, your best bet is to first try a test with a small WordPad file, to make sure the two mail systems can handle the package properly. 99

- Finally, you can **receive messages** from anyone who knows your e-mail address.

Who can I send a message to?

When you address a letter to your next-door neighbor and drop it in your local mailbox, you can be reasonably sure that your local mail carrier will deliver it. After all, it's on his route. What if you send a postcard to Moscow? It'll get there, too, as long as the Postal Service and its counterparts in Russia have an agreement to exchange mail. But if you try to send a package to Mr. Floyd on the dark side of the moon, it'll probably come back marked "Undeliverable."

E-mail works the same way. Microsoft Exchange has its own local delivery route, plus agreements with foreign e-mail systems to swap mail. Depending on how you and your network administrator have it set up, Exchange lets you communicate with the following people:

- Other Windows users on your company's network

- Anyone with an account on The Microsoft Network online service

- Anyone with a fax machine

- Anyone with an account on the Internet

TIP   **For more information about The Microsoft Network and the** Internet, see Chapters 24 and 25.

E-mail etiquette

Once you've used e-mail for awhile, you'll wonder how you ever got along without it. You'll get rid of those stupid pink "While You Were Out" message slips. When you come back from lunch, you'll find easy-to-read electronic messages instead of indecipherable scribblings on yellow sticky notes all over your computer screen. Maybe you'll even use e-mail to send love letters to your sweetheart or instant expressions of outrage to your Congressman.

After awhile, you may think the *e* in e-mail stands for *easy*, and there's the problem. E-mail is so effortless that it's easy to send the wrong kind of message, and once you've hit the Send button, there's no way to bring it back.

Want to avoid the most common e-mail boo-boos? Memorize these helpful tips:

- Be extra clear when you write e-mail. If you're responding to someone else's message, include a snippet of the original message so the person at the other end knows what you're talking about. Don't just send a message saying "Great idea. Go for it!" You're likely to get a message back—"Go for what?"

- Include a meaningful Subject line. Your message is more likely to get read if the Subject line gives a strong clue about the message contents.

- Avoid sarcasm and subtle humor unless you're positive the recipient will get your joke. If you must, at least add a "Just kidding!" afterwards. Better yet, pick your favorite smiley icon and tack it onto the message.

- Never, ever send a message when you're angry. Mad at your boss? Go ahead and write that memo telling him what you really think, but *don't* send it. You'll probably feel a lot cooler in the morning, so go home, get a good night's sleep, and when you get to work the next day delete the message without re-reading it. Start a new message and send it instead. Remember: e-mail is forever. Especially when it's embarrassing.

- Don't put people on the Cc: list unless they really need to see a copy of your message. Electronic junk mail is just as irritating as the paper variety.

- Be extra careful when you use the Reply To All button. One infamous e-mail writer at a large computer company accidentally sent a steamy love letter intended for his sweetheart to all 5,000 employees at his company. People still whisper behind his back when they see him in the hallways.

I want to send an e-mail message...

To send an old-fashioned paper letter, you'll need a piece of paper, an envelope, an address book, and a stamp. To compose an e-mail message, you'll need the electronic equivalent of everything but the stamp. Fortunately, all of this is usually just a click or two away.

Here's how to get started:

1 Click the new message button (you can also press Ctrl+N). You'll see the New Message form shown in figure 23.2.

*Want to send a data file along with your message? Click the **Insert file** button to attach it to your message.*

*Not sure what the buttons on the **toolbar** do? Aim the mouse pointer at a button and leave it there for a few seconds to see a helpful **ToolTip**.*

*Use the **formatting toolbar** to quickly change fonts, add bullets, or adjust the text alignment.*

Fig. 23.2

The electronic letter, complete with envelope.

*Click here to **Send** your message to the Outbox.*

*Put a short summary of the message in the **Subject** line.*

*The **envelope**. Click the To and Cc buttons to tell Exchange where to deliver your message.*

*Enter the **message text** in this window. You can use fancy fonts, bold and italic formatting, even colors. If your recipients are also Exchange users, they'll see exactly what you sent.*

66 *Plain English, please!*

When you use Microsoft Exchange, you may occasionally see a reference to **MAPI**. The acronym, pronounced "mappy," stands for the Messaging Application Programming Interface, a common set of software widgets that let different e-mail programs communicate reliably with one another. Thanks to MAPI, you can use Microsoft Exchange to swap e-mail with a coworker who uses Lotus Development's cc:Mail or Novell's GroupWise. 99

2 Enter one or more addresses for the primary recipients. Press the To button to search through the Address Book (see fig. 23.3). Highlight the name you want to add, then press the T**o** button to add the name to the Recipients list. If you want to send copies to other people, add their names to the C**c** list here. (You can add a new name to your address book here by clicking N**ew**.) You can send the same message different ways—via fax, e-mail, and the Internet, for instance.

TIP Want to send a secret copy to someone? Use Bcc, for blind carbon copy. As you're composing a message, select Bcc Box from the V**iew** menu to add this capability.

Fig. 23.3
Your Address Book contains the details you need to send a message to anyone that Exchange can reach.

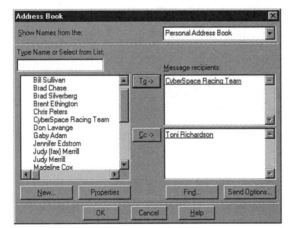

TIP **You don't have to enter the full name of a recipient, as long as** there's an entry in your Address Book. Just enter some or all of the name, and Exchange will search for the nearest matching name. For example, if there's only one Bill in your Address Book—the entry for Bill Gates—you can type **Bill** in the address field and Exchange will automatically fill in the rest of the name when you press the Send button. If there's more than one Bill, Exchange will show you a list of possible addressees and let you pick the right one.

3 Enter a Subject. Be as clear and detailed as possible. For example, `Copy machine is broken!` is a better Subject line than `Big problem!!!`

4 Attach any files, if necessary.

CAUTION **Be careful when sending files to other people who aren't using** Exchange. You have no guarantee that the programs they use to receive mail will correctly receive the attachment you send. Try a test run before you send a crucial file.

5 Select any options. For example, if you want to be notified when the person at the other end reads your message, click the Receipt button.

6 Click Send or press Ctrl+S. Your message goes into the Outbox and will be sent the next time Exchange checks for mail.

How do I send mail to people on different services?

Good question. The answer depends on several factors.

If you're sending and receiving mail through The Microsoft Network, which has an Internet connection, you can address mail to any online service using the standard Internet addressing scheme: *name@location.location.etc.* For instance, the developer on this book was lwagner@que.mcp.com—e-mail her and tell her what you thought of the book! Addresses at online services look like this: *IDnumber*@compuserve.com, *IDnumber*@prodigy.com, *nickname*@aol.com.

If you're on a local area network, your e-mail administrator may have set up mail **gateways** to connect to various services, such as CompuServe. Ask about this—there may be a special way that messages need to be addressed.

What do I do with these messages?

Sooner or later (usually sooner), your Exchange mailbox will start overflowing with messages, and you'll have trouble keeping up with your mail. The solution? Create a filing system, and move related messages into folders so you can find them easily later.

To read a message, just double-click on it.

What are those funny-looking symbols I see in some e-mail messages?

It's hard to be humorous in e-mail. Subtle humor is the worst of all. When you're face-to-face, you signal a joke with a smile and a wink. So how do you pass the same message along in an e-mail message?

I sometimes add **<g>** (for "grin") after a remark that might leave the reader wondering what I meant. You can do the same. But if you want to really be creative, try using an **emoticon**—a clever word that packs *emotion* and *icon* into the same space. The most common of all is the **smiley**, a little grinning face turned on its side to suggest that that last remark was not meant to be taken seriously.

There are literally thousands of smileys. Here's a sampling of some of the more useful ones. (If you can't figure them out, try turning your head 90 degrees to the left.)

:-) or :)   Plain ol' smiley. "Just kidding."

;-)   Winky smiley. Used for slightly more sarcastic remarks. "Just kidding. Really!"

:-(Frowning smiley. "I didn't like that last remark." Also used to express unhappiness.

>:->   Devilish smiley. For really caustic comments.

:*)   Drunk smiley.

:-{)   Smiley with moustache.

{:-)   Wearing bad toupee.

:'-(Crying.

:-@   Screaming.

O :-)   Angel smiley (see the halo?).

:-D   Laughing (at you!).

:-/   Skeptical smiley.

:-o   Uh-oh!

X-(Dead smiley.

—<—{(@   Long-stemmed rose (for when you're feeling romantic).

To reply to a message, click the Reply to Sender button. To reply to everyone on the list for the original message, use the Reply to All button.

To delete a message, click the Delete button. Exchange doesn't actually delete the message; it just moves it to the Deleted Files folder, where you'll need to delete it again to really get rid of it.

To store a message in a folder, drag the message from the right-hand pane and drop it on a folder icon in the Folders list on the left side of the Exchange window.

Q&A *I don't see the Folders list. Is Exchange broken?*

 No, it's just not set up to show that view when you click on the Inbox icon on the desktop. To reveal the Folders list, click the Show/Hide Folder List button on the Exchange toolbar.

CAUTION If you use Exchange for your regular e-mail, you'll quickly fill it with irreplaceable messages. Don't run the risk of losing them forever! Keep backup copies of your mail file. Use the Find, Files or Folders option to search for files called *.PST, then copy the results to a safe place.

What do these default folders do?

When you first use Exchange, it has only four folders. Here's what they're used for:

The **Inbox** is the place where incoming mail is delivered.

When you send a message, it goes into the **Outbox** until Exchange is ready to deliver it. (It'll deliver the message the next time you connect to the network or service that's supposed to carry it. When's that? It depends on how you've got Exchange configured.) Exchange must be running to send or receive messages.

Sent Items keeps a copy of each message that you send. You can tell Exchange not to save these messages by choosing Tools, Options and checking the appropriate box.

Deleted Items is the Exchange equivalent of the Recycle Bin. Messages you delete go here. When you select a message in this folder and delete it, Exchange gets rid of it permanently. If you're pressed for space on your hard disk, it's a good idea to get in the habit of deleting unimportant messages as soon as you've read them.

Sending and receiving faxes

It's easy to tell a fax that was sent by a computer because it's usually so sharp and clear. The reason, of course, it that it doesn't have to be scanned in through the fax machine, where the glass is covered with fingerprints, scratches, and stray bits of blueberry muffin somebody dropped there last month.

When you set up Exchange to handle faxes, Windows turns your fax modem into the full-fledged equivalent of a fax machine. You can receive any fax, anytime, from anyone, anywhere. You can send faxes, too—if you can print a document, you can fax it. The only thing you can't do is fax a paper document to someone else—with or without blueberry muffin crumbs.

TIP   **Actually, you *can* use Exchange to fax a piece of paper to some-** one else if you have a special kind of hardware called a **scanner**. It's a big hassle to make your scanner and fax modem work together, though. If you fax lots of paper documents, you're better off using a plain old fax machine and saving the fax modem for the documents you create on your computer.

Setting up the fax

The fax component of Microsoft Exchange is not installed automatically when you set up Windows 95. Here are the three steps you have to go through before you can set up Exchange to handle faxes:

1 Install the fax software. Use the Add/Remove Programs icon in the Control Panel and check the box labeled Microsoft Fax, then follow the instructions.

2 Tell Exchange that you want to use the fax capabilities. Double-click on the Inbox icon and choose Tools, Services. If you see the words Microsoft Fax in the list, you can stop here. Otherwise, click the Add button and choose Microsoft Fax from the dialog box that appears.

3 Tell Exchange about your fax modem. At this point, the Exchange setup program automatically offers to do this for you. Just click OK and fill in your fax number in the dialog box that appears. Then click on the modem tab and make sure your modem is listed correctly.

You're ready to fax!

Composing a fax

You have two options when you want to send a fax to someone else. In either case, you can ask Exchange to send over a wizard to help with the details.

I just want to fax a quick note...

The easiest way to send a quick note to someone who isn't on your e-mail system is to jot a quick fax. Open Exchange and choose Compose, New Fax. You'll instantly invoke the wizard. Follow the instructions, and type the message you want to send on the screen with the box for Notes. Click Finish, and Exchange will go to work, converting your input into the right format, then dialing the phone, squealing at the machine on the other end to establish communications, and sending the fax.

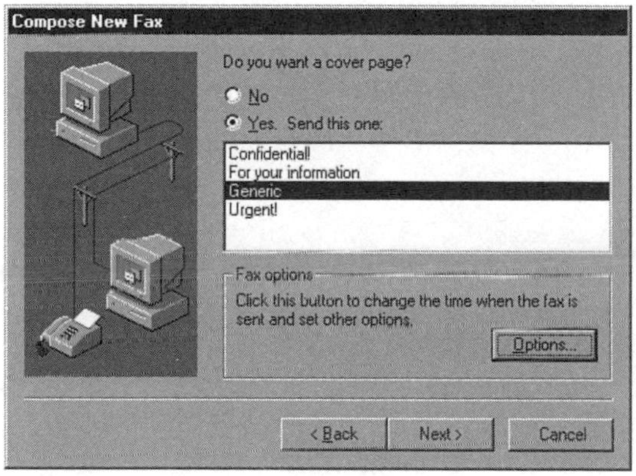

Fig. 23.4

The Compose New Fax Wizard walks you through the process of creating a fax. If you attach a file (such as a word processing document) to your fax, Windows "prints" it and sends the page to the recipient's fax machine.

I just created this document. How do I fax it?

If you've just used an application program (WordPad, for example) to create a beautiful document, complete with fancy fonts and formatting, it's a snap to fax it. Just print the file the way you normally would, but when Windows asks which printer you'd like to use, choose Microsoft Fax from the list. At this point, the Exchange Wizard will pop up, giving you the opportunity to add a cover sheet or a quick note. Follow the same steps you'd use to send a fax from Exchange.

> **TIP**   **Use the Windows built-in cover page editor to put together**
> attention-getting cover pages for the faxes you send out. You'll find it on
> the Start menu, under Programs, Accessories, Fax. If you prefer, you can skip
> the cover page completely.

Sending the fax

Most of the time, Exchange assumes you want your fax to go out right now. But what if you're sending a 10-page fax halfway around the world? Wouldn't you rather wait till the phone rates are less expensive? Exchange lets you do exactly that. When you get to the dialog box where the Wizard asks which cover page you want to use, click the Options button (you'll see a dialog box like the one in figure 23.5), and then click the Set button in the section labeled Time to send.

Fig. 23.5

Want your fax to go out later, when telephone rates are lower? Use the Send Options dialog box to set it up for delayed delivery.

Receiving faxes

Sending faxes is easy, but what if you want to use Exchange to receive a fax? You have three choices. To set this option, double-click on the fax icon in the lower right corner of the taskbar, then choose Options, Modem Properties. You'll see the sheet in figure 23.6.

- If you never want Exchange to answer the phone, choose Don't answer.

- If you want to decide when to pick up a fax, choose Manual.

- If you want to use your modem as a full-time fax machine, just tell Exchange how many rings to wait before picking up. The default is four.

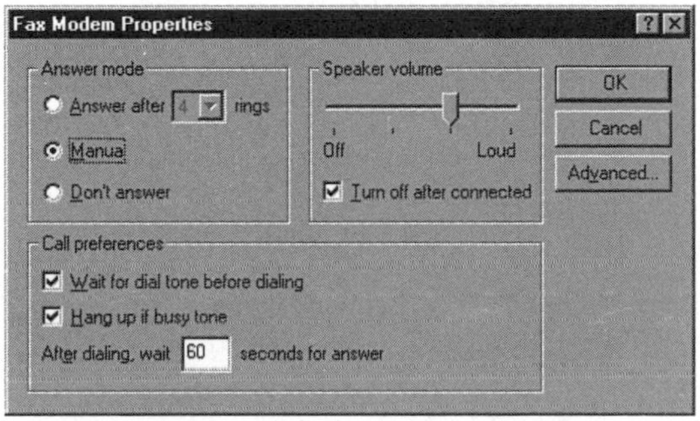

Fig. 23.6

Set your telephone to answer after a specified number of rings, or only when you click this button.

Fax Modem Properties	? X

Answer mode
- ○ Answer after 4 ▼ rings
- ⊙ Manual
- ○ Don't answer

Speaker volume
Off ——————— Loud
☑ Turn off after connected

OK
Cancel
Advanced...

Call preferences
☑ Wait for dial tone before dialing
☑ Hang up if busy tone
After dialing, wait 60 seconds for answer

TIP   **What's the best way to find someone's e-mail address? If they're** not on your network, call them on the phone and ask! Seriously. There's no comprehensive Yellow Pages or Directory Assistance for e-mail. Not yet.

24

Connecting to The Microsoft Network

● In this chapter:

- What is The Microsoft Network?

- How do I sign up?

- Logging on and logging off

- Communicating with other people online

- Files, references, and more!

Looking for stimulating conversation? The latest games? That piece of trivia that you can't quite recall? The Microsoft Network is a great starting point . . . . >

Most of the time, Windows 95 is strictly personal. It's you, your PC, and your work. Sure, you can share files with other people, but, for the most part, you and Windows have a one-to-one relationship. There's one giant exception to that rule, though. The Microsoft Network (MSN), an online service that's included with Windows 95, lets you interact with people from all over the world, sending messages, chatting, looking up facts and figures, and generally exploring the outside world.

To use The Microsoft Network, all you need is a modem and a copy of Windows 95. (It doesn't hurt to have a healthy sense of curiosity, too!)

The more things change...

They say life is full of surprises. That's especially true of an online service like The Microsoft Network, where new sections come and go literally at a moment's notice. Part of the appeal of this online service is the way it's constantly growing and changing. It's like the weather in Boston: if you don't like it today, just come back tomorrow.

That also explains why the screens you see in these pages probably look a little different from the ones you'll see when you log on to The Microsoft Network. The basic building blocks don't change, though—and fortunately, most of the changes are designed to make it easier for you to get around!

How do I sign up?

 Before you can explore The Microsoft Network, you have to make sure it's installed. If you can't find the files on your computer, open Control Panel, choose Add/Remove Programs, then check The Microsoft Network box (if you haven't already installed the Exchange e-mail program, you'll need to add it, too).

Going online with The Microsoft Network

Each time you dial up The Microsoft Network, this is your home base. It's called Microsoft Network Central, and it's your gateway to literally everything inside the service.

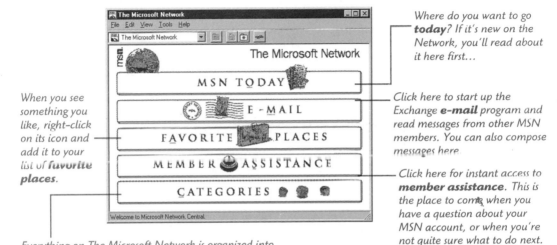

Where do you want to go today? If it's new on the Network, you'll read about it here first...

When you see something you like, right-click on its icon and add it to your list of favorite places.

Click here to start up the Exchange e-mail program and read messages from other MSN members. You can also compose messages here.

Click here for instant access to member assistance. This is the place to come when you have a question about your MSN account, or when you're not quite sure what to do next.

Everything on The Microsoft Network is organized into a series of folders, each representing a different broad category. Click here to start discovering what's inside MSN.

Jump to Microsoft Network Central.

Jump to your personal favorite places folder.

Disconnect from The Microsoft Network.

Go to the parent of the current folder.

See the properties for the selected item. Same as right-clicking.

Create a shortcut to selected icon(s) and add to your favorite places folder.

Change the view of the contents of the current window—choices are Large Icons, Small Icons, List, and Details.

See an Explorer-style tree view of The Microsoft Network.

Double-click on any of these icons to drill down into the many categories of information available on MSN.

Once the MSN software is properly installed, the next step is to register your name (and credit card number) with the folks who run The Microsoft Network. Windows normally walks you through this process when you first install MSN. If you choose not to configure The Microsoft Network but change your mind later, just follow these steps:

First, look in the root folder of your hard drive for a folder called Program Files. Inside that folder you should find another folder for The Microsoft Network. Look inside *that* folder, and you'll see an application called Signup. Double-click here—you'll be transported to the dialog box shown in figure 24.1. (If you still can't find it, try the Find, Files or Folders option on the Start menu.)

Fig. 24.1

Signing up for The Microsoft Network isn't difficult. Just answer three sets of questions: Who are you? What do you want to do? And how do you plan to pay for it?

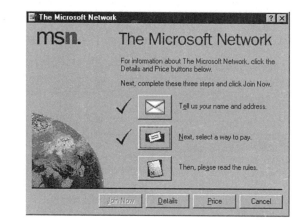

The Microsoft Network needs some crucial bits of data from you before it will let you join in the fun: it wants your name, your credit card number, and your formal agreement to the MSN rules (all you have to do is read a dialog box and click OK). Once you've gotten over these hurdles, you get to choose a sign-up name and a password. Assuming the name you've chosen hasn't been taken already, you're ready to go.

TIP **It's a good idea to change your password regularly. With MSN, this** task takes only a few seconds. From The Microsoft Network Central screen, choose Tools, Password, and follow the prompts. Don't forget to write your new password down and store it in a safe place!

How much is this going to cost me?

Cruising around an online service like The Microsoft Network is a little like riding in a taxi through Manhattan. It's a fascinating place to visit, but you're paying for every second that the meter is ticking. You certainly wouldn't sit in the back of a cab with the meter running for 20 minutes while you read your mail. So why do the same online?

If money matters, you should do as much work as possible on your own nickel, and save the pay-as-you-go trips for those times when you're trying to get from point A to point B. Here are a few tips to keep your MSN budget under control:

- Never read messages while you're connected to MSN. Download your mail and log off. Then you can read your messages at your own pace, and reply as thoughtfully as you need to. When your outbox is stuffed with all your replies, *then* it's OK to do a second pass to send the new messages.

- Set up MSN so it will automatically disconnect if you've been sitting idle for a certain period of time (the default value is 10 minutes). Go to Microsoft Network Central, choose <u>V</u>iew, <u>O</u>ptions, click on the General tab, and make sure the proper options are set. And don't worry—MSN will never deliberately break the connection without asking your permission first.

- For a constant visual reminder of how long you've been online, check out the small modem icon in the lower right corner of the taskbar. The red and green lights flash each time your modem talks to the one on the other end of the connection. Double-click the modem icon; you'll see a display that tells you how long you've been connected.

- Make sure you get your money's worth. There are plenty of places on The Microsoft Network where you can spend significant amounts of money. Some are worth every penny. Make sure you know up front how much you're spending, and what you're getting for your hard-earned dollars. Each additional-cost feature will state clearly what the charge is, and you can find the current MSN basic rates by going to Member Assistance.

Starting up and shutting down...

Once you've got a login name and password, you're ready to connect to The Microsoft Network. Start by double-clicking the MSN icon on the desktop. That takes you to the Sign In window (see fig. 24.2), where all you have to do is click a button to get online.

Fig. 24.2

Double-clicking the MSN icon on the desktop takes you here. Click Connect to go straight to MSN. Click one of the other buttons if you're away from home and want to change the number you normally call or tell Windows to use a different set of Location settings.

Each time you dial in, you have a chance to choose another number to call or specify that you're dialing from a different location. Both options are handy if you have Windows 95 installed on your notebook PC, and you want to check your mail or browse a bulletin board from somewhere other than your usual stomping grounds.

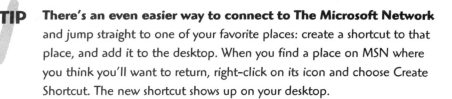

TIP   **There's an even easier way to connect to The Microsoft Network** and jump straight to one of your favorite places: create a shortcut to that place, and add it to the desktop. When you find a place on MSN where you think you'll want to return, right-click on its icon and choose Create Shortcut. The new shortcut shows up on your desktop.

The first thing you'll see every time you connect is the MSN Today screen (see fig. 24.3). You can set up MSN so you don't see this screen automatically, but why would you want to do that? MSN Today takes only a few seconds to read, and it gives you valuable information about new sections that have been added, and about upcoming special events. If you see something you like on MSN Today, you can usually click on one of the highlighted words to jump straight there and check it out for yourself.

These **jumps** are one of the coolest parts of MSN. Whenever you see a word or phrase in a different color, chances are it's a jump. (You can tell for sure by aiming the mouse pointer at it. If the arrow turns to a small hand, it's a jump.) Click on any jump, and it's just as though you've stepped into the Star Trek transporter room. "Beam me down, Scotty." Even if your ultimate destination would normally require double-clicking through ten levels of folders, this shortcut can save you time.

Fig. 24.3
The MSN Today page keeps you up to date on new developments on The Microsoft Network. Click on one of the highlighted "jump" words and you'll be transported—Star Trek-style—straight there.

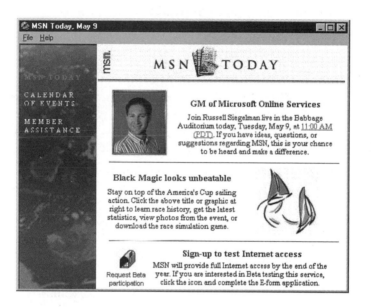

 To disconnect from The Microsoft Network, right-click on the MSN icon at the right side of the taskbar and choose Sign Out. Don't worry—you'll get a chance to change your mind before MSN actually pulls the plug.

Q&A *Every time I log on to The Microsoft Network, the graphics seem fuzzy for a few seconds, although they eventually clear up. Is there something wrong with my modem?*

No, that's exactly the way MSN is supposed to work. The idea is to quickly show you the general, very rough outline of each graphic image instead of forcing you to wait while the screen slooooooooooowly redraws the image. If, after you see the first pass, you decide you don't need to see more, you can move on without wasting too much time. If you choose to stay and watch, though, the graphics will gradually get sharper and clearer.

What can I do with The Microsoft Network?

If you've ever sampled another online service, such as CompuServe or America Online, you have a pretty good idea of what you can do on The Microsoft Network. The most popular sections are the ones where you can talk directly with other people who have similar interests, either live in a "chat" area, or on a bulletin board, where you follow a more leisurely discussion with longer messages and responses posted over days or weeks—for all to read.

" Plain English, please!

There are several ways to communicate with other people on an online service. Chat is an immediate-gratification thing, where the person you're typing back and forth with is online at the same time as you. It's a real conversation, only slower, because no one can type as fast as they talk. A bulletin board is more like public e-mail. Just like the bulletin board in the company kitchen, people can write down their comments and pin them up in a public place for others to see. "

But there are plenty of other things to do on MSN, too, and the best way to find them is to explore. Chances are you'll get a special offer of free connect time when you first sign up. Take advantage of those free hours to look around MSN to see whether it has what you want.

Q&A *Each time I double-click on an MSN icon, the window I was looking at goes away. Can't I keep two windows open at once?*

Yes, you can. Choose <u>V</u>iew, <u>O</u>ptions, and click on the Folder tab. Now tell MSN you want to browse with a separate window for each folder. If you prefer the clean, uncluttered, single-window approach, you can still open a separate Explorer-style window on demand by right-clicking on an MSN icon and then choosing Explore from the popup menu.

I want to send electronic mail

The most popular form of communication online, by far, is e-mail. If you're a member of The Microsoft Network, you can use Microsoft Exchange to send a message to any other MSN member. You can also send messages to anyone who has an Internet address—a group that includes members of other online services that are connected to the Internet, such as America Online, CompuServe, and Prodigy. (To read more about how Microsoft Exchange works, see Chapter 23.)

- To check your e-mail, click on the E-mail bar in Microsoft Network Central. That starts the Exchange software, if it isn't already running.

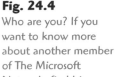

- When you create a message intended for someone on The Microsoft Network, you'll need to know his address. That means looking in the MSN Address Book. Switch to Exchange, and click on the Address Book icon. Select The Microsoft Network in the drop-down list box titled "<u>S</u>how Names from the:"

- You can get extra information about any MSN member, once you find her entry in the MSN Address Book. Just right-click on the name and choose P<u>r</u>operties to see a sheet like the one in figure 24.4.

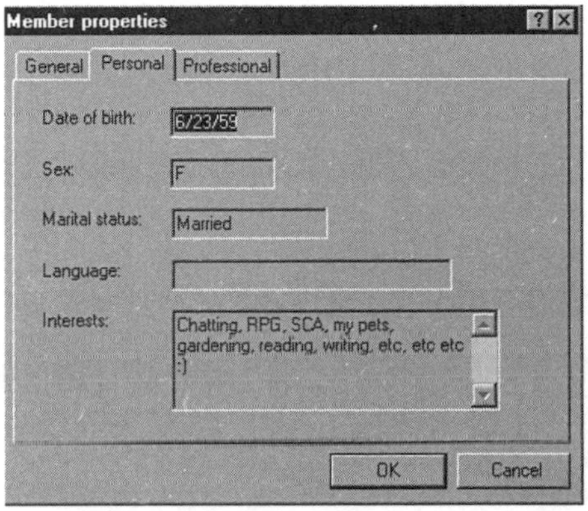

Fig. 24.4

Who are you? If you want to know more about another member of The Microsoft Network, find his or her entry in the MSN Address Book, and look at the properties.

Member properties	? X
General	Personal	Professional

Date of birth: 6/23/59

Sex: F

Marital status: Married

Language:

Interests: Chatting, RPG, SCA, my pets, gardening, reading, writing, etc, etc etc :-}

OK   Cancel

TIP   **It's usually faster to find a personal Address Book entry than it is** to go through the entire MSN Address Book over the phone. To copy the MSN address of a person you write to regularly into your personal address book, highlight the name, right-click, and choose <u>A</u>dd to Personal Address Book from the popup menu.

Q&A   *Whoops! I'm lost in The Microsoft Network. How do I get back to the beginning?*

Like anything in Windows, the trick is to use the right mouse button. While you're connected to MSN, you'll see a small icon in the lower right corner of the taskbar. Right-click there for a handful of extremely useful options, including shortcuts that take you straight to MSN Central or your Favorite Places folder, plus a bold entry that lets you sign off *right now*.

I want to have a serious conversation

Online bulletin boards can be like big cocktail parties. At any given time, there may be dozens of conversations going on, all at the same time. Some are serious, some are just silly. But because it's a public place, you're free to stop by, listen in, and even contribute to the conversation. (Just like at a cocktail party, though, it's best to listen for a while to make sure you understand the conversation before you jump in!)

Unlike chat areas, where everyone talks at once and confusion is normal, bulletin boards allow you to spend as much time as you need reading and writing your contributions. Each separate conversation gets its own **thread**, and every time you reply to a message instead of starting a new one, the reply is indented under the original message. Eventually, a thread can become filled with back-and-forth dialog, as figure 24.5 shows.

Fig. 24.5

In a threaded discussion, each reply is indented so you can easily follow the entire dialog.

Subject	Author	Size	Date
⊟ RE: Taking Up Sod	Phil Ash	852 bytes	5/3/95 9:48 PM
⊟ RE: Taking Up Sod	Peter Delaney	887 bytes	5/4/95 5:27 PM
📄 RE: Taking Up Sod	Steven Rothweiler	687 bytes	5/4/95 8:24 PM
📄 RE: Taking Up Sod	Aaron Contorer	826 bytes	5/5/95 11:02 AM
📄 Patio and Pergola	Peter Delaney	609 bytes	5/4/95 5:31 PM
📄 Herbs (Basil and Cilantro) - ...	Aaron Contorer	679 bytes	5/5/95 10:58 AM
⊟ Roses	Paul St Denis	390 bytes	5/5/95 10:32 PM
⊟ RE: Roses	Sharron Mik	594 bytes	5/6/95 8:47 AM
📄 RE: Roses	Steven Rothweiler	557 bytes	5/6/95 8:11 PM
📄 RE: Roses	Steven Rothweiler	557 bytes	5/6/95 8:13 PM
⊟ RE: Roses	Paul St Denis	605 bytes	5/7/95 8:14 PM
📄 RE: Roses	Sharron Mik	564 bytes	5/8/95 2:40 PM
📄 RE: Roses	David Soper	456 bytes	5/8/95 11:29 PM
⊟ Dog Spots	Mark Lamphier	466 bytes	5/6/95 6:54 PM
📄 RE: Dog Spots	Steven Rothweiler	534 bytes	5/6/95 8:13 PM
⊟ Getting Rid of Bermuda Grass	Dennis Nunes	459 bytes	5/7/95 7:59 AM
📄 RE: Getting Rid of Bermuda Gr...	Greg Smith	514 bytes	5/9/95 3:19 AM

10 conversations, 9 with unread messages

To start a new thread, use the Compose menu to create a new message. Give the message a meaningful title, so other people will read it. When you click the Send button, MSN will post the message to the discussion, and add a small document icon to its left to signal that it's a new conversation.

To follow a thread, double-click on the original message, which will pop up in its own window. Click the Next Message button (with a single down arrow) to jump to the next message in the same conversation. Click the Next Conversation button to walk away from a boring discussion and see what's happening in the next thread.

To reply to a message in a conversation, use the Compose menu and choose Reply to BBS. Type in your reply, as shown in figure 24.6. When you're satisfied with what you've written, press the Send button; your message will be added to the list for all to see. (To send a private message to someone, use the Reply by E-mail choice instead. Unless you're discussing very personal issues, though, it's considered good etiquette to keep the conversation public so everyone can read what you have to say.)

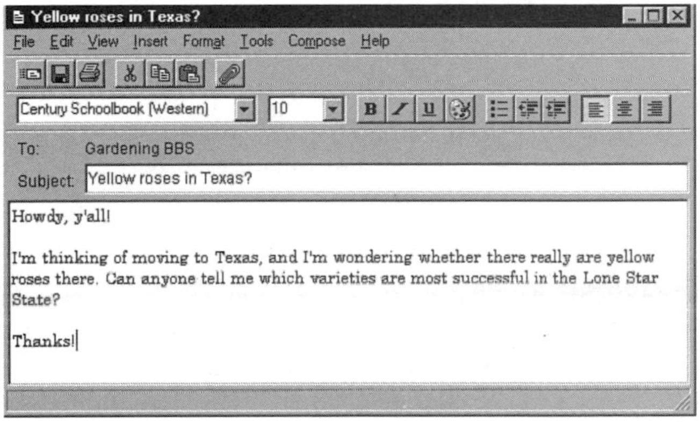

Fig. 24.6

To post your own message in an online conversation, just compose a new message and click the Send button (at left).

I want to have an instant conversation

Like other online services, The Microsoft Network includes areas where you can chat with other people who are online right now. There's nothing permanent about these sessions, and there's rarely anything serious that goes on. (How can there be? You only have one line for each comment, and everything scrolls by so quickly that it would tax even The Amazing Kreskin's powers of concentration.)

If bulletin boards are like cocktail parties, chat areas are like crowded bars. There's so much noise you might not even be able to hear yourself think. And you certainly won't be able to have an in-depth conversation. In some areas, in fact, most of the comments will be of the "What's your sign?" variety.

Chat isn't for everyone, but it's fun occasionally. When you find yourself in a chat area, the window will look like the one in figure 24.7.

Fig. 24.7
Inside the chat window. Things move quickly here!

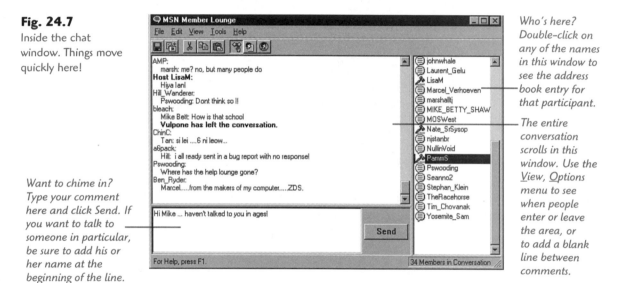

Who's here? Double-click on any of the names in this window to see the address book entry for that participant.

The entire conversation scrolls in this window. Use the View, Options menu to see when people enter or leave the area, or to add a blank line between comments.

Want to chime in? Type your comment here and click Send. If you want to talk to someone in particular, be sure to add his or her name at the beginning of the line.

There's one in every crowd. When you're in a crowded bar and a rowdy patron starts annoying you, you can turn your back. Do the same thing online if a fellow chat participant gets out of hand. To tell MSN you want to turn your back on someone, highlight his or her name in the list at the right, then choose View, Ignore Members. The comments will no longer appear in the chat window.

But wait! There's more...

There's much, much more in MSN, and there's no way to cover it all here. Just to give you an idea of what's out there, though, look for the trial edition of Microsoft Bookshelf, a collection of reference books that includes an atlas, dictionary, encyclopedia, and much more. The version of Bookshelf on MSN is smaller than the one you can buy on CD, but it's still fun to use.

To find Bookshelf, click on the Start menu and choose Find, On The Microsoft Network. In the dialog box that pops up, type **Bookshelf** and then click Find Now. The results appear at the bottom of the Find dialog box, as shown in figure 24.8.

Fig. 24.8

Click the Start menu and use Find to track down anything on MSN. In this case, we've found the Bookshelf Intro Edition.

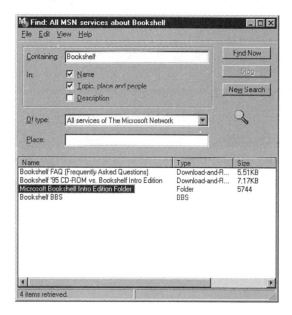

To install the introductory edition of Bookshelf, jump to the folder where it's stored, and follow the online instructions. Now, anytime you need to know an obscure fact, you can go straight to the source (see fig. 24.9). The program looks different from anything you've ever seen in an online service, and it's just a sample of what you can expect to find on The Microsoft Network.

Fig. 24.9

For a great glimpse of what MSN can do, try the introductory edition Microsoft Bookshelf. Look in any of the books—dictionary, atlas, encyclopedia, and more—for just about any conceivable fact.

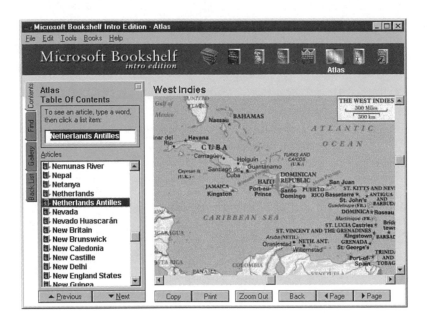

25

Getting On the Information Superhighway: Accessing the Internet

● In this chapter:

- What is the Internet, anyway, and what can I do there?

- How do I join up?

- Setting up the software to get yourself connected

- What else is out there?

Don't be a "technophobe"—jump on the Information Super-highway straight from Windows 95. All you need is a modem and a little cash . . . . ➤

Douglas Adams, the author of *The Hitchhiker's Guide to the Galaxy* and all its sequels, said it better than I can: "The Internet is big. Really big. It gives the idea of infinity much better than infinity itself."

With that kind of introduction, it seems a bit presumptuous to try to explain the Internet in one small chapter of this book. So let's start with a general disclaimer: if you want to know everything about the Internet, you'll have to read several big books (including some excellent ones published by the people who brought you this one). You'll also have to master some hard technical terms, because there's very little plain English to be found when you start talking about the Internet!

Fortunately, it's all worth the effort. The Internet is a very cool place, and this chapter can help get you moving in the right direction.

What is the Internet?

Without getting into too many boring technical details, suffice it to say that the Internet was originally set up in the late 1960s and early 1970s. The basic principle was to share ideas and computer time (which was incredibly expensive back then). The name itself is short for **internetworking**, which is a fairly accurate description of the way many small groups of computers at research institutes and universities were hooked into one immense worldwide network with the help of telephone lines and modems, and a lot of cooperation.

Today, all those folks—genuine rocket scientists and propellerheads alike—are still using the Internet, but they have to share the space with ordinary people like you and me. And where commercial activity was once strictly forbidden on "the Net," today it's the single most important force driving its growth. Depending on who you listen to, there are upwards of 30 million people who now use some part of the Internet for business or pleasure.

 TIP **Its official name is the Internet (there's even an Internet Society** that manages the business of keeping track of Internet names and addresses) but real experts just call it the **Net**, as in "Let me look for that information on the Net and I'll get back to you."

When you connect your computer to the Internet, you can do all sorts of interesting things. You can also get hopelessly lost. Aside from being frustrated, though, or getting some nasty e-mail (called **flames**) from other Internet users, nothing bad can happen to you or your computer. (Unless, of course, you encounter a computer virus. See the following for details.)

Q&A *Do I need to worry about computer viruses?*

A **computer virus** is a renegade piece of computer software that does something other than what it's supposed to do, usually without any warning. Like their human counterparts, computer viruses are transmitted through contact, most often by infected disks and programs. If you ever contract a computer virus, the effects can range from mildly annoying to catastrophic.

You don't run any risk of your PC contracting a computer virus through the Internet, as long as you don't download any programs. Follow that rule, and you'll be absolutely safe. What if you do want to download programs? Well, make one of your first downloads a virus-checking-and-removal program, or bite the bullet and go buy a commercial virus-detection-and-repair program such as Norton Antivirus.

How does the Internet work?

I'd rather answer a month's worth of Final Jeopardy questions than try to explain the Internet in 50 words or fewer! But OK, here goes...

On the Internet, every computer is connected to every other computer—directly or indirectly. If you have information on your computer and you're willing to share it with me, then our computers can use the Internet to contact each other. Before they can communicate, though, they have to agree on names and a common language. That's where the Internet comes in.

Every computer that is connected to the Internet has a unique address (called an **IP address**) that consists of one long number broken into four groups of up to three digits. Like your Social Security number (if you live in the United States) or your government ID number in another country, it's associated with one and only one individual. So, for example, the main machine at Macmillan Computer Publishing, the company that produced this book, is called 198.70.48.1.

That's all fine and dandy if you're a computer, but human beings are more comfortable with words than with numbers. So all those Internet addresses also have corresponding names. Instead of having to remember my 12-digit Internet ID number, all you have to know is that my Internet name is ed@bott.com. Special machines called **name servers** make sure that our computers can translate names to numbers, and vice versa.

When two computers want to exchange information over the Internet, all the data gets chopped into small pieces and sent out into the Internet. Every one of these **packets** is exactly the same size, just like a boxcar on a freight train, and each packet has a label that includes the address it came from, the address it's going to, and enough information to help the computer, at its ultimate destination, reassemble all the packets into their original form. Each time a computer on the Internet sees one of these packets, it reads the label and sends it along in the right direction.

Connecting the dots

What's in a name? On the Internet. the answer is: a lot of dots.

Internet names typically consist of two parts: a **host name** and a **domain name**, separated by an "at" symbol (@). Individual pieces of both the host and domain names are separated by dots, or periods.

The domain name helps narrow down the group of computers and people I'm associated with. If I work for a big company like Macmillan Computer Publishing, for example, my domain name might be mcp.com (pronounced *em cee pee dot com*). The *com* tells other people that this group is a company. If the extension were *edu* or *org*, they'd know that mcp was affiliated with an educational institution or a nonprofit organization instead.

Large domains can be broken into **subdomains** to make life easier for the people who have to keep track of all these computers. So if I ran

mcp.com, I might create a subgroup called que.mcp.com (remember, you pronounce each of the periods between the parts of a domain name as *dot*).

Finally, all the people who have individual access to computers in the organization would get their own unique **host name.** There's no rule that says you have to use your real name, either: You could call yourself jean-luc.picard@que.mcp.com if you wanted, and that would be a perfectly legal Internet name. (When you say your Internet address out loud, remember to pronounce the at-sign as "at.") Generally, though, your host name will be some combination of your first and last name or initials.

There might be another jean-luc.picard elsewhere on the Net, but the unique combination of a host name and domain name, separated by an at sign, guarantees that you can always reach someone, as long as you know his name.

All these packets travel at lightning speeds around the Internet, and because the network is so big and interconnected, there's always a way to get from here to there.

How do I join the Internet?

You don't. The Internet is not a company or an organization. Nobody runs it, really (although there's a group that keeps track of all the names and numbers). When you get on the Net, you're pretty much on your own.

OK, how do I get hooked up?

One way or another, before you can get on the Internet, you have to find a set of wires that can carry information between you and all those other computers.

- If your company already has an Internet connection, it's easy. The same wires that carry your information around your company's local network can also connect to the Internet. Ask your network administrator to get you hooked up.

- If you want to use the Internet from home, you'll need a modem and a place where you can call and establish a connection to the rest of the Internet. Companies that sell this service are called **service providers**.

TIP   **The coolest part of the Internet, the World Wide Web, is stuffed** with enormous graphics files that practically crawl across your screen if you try to use a modem that's too slow. So if you want to be a happy Net surfer, find a fast modem. Look for the numbers 14400 (good enough) or 28800 (much better). The numbers indicate transmission speeds; the higher the number, the faster those bits will move across the phone wire and into your computer and down your screen. If you do get a fast modem, though, make sure your Internet service provider has a local number that runs at the same speed!

Finding an on-ramp: service providers

You can take your choice of service providers, from small companies in storefronts to huge organizations like CompuServe and Microsoft. You can find ads for service providers in the business section of most big-city newspapers. If you have a friend who's already connected to the Net, ask for a recommendation. In any case, it shouldn't cost more than about a dollar a day for all the access an average user needs.

Getting Windows 95 ready for the Internet

Maybe your company network already has a gateway to the Internet, or you've decided to spring for a fast modem and a dial-up account. It doesn't really matter *how* you get there—before you can take advantage of all the cool things out on the largest network in the known universe, your computer has to be configured to be part of the Internet. And as soon as you start talking about networking, things get just a little...well, complicated.

If you don't have a lot of technical experience, the very best way to get yourself connected to the Internet is to beg or bribe an experienced friend. It shouldn't take that long, really—assuming you've handled the prerequisites of signing up with a service provider, getting an IP address, writing your password down in a safe place, and so on, the whole job shouldn't take more than an hour in the hands of someone who knows networks.

Still, if you're bound and determined to do it yourself, here's what you'll have to do.

1 Install the TCP/IP software. Think of this as a Berlitz course in Internet-speak for your PC. Open Control Panel, double-click on the Network icon, then click the <u>A</u>dd button. TCP/IP is a protocol, so you'll need to highlight that entry in the list and then click another <u>A</u>dd button.

When the Select Network Protocol dialog box appears, highlight Microsoft in the left pane and choose TCP/IP in the right. (The dialog box looks something like the one shown in fig. 25.1.) Click OK, and you're done with the first step.

2 Next, **set up a network adapter** and make sure the TCP/IP software is hooked up to it. If you have a network card in your computer already, you probably don't need to worry about this step, because Windows should have detected the hardware and added the right software automatically.

If you plan to use a modem to dial in to an Internet service provider, click the Add button again, highlight Adapter, click the second <u>A</u>dd button, and find the Microsoft Dial-Up Adapter. Click OK.

In the Configuration section of the Network dialog box, you should see an entry that includes the protocol (TCP/IP) and the network adapter, connected by an arrow. (See fig. 25.2 for an example.) So far, so good...

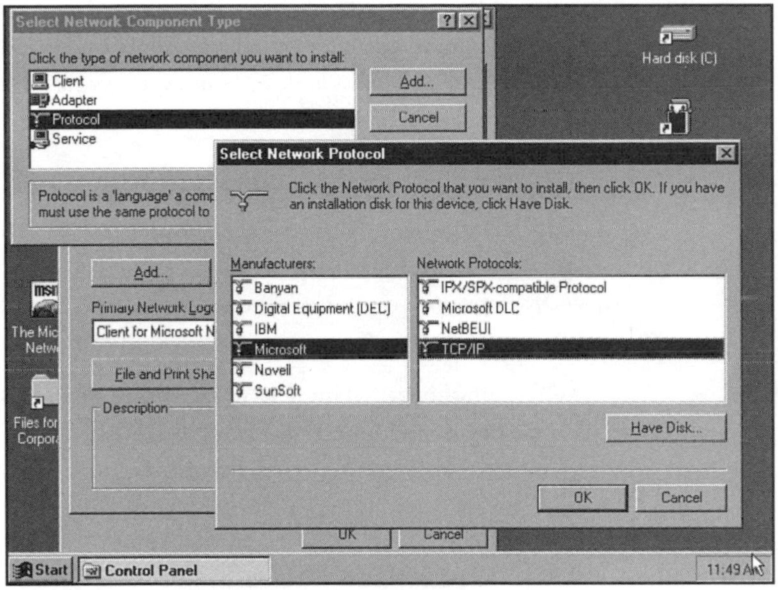

Fig. 25.1

Before your computer can talk to other computers on the Internet, you have to install software that lets it speak TCP/IP, the universal language of the Internet.

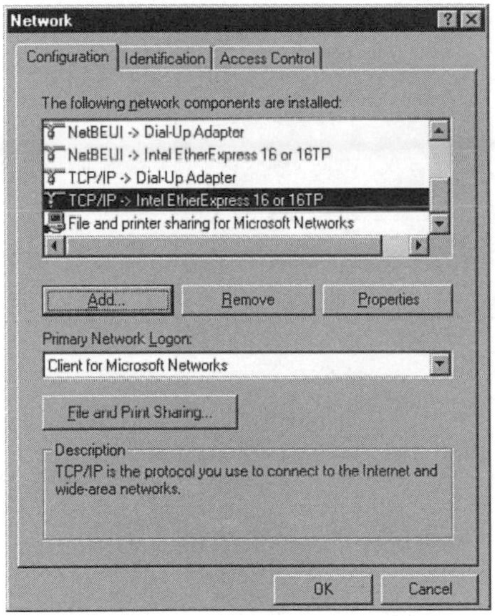

Fig. 25.2

Here's where you check to see which protocol is connected to which adapter.

CAUTION **Be sure that the TCP/IP protocol is hooked up to the right** network adapter. If you use a network card to hook up to your company network but access the Internet over the telephone, highlight the entry that has TCP/IP connected to your network card, and click the Remove button. At that point, you'll be left with just the connection to the Dial-Up Adapter. This keeps Windows from wasting your PC's horsepower (and your patience) searching for an Internet connection that doesn't exist.

3 Highlight the TCP entry in the Network dialog box, click the Properties button, and **enter your configuration information.** Your dial-up service provider should have given you a "cheat sheet" with all the right settings printed on it. For a company network, you'll need to get the same information from your network administrator.

At a minimum, you'll have to check three of the six tabs in the TCP/IP Properties dialog box: IP address, Gateway, and DNS Configuration (see fig. 25.3). Don't worry if you don't understand a word; concentrate on entering the numbers correctly, and you'll be fine.

Fig. 25.3

Do you speak TCP/IP? Of course you don't, but if you expect your computer to communicate on the Internet, you'll have to make sure that this dialog box is filled out flawlessly.

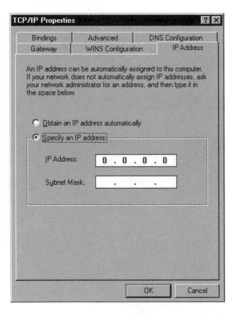

4 Make the connection. Open My Computer, double-click on the Dial-Up Networking icon, and follow the wizard's instructions to set up the name and phone number for a new connection. If you plan to have multiple Internet connections—one over your company network and another over the phone, let's say—right-click on the connection icon, choose Properties, click the Server Type button, and then click the TCP/IP properties button to enter all those numbers again.

When you're satisfied that everything's working right, double-click on the icon you just created to hook your PC up with the computer in your Internet service provider's office.

The next time you click OK, Windows should remind you that you'll have to restart your computer before your new software can kick into gear. Go ahead—restart now. When you get back, your TCP/IP connection should be ready to go. If you've got a direct Internet connection over your company network, you'll be able to hook up without doing anything else. If you're planning to rely on a dial-up connection, double-click the Dial-Up Networking icon you just created and wait for it to connect; then you can start **surfing** the Net in earnest.

66 *Plain English, please!*

Occasionally, you'll see a reference to something called **Winsock**. That's the technical term for the Windows Sockets standard. In essence, it's the bit of software that lets Windows plug into the Internet. There are at least three different versions of the Winsock software floating around, including the one that comes with Windows 95. If you start getting Winsock error messages, it's time to call for technical support! 99

What's out there?

You could fill a book with all the great things you can do with an Internet connection. (In fact, there's an excellent book filled with worthwhile information from the same people who created this one. If you're curious about the Internet, get *Using the Internet*, available from Que Corporation.)

Meanwhile, here's a sampling of the things you can do once you're connected to the Net.

Newsgroups

You can drop in on discussions of every imaginable topic, from championship dog breeding to astrophysics, on public bulletin boards called **UseNet newsgroups**. You don't have to say a word; you can just **lurk** (watch without participating) and learn. Or you can chime in and add your own comments to a newsgroup.

Interesting databases

Every conceivable fact and figure is available somewhere on the Internet. When a friend of mine discovered that his son had been diagnosed with a rare disease, he used the Net to track down more information. Within two hours, he had found 1800 relevant articles, including detailed descriptions of the symptoms and treatments, along with names of the world's top specialists. (His son's doing just fine now, by the way.)

New programs, shareware, and freebies

The Internet is stuffed to bursting with software. Look for **FTP servers**—those are central storehouses that use the Internet's **File Transfer Protocol** to exchange files with computers like yours.

The World Wide Web

The hottest of all Internet destinations is the **World Wide Web**. At last count, there were more than four million pages of information on the WWW, ranging from the extremely silly to the enormously valuable. Web pages include text, graphics, and links that you can click to jump instantly to other Web pages. (See fig. 25.4 for a close-up of the Web page at the U.S. Library of Congress.)

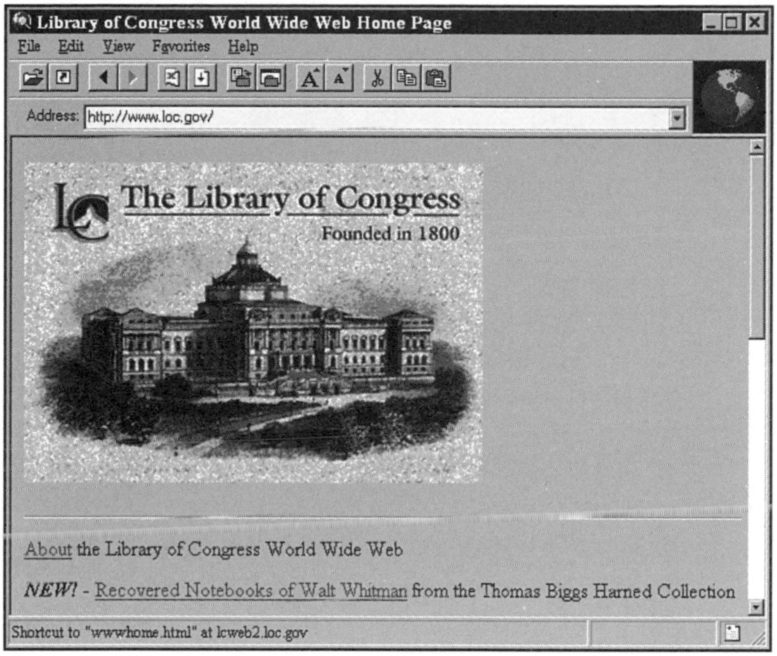

Fig. 25.4

The hottest ticket on the Internet? No doubt about it—the World Wide Web, with its cool graphics and unpredictability, is the place to see.

Library of Congress World Wide Web Home Page

File   Edit   View   Favorites   Help

Address: http://www.loc.gov/

The Library of Congress
Founded in 1800

About the Library of Congress World Wide Web

NEW! - Recovered Notebooks of Walt Whitman from the Thomas Biggs Harned Collection

Shortcut to "wwwhome.html" at lcweb2.loc.gov

TIP **If you want to access the Internet using software designed** especially for Windows 95, check out a program called Microsoft Plus! for Windows 95. It includes a wizard that helps set up an Internet connection for you, plus special utilities that let you browse the World Wide Web and save interesting pages as Windows 95 shortcuts.

Part VIII: Troubleshooting Windows 95

Troubleshooting Windows 95

Troubleshooting
Windows 95

● In this chapter:

Got a problem or question? This is the place to look for quick answers . . . . ⬤

Getting started

Here are some tips and answers to commonly asked questions about getting Windows 95 started and properly configured.

Why does it take so long for Windows to get started?

You probably have a morning routine you go through before you do any real work—and so does Windows. There's a long, long checklist that Windows goes through before it lets you get to work, so it's normal for startup to take a little while.

First, Windows checks your computer's memory and disk drives. Then it searches the hard disk for the simplest Windows startup files. Next comes the Plug and Play scan to take inventory of what's plugged in. At this point, Windows loads the rest of its files and programs. If you're on a network, this is when you'll have to type in your password. Once Windows is fully loaded, it launches any programs in your StartUp folder before handing the whole thing over to you.

My computer won't start up properly

It *is* plugged in, isn't it? The monitor's turned on, too, and the brightness and contrast controls are set properly? If you pass those checkpoints, try to restart your computer by pressing the on-off switch. When you see the words `Starting Windows 95`, press the F8 key, and choose Safe Mode from the menu. This starts up a special simplified version of Windows. Once you start in Safe Mode, you can try to figure out where the problem is. If Safe Mode doesn't work, you may need to resort to your emergency startup diskette.

Emergency diskettes... because you just never know

You need an emergency diskette, just in case something happens and Windows won't start up on your PC. If that happens, you just pop the emergency diskette in your A: drive, and turn the computer on. It's kind of like a secret back door to use when you're locked out of the main entrance.

To create an emergency diskette, open Control Panel, choose Add/Remove Programs, then select the Startup Disk tab and follow the instructions. Store your emergency diskette in a safe place.

I usually shut down my computer by just pressing the power switch. Is that OK?

No, it's *never* OK to press the big red switch unless you've first used the Windows Shut Down command (found on the Start menu). Windows keeps track of all sorts of important things in the background while you work. When you use the Shut Down command, Windows makes sure that that information is saved properly. If you turn off the power before shutting down, you risk losing data.

Where did CONFIG.SYS and AUTOEXEC.BAT go?

If you've ever struggled with DOS, you've met its two startup files, CONFIG.SYS and AUTOEXEC.BAT. They're still here in Windows 95, but you won't see them nearly as often. Windows uses them if it must, but it prefers not to.

A lot of data that used to clutter up these files is unnecessary in Windows 95. The only reason these files are still around is because some kinds of hardware absolutely, positively have to have their own translation programs, called **drivers**, in order to work. Windows does a thorough job of stripping away unnecessary programs when you first install it, so you shouldn't need to worry about AUTOEXEC.BAT or CONFIG.SYS ever again.

Windows told me that some of my files are out of date. What's that all about?

The Setup program that came with older Windows programs probably tried to add files to the Windows\System folder on your computer. While it may have been a good idea to update the version of Windows that you bought in 1992, it's definitely a no-no to put those files in Windows 95.

Fortunately, Windows anticipates this, and keeps a safe copy of these essential files. If a Setup program wrongly replaces some system files, Windows will give you a chance to put the right ones back. Just say yes.

Finding your way around the desktop

This section presents tips on using the common desktop items—the taskbar and shortcut icons.

The taskbar hides part of my application's dialog box

Want a little extra room on the screen? Then "hide" the taskbar. Right-click in any empty space on the taskbar, and choose Properties from the popup menu. To give yourself a little extra room on the screen, click on the tab labeled Taskbar Options, and find the box that says Auto hide. Click in the box to make a check mark appear, then click on OK to close the dialog box. The taskbar disappears, giving you a little more working room. To make it reappear, just bump the mouse pointer into the bottom edge of the screen. Shazam! Up pops the taskbar.

The taskbar buttons are too small to read the full label

When you've got a lot of windows open, the buttons on the taskbar become unreadable. No problem—just point to any button and let the pointer sit there for a few seconds. Eventually, a little label called a **ToolTip** will pop up, telling you the full name of that button. After the first tip appears, you can slide the pointer from button to button, and the remaining ToolTips will appear instantaneously.

I need to make room on the taskbar for more buttons

Another fix for a full taskbar is to increase its height. Point to the top border of the taskbar until you see a double-headed arrow. Then drag upward to make the taskbar tall enough for two rows of minimized programs.

My taskbar disappeared, and the Auto hide option isn't checked. Where did it go?

While resizing the taskbar, you might have accidentally dragged the taskbar down instead of up, so that it's set to be zero buttons high. To put it back to normal, aim the mouse pointer at the very bottom of the screen until it turns to a two-headed arrow, then drag the pointer up slightly. The taskbar will pop back into position.

How can I get all these windows off my desktop? Now!

Right-click on a blank area of the taskbar and then choose Minimize All from the popup menu. Watch each window shrink down onto the taskbar, one after another. When the job's all done, you have a sparkling clean desktop.

I know I worked with a file this morning, but it's not on the Documents menu. What did I do wrong?

Nothing, probably. Windows can only keep track of files that are opened from a folder window, from the Windows Explorer, or from a program that was designed for Windows 95. If you use the File menu to open or save a document with an older Windows application, it won't be added to the Documents list.

I want to clear the Documents list and start over

First, right-click on the taskbar (not on a button), and choose Properties from the popup menu to open the taskbar Properties dialog box. Click on the Start Menu Programs tab, then click the Clear button in the bottom half of the dialog box to empty the list and start with a clean slate.

Can I use a keyboard shortcut to switch between applications?

If you learned to switch between applications using the Windows 3.1 keyboard shortcut Alt+Tab, you'll be happy to know it works in Windows 95, too. When you have more than one program running (or several folders open), hold down the Alt key and keep holding it down as you Tab from one program to the next. When you find the one you're looking for, release both keys to switch to that window.

What's that arrow in the corner of an icon mean?

The little arrow in the lower left corner of an icon means it's a **shortcut** to an original file. If you've gotten used to DOS and Windows 3.1, you've never seen anything like shortcuts before. But once you learn what they do, you'll find yourself using them everywhere.

Shortcuts work like small pushbuttons that let you jump straight to a file stored somewhere else. When you double-click a shortcut, you tell Windows to find the **target file** and open it.

I added some shortcuts to the Start Menu, but they don't show up

You can drag-and-drop shortcut icons for your most-used programs onto the Start button to add them to the top of the Start menu. That way, you don't have to work your way through the cascading menus to find your favorite programs. However, if you place too many items on the menu, it might get too long to fit on the screen and the top items won't show. To fix the problem, open the Start menu, and choose S̲ettings, T̲askbar. Click the Start Menu Programs tab and the Advanced button. In the Explorer window, drag the excess items from the Start Menu folder and drop them in the Programs folder.

Can I have only one shortcut for a program or document?

Use lots of shortcuts! There's no law that says you can only have one shortcut for any program or document. If you have a favorite program, scatter shortcuts for it everywhere.

My shortcut isn't working. What's wrong?

Usually, if a shortcut doesn't work, it's because you've deleted the target file the shortcut refers to. Occasionally, just moving the target file will cause a problem with a shortcut, despite Windows' efforts to keep things straight. If you know where the missing file is, you can use the Browse button in the Missing Shortcut dialog box to help Windows find it. Another possibility is that you need to tell Windows to start a program in a different folder—the one where your data files are stored, for example. To fix the problem, right-click on the shortcut icon, click Properties, and look at what's in the box labeled Start in.

I can't seem to get some icons to move off my desktop

Windows puts a few things on the desktop, whether you want them there or not. My Computer, the Recycle Bin, The Microsoft Network, and the Network Neighborhood—you can't get them off the desktop with dynamite. But that still leaves plenty of room on the desktop for the things you use every day. When they're on the desktop, you can get to them with a click or two.

Working with windows

If you have questions about clicking, double-clicking, finding the DOS prompt, or manipulating windows, check out this collection of tips.

You really want a command line?

If you learned to use a PC with MS-DOS on it, you might want to return to the familiar DOS environment occasionally. One way to do it is to click the Start button, then choose Programs, MS-DOS Prompt to open a window with a DOS prompt. You can type commands and run programs in the DOS Prompt window   although some of them won't work properly with Windows 95.

The other option for anyone who wants to just type a DOS command is the Run command, also found on the Start menu. It gives you a tiny box, big enough to hold a single command, plus a Browse button that lets you search for a specific file to run.

Why do you have to double-click on an icon?

Because otherwise, you'd constantly be opening windows, looking inside folders, and starting up programs when you really didn't want to. Think of it this way: the first click tells Windows to get ready. If there's another click almost immediately, it opens the window. If not, Windows assumes that you don't really want to open the window, and you're going to do something else instead.

I double-clicked, but I didn't get the expected results

Be careful when double-clicking an icon, or you might accidentally rename a file! Watch what happens when you click the name of an icon twice, slowly. The highlighting changes and Windows assumes you want to start typing a new name. To avoid this, always aim at the picture, not the label. (Press Esc to quit renaming this time.) And practice double-clicking until you can do it flawlessly.

I have trouble double-clicking fast enough

Windows expects that when you double-click, the clicks will come one right after the other, as fast as lightning. But you can slow down the double-click rate so that Windows will wait a little longer for that second click. To retrain the mouse, open the Control Panel window and double-click on the Mouse icon. Slide the <u>D</u>ouble-click speed lever all the way to the left, and test the new settings by double-clicking the jack-in-the-box. There—isn't that better?

Why can't I move or resize this window?

Remember, some windows, like the Windows Calculator, are a fixed size and can't be resized. The other explanation is that you maximized the window so that it occupies the entire screen. As long as the window is maximized, you can't move it around, resize it, see its borders, or see anything else on your desktop (except the taskbar). But don't worry, all you need to do is click the Minimize or Restore buttons in the title bar.

I accidentally made a window so small I can't see the menus anymore. What do I do now?

No problem. It may not look like a window, but it still acts like one. Aim the mouse pointer at the lower right corner of the window until it turns to a diagonal, two-headed arrow. Now click the left mouse button and drag the window's borders out until the window is a more useful size.

I moved a window off the screen! How can I get it back?

If you move the window so far off the screen that you can't get to the title bar to drag it back, here's the secret fix: hold down the Alt key, and press the spacebar. That will pull down the window's Control menu. Press the letter **M** (for Move), and then use the arrow keys to slide the window back toward the main screen. When you can see enough of the title bar to grab, press Enter, and move the window using the mouse.

I can't remember what all these buttons do

Can't remember what a button does? Look for the ToolTips. Let the mouse pointer rest over any button, and a helpful label will pop up to tell you what the button does. This tip works in the taskbar, and for most buttons you find in the ribbons and toolbars of many Windows accessories and Windows 95 applications.

What do I do if the pointer seems to disappear?

 What do you do if the pointer seems to disappear every time you turn your head? Make it bigger. Make it darker. Make it leave a trail so you can spot it the instant it moves. To do any or all of these things, double-click on My Computer, open the Control Panel folder, and double-click on the Mouse icon. Experiment with the options till you find the settings that work best for you.

Using menus and dialog boxes

If you're having trouble telling Windows what to do, check out these tips. They may answer your questions.

Why don't some menu commands work?

Sometimes, choosing a menu item does something right away. If you choose File, Save, for example, and you've already given your file a name, a program like WordPad will simply save your most recent work using the existing file name, and then return you to what you were doing.

But sometimes a menu choice does nothing at all. You can point and click till your finger falls off and nothing happens. Windows **grays out** a menu choice that's temporarily unavailable. It's still there—it's just not available for you to use right now.

I chose a command, but nothing seemed to happen. It wasn't grayed out, but it isn't working. What's up?

Is there a check mark next to the command you think is not working? If there is, click the command again. Now is it doing what you expect? Some commands are like on-off switches. A check mark means it's "on"; no check mark means it's "off."

Cascading menus disappear before I can make my choice

Cascading menus take a little getting used to. If you find that they disappear too quickly, try slowing down a little. When the menu appears to the right, move the cursor slowly, in a straight line, to the new menu. Now you can move up or down as fast as you like.

How do you know when a popup menu is available?

You don't. So, anytime you're not sure what to do, just point at something and click the right mouse button. Trust me: there's no way you can hurt your system just by displaying a menu, so click away.

My mouse works, but I prefer the keyboard. How can I make menu choices without a mouse?

Press the Alt key and the underlined letter of a menu name to open a menu or highlight a command. Press the down arrow to move the highlight down the list of commands in a menu. Press Enter to choose the command, or Esc to close a menu and say, "Never mind, I don't want any of these."

How can I move the dialog box out of the way?

Sometimes, a dialog box gets in the way of the very thing you need to see to answer one of its questions. Although you can't resize dialog boxes, you *can* move them around the screen and out of the way. Put the mouse pointer on the title bar, click and hold down the left button, and drag the box to another location. That way, you can deal with those persistent questions without losing sight of your work.

My mouse isn't working. How do I get around a dialog box without it?

When you press the Tab key, you move forward to the next option in the tabbing order of a dialog box. As you move, the option that is currently chosen has a dotted line around it or is highlighted. (Sometimes the highlight can be hard to see. If you're not sure which option is highlighted, press the Tab key repeatedly until you're sure where it's ended up.)

Press Shift+Tab to return to the previous option in the tabbing order. Press Enter to carry out the options you have chosen.

If one of the letters in a button or a label is underlined, you can use that letter to move directly to an option. Press Alt and the underlined letter at the same time. For example, to move to the File Name option, press Alt+N.

Working with folders and files

Files and directories (make that icons and folders) are the topic of discussion in this section. Even if you're an old hand at working with files in DOS, you'll probably have some questions because Windows 95 does things differently.

What can I put inside a folder?

Folders hold icons. Most of the folders you work with every day hold icons representing your program files and documents. But folders can also hold other folders. If you want all your work filed in one place, for example, you might create a folder called Projects and fill it with other folders, one for each iron you and your fellow workers have in the fire right now.

How can I create a new folder?

To create a new folder, double-click on the My Computer icon, and keep double-clicking on folders until you've opened the one where you want to create a new folder. Right-click in any empty spot in this folder window and click on Ne<u>w</u>. Choose Folder from the cascading menu. The same technique works in Explorer.

Help, I'm drowning in windows for all the folders I had to open to get to the one I wanted

Do you get a new window (and a bunch of unwanted clutter) every time you double-click on a folder? If you prefer, you can see the contents of each new folder displayed in the same window instead of opening a new window for each folder. Open a window for My Computer (or any folder), and choose <u>V</u>iew, <u>O</u>ptions. On the dialog tab labeled Folder, make sure there's a dot next to the choice that reads, Browse folders by using a si<u>n</u>gle window that changes as you open each folder. Click OK, and from that point on, whenever you open a new window, it will automatically close the previous window.

How can I sort the files in a folder?

No matter what kind of window you use, you can sort files in any order you like. Choose <u>V</u>iew, <u>D</u>etails, and then sort the list by clicking the column headings—they act like buttons. Click the headings again to sort in reverse order.

How can I control whether the file I drag gets moved or copied?

When you drag-and-drop a file onto a folder, Windows moves the file— provided you're moving it to another folder on the same disk. But if the destination folder is on another drive, then the file will be copied. Unless it's a program file, in which case… Well, the rules are incredibly confusing. Fortunately, there's a foolproof alternative.

Whenever you want to move something, copy something, or create a short-cut, click with the *right* mouse button and drag it. When you release the button, you'll see a popup menu with a list of choices. You can decide whether you want to move the file, make another copy of it, or cancel the whole thing.

What can I include in a long file name?

You can make an icon's name up to 255 characters long, and you can even use some punctuation marks: periods, commas, semicolons, ampersands, parentheses, and dollar signs. There are a handful of characters you can't use to name a file or folder, though. Here are the keys that you're not allowed to use in an icon's name:

: ' " \ / * ? |

What happened to the three-letter file extensions?

Those three-letter file extensions, like .TXT, that you used to tack onto the end of files are still there. Whenever possible, though, Windows hides the extensions and gives you a more meaningful explanation. Instead of .TXT, Windows labels those files as Text Documents. Your eight- and three-letter file and extension names are still there, though, so they get along with older programs.

I have two files in the same folder with the same name. How can that be?

They have the same first name, but their last names are different. One might be called WINDOWS.EXE, while the other is WINDOWS.INI. You can tell them apart in one of two ways: by the icon that the files use, or by right-clicking and looking on each file's Properties sheet to see its file type.

How does Windows know what kind of file this is?

To start a program, you don't have to click on its icon. If you've found a file that was created by that program, you can double-click on that file's icon, and launch the program instantly, with the file you clicked on already loaded.

How does it work? Well, Windows knows that every file on your PC has a first name and a last name. The first names have to be unique, but the last name (also known as the **file extension**) works just like your family name to identify a bunch of files that look and act somewhat alike. When you double-click on one of these files, Windows looks up its file type and says, "Oh, the .DOC extension means this is a document, and I need to use WordPad to open it."

Here are a few important facts about this whole process:

- File types are based on file extensions.

- Extensions have to be registered with Windows before your applications can automatically start up when you double-click on a document.

Why does my program have to be registered?

What does **registered** mean? Well, each program has certain file types that it can open and save. For instance, Microsoft Word uses .DOC extensions. When a program is installed, it tells Windows which extensions it uses, and the extensions are "registered" in a master list of them. That way, when you double-click on a data file to open it, Windows knows which program to use.

How can I use a different program to open a file?

Select the file, then hold down the Shift key and right-click on the file. This adds the Open With command to the popup menu, in addition to the Open command. Choose Open With; Windows will open a dialog box where you can choose what program you want to use to open the file. This technique can come in very handy if you have two programs (like Microsoft Word and WordPad, for example) that you might want to use at different times to open up .DOC files. Only one of the applications can be associated with .DOC files, but the Open With menu lets you pick either one.

I need to find a file that's lost somewhere among the thousands of files on my disk!

With Windows 95, you can search through an entire hard disk quickly to find any file, any time—even if you only remember a tiny scrap of information about it. To set the Windows bloodhound on the trail, click on the Start button, and choose Find, Files or Folders. Use the Find Files command. What do you do next? That depends on how much you remember about the file in question. See Chapter 7 for full instructions.

How much space do I have left on my disk?

Every time you save a file to a disk, it occupies some of the space on that disk, and sooner or later you'll use up all the empty space. You'll need to keep a watchful eye on free disk space, especially if you're planning to install a new program. To see how much space is left on a disk:

1 Double-click to open My Computer.

2 Click on the icon for the drive you want to check. The total disk capacity and free space appear in the status bar at the bottom of the My Computer window. (If the status bar isn't visible, pull down the View menu and check Status Bar.)

3 To see a graphical display of free disk space, right-click the drive icon, then choose Properties from the popup menu.

I threw away a file by mistake. How do I get it back?

Stop! Before you do anything else, double-click on the Recycle Bin icon on your desktop. The Recycle Bin is really just a special folder where Windows stores your recently discarded files and other icons. To recover a file, just drag it out of the Recycle Bin window and into another folder.

What happens when the Recycle Bin gets full?

The Recycle Bin isn't a bottomless pit. Sooner or later (probably sooner) you'll fill it up. When that happens, Windows automatically deletes files to make room for the freshly deleted ones. Of course, you can always tell Windows to take out the trash. Right-click on the Recycle Bin, then choose Empty Recycle Bin.

I deleted a bunch of files, but that didn't free up any space on my disk

When you're trying to make room on your hard disk to install a new program, the Recycle Bin can drive you crazy. You delete some old files, thinking that you're clearing space. Instead of freeing up room, though, Windows just moves the deleted files to the Recycle Bin, where they still gobble up the same amount of space. The moral: when space is at a premium, always remember to empty the Recycle Bin.

I'm sure I want to get rid of an icon and I don't want it saved in the Recycle Bin

What if you're absolutely, positively certain you want to get rid of an icon once and for all? Right-click on it, then hold down the Shift key as you choose Delete. When you use this trick, you'll bypass the Recycle Bin completely and simply vaporize the rascal.

Can I cut down the number of files saved in the Recycle Bin?

If you're running tight on hard disk space, you might want to restrict the amount of space that Windows sets aside for the Recycle Bin. To adjust this setting, right-click on the Recycle Bin icon, choose Properties, and move the slider control left or right. Using the controls here, you can even turn off the Recycle Bin completely, although you can't remove its icon from your desktop.

I always find errors when I check my hard drive with ScanDisk. Is that bad?

Maybe. If you constantly experience disk errors, you might have a hard disk that's on the verge of failing, or there might be a bug in one of the programs you use that's leaving a mess behind when you close it. Double-click on the icon for the disk that's giving you trouble, and look for files with names like FILE0000; ScanDisk creates those files as part of its cleanup process. Try opening those files with WordPad. If you recognize the data inside the files, you might be able to tell which program is causing the disk problems.

What's the Defragmenter?

Windows slices each file into small **clusters**, which then get saved in their own locations on your hard disk. Windows keeps a master list of which piece went where, so it can reassemble the file later. That's fine, unless the fragments of your file get scattered on parts of the hard disk that are miles apart. This fragmentation can cause your whole system to slow down while Windows scurries around putting a file together.

The solution? Use the built-in Windows Disk Defragmenter. To start it up, right-click on any drive, choose Properties, and select the Tools tab. The status window at the bottom of the dialog box will tell you how long it's been since you last used the defragmenter. Choose the button labeled Defragment Now to start up the program.

How can I keep files current on both my desktop system and my notebook computer?

Windows 95 has a special utility designed especially for notebook users. It's called the **Briefcase**, and it works much like a smart version of the fancy leather briefcase you use to carry paperwork to and from the office. Here's how it works:

You tell Windows to create a special briefcase folder on your notebook PC. You can then connect your notebook PC to your desktop PC, and drag data files from your desktop PC into the briefcase folder. Once the briefcase is set up, you can work with those files on your notebook while on a trip. When you return, you can reconnect the computers, and ask Windows to compare the briefcase files with the originals. It will offer to add, delete, and copy newer versions of files to update older versions on the other machine. See Chapter 19 for more details.

Windows and your hardware

One of the more challenging aspects of working with computers is getting all the pieces of hardware to work together with Windows and with each other. These tips may help.

Never overlook the obvious when your equipment isn't working

Sometimes, the simplest steps are the easiest to overlook. If you're having equipment problems, always check the obvious. Before you ask for help, ask yourself these questions:

- Is it plugged in?

- Is the power turned on?

- Have I checked the connections carefully? Any loose wires?

- Is the modem connected to the phone line?

Windows says the device has a resource conflict. What's that mean?

A **resource conflict** happens when more than one piece of equipment is trying to use a port or other piece of hardware. Windows 95 has built-in help for this problem, in the form of the **Hardware Conflict Troubleshooter**. To start up this wizard, click on the Start button, and choose Help from the menu. On the Contents tab, double-click on Troubleshooting, then click on the entry labeled If you have a hardware conflict. You'll see a dialog box. Click on the appropriate button to get the process started, then follow the detailed instructions. (They're written in plain English.)

My PC is getting really slow. What could be wrong?

You might be running low on memory. When Windows runs out of RAM, it first tries to use the hard disk to simulate extra memory. Windows takes the chunk of RAM your first program is using and **swaps** it from memory onto the hard disk (which is about a thousand times slower than RAM). That frees up a chunk of RAM for your second program to use, but when you switch back to the first program, Windows has to swap both chunks of data. Add another program, and pretty soon Windows is spending all its time swapping data onto your hard drive and back again instead of running programs. The result is a lot of noise from your hard disk, and a PC that's running in super-slo-mo. If your system slows to a crawl too often, you need more memory.

My mouse is acting funny—it hops and skips across the screen, or leaves little "mouse droppings"

You probably have a non-Microsoft mouse, and Windows is having trouble communicating with it. Call the store that sold you the mouse (it probably came with your PC), and ask if there's a new driver for Windows 95. (A **driver** is a small software program that tells Windows how to talk to a piece of hardware.) If they say no, demand to exchange it for a new mouse that's compatible with Windows 95.

Why do I need a larger hard drive just to work with a few multimedia files?

Data files for some of these multimedia types are huge. A 10-second sound clip, for example, might take up a healthy 100K of disk space, while a single four-minute music video file could consume more than 40 megabytes of disk space! That's why CD-ROMs (which can hold more than 600M) are so widely used for multimedia software.

Why does this video look so jerky?

You don't have adequate hardware. Video is incredibly demanding, hardware-wise. If you don't have a fast CD-ROM and a Pentium, you can expect to see some problems with your video. What kind? Dropped frames, jerky motion, or sound that doesn't keep up with the picture. There's no real cure, unfortunately, short of getting a new PC.

My sounds don't sound right. Most are tinny, and some won't play at all

You probably have an old 8-bit sound card. That's a low-end card that handles some (but not all) files well. It might be time to think about getting a new 16-bit sound card—or, better yet, a Plug and Play card.

The CD Player program says it's playing just fine, but I don't hear any music

You need to make a special connection between your CD player and your sound card before you can hear the sound from a music CD. If you have an external CD-ROM reader—one that sits on your desktop outside your PC—there will be a cable that runs from the back of the CD reader to a jack on the sound card. Internal CD-ROM players—those that are installed directly in your computer's case—use a special wire that is connected inside the PC. Talk to the company that sold you your PC for details on how your drive works.

Which drive letter does my CD-ROM get?

Every drive in your system uses a letter of the alphabet, followed by a colon, for its name. Your first floppy drive is always A:, your main hard drive is always C:, and so on. Which letter gets assigned to your CD-ROM? That depends. Windows usually takes the next available letter, but that isn't always D:. If you have two hard drives, for example, if you've used DriveSpace disk-compression, or if you're on a network and you've assigned drive letters to various folders on different file servers, your next available drive letter could be anything between E: and Z:. And it could change from one day to the next, depending on your network setup.

That can play havoc with programs that expect to see the same drive letter every time you start them up. So Windows lets you permanently assign a drive letter to your CD. On my system, for example, I've set the CD-ROM reader up so it always appears as drive E:. See Chapter 20 for instructions on how to do it.

How can I keep a CD from starting by itself when I insert it into the drive?

AutoPlay is great most of the time. But what if you don't want your AutoPlay CD to start automatically? Hold down the Shift key as you insert the CD-ROM, and Windows will ignore the AutoPlay instructions. Now you can open the My Computer window, right-click on the CD-ROM icon, and use other options like Open to see the files on the CD-ROM.

I need to remove a PC card safely

Before you attempt to remove a PC card from your notebook computer you first have to tell Windows you're planning to remove it. Why? Because some programs may depend on that card, and it's Windows' job to notify them in advance before you slice the lifeline. To give Windows proper notice, use the PC Card icon on the taskbar. Double-click to pop up a full-sized window that lets you adjust all the settings for each device, or just click on the icon to pop up a quick list of cards that can be removed.

Windows and your software

Your software programs let you get some real work done. But with the mixture of DOS programs, old Windows programs, and new Windows programs you're likely to be using, you may have questions about installing and using the software, and cutting and pasting data between programs.

What do I do with these old DOS programs?

Most DOS programs work just fine under Windows 95. The easiest way to set up a DOS program is to drag it onto the Start button; to launch it, click on its entry in the Start menu.

Some DOS programs, especially games, need a bit of special treatment to run successfully in Windows, and the first place to look when you're having trouble is on its Properties page. Right-click on the program icon, then choose Properties. You'll see a big, complicated set of dialog boxes in which you can adjust the way Windows tries to run the program. See Chapter 11 for more details on how to adjust the settings.

I started a DOS program, and now I can't get back to Windows. What do I do?

DOS runs in a window most of the time, but you can also start up a full-screen DOS prompt that looks just like you've quit Windows. If you're absent-minded, you might even forget you're still in Windows. Appearances to the contrary, you haven't left Windows. To make the DOS program shrink down into an icon on the taskbar, just click its Minimize button (the button with the underline on it). To make it go away, get to a DOS prompt and type **EXIT**.

Why doesn't Windows know how to remove the program I just installed?

The Add/Remove Programs dialog box in Control Panel not only helps you install programs; it also lets you remove them. In fact, using the Remove button is the only way to be sure you delete all the files and settings a program installed on your system. For the feature to work, however, the program must provide an uninstall utility designed to work with Windows 95. Older Windows 3.1 applications, and smaller utility and accessory programs don't provide Windows with the necessary information. You're on your own if you need to remove them.

Why doesn't this program work right?

When is a Windows program not a Windows program? When it's an old Windows program that doesn't understand how to work with Windows 95, of course.

Now, there's nothing wrong with being old—sooner or later it happens to all of us. But the problem with Windows programs that were developed before Windows 95 came around is that they don't understand how to deal with long file names. If you use one of these older programs, any files you use with that program will be limited to eight characters and a three-character extension.

How do I know if I have a bug in my program?

Here are some symptoms:

- Your system freezes up. You might be able to move the mouse, but nothing happens when you tap the keys or click the mouse button. The usual cure is to turn the PC off and then back on again. (You'll lose any unsaved work, unfortunately.)

- The picture on your monitor starts to act up. Windows might refuse to go away, or you'll see dark holes in the background. If you're lucky, you can save your work before you restart your computer.

- Everything begins to move at a glacial pace. When your PC gets reeeeeeeeaaaaaaaallllllll slllllooooooowwwwww like this, you might be moments away from losing all your work. Save what you can, and prepare to restart your PC.

- You see a bright blue screen with a white error message on it. That generally means Windows did something bad. If you're lucky, you can hit the Enter key and get back to work.

- You see a Windows dialog box, telling you your application has caused a general protection fault. Click OK and see if you can get back to work. You'll probably lose anything you haven't saved lately.

I don't have all the Windows accessories mentioned in the book. Why not?

If your copy of Windows 95 arrived on floppy disks instead of on a CD-ROM, then you might not have everything I talk about in this book. But the more likely explanation is that the little programs you're looking for were never installed on your PC. Fortunately, it's easy to install the missing programs. See Chapter 12 for the instructions.

The Add/Remove Programs utility is confusing. Which programs will be added?

The Windows Setup portion of the Add/Remove Programs dialog box is confusing until you understand how it works. A check mark beside an item in the Components list means the item is already on your PC. If a box is empty, clicking to add the check mark tells Windows to add the program. Clicking to remove a check mark removes the program, too. Don't touch those check marks unless you want to take a program off your computer!

I seem to have the same document open in two different windows. How can that be?

Be sure you don't accidentally open two copies of the same document! With some programs and most folders, when you click on the icon and the window is already open, Windows just switches you to that window. But other programs (including WordPad) let you open two or more copies of the program, each in its own window. If you're not careful, you can wind up editing the same file in two places. If you save the file in the second window, you might accidentally overwrite the changes you made in the first one. The only cure is to keep an eye on the taskbar and watch out for duplicate windows.

How can I open a text file that's too large to fit in Notepad?

You can't use Notepad to open large files. But don't worry—if you select a file that's too big, Windows will pop up a gentle warning message that offers to let you use WordPad instead. That's the right choice to make.

Most of my words are disappearing into the right side of the WordPad window. What's going on?

You need to set the **word wrap** option. When you do that, WordPad puts up a solid wall along the right edge of the document. When the text gets there, it has to turn and run into the next line instead. Choose <u>V</u>iew, <u>O</u>ptions, and then select one of the Word Wrap settings. Most of the time, you'll wrap to the window, so you can read your text more easily. But sometimes, you'll want to wrap to the ruler, especially when you want to see what your document will look like when printed.

I copied some things, but they disappeared before I could paste them into another document

The **Clipboard** can only hold one thing at a time. If you copy or cut something, it will wipe out anything that was previously being stored on the Clipboard. That's why, if you're shuffling a lot of data around, it's always a good idea to paste it into its new home *immediately* after you've cut or copied it to the Clipboard.

What happens when I paste data?

When you paste something from the Clipboard, Windows tries to figure out the most appropriate action to take with the specific type of data you've put there. It's easiest when the type of data is exactly the same, and less predictable when the data types are very different. Here's a sampling of what you can expect:

- **Words and numbers** usually move easily from one place to another. The formatting may or may not survive the trip, though. For example, if you copy a fat, bold headline from a WordPad document and paste it into a Notepad file, the words appear, but the bold attribute disappears.

- **Pictures** can move from one place to another in a variety of formats. Most of them are simple bitmaps, which means you have to paste them in at exactly the same size and shape as the original, unless you want them to be distorted.

- You can even use the Cut, Copy, and Paste commands to move **files** from one place to another. Open My Computer, and keep double-clicking until you reach the folder window that contains the file or files you want to move. Highlight one or more files, right-click, and choose Cut or Copy from the popup menu. Now you can move to another folder window, right-click, and use the Paste command to insert the files in that folder.

What's so special about Paste Special?

If you choose the Edit, Paste Special command, Windows opens a dialog box and waits for more instructions from you before it actually inserts the contents of the Clipboard into your document. This gives you the opportunity to control the formatting of the item you're pasting, or create a link between the pasted copy and the original item you copied. See Chapter 13 for more on the Clipboard and Object Linking and Embedding (OLE).

I pasted something into a document, and now there's a box around it. What's that all about?

Congratulations! You just embedded one document inside another without even realizing it. If that's not what you wanted to do, you'll have to tell Windows to do the paste differently. Go the to Edit menu, and choose Paste Special. This time, you'll see a dialog box with a list of the options available to you. As you highlight each option in the list, look in the Results area at the bottom of the dialog box to see what will happen, then choose the one that matches what you want.

Why do I have trouble when I try to use OLE?

Object Linking and Embedding (OLE) demands a lot of RAM to do its magic. If your computer has only 4M of RAM, you should probably forget about using OLE—if it works at all, it'll be creepingly slow. Even with 8M, extensive OLE use can be an exercise in frustration. (Before I upgraded my computer's memory, I had only 8M of RAM, and Windows was forever crashing and locking up when I tried to link and embed Microsoft Excel charts in a Microsoft Word document.)

My program just stopped and I can't close the window

There's one sure way to close a window, but it's *strictly for emergencies*. If a program just stops with no explanation, you can shut it down by pressing the Ctrl, Alt, and Delete keys simultaneously. Choose the name of the window from the popup list, and click the End Task button.

It's a great way to get back to work when your program has failed, but the Ctrl+Alt+Delete should only be used as a last resort. Don't use it to close an application, unless you're absolutely sure it's stopped working.

Personalizing Windows

Windows lets you put the "personal" in personal computers by changing settings to suit your preferences. The tips in this section help to make your Windows system your own.

I'm left-handed. Is there an easier way to use this mouse?

Windows lets you reverse your mouse settings, so that the right button does the jobs normally handled by the left button (and vice-versa). To switch mouse buttons, double-click on the Control Panel's Mouse icon, and follow the instructions. It's a handy trick for left-handers. If you try it, though, remember to do a mental translation from now on: every time we talk about clicking and right-clicking, just reverse the directions.

Can I make the borders easier to grab when I resize a window?

When you're aiming at a window's border, the tip of the arrow is the only part that counts. That end consists of one tiny dot, and you're trying to use that dot to hit a window border that's as thin as a piece of thread. If you're having trouble resizing windows, why not make the borders a little bigger?

Right-click anywhere on the desktop, choose Properties from the popup menu, and, when the Display Properties dialog box appears, click on the tab labeled Appearance. Click inside the box labeled item, then type the letter **A**. The words Active Border should now be highlighted. Click in the box labeled Size, and use the up arrow to increase the setting from a measly 1 to a wider 3 or 4. Click OK and try again. There—isn't that easier?

How can I enlarge the buttons in the title bar?

You won't find a setting for adjusting the Minimize, Maximize, and Close buttons, but you can adjust their size just the same. Open the Display Properties dialog box by right-clicking on the desktop and choosing Properties from the popup menu. Click on the Appearance tab and begin experimenting with the size of the type in the active and inactive title bars. When you change the type size, the size of the buttons changes, too. To make the buttons bigger, just make the title bar font bigger.

Where did all my colors go?

When you're selecting a desktop color scheme, it doesn't matter how many colors you've told Windows you want to use. When you pull down the color list in the Display properties dialog box, you see only 20 colors. What happened to the others? Well, you'll have to mix them yourself (you'll find instructions in Chapter 14).

I can't see the window border (or some other part)—it blends into the background!

If you accidentally make the background color and the foreground color the same somewhere in Windows, you won't be able to see what you're doing.

To fix it, just open the Desktop Properties dialog box (right-click on the desktop and choose Properties from the popup menu), click on the Appearance tab, select the Windows Standard scheme, and click Apply.

When I changed the resolution, the color palette changed, too!

Your video card needs more memory to display higher resolutions. It also needs more memory to display more colors (most video cards don't have enough memory to handle all those colors at all resolutions). If you want to see photos in True Color, you may have to choose the smallest desktop area: 640×480. If you want to pack more **pixels** (picture dots) on the screen (at 1024×768, for example), you'll probably have to settle for fewer colors.

Why does my screen redraw seem slower at some settings?

Manipulating more information simply takes more time. Unless you have an extremely fast, accelerated video card, you'll notice significantly slower screen response as you push your system to higher resolutions and more colors. If you need more speed, reduce the display resolution, the colors, or both.

I selected a pattern for my desktop and clicked OK, but I don't see it

Make sure that you don't have any wallpaper selected. Wallpaper always covers up the desktop pattern, which in turn covers up the background color. To clear the wallpaper selection, open the Desktop Properties dialog box, choose the Background tab, and highlight the (None) entry in the wallpaper list.

Why can't I use this image as wallpaper?

You're not restricted to the wallpaper selections that come with Windows. You can use your own images as wallpaper, too. However, to use a picture as wallpaper, it must be saved as a Windows **bitmap (.BMP) file**.

You can find .BMP files suitable for use as wallpaper from a variety of sources, including the Internet and online services. Most of the popular graphics and scanning programs can also save files in this format.

My picture doesn't fill the screen as wallpaper

If you want one picture to completely cover your desktop without tiling, the size of the picture must match your display resolution. For example, if your resolution is set at 640×480 pixels, you'll need a picture that measures exactly 640×480. For a higher resolution, you'll need a larger picture. Obviously, the same picture file won't work at different resolutions.

Printing and fonts

This section will help you with the questions that may arise as you move your work through the transition from the screen to the printed page.

My printer just installed itself. How'd that happen?

The ridiculously easy way to set up a printer is to make sure you have a Plug and Play printer. All you have to do is connect the printer cable to your PC, and turn on the power to the printer. The next time you start Windows, it will detect the addition of the printer, and then automatically configure it for you.

How do I know my printer is installed correctly?

When you first install a new printer, Windows offers to print a test page for you. Just say yes! This is the best way to make sure that the printer works correctly. Later, if you have any problems, Open the Printers folder, right-click on a printer, choose Properties, and click the Print Test Page button in the General tab to print another test page. It's a good way to determine whether the problem is with your printer or your application.

Why is MS Fax listed as a printer connected to the FAX port?

If you look at the list of ports, you may see Microsoft Fax listed as a printer, hooked up to the FAX: port. That's not a mistake. As far as Windows is concerned, any fax machine is just a special printer, even if it's halfway around the world. It puts images on paper, just like any printer, and the telephone line acts just like a ve-e-e-e-e-e-ery long version of a printer cable.

Why can't my old favorite Windows program use all my printer's features?

Because old Windows programs don't use the same dialog boxes as new ones written especially for Windows 95, you may not be able to set up your pages and printers completely. If this is the case, you probably need to contact the company that made the program and ask them if they have a new version designed for Windows 95.

Why is this print job taking so long?

When you print to a shared printer, especially a slow one like a color printer, you sometimes have to wait in line while other jobs work their way through the printer. Sometimes delays are caused by hardware problems: the printer might be out of paper, jammed, or just not turned on. (Don't laugh—it happens.) You won't know exactly why your print job is moving like rush hour traffic on an L.A. freeway unless you check your place in the print queue.

Did I say freeway? Actually, the print queue is more like a one-lane highway. When four or five people try to print at once, only one job gets to actually go to the printer. The others have to slow down, line up single file, and wait their turns. If you tell Windows to pause one of the jobs, it's just as if you've put on your emergency brake in the fast lane. Everything comes screeching to a halt until the stalled job gets moving again.

Double-click on the printer icon in the Printers folder and you'll see a list indicating the status of all the jobs waiting to be printed, including yours.

Oops—I didn't mean to print that!

Sooner or later, it happens to everyone: you send a big job (40 pages? 100? 400?) to the printer, and the instant you finish clicking the Print button, you realize that you left out a paragraph on page 1. You could just let the printer chew through all those pages, then throw everything away and start over. But if you're quick enough, you can jump in right now and stop everything.

You have to be quick, though, because you can only cancel a print job if the job is still in the queue. Open the printer window, select the job, right-click, and choose Cancel Printing from the shortcut menu. If you don't want to kill the job, but just want to stop it temporarily, choose Pause Printing instead.

My printer is installed correctly, but I can't find the Sharing command on the shortcut menu. Where did it go?

 You need to add File and Printer Sharing services. Open the Network folder in Control Panel, click the <u>A</u>dd button, and choose Service. Click <u>A</u>dd again. Highlight Microsoft, and choose the File and Print sharing entry that matches your network. Click OK and follow the instructions. You'll need to restart your computer before the changes will take effect.

How can I control separator pages on a remote printer?

You can only control the option for **separator pages** if the printer is attached directly to your computer. If you want Windows to print a special page to help you spot the beginning of each new document you print on a shared printer, you'll have to ask the owner of the PC the printer is hooked up to.

I need this rush print job. Now!

If you find your rush print job stuck in the print queue behind 27 big jobs submitted by Bob in Accounting, you can cut in line in front of Bob. First, open the Printers folder and double-click the icon for the printer where your print job is waiting. Then, select your print job and drag it to the top of the list. Voilà! You're now next in line.

My fonts are all messed up. What went wrong?

You chose a non-TrueType font that isn't available on your printer. When that happens, Windows looks around for the best available match, and tries to print it. If its best guess isn't good enough for you, choose a new font, preferably one with the **TT (TrueType)** symbol next to it.

I changed the font formatting, but my document still looks the same. What happened?

If you chose formatting without having any text selected, you won't see the results until you type some new characters. Windows adds the formatting information at the insertion point, so it affects whatever you type from that point on. If you want to format the existing document, try it again with the text you want to see changed.

How can I get rid of these ugly raster fonts?

 You can tell Windows that you don't want to see those nasty fonts anymore. In the Control Panel, open the Fonts folder, and choose Options. On the last tab, there's a check box that tells Windows to show you only TrueType fonts.

How many fonts can I install?

There used to be a limit on the number of fonts you could install under Windows. No more. Now, as long as you have room on your hard disk, you can have a thousand fonts or more. Of course, you might have trouble keeping track of them all, but that's a different story...

I've got too many fonts. How can I get rid of some of them?

To delete fonts, open the Fonts folder, select the font icons, and drag them into the Recycle Bin. It's OK to delete fonts you've added, but don't delete any of the raster fonts that come with your system, like MS Sans Serif and MS Serif. All sorts of programs depend on them. Likewise, don't delete the Times New Roman, Arial, or Courier TrueType fonts.

Communicating with others

In today's interconnected world, nearly every computer needs to communicate with others over modems and networks. This section addresses some of the questions that come up when you try to send e-mail, faxes, and network communications.

My system seems to hang when I double-click the Entire Network icon

Be prepared to wait when you double-click on the Entire Network icon. If you're part of a big network, it can take a few minutes, literally, for Windows to track down all those pieces and build the list of icons to show you.

Some features don't seem to work on our network

Some of the network techniques described in this book may not work on your network. It all depends on how much trust the person who set up your network had in you and your fellow workers. If you work for the CIA, security will surely be a lot tighter than if you work for a real estate agency.

Help! I forgot my password!

Call your network administrator. It takes special management tools to erase your old password and give you a new one when you've forgotten the original password. Why the runaround? Well, the whole point of passwords is to offer security. If you forget your password, there's no way Windows can tell that it's really *you* instead of some snoop trying to steal your files.

I don't see the Folders list. Is Exchange broken?

No, it's just not set up to show that view when you click on the Inbox icon on the desktop. To reveal the Folders list, click the Show/Hide Folder List button on the Exchange toolbar.

Why don't I see any fax options in Microsoft Exchange?

The fax component of Microsoft Exchange is not installed automatically when you set up Windows 95. Before you can use Exchange for faxing, you'll need to install the fax software, add faxing to the list of services Exchange provides, and tell Exchange about your fax modem. (The steps are explained in more detail in Chapter 23.)

I want to receive faxes with my fax modem

First of all, Exchange must be running in order to receive faxes. It can be running in an open window or minimized to a button on your taskbar, but just having the Exchange or Inbox icon on your desktop is *not* enough. Next, you need to give Exchange instructions on how you want the fax component to answer the phone. To set this option, double-click on the fax icon in the lower right corner of the taskbar, then choose Options, Modem Properties in the Microsoft Fax status dialog box. You can choose Don't Answer, Manual, or set the number of rings before Exchange answers automatically.

How can I fax a paper document?

Exchange and a fax modem work best when sending documents you create on the computer. However, you *can* use Exchange to fax a piece of paper to someone else if you have a special kind of hardware called a **scanner**. It's a big hassle to make your scanner and fax modem work together, though. If you fax lots of paper documents, you're better off using a plain old fax machine and saving the fax modem for the documents you create on your computer.

The people I send e-mail to don't get the files I attach

There are many different e-mail programs in use, and they don't all handle attachments the same way. Be careful when sending files to other people who aren't using Exchange. You have no guarantee that the program they use to receive mail will correctly receive the attachment you send. Try a test run before you send a crucial file.

How can I make a backup copy of the e-mail messages in Exchange?

If you use Exchange for your regular e-mail, you'll quickly fill it with irreplaceable messages. Don't run the risk of losing them forever! Keep backup copies of your mail file. Use the Find, Files or Folders option to search for files called *.PST, then copy the results to a safe place.

How can I tell if I've established a successful modem connection?

Look in the notification area, right next to the clock on the right side of the taskbar. You'll see a small modem icon with two lights that blink on and off to indicate that data is going back and forth. Double-click on the icon to display a big window with more information about the current connection.

This @%&#!! modem doesn't work!

Murphy has a special book of "Murphy's laws" reserved just for modems and communications issues. It's a thick book, too. The best starting place for fixing modem problems is the Windows online help system. Search for Troubleshooting—virtually all the tough modem problems are well explained here, with helpful step-by-step instructions.

How can I skip all the opening navigation screens and go straight to a location on The Microsoft Network?

You can connect to The Microsoft Network and jump straight to one of your favorite places if you create a shortcut to that place, and then add it to the desktop. When you find a place on MSN where you think you'll want to return, right-click on its icon and choose Create Shortcut. The new shortcut shows up on your desktop. The next time you want to visit that place, just double-click the shortcut icon. If necessary, Windows will offer to log on to MSN in order to take you there.

Every time I log on to The Microsoft Network, the graphics seem fuzzy for a few seconds, although they eventually clear up. Is there something wrong with my modem?

No, that's exactly the way MSN is supposed to work. The idea is to quickly show you the general, very rough outline of each graphic image instead of forcing you to wait while the screen sloooooooooowly redraws the image.

If, after you see the first pass, you decide you don't need to see more, you can move on without wasting too much time. If you choose to stay and watch, though, the graphics will gradually get sharper and clearer.

Each time I double-click on an MSN icon, the window I was looking at goes away. Can't I keep two windows open at once?

Yes, you can. Choose View, Options, and click on the Folder tab. Now tell MSN you want to browse with a separate window for each folder. If you prefer the clean, uncluttered single-window approach, you can still open a separate Explorer-style window on demand by right-clicking on an MSN icon and then choosing Explore from the popup menu.

Whoops! I'm lost in The Microsoft Network. How do I get back to the beginning?

Like anything in Windows, the trick is to use the right mouse button. While you're connected to MSN, you see a small icon in the lower right corner of the taskbar. Right-click there for a handful of extremely useful options, including shortcuts that take you straight to MSN Central or your Favorite Places folder, plus a bold entry that lets you sign off *right now.*

Where did the file I downloaded from MSN go?

The folder where Windows stores the files you download from MSN is deeply buried on your hard disk; it's easy to miss its location unless you're paying very close attention. You'll find the folder (Transferred Files) inside the The Microsoft Network folder, which is, in turn, inside the Program Files folder. In other words, its address is: `C:\Program Files\The Microsoft Network\Transferred Files`.

Of course, you can always use the Find, Files and Folders command on the Start menu to find the file, provided you remember its name or another distinguishing characteristic.

What about viruses? Can I "catch" them on the Net?

First, don't panic. A computer **virus** is a renegade piece of computer programming that does destructive things to your PC, usually without any warning. It's transmitted through infected disks and programs. Sounds scary, doesn't it?

Actually, you don't run any risk of your PC contracting a computer virus through the Internet, as long as you don't download any programs. Follow that rule, and you'll be absolutely safe. What if you *do* want to download programs? Well, make one of your first downloads a virus-checking-and-removal program, or bite the bullet and buy an antivirus program such as Norton Antivirus.

Part IX: Indexes

Action Index

Index

Action Index

Basics: hardware, DOS, and Windows

Rearranging windows and icons

When You Need to...	You'll Find Help Here...
Move a window	p. 159
Close a window	p. 161
Put a program or folder back into a window	p. 166
Resize a window	p. 169

Installing, starting, and switching between programs

When You Need to...	You'll Find Help Here...
Start a program	p. 154
Switch between two windows	p. 157
Create a shortcut	p. 148
Install a new Windows program	p. 198
Install a new DOS program	p. 205
Install a new program from a CD-ROM	p. 345
Play a music CD	p. 347
Run a program from a CD-ROM	p. 350

Windows applications and accessories

When You Need to...	You'll Find Help Here...
Use the Windows Explorer	p. 141
Use the Quick Viewer	p. 143

When You Need to...	You'll Find Help Here...
Find any file, anywhere, anytime	p. 144
Bring back a file you just deleted	p. 145
Control the Recycle Bin	p. 147
Jot down some notes	p. 215
Write a letter	p. 215
Create a picture	p. 219
Add up some numbers	p. 223
Adjust the volume on your sound card	p. 326
Record sounds	p. 329
Play a multimedia game or a video clip	p. 346
Use the Briefcase to carry files from one computer to another	p. 338
Set up your Briefcase	p. 339
Use HyperTerminal	p. 378
Set up a new HyperTerminal location	p. 379
Set up the Windows Phone Dialer	p. 380
Cut, copy, and paste from one window to another	p. 230
Cut, copy, and paste in a DOS program	p. 231
Send an e-mail message	p. 389
Send mail to people on different services	p. 391
Send or receive a fax	p. 394
Use ScanDisk	p. 124
Use the Defragmenter	p. 125
Protect files	p. 126

Making Windows look a little better

When You Need to...	You'll Find Help Here...
Decorate the desktop	p. 243
Adjust the screen resolution	p. 245
Change the wallpaper pattern	p. 248
Change the color of the desktop	p. 249
Change the font used on the desktop	p. 252
Resize buttons	p. 254
Install a screen saver	p. 255
Add a shortcut	p. 263
Add a shortcut to the Start menu	p. 265
Organize the Start menu	p. 267
Put a Favorite Places folder on the Start menu	p. 268
Hide the taskbar	p. 272
Make the taskbar bigger	p. 272
Move the taskbar	p. 273

Printing, fonts, and special characters

When You Need to...	You'll Find Help Here...
Install a new printer	p. 284
Print on a network printer	p. 294
Share your printer with someone else	p. 295
Tell Windows which font to use	p. 305
Add a new font	p. 310

When You Need to...	You'll Find Help Here...
View a font	p. 311
Use a special character	p. 313

Managing disks, drives, directories, and files

When You Need to...	You'll Find Help Here...
Copy files to a floppy disk	p. 128
Format a floppy disk	p. 129
Copy the whole disk	p. 129
Copy files from a CD-ROM	p. 130
Use ScanDisk	p. 124
Use the Defragmenter	p. 125
Protect files	p. 126
Keep your files organized	p. 132
Move files and folders around	p. 137
Use the Windows Explorer	p. 141

Networking

When You Need to...	You'll Find Help Here...
Understand the Network Neighborhood	p. 358
Connect with other computers	p. 80

continues

When You Need to...	You'll Find Help Here...
Change your password	p. 362
Use the files on a file server	p. 364
Map to a drive letter	p. 364
Share information with other people	p. 366

The Microsoft Network

When You Need to...	You'll Find Help Here...
Learn more about The Microsoft Network	p. 410
Connect to The Microsoft Network	p. 399
Sign up with MSN	p. 400
Start up and shut down MSN	p. 404

Index

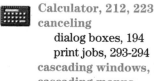

PLUG YOURSELF INTO...

THE MACMILLAN INFORMATION SUPERLIBRARY™

Free information and vast computer resources from the world's leading computer book publisher—online!

FIND THE BOOKS THAT ARE RIGHT FOR YOU!

A complete online catalog, plus sample chapters and tables of contents give you an in-depth look at *all* of our books, including hard-to-find titles. It's the best way to find the books you need!

- ● STAY INFORMED with the latest computer industry news through our online newsletter, press releases, and customized Information SuperLibrary Reports.

- ● GET FAST ANSWERS to your questions about MCP books and software.

- ● VISIT our online bookstore for the latest information and editions!

- ● COMMUNICATE with our expert authors through e-mail and conferences.

- ● DOWNLOAD SOFTWARE from the immense MCP library:
    - Source code and files from MCP books
    - The best shareware, freeware, and demos

- ● DISCOVER HOT SPOTS on other parts of the Internet.

- ● WIN BOOKS in ongoing contests and giveaways!

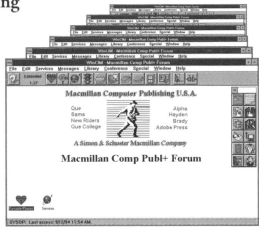

User-Friendly References for All Your Computing Needs

**Using Word
for Windows 95**
0-7897-0085-9, $19.99 USA
Publication Date: 9/95

**Using Excel
for Windows 95**
0-7897-0111-1, $19.99 USA
Publication Date: 8/95

**Using PowerPoint
for Windows 95**
0-7897-0365-3, $19.99 USA
Publication Date: 9/95

**Using Microsoft
Network**
0-7897-0398-x, $19.99 USA
Publication Date: 8/95

The new *Using* series gives readers just the information they need to perform
specific tasks quickly and move on to other things. *Using* books provide
bite-sized information for quick and easy reference, along with real-world
analogies and examples to explain new concepts.

QUE® For more information on these and other Que products, visit your local book retailer or call 1-800-772-0477.

Copyright © 1995, Macmillan Computer Publishing-USA, A Simon & Schuster Company

Source code ISBN: 0-7897-0092-1

Complete and Return this Card for a *FREE* Computer Book Catalog

Thank you for purchasing this book! You have purchased a superior computer book written expressly for your needs. To continue to provide the kind of up-to-date, pertinent coverage you've come to expect from us, we need to hear from you. Please take a minute to complete and return this self-addressed, postage-paid form. In return, we'll send you a free catalog of all our computer books on topics ranging from word processing to programming and the internet.

Mr. ☐   Mrs. ☐   Ms. ☐   Dr. ☐

Name (first) [＿＿＿＿＿＿＿＿] (M.I.) ☐   (last) [＿＿＿＿＿＿＿＿＿＿＿＿]

Address [＿＿＿＿＿＿＿＿＿＿＿＿＿＿＿＿＿＿＿＿]

[＿＿＿＿＿＿＿＿＿＿＿＿＿＿＿＿＿＿＿＿]

City [＿＿＿＿＿＿＿＿＿＿＿]   State [＿＿]   Zip [＿＿＿＿＿] [＿＿＿＿]

Phone [＿＿＿] [＿＿＿] [＿＿＿＿]   Fax [＿＿＿] [＿＿＿] [＿＿＿＿]

Company Name [＿＿＿＿＿＿＿＿＿＿＿＿＿＿＿＿＿＿＿＿]

E-mail address [＿＿＿＿＿＿＿＿＿＿＿＿＿＿＿＿＿＿＿＿]

1. Please check at least (3) influencing factors for purchasing this book.

Front or back cover information on book .... ☐
Special approach to the content .... ☐
Completeness of content .... ☐
Author's reputation .... ☐
Publisher's reputation .... ☐
Book cover design or layout .... ☐
Index or table of contents of book .... ☐
Price of book .... ☐
Special effects, graphics, illustrations .... ☐
Other (Please specify): _____ ☐

2. How did you first learn about this book?

Saw in Macmillan Computer Publishing catalog .... ☐
Recommended by store personnel .... ☐
Saw the book on bookshelf at store .... ☐
Recommended by a friend .... ☐
Received advertisement in the mail .... ☐
Saw an advertisement in: _____ ☐
Read book review in: _____ ☐
Other (Please specify): _____ ☐

3. How many computer books have you purchased in the last six months?

This book only .... ☐   3 to 5 books .... ☐
2 books .... ☐   More than 5 .... ☐

4. Where did you purchase this book?

Bookstore .... ☐
Computer Store .... ☐
Consumer Electronics Store .... ☐
Department Store .... ☐
Office Club .... ☐
Warehouse Club .... ☐
Mail Order .... ☐
Direct from Publisher .... ☐
Internet site .... ☐
Other (Please specify): _____ ☐

5. How long have you been using a computer?

☐ Less than 6 months   ☐ 6 months to a year
☐ 1 to 3 years   ☐ More than 3 years

6. What is your level of experience with personal computers and with the subject of this book?

	With PCs	With subject of book
New	☐	☐
Casual	☐	☐
Accomplished	☐	☐
Expert	☐	☐

Source Code ISBN: 0-7897-0092-1

7. Which of the following best describes your job title?

Administrative Assistant .... ☐
Coordinator .... ☐
Manager/Supervisor .... ☐
Director .... ☐
Vice President .... ☐
President/CEO/COO .... ☐
Lawyer/Doctor/Medical Professional .... ☐
Teacher/Educator/Trainer .... ☐
Engineer/Technician .... ☐
Consultant .... ☐
Not employed/Student/Retired .... ☐
Other (Please specify): _____ ☐

8. Which of the following best describes the area of the company your job title falls under?

Accounting .... ☐
Engineering .... ☐
Manufacturing .... ☐
Operations .... ☐
Marketing .... ☐
Sales .... ☐
Other (Please specify): _____ ☐

9. What is your age?

Under 20 .... ☐
21-29 .... ☐
30-39 .... ☐
40-49 .... ☐
50-59 .... ☐
60-over .... ☐

10. Are you:

Male .... ☐
Female .... ☐

11. Which computer publications do you read regularly? (Please list)

_____
_____
_____
_____
_____
_____
_____
_____
_____
_____

Comments: _____
_____
_____

Fold here and scotch-tape to mail.